Interactive
Data
Warehousing

ISBN 0-13-080371-5

Interactive Data Warehousing

Harry Singh

Prentice Hall PTR
Upper Saddle River, NJ   07458
http://www.phptr.com

Library of Congress Cataloging-in-Publication Date
Singh, Harry,
    Interactive data warehousing / Harry Singh.
      p. cm.
    Includes bibliographical references and index.
    ISBN 0-13-080371-5 (alk. paper)
    1. Data warehousing. 2. Distributed databases. 3. World Wide Web
  (Information retrieval system) I. Title.
  QA76.9.D37S563   1999
  551.22—dc21   98-30045
                                          CIP

Editorial/Production Supervision: *Craig Little*
Acquisitions Editor: *Michael Meehan*
Buyer: *Pat Brown*
Marketing Manager: *Kaylie Smith*
Cover Design: *Bruce Kenselaar*
Cover Design Direction: *Jayne Conte*
Interior Design: *Gail Cocker-Bogusz*

 © 1999 Prentice Hall PTR
Prentice-Hall, Inc.
A Simon & Schuster Company
Upper Saddle River, NJ 07458

Prentice Hall books are widely used by corporations and government agencies for training, marketing, and resale.

The publisher offers discounts on this book when ordered in bulk quantities.
For more information, contact the Corporate Sales Department, Phone: 800-382-3419; Fax: 201–236-7141; email: corpsales@prenhall.com; or write: Corporate Sales Department, Prentice Hall PTR, One Lake Street, Upper Saddle River, NJ 07458.

A number of entered words in which we have reason to believe trademark, service mark, or other proprietary rights may exist have been designated as such by initial capitalization. However, no attempt has been made to designate as trademarks or service marks all personal computer words or terms in which proprietary rights might exist. The inclusion, exclusion, or definition of a word or term is not intended to affect or to express any judgment on, the validity or legal status of any proprietary right that may be claimed in that word or term. All product names mentioned herein are the trademarks of their respective owners.

Every effort has been made to make the contents of this book as accurate and understandable as possible. However, neither the author nor the publisher makes any warranty, and neither assumes any liability with regard to the uses to which its contents may be put.
Printed in the United States of America

10 9 8 7 6 5 4 3 2 1

ISBN 0-13-080371-5

Prentice-Hall International (UK) Limited, *London*
Prentice-Hall of Australia Pty. Limited, *Sydney*
Prentice-Hall Canada Inc., *Toronto*
Prentice-Hall Hispanoamericana, S.A., *Mexico*
Prentice-Hall of India Private Limited, *New Delhi*
Prentice-Hall of Japan, Inc., *Tokyo*
Simon & Schuster Asia Pte. Ltd., *Singapore*
Editora Prentice-Hall do Brasil, Ltda., *Rio de Janeiro*

Dedication

To my children, Sarita, Sushila, Sanjay, and Samita, for their love,
to my brothers, Narinder, Ishar, and Shamsher,
to my sisters, Jiswant and Rajinder, for their prolonged faith,
and to my parents, for their high ethics and convictions during my growing years.

CONTENTS

CHAPTER 1   INTRODUCTION

PREFACE

As technologies and industries converge, what is emerging is a new global information industry. There may not be cable or phone or computer companies, as such.... There will be information conduits, information providers, information appliances, and information consumers.

Interactive Web-enabled and distributed computer systems will be of increasing importance in our society, especially from the desktop. In such systems, shared data may be the only thing that binds together different subsystems. Thus the key paradigms and concepts of distributing information over the large expanse of the enterprise should be associated with data considerations. Designing a data warehouse system so that the data required by its individual components, applications, and processes will be available when needed in the proper form, and with appropriate security, etc. is a substantial engineering task.

If the sharing or exchange of information plays a key role in data warehouse systems, then both communication and database issues are of great importance. Those issues extend far beyond the classical transport perspective of communications engineering and centralized databases. That trend is driven by ever-expanding technological capabilities, the desire of computer users to more fully integrate their information systems, the existence of heterogeneous systems that must pragmatically be evolved, not redone, and the certainty that in the foreseeable future users will continue to implement and introduce new systems that are not members of a homogeneous family.

Data warehousing technologies are the future way to accomplish Decision Support. Sooner or later, every enterprise WILL implement a data warehouse solution. The question is NOT IF, BUT WHEN & HOW. The overriding architectural challenge is the development of an Internet or Intranet structure and framework that will permit heterogeneous data warehouse systems to work together.

Data warehouses come in all shapes and sizes. Some are small and trivial. Some are diverse and complex. Some span a single database, while others span the heterogeneous mix of the entire enterprise, across the boundary-less network. But whatever they may look like and whatever their complexity, data warehouses hold the promise to transform data into knowledge and help businesses compete. This book is about sharing knowledge from concepts to systematically building and implementing a data warehouse in Internet/Intranet environments.

This book exploits the World Wide Web technologies and the techniques essential for successful deployment of decision-support processing, in data warehouse environments. This book analyzes and discusses key issues such as construction of Intranets, distribution of functions over the enterprise, Web-enabled computing technologies, Web information flow across multiple systems, Object technologies and their inter-relationships, and more.

Acknowledgments

One of my English literature teachers, Pathak, taught me a lot about books and reading. He used to say that no one should invest time in reading a book until it has stood the test of a hundred years. I hope this book is an exception.

I acknowledge many debts: to Belen Balaba and to my many colleagues, for stray remarks that pushed me to complete this manuscript; to Mike Meehan, for painstaking scrutiny; to many data warehousing enthusiasts, vendors, and technologists, for providing much of the food for thought; and finally to my parents and children for their perseverance.

Harry Singh, Ph.D.

TRADEMARKS

The following are registered trademarks of International Business Machines Corporation: *DB2, IMS, IMS/DB, CICS, MVS, AIX, AIX/6000, IBM 370,IBM System/390, PC-LAN, VTAM, VSAM, ISAM, LU6.2, ACF2.*

The following are registered trademarks of Oracle Corporation: *ORACLE7, Oracle Server, PQO, Express.*

The following are registered trademarks of Informix Software, Inc.: *Informix, On-Line Dynamic Server, DSA, PDQ, Metacube.*

The following are registered trademarks of Sybase, Inc.: *Sybase System 10, SQL Server.*

The following are registered trademarks of Digital Equipment Corporation: *VAX, VMS, ULTRIX, DEC, Rdb, VT, OpenVMS, VAXclusters, RMS.*

The following are registered trademarks of Novell, Inc.: *NetWare, IPX/SPX.*

The following are registered trademarks of Apple Computer Corporation: *Mac, Macintosh.*

The following are registered trademarks of Microsoft Corporation: *Microsoft, Windows 3.1, Windows95, NT, Windows NT, MS-DOS, NT Advanced Server, SQL Server, ActiveX, Excel.*

The following are registered trademarks of Hewlett-Packard Company: *Hewlett-Packard, RPC, Open Warehouse.*

The following are registered trademarks of Sun Microsystems, Inc.: *Java Sun, Solaris, SunOS, NFS, SunNet Manager.*

The following are registered trademarks of X/Open: *UNIX, Motif.*

The following are registered trademarks of Massachusetts Institute of Technology: *X-Windows.*

The following are registered trademarks of MicroStrategy, Inc.:*DSS Agent, DSS Server.*

The following are registered trademarks of Kenan Systems Corp.:*Acumate ES.*

The following are registered trademarks of Lighten, Inc.: *Advance.*

The following are registered trademarks of Comshare, Inc.: *Commander.*

The following are registered trademarks of Dimension Data Systems.: *Dimension Control.*

The following are registered trademarks of Kelly Information Systems, Inc.: *DSPlus.*

The following are registered trademarks of Planning Sciences Corp.: *GENTIUM.*

The following are registered trademarks of Holistic Systems, Inc.: *Holos.*

The following are registered trademarks of Hyperian Software, Inc.: *Hyperian.*

The following are registered trademarks of Andyne, Inc.: *PaBLO.*
The following are registered trademarks of Cognos, Inc.: *PowerPlay.*
The following are registered trademarks of CorVu Pty. Ltd.: *CorVu.*
The following are registered trademarks of IQ Software Corp.: *IQ/Objects, IQ/Vision.*
The following are registered trademarks of Lotus Corp. (IBM): *Lotus 1-2-3.*
The following are registered trademarks of SPSS, Inc.: *SPSS.*
The following are registered trademarks of Arbor Software: *Essbase.*
The following are registered trademarks of Pilot Software: *Lightship.*
The following are registered trademarks of Visigenic Software, Inc.: *DriverSet.*
The following are registered trademarks of Simba technologies, Inc.: *Simba.*
The following are registered trademarks of UNISYS, Inc.: *OPUS.*
The following are registered trademarks of Intel, Corp.: *x86, Intel.*
The following are registered trademarks of Computer Associates, Inc.: *Ingress, Open-Ingress.*
The following are registered trademarks of Boreland Software, Inc.: *Interbase.*
The following are registered trademarks of AT&T (NCR) Corp.: *NCR 3600, GIS, 3500 SMP, 3600 MPP.*
The following are registered trademarks of Pyramid, Inc.: *MIServer.*
The following are registered trademarks of Tandem Corp.: *SQL/MP, Teradata.*
The following are registered trademarks of Silicon Graphics: *VRML.*
The following are registered trademarks of Netscape: *LiveMedia, SSL.*

Interactive
Data
Warehousing

1

INTRODUCTION

Casual web users typically are less frequent users of data warehouse decision support than traditional decision-support analysts. They demand products that are easy to use and based on metadata-driven middleware using industry-standard Open Data Base Connectivity (ODBC) interfaces, so that nearly all decision-support tools and combinations of tools can take advantage of it.

In order to support large numbers of internal and potentially external web users accessing the data warehouse, it becomes imperative to have strong warehouse-management facilities. Some warehouse implementations have powerful query-management capabilities for monitoring and maintaining audit trails of warehouse usage and for graphically advising administrators as to how to tune the warehouse based on usage patterns. Warehouse tuning is achieved through summary population, index creation, and problem-query handling.

The three-tier architecture is ideally suited for Web environments due to its support for ease of use and query-management functionality on the server rather than on traditional "fat clients." Thus, users can now have easy access to corporate data in a managed environment with no additional desktop software besides the Web Browser.

World Wide Web as Information Accelerator

As we come into the 21st century, our world is experiencing the unprecedented growth of a technology that promises to bring people closer together in both business and society.

Corporations recognize that information placed in the hands of decision-makers is a powerful tool. To meet decision-makers nearly insatiable appetite for information, data is being extracted from operational systems and placed in data warehouses.

The delivery of data warehouse information to decision makers throughout the enterprise and around the world has been an expensive challenge. Once data has been extracted and organized for user access, analytic software must be loaded on each user's workstation, users must be trained, and ongoing user support staffs must be recruited. User requirements and even the users themselves change constantly, resulting in a significant support burden.

The Internet, the World Wide Web, and the emerging object technologies (OO technologies) offer a solution. In addition to simplifying the deployment of data warehouse access, an intranet can introduce a new level of collaborative interactive analysis and information sharing among decision-makers. Moreover, the OO technologies can make application development simpler and the by-products re-usable.

Today's businesses are operating very differently (and in a very different environment) from businesses of only a few years ago. Information is proliferating at dizzying rates. Data marts and data warehouses are springing up to accommodate the ever-growing stores of data that are the lifeblood of business. Flatter organizational structures are spawning more users of critical business data. More importantly, these users must quickly turn data into meaningful information on which key business decisions can be based.

Part of the reason for this change is the pervasiveness of the Internet and the World Wide Web which have made fast, easy global communications a reality. The Internet has opened the door to a global business community where being able to make informed decisions and move quickly is key to success. In this environment, finding effective ways to get meaningful information to the people who need it, wherever they are and at any hour of the day or night, is a major business challenge.

Data warehouse systems are an essential technology in allowing the enterprise to be more intelligently responsive to customers and other stakeholders. These warehouses provide analysts and management the information they need to understand customer buying habits, product performance, and the success or failure of marketing efforts. Many companies have made competitive gains in the marketplace as a result of using data warehousing technology.

But a data warehouse is only as good as its data. The old "garbage in-garbage out" analogy has never been more appropriately applied than it is to data warehousing. For a data warehouse project to be successful, you must:

- Extract data from disparate legacy systems, production systems, relational databases, and outside external data sources.
- Cleanse and validate the data.
- Integrate the data into a logically and syntactically coherent enterprise view.

Web-Enabled Decision Support

Web-enabled decision-support tools have come a long way in a relatively short time. However, the level of sophistication of the solutions can vary widely. Web-enabled decision-support tools can be classified as:

- *Web client-based*: Such tools deliver the ability to publish static information in HTML format that can be read by browsers. They provide basic file distribution services using a two-tier architecture. These tools also save or convert reports and documents as HTML files and store them on the web server.

- *Web client and server shared functions*: These tools deliver the ability to publish static reports on a scheduled basis, deliver on-demand reports and/or initiate a report for dynamic execution via the browser. They provide dynamic HTML publishing, which means that HTML documents are created on the fly in response to user requests. The output is a static HTML page or document. These architectures implement a four-tier architecture (web browsers, web servers, application servers, and databases) and most use Common Gateway Interface (CGI) to link web servers to external programs.

- *Interactive web-enabled environments*: These tools deliver the ability to deploy applications in an interactive and content-rich browser environment, and have some components written in Java or ActiveX. They provide Java-assisted publishing, adding Java applets or other client-side programs to second-generation architectures to provide an enhanced interface, provide support for localized processing, or convey interface events to back-end CGI servers.

- *Dynamic use of Java* and *OO technologies*: These technologies provide dynamic Java publishing. Fourth-generation web architecture is designed, maintained, and executed entirely on the web using Java code. It employs a classic three-tier architecture (Java applets, a Java application server, and a back-end database or resource manager) and is not constrained by HTML and HTTP.

These definitions provide a useful starting point for understanding the functionality of the various web-enabled decision-support tools and Web architectures available today.

Warehousing in Brief

The initial concept behind data warehouses was one of an enterprise-wide repository (**Figure 1.1**) that homogenized and coalesced all of the organization's data into a single unified structure, from which all departments could glean a comprehensive view of the organization. In this early concept, all production systems would feed their pieces of the puzzle into the single enterprise warehouse, and therefore all extractions and transformations within the entire organization came under the control of a single process.

Demand for data access is growing in direct proportion to the success of the warehouse. Initial deployment of a pilot warehouse is often limited to a

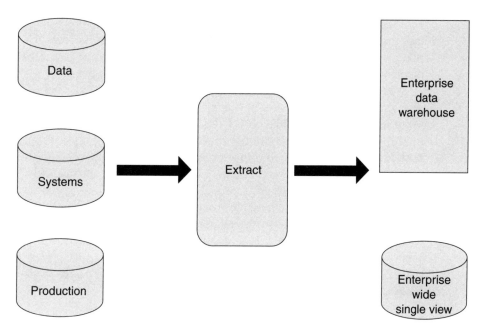

Figure 1.1 Enterprise Data Warehouse

small set of corporate users in a functional department like marketing. As the value of the investment in information access comes to be realized, demand increases dramatically, spreading from a few corporate users to multiple sites.

Web-Enabled Data Access

A corporate intranet is the ideal vehicle for widespread information access within an organization. Such an approach takes advantage of Internet technologies and familiar web browsers to deliver access to information across internal corporate networks from anywhere in the organization—regardless of platform or the location of the user. "Thin clients" for web-enabled data access mean that mobile computing environments have easy access to data as well. Many third-party data access tools are already web-enabled. By leveraging Java and other application-building tools, organizations can also deploy custom data access applications that are available from anywhere within the corporation.

Web-enabled applications mean that neither the user's physical location (assuming access to the corporate intranet exists) nor limitations of a desktop platform are obstacles to accessing the data warehouse. As a result, previously insurmountable barriers to application deployment disappear.

From a systems management perspective, moving from a desktop-centric model to a network-centric one is revolutionary. Installing and maintaining point-and-click access tools on the desktops of a few users—all located in corporate headquarters—may not be overwhelming during a pilot implementation. However, widespread adoption could result in huge costs to the organization, and installing data access software on every desktop quickly becomes overwhelming.

This so-called "fat client" approach is outdated in today's computing environment. By deploying browsers on all enterprise desktops, the organization can move toward a "thin client" computing model with a fraction of the systems management cost of the "fat client" model. With a network-centric approach, it is no longer necessary to install software on every desktop each time a new application is deployed.

Network Management Considerations

The Internet plays two major roles in an enterprise data warehouse deployment:

- Data transfer from source systems to the enterprise warehouse and data marts.
- End user access to data stored in the warehouse and data marts.

Each of these functions places a different kind of stress on the network, which must be explicitly managed to ensure acceptable service levels to users. In the future, additional network considerations will likely come into play to support cooperation among distributed database environments. The following sections describe the implications of these requirements.

Data Transfer Requirements

Most enterprise data warehouses will be sourced from mainframe databases for years to come. Legacy systems house corporate data, often organized as repository systems, that must be integrated and maintained historically in the data warehouse environment. High-speed access to these mainframes is necessary for efficient transfer of data to the warehouse environment. While the mainframe can attach to multiple networking services, high-speed interfaces ensure a practical way to transfer data into the enterprise warehouse. Most local area networks do not have the bandwidth for large data transfers without seriously impacting service levels.

Many mainframe suppliers have embraced IBM's Enterprise Systems Connection (ESCON) standard (the ANSI standard is SBCON). ESCON provides inherent advantages for the distributed environment, with data transfer rates up to 17 megabytes per second and extended distances up to 60 kilometers. For system success, new server-based warehousing solutions must coexist with mainframes and maximize the speeds and feeds of data movement between these two critical components.

As LAN technologies supporting 100 Mbps become more common, supporting multiple data marts within network bandwidth constraints will become enormously simplified.

User Access Requirements

With web-enabled applications critical to the success of information access within the organization, an intranetworking infrastructure becomes extremely important. With the advent of new technologies, it has become more economically efficient as well. Most enterprises consider intranetworking as a private internet for the entire enterprise. As a result, the enterprise must rethink its hierarchy of computing—from the desktop to enterprise server to mainframe. Methods of connectivity, connectivity protocols, bandwidth considerations and, importantly, software platforms that support enterprise needs must be considered when making design and implementation decisions.

Any enterprise network solution must include both a WAN and a LAN strategy. A solid WAN strategy brings together divisions of the enterprise where geographical distances must be overcome. WAN designs must consider economics, bandwidth, and reliability. Previous WAN technology relied on expensive, high-speed leased-line circuits, providing connectivity only to those sites with a hard requirement. Today, as the enterprise considers total connectivity, it must look at newer technologies such as frame relay and, as the technology matures, ATM technology to gain better efficiencies and higher bandwidth for the overall enterprise network.

The standard use of LAN technologies is also undergoing change. The need for higher bandwidth connections internally and the continued focus on commodity componentry is bringing even higher bandwidth and lower LAN implementation costs.

The variety of interconnect technologies and protocols, along with the organization's ever-increasing reliance on a network-centric computing model, makes systems management in the network environment a critical and complex challenge. In addition, performance monitoring, availability, and backup and disaster recovery must be managed with particular attention to the increasing demand for network computing. Systems management tools must be able to perform these tasks from remote sites in today's distributed computing environment. Adaptability to emerging protocols and technologies must be built into any systems management strategy in this area.

Future Distributed Database Requirements

The quantity of information organizations must manage is ever increasing. Rather than using a central information resource that is connected into the computing hierarchy, some organizations are moving toward the concept of a workgroup server architecture. The workgroup server provides the information resource for a department, which becomes a distributed information environment requiring a distributed database environment. These workgroup servers are then connected into a hierarchy of enterprise servers, yielding a truly distributed data computing environment.

A key application in this environment is the distributed database. A distributed database environment creates a number of challenges:

- The complexity of making the distributed database transparent to users, while simultaneously delivering the highest levels of performance, reliability, and availability.
- From the desktop to the highest level in the computing hierarchy, the distributed environment is one in which heterogeneity is a reality in terms of computing hardware, network connectivity, operating systems, network protocols, and multi-database software platforms.
- Systems management tools must manage the heterogeneous environment over a network infrastructure throughout the organization.
- Managing the Network

Why a Data Warehouse?

For some businesses, a data warehouse is an essential tool necessary to gain or maintain a competitive advantage. Or it can be an unnecessary, costly, and time-consuming distraction preventing you from leveraging more value from current systems. Here's how to determine if a data warehouse is the best way to improve information access and facilitate decision-support activities.

Data warehouses are essentially databases designed to improve access to a wide range of information. And when data warehouses are accompanied by on-line analytical processing (OLAP) software, which provides the tools to access the information in the data warehouse, information queries can be much faster than they would be using traditional relational databases.

In short, data warehousing and OLAP means faster and better access to widespread information. The idea of a data warehouse is to put a wide range of operational data from internal and external sources into one place so it can be better utilized by executives, line of business managers, and other business analysts. Once the information is gathered, OLAP software comes into play by providing the desktop analysis tools for querying, manipulating and reporting the data from the data warehouse.

Keep in mind that while a data warehouse may contain data gathered from many different sources and satisfy a diverse range of analysis needs, its smaller version, the data mart, is intended to focus on a subset of data such as sales and marketing data or financial data only.

Why Do You Need a Data Warehouse?

Larger, more complex businesses suffer from a common information management problem: data is stored in a variety of operational systems, in a variety of formats, and on different computing platforms. In some cases, information is essentially locked away in legacy systems that are difficult to access without having the IS department write special programs to extract the data. Consequently, it can be very difficult to get a complete picture of the business as a whole from an information perspective, to consolidate data across functional systems, and to compare data between functional systems. Also, in many cases, data is stored in transaction collection systems—billing, reservations, inventory, production control—and is not organized or aggregated in a way that facilitates decision-support activities. A data warehouse is a mechanism for delivering improved information access and higher quality decision support.

What Is a Data Warehouse?

A data warehouse is not a single product but an environment, typically consisting of multiple products from multiple vendors. The data warehouse environment consists of:

- The source systems from which data is extracted
- The tools used to extract data for loading the data warehouse

- The data warehouse database itself where the data is stored
- The desktop query and reporting tools used for decision support

The source systems for the data warehouse can include: mainframe and minicomputer "legacy" systems, desktop database and spreadsheet data, data provided by external sources, and data from other client/server systems that is stored in relational databases.

The tools used to feed the data warehouse database, usually termed "middleware," are responsible for the transformation of the data from the source systems. This data transformation can be very complex and can include:

- Field translations (such as from mainframe to PC formats)
- Data formatting (such as decimal to binary data formats)
- Field formatting (to truncate or pad field data when loaded into the warehouse)
- Reformatting data structures (such as reordering table columns)
- Replacing field data through table lookups (such as changing alpha codes to numeric IDs)
- Remapping transaction codes to summary reporting codes
- Applying logical data transformations based on user-defined business rules
- Aggregating transaction level values into "roll-up" balances

The data transformation tools may also be able to schedule the extracting and pumping of the data into the warehouse. The maintenance of this data transformation is often the most difficult and expensive ongoing task required to manage a data warehouse and definitely requires the support of your IS department.

The data warehouse depends on a database to store the warehouse data. The most popular databases for this task are relational databases such as ORACLE or DB2, which are used for some of the world's largest data warehouses and can manage multiple terabytes of information. Because data warehouses may contain a variety of different data types, new "universal" data servers such as those from Oracle or Informix may be a good choice for the warehouse database server. Multidimensional databases are also becoming more popular for use in data warehouses of less than five gigabytes in size. These databases typically run on single- and multi-processor hardware using either the Microsoft NT or the UNIX operating system.

Users query the data warehouse with graphical desktop tools that are often termed OLAP or ROLAP (relational on-line analytical processing) tools.

Some of these tools function as add-ins to popular spreadsheets so they can extract data from the warehouse into a worksheet for further analysis. The essential difference between OLAP and ROLAP tools is that OLAP tools work against data stored in multidimensional databases, whereas ROLAP tools are designed to work specifically against data stored in relational databases. These tools are designed to provide users with a feature set that is aimed at making ad hoc decision support easier, providing functions such as:

- Data navigation using drill down to manage summary and detail information
- Multidimensional "views" of the data not limited to a conventional two-dimensional view
- Rotation of dimensions for alternate views of the same core data set
- Charting and trend analysis to visualize the data relationships more easily
- Ranking and exception reporting to see highs and lows or isolate key data
- Data mining to search out unexpected relationships between data
- Row/column matrix and cross tabulation reporting to show total or average balances

Many of the OLAP and ROLAP implementations use web-enabled tools so queries can be run from standard Internet/intranet browser software, and data published as standard web pages can be accessed by any Internet/intranet user.

There are a few vendors that provide an end-to-end, single-vendor data warehouse solution, but most data warehouses involve cooperation between multi-vendor products.

Data Warehouse Operation

Data warehouses are seldom updated in real time. When a transaction is posted to a source transaction system, the data warehouse is not updated instantly. Instead, data is uploaded in batches to the data warehouse on a scheduled basis, say at the end of a trading day or the end of a fiscal period. Consequently, data warehouses are always slightly out of step with the transaction systems they reflect.

Data warehouses usually store data that has been aggregated by comparison with the original transaction data so the warehouse may store balances at product line, account code, customer or financial statement line level. Some

OLAP and ROLAP tools may provide the ability to "drill down" to reach the systems where the original transactions are stored in order to view the source for the balance numbers.

These OLAP and ROLAP tools take advantage of the data that is stored in formats and structures that are optimized for fast extraction and manipulation of data for decision support rather than transaction auditing. In ROLAP tools, this usually means data is stored in denormalized forms or in "fact" or "star" tables where a single value, such as a balance, is stored for a combination of multiple information dimensions, such as the total sales dollar value for each combination of products, salespersons, territories, and months. In OLAP tools, the data is stored in a multidimensional "cube." This organization makes it easy for ROLAP/OLAP tools to zero in on specific values and quickly retrieve alternate views of different combinations of the information dimensions.

Building a Data Warehouse

You may imagine "Isn't my general ledger an accounting warehouse?" This is a great question because in many ways it should be. If your general ledger is structured to receive summary data only from the sub-ledgers, has a flexible multi-segment account structure, can import data from external files, and can also store statistical and budget information, then the general ledger may already be well-equipped to function as a basic accounting warehouse. Many client/server general ledgers satisfy these requirements and, through partnerships with OLAP vendors, can also provide excellent decision-support tools. Some vendors have essentially repositioned their client/server general ledgers as "accounts warehouses" by linking them with OLAP packages and providing tools to automate the extraction and transformation of data from other accounting and non-accounting systems.

An alternative approach for such a data warehouse is to manage the data from multiple source systems through an independent report writer that has the ability to reach out to multiple systems and other files such as spreadsheets. In this scenario, data is never "staged" from your systems into a separate data warehouse database but accessed in real time by a report writer that may allow you to consolidate, compare and contrast data at various levels.

Data Mart Strategies

Global warehouses are very difficult to design and build for a number of reasons, including political, financial, performance, and strategic issues. The political issues primarily involve data ownership and provincialism, refusing to share their data, while others have other agendas. Financially, these large projects often involve expenditures in the millions of dollars and take many months to produce anything useful.

Large warehouses sometimes have difficulty in handling requests from many users among multiple departments in a timely manner, which causes performance problems. The length of time it takes to produce a workable solution often discourages potential users, who argue that by the time the project is scheduled to be completed, their requirements have long since either changed or disappeared altogether.

Dependent Data Marts

For these and other reasons, the architectural principles evolved into the concept of dependent data marts, which are smaller subsets of the enterprise warehouse specifically designed to respond to departmental or line-of-business issues. In this strategy, data is loaded from production systems into the enterprise warehouse and then subdivided into the smaller data marts (**Figure 1.2**). These marts are called "dependent data marts" because they rely on the central warehouse for their data and metadata rather than obtaining these from the production systems. While these data marts solved some of the performance issues and even some of the political issues, the financial problems and strategic issues were, if anything, exacerbated because the enterprise warehouse must be built before the data marts can be implemented.

Independent Data Marts

Some see independent data marts as a viable alternative to the top-down approach of an enterprise warehouse. An organization can start small and move quickly, often realizing limited results in three to six months. Issues of political parochialism are ignored by this strategy, although they come up later on. Proponents of this approach argue that after starting with a small data mart, other marts can proliferate in departments or lines of business (**Figure 1.3**) that have a need, and that by satisfying the various divisional needs, an organization can build its way to a full data warehouse by starting at the bottom and working up. The consequences are that multiple marts require multiple (and somewhat redundant) data to be extracted from production systems as shown below.

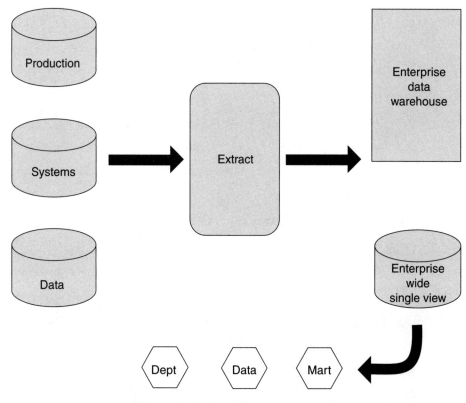

Figure 1.2   Dependent Data Marts

Data-Related Warehousing Issues

The challenge of populating data warehouses or data marts with usable data is material. To avoid the "garbage in, garbage out" syndrome, a number of issues surrounding the acquisition and utility of data must be resolved.

Multiple Sources

The problem is the number of internal legacy systems that exist and their incredible diversity. Many legacy systems, by their nature, are relics from bygone computing eras. These antediluvian remnants often were constructed

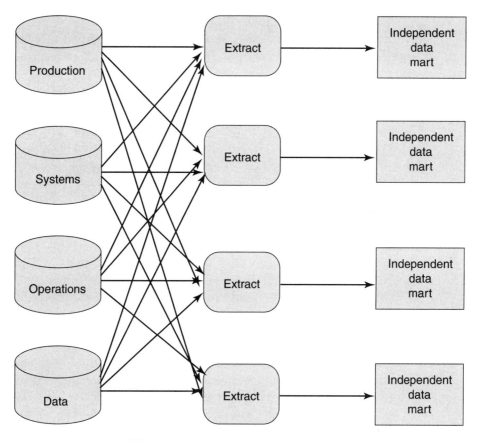

Figure 1.3   Independent Data Marts

around flat files, network databases, or hierarchical databases. Some are EBCDIC and others are ASCII encoded. And even within the classifications of network and hierarchical, there are numerous products and packages that were used to construct the data, including the ubiquitous COBOL home-grown files. Of course, newer generations of systems have implemented SQL-based relational structures.

In addition, external sources of data are being added at the request of business line users who want to enhance the value of the information in a data warehouse. These sources come in different formats and must be matched to internal sources of data.

Each of these generations, products, and home-grown systems have their own unique quirks with regard to data storage and the best mechanism for wresting the data from them.

Multiple Targets

Diversity is also a challenge in the data mart arena, particularly if the desired implementation is independent data marts. If the system architect is not careful, it is easy to wind up in a situation where each mart requires its own independent extract from each of the production databases.

The jumble of arrows (**Figure 1.3**) indicating duplication of uploads and extractions to the various data marts from each production database points out the challenge. Not only is it expensive to replicate the extraction and cleansing process for each additional mart that gets placed online, but the drain on the production systems from servicing multiple overlapping requests for data extractions eventually takes its toll on the availability of the production systems. They simply wind up with insufficient time to do the work they are intended to do because they spend so much time feeding the data marts. Alternatively, reducing their availability to the data marts causes users of the data marts to work with outdated information.

Further adding to the challenge is the fact that the independent data marts are often created with no overall enterprise data model. The result is that any given data element may be extracted and transformed into multiple different versions of the same element, depending on the point-of-view of each specific data mart requesting the data element.

Data Consistency Issues

The isolationism of the multiple legacy systems fragments data consistency. Multiple legacy systems may, in fact, capture and process similar information, such as gender, marital status, order information, etc. However, there may be dozens of different mechanisms for structuring that data syntactically and semantically.

Data may be captured using multiple different units of measure, such as pounds vs. tons. One system may encode gender via single letter designators (M/F), while another may have binary designators (1/0), a third may have a full word (male/female) and yet a fourth may have two data elements (one for male, one for female) in which a user may enter an X. Marital status, conventions for capturing names (use of Jr., Dr., Mr. Ms.), all of these are candidates for yet another form of diversity that presents problems in data consistency.

A favorite area of potential conflict is the designation of international business. Many consider Canada as domestic, while others see it as international. It is easy to see how sales and finance might treat a Canadian account differently in terms of classification, which would result in drastically different revenue reports produced by the two systems.

In order to avoid these kinds of issues, the data warehouse architect must develop mechanisms for ensuring consistent data into the data warehouse or data marts in the organization.

Data Quality Issues

Once we have consistent semantics and syntax, there is the not so minor issue of data content. Is the data in the legacy systems accurate? Are there misspellings of proper nouns that will cause multiple records when there ought to be only one? Have poor data entry validation practices allowed such anomalies as "dummy" social security numbers or customer accounts, so that we find multiple people with the same (999-99-9999) social security number, or multiple customers with the same customer number? Do we have zip codes that do not exist in our system or do not correlate with the city and state in the address fields?

Issues with Emerging Technologies

Is This Solution Really Complete?

Look for a solution that can handle all aspects of implementation from designing and building reports to deployment, administration, and management of decision support applications. Depending upon resources available and the skill level of people who will be using the tools, organizations may also want to look for a solution that requires no programming or scripting.

Does the Product Support Internet Standards?

To be most useful and effective, web-enabled decision-support tools should support Internet standards such as HTML output, hot-linking, and CGI scripts. The tools should also take advantage of JPEG and GIF formats to extend HTML's output capabilities for richer content and may have Java applets and ActiveX controls either in place or planned for the near future. Deployment of Java applets, in particular, can allow the product to provide interactive and content-rich web decision-support environments. Beyond this, be certain that the web-enabled solutions vendor has a strategy for the future that allows easy migration as new and emerging technologies and standards mature.

What about Server-Based Processing?

According to many industry experts and analysts, server-based processing is key to successful web-enabled decision support. The web-enabled products that lack server-based processing, including many of the popular client-centric query and reporting tools, are going to be at a distinct disadvantage when it comes to delivering complete web-enabled decision support. Without server-based processing capabilities, users will not be able to take advantage of the benefits of automated scheduling and on-demand reporting.

It is also important that the product support server-based processing on both UNIX and Windows NT platforms. Being able to use the tool with both UNIX and NT increases scalability options and ensures that the large number of medium-to-large organizations that use both platforms can deploy a single seamless solution to all their users. It is very important to understand what level of support for server-based processing a product is actually delivering.

Some products have the ability to perform all of their processing on the server. Others offer only partial implementations, with only a portion of the processing (scheduling, for example) actually being performed on the server. Since the Internet is a server-based environment, if a web-enabled decision-support solution requires any processing to be executed on the client (SQL generation, calculations, sorting, correlation or result sets, formatting), it may not be satisfactory either in terms of performance or functionality.

Can the Product Access All Popular Data Sources?

Whether organizations choose to deploy their web-enabled decision-support solution within UNIX or Windows NT environments or both, it is essential that they have complete flexibility in mapping to back-end data sources. This includes access to data warehouses, data marts, and corporate, departmental, and personal databases.

Is there a Single Solution for Both Web and Client/Server Users?

Current research indicates that the vast majority of people who need to use corporate data are occasional users who want to look at previously-created reports or do simple information look-ups. For these users, the Web is an extremely cost-effective way to meet their needs. At the same time, it is important that the needs of the 20 to 30 percent of the user population who need more capabilities (primarily analysts, power users and developers) be met. These users' needs are usually addressed most effectively in a client/server environment.

For these reasons, it is likely that most organizations will want to deploy both client/server and web-enabled decision-support solutions. Compatibility between the client/server and web solutions is an important consideration. With a single decision-support tool that is architected to provide robust support for both environments, an organization can cross-leverage its client/server and web investments—reusing and re-deploying assets for both environments, eliminating the need to maintain separate systems that require separate administration and training, and saving time and money in the process.

The Technologies Exploited

As technologies and industries converge, what is emerging is a new *global information industry*. There may not be cable or phone or computer companies, as such. But there will be information conduits, information providers, information appliances, and information consumers.

Interactive web-enabled and distributed computer systems, especially those accessible from the desktop, are becoming of increasing importance in our society. In such systems, shared data may be the only thing that binds together different subsystems. Thus the key paradigms and concepts of distributing information over large expanse of the enterprise should be governed by data considerations. Designing a data warehouse system so that the data required by its individual components, applications, and processes is available when needed in the proper form, and with appropriate security and integrity safeguards, is a substantial engineering task.

If the sharing or exchange of information plays a key role in data warehouse systems, then both communication and database issues are of great importance. Those issues extend far beyond the classical *transport* perspective of communications engineering and centralized databases.

Data warehousing technologies are the future underpinnings of decision support. Sooner or later, every enterprise *will* implement a data warehouse solution. The question is not if, but when and how. The overriding architectural challenge is the development of an Internet or intranet structure and framework that will permit heterogeneous data warehouse systems to work together.

Data warehouses come in all shapes and sizes. Some are small and trivial. Some are diverse and complex. Some span a single database, while others span the heterogeneous mix of the entire enterprise, across the boundary-less network. But whatever they may look like and whatever their complexity, data warehouses hold the promise to transform data into knowledge and help businesses compete. This book is about sharing knowledge from concepts to systematically building and implementing a data warehouse in the emerging paradigm of Internet/intranet environments.

Guide to the Reader

Essentially every enterprise is implementing some type of a "data warehousing" solution, may it be for a full-fledged comprehensive data warehouse, virtual data warehouse, or simple departmental data mart. The options and potential are limitless.

Most large enterprises have databases, workstations, and access to the Internet. Most of them have also developed their private intranets, developed a need to provide information access to their business partners, recognized the need to exploit emerging technologies, and have legacy data running either on departmental or central enterprise servers.

This book explains how to exploit World Wide Web technologies and the techniques essential for successful deployment of decision-support processing, in data warehouse environments. This book analyzes and discusses key issues such as construction of intranets, distribution of functions over the enterprise, web-enabled computing technologies, web information flow across multiple systems, object technologies and their interrelationships, and more.

This book describes techniques necessary to use technologies to face the challenge of the '90s and beyond, to store data to meet an organization's decision-support needs, and to provide users with common, simple, transparent access to information, regardless of where it resides. It contains detailed discussions and analysis of major issues including why a split between operational and informational databases is necessary and how to accomplish it, the lack of data creditability, integration of decision-support system (DSS) data, and how the web and data warehousing technologies fit with DSS needs.

The Issues Addressed

This book addresses the issues and techniques essential for successful migration to a data warehouse, the core of decision-support processing. Throughout the book, you will find step-by-step descriptions of the emerging technologies that are essential for the multi-tier paradigms. The author:

- Lays the foundation for data warehouse concepts with a discussion of the components and the environments, leading to various types of data warehouse solutions suited to the web-distributed and desktop environment.
- Describes the implementation development cycle, architecture, data models, and the data sources needed to implement and access a web-enabled data warehouse.
- Describes techniques necessary to use technologies to face the challenge of the new paradigms—how to store data to meet an organization's decision-support needs and provide users with a common, simple, transparent access to information regardless of where it resides.
- Analyzes and discusses such key topics as granularity of data, partitioning data, metadata, the time basis for decision-support system data (DSS), system of record, migration and more.
- Provides detailed discussions and analysis of major issues.
- Focuses on exploiting technologies, including the Internet, object oriented tools, parallel databases, and decision-support systems that may form the basis of tomorrow's requirements. It also explores the analysis options and techniques.
- Builds upon the implementation development processes discussed in previous chapters that are required for an effective data warehouse, describes the processes for populating and managing the warehouse, and finally provides the know-how to access and use it, with emphasis on analysis tools for decision support and reporting.

The Bottom Line

The reader should be able to take away the following knowledge from this book:

- Data warehouse architecture
- Role of the Internet and object technologies in implementing today's data warehouses
- The importance of data mart warehouses
- Client/server technologies in web-enabled implementations
- Data warehouse modeling
- Importance of security and Web-based implementations
- Standards for graphical interfaces and object-oriented technologies
- Building a practical data warehouse
- Managing the growing data warehouse

In addition, the book focuses on a number of aspects of data warehouse development and on the issues to consider when building a warehouse. You will learn why current skills may need to be enhanced for data warehousing and you will be introduced to new and adapted techniques needed to independently develop source data, warehouse data, and metadata models. The book concludes with a comprehensive bibliography, glossary, and index.

Prerequisites

This book is not a beginner's introduction to computers or data warehousing, or the World Wide Web. It assumes that you know the fundamentals of computing and have some knowledge of database technologies, client/server and Internet technologies, and a basic knowledge of decision-support systems.

Commonly Used Abbreviations

COM: DEC and Microsoft's Common Object Model
CORBA: Common Object Request Broker Architecture
DCE: OSF's Distributed Computing Environment
DBA: Database Administrator
DBMS: Database Management Systems

DSS: Decisions Support System.

EIS: Executive Information Systems.

IDL: Interface Definition Language.

IIOP: Internet Inter-ORB Protocol.

IOP: Inter-ORB Protocol

IPX: Novell's Internet Packet Exchange

ISO: International Standards Organization

MPP: Massive Parallel Processing. The "shared nothing" approach of parallel computing.

ODBC: Open Database Connectivity. A standard for database access developed by Microsoft from the SQL Access Group consortium.

OLAP: On-Line Analytical Processing, originally introduced in 1994 in a paper by E.F. Codd, is a decision-support counterpart to On-Line Transaction Processing. OLAP allows users to derive information and business intelligence from data warehouse systems by providing tools for querying and analyzing the information in the warehouse. In particular, OLAP allows multidimensional views and analysis of that data for decision-support processes.

OLTP: On-Line Transaction Processing. OLTP describes the requirements for a system that is used in an operational environment.

OMG: Object Management Group

ORB: Object Request Broker

ORB Core: The ORB component that moves a request from a client to the appropriate adapter for the target object.

OSF: Open Software Foundation

OSI: ISO's Open Systems Interconnection

Query: A (usually) complex SELECT statement for decision support. See Ad Hoc Query or Ad Hoc Query Software.

ROLAP: Performing OLAP functions against a Relational DBMS is known as ROLAP, for Relational OLAP. Many relational products will offer star and snowflake schema for allowing OLAP queries in a relational environment.

RDBMS: Relational Database Management System.

SMP: Symmetrical Multi-Processing. The "shared everything" approach of parallel computing.

SNA: IBM's System Network Architecture.

SQL: Structured Query Language. A structured query language for accessing relational, ODBC, DRDA, or non-relational compliant database systems.

T1: (1) Digital transmission facility operating with a nominal bandwidth of 1.544 Mbps. Also known as Digital Signal Level 1 (D1). Composed of 24 DS-0 channels in many cases. The T1 digital transmission system is the primary dig-

ital communication system in North America. (2) A high-speed 1.5 Mbps leased line often used by companies for access to the Internet.
TCP/IP: Transmission Control Protocol/Internet Protocol.
WWW: World Wide Web.

Conclusions

Organizations are building more and more data warehouses for decision support as the business value of this technology grows. In doing so, they have to access their operational systems to extract the data they need for their warehouses and/or data marts.

Organizations then have a choice as to whether they use an integrated suite of tools designed to work with each other, or they invest in multiple disparate individual tools, which do not provide integrated support and must be stitched together.

From a business and technical perspective, the choice seems relatively clear that the overall advantage lies squarely with an integrated approach that combines good planning with a robust tool set that allows developers to focus on the business problem rather than the technical problem, such as writing, debugging and maintaining procedural code that is only going to be used as a tool to get to the business objective.

Those organizations that choose the integrated approach will meet their business objectives sooner, with fewer resources and lower expenditures, translating to competitive advantage and increased market share.

You may not need a data warehouse at all. You may be able to leverage your general ledger better or simply improve your existing reporting and query tools. You may only need a specialized, less costly data mart to address a specific need such as providing selective executive-level or line-of-business information sourced from a handful of operational systems.

If you decide you need a data warehouse, then you will likely need to figure on building and maintaining three types of products: data extract and transformation tools, a data warehouse database (either relational or multidimensional), and one or more desktop OLAP or ROLAP tools for deployment on every business analyst's desktop. Nurturing the data warehouse, feeding it with information, and maintaining its structures to reflect ever-changing business needs will be a constant struggle for your IS department.

For some businesses, particularly those that have a high volume of transactions, such as retail and utilities, or those that exhibit high risk, such as financial services, a data warehouse may simply be an essential tool to maintain and improve competitive advantage. For businesses saddled with dozens of difficult-to-access and impossible-to-restructure legacy systems, a data warehouse may be a cost-effective way to keep those systems running while delivering enhanced decision-support value from the legacy data.

On the other hand, a data warehouse can be an unnecessary, costly, and time-consuming distraction from managing your operational systems more effectively and leveraging more value from the systems that you have. Make sure you know which category your business fits into before moving forward with your data warehousing initiative.

2

DATA WAREHOUSE
ARCHITECTURE

Introduction

In a successful data warehouse implementation, thousands of users access and analyze the warehouse data, share information, and collaborate in the decision-making process. Building a data warehouse is a time-consuming and expensive task. The promise of data warehousing is information access for the decision-making majority, not just a handful of users. If data warehousing only meets the needs of a small user community, this initiative will not fulfill that promise, just as decision-support systems (DSS) and executive information systems (EIS) have failed in the past to achieve broad enterprise acceptance.

Who Needs a Data Warehouse?

Corporations must address and respond to marketplace pressures such as competition engendered by a global economy, deregulatory changes in the utilities and telecom industries, and potential government intervention in the health care sector. Since the empowerment of the desktop user, web-enabled applications accessing remote data warehouses have become a necessity.

Corporations are facing issues demanding attention to such trends as customer-focus target marketing to achieve efficient use of marketing resources. The demand will continue to increase for cross-functional use of information sourced from multiple operational information systems. In addition, corporate downsizing has forced the productivity of the knowledge worker to become a premier issue. Increasingly, corporations worldwide are adopting the data warehouse concept as the architectural foundation to make better decisions and respond more rapidly to the changing business environment.

If the end user is not included in the architectural process, their requirements will never fully be met, thus limiting the effectiveness of the data warehouse project. Managers from all business disciplines want enterprise-wide information access, as well as the ability to manipulate and analyze information that the company has gathered, for perhaps a different purpose, in order to make more intelligent business decisions. Business analysts, for their part, use the information in the data warehouse to identify business trends, analyze customer buying profiles, formulate marketing strategies, perform competitive cost analyses, and support strategic decision making.

Whether to increase customer value, identify new markets, or improve the management of the firm's assets, the data warehousing concept promises to deliver the information necessary to accomplish these tasks quickly and efficiently. However, the users and ultimately all corporate decision making based on corporate data will benefit only when these processes and tools for collection and distribution of information involve the end users.

An Architecture Definition

An architecture is a high-level description of the organization of functional responsibilities within a system. However, an architecture is not a description of a specific solution to a problem or a roadmap for success in design. It does not provide guidance in determining where functionality should reside or how to organize it. An architecture does not direct a designer to a successful, powerful or elegant solution to a specific problem.

The goal of architecture, in this book, is to convey information about the general structure of systems. In that sense, architecture defines the relationship of system components, but does nothing to describe the specific implementation of those components. Client/server is architecture in the sense that it defines a relationship between system components. It should be kept in mind that architecture is not a solution in itself, just a framework for developing any number of specific solutions.

Computing architectures do not address the detailed design of an application. Today, most developers create an application as though it were the only one they will ever develop. There is no grand design of which technologies should be employed or why; no thought to how information should be encapsulated, accessed, and assembled into applications; and no common framework for interaction with existing applications.

Effective data warehousing require the definition of architecture—an overall plan for the infrastructure of information and technologies. Although there is no single, all-encompassing architecture for computing, before the development of any next-generation applications, two architectures should be devised. These are a *technical architecture* and an information *architecture*.

Types of Architectures

A *technical architecture* provides a blueprint for assembling technology components. A technical architecture defines what tools and technologies will be used and how. The definitions may include the definition of objects that encapsulate several databases, middleware, and other technologies, as well as which development tools to use and how they will be integrated to provide a complete support environment for the software project.

Information *architecture* describes the content, behavior, and interaction of business objects. These concepts build a semantically rich model of the problem. The information architecture prescribes the building blocks for application development. Business objects use the services of the technical architecture objects. Information architecture provides a framework for the information components of the business: subjects, events, roles, associations, and business rules.

Role of Data Warehousing

Recent years have seen an explosion in the growth of data warehousing. The goal of integrating data to provide accurate, timely, and useful information to an organization's decision-makers is not a new idea. Corporations have sought to create corporate-wide information centers that would enable them to better understand their customers, products, and markets. Now, business conditions and exciting new technologies, such as the Internet, are creating a new wave of interest in decision-support systems in the form of web-accessible data warehousing solutions.

Successful data warehousing requires architecture. This architecture must be flexible enough to provide for the inevitable, inherent changes the data warehousing environment will require as it matures within a company.

Changing Environments

Today, the way companies do business has been fundamentally altered. Centralized markets and competition have created pressure on product cycles and costs. Rightsizing, Internet, business process reengineering, and shorter time-to-market cycles are forcing companies to do more with less. All of these pressures have combined to accelerate the pace of business, requiring organizations to recognize and adapt to change more rapidly. Timely strategic planning and decision making have become critically important as companies seek to cut costs and gain an advantage over their competition. In this environment, businesses need constant, continuous access to information.

Mass of Data

As the information needed to make decisions has become more important, it has also proliferated. The overwhelming market acceptance of the Internet databases (especially relational databases) and the availability of inexpensive platforms has created a massive amount of data for organizations to work with. This data can help companies to understand customer patterns, to know who buys what, when, and where.

Waves of Technology

Several new technologies that are of significant value for analyzing data have emerged. The Internet with enhanced security has revolutionized the thought processes. Online Analytical Processing (OLAP) software has matured. This relatively new breed of software provides significant performance boosts and delivers data to users in a more suitable form for decision support. Some OLAP products are based on popular relational technology (ROLAP). Others are based on more recent database technologies called Multidimensional Databases (MDD) and Multidimensional Online Analytical Processing (MOLAP).

These advances in data storage and retrieval have, in turn, led to advances in data querying products and techniques. Among the new technologies showing great promise for data warehousing are the Internet and the World Wide Web. These technologies have the capability to provide every employee throughout a global organization with easy access to data. The question still remains as to how these masses of non-technical but business-savvy knowledge workers will find what they need in a data warehouse. Although the web exaggerates the problem, the solution is the same for all *levels* of data warehousing that we will investigate.

Data warehousing must not only provide data to knowledge workers, but also deliver information about the data that defines content and context, providing real meaning and value. This information about data is called metadata. We will also examine metadata and its importance to achieving the potential of data warehouses.

Data Warehouse Definition

The idea behind data warehousing is to create competitive advantage by tapping the huge quantities of raw data being captured by operational systems. Corporations know that databases from marketing, distribution, sales, and finance contain information, which, if properly accessed and analyzed, can dramatically increase the effectiveness of the decision-making process. A well-designed and accessible data warehouse can provide a company's knowledge workers with the information they need to ensure the company's success.

It is hard to find an organization that is not implementing a data warehousing solution. Many corporations, however, refer to data warehousing with different terms. And nearly every company implementing data warehousing is doing so in a unique way.

An Architecture for Data Delivery

A data warehouse is an architecture for delivering information to knowledge workers. It is not a product or a database. It is an architecture that defines what information will be delivered to users, how the information will look, and what tools employees will use to access the information. This architecture can take on many forms.

Data warehouses assemble data from all over an organization—from legacy databases, desktop databases, credit reports, sales call reports, and more. This collective database makes a larger amount of summarized data available to a wider group of users. It can be mined or queried in ways that are useful for decision making through a common, centralized database or through distributed data marts and easy-to-use query software.

How do data warehouses differ from operational systems? Quite simply, operational systems exist for a different purpose and thus have a different set and number of users within a corporation. Therefore, you would expect a data warehousing architecture to be very different from that of operational systems.

Parallel Universes

Operational systems have different structures, needs, requirements and objectives from data warehouses. These variations in data, access, and usage prevent organizations from simply using existing operational systems as data warehouse resources. For example, operational data is short-lived and changes rapidly, while warehouse data has a long life and is static. Operational systems feature standard, repetitive transactions that use a small amount of data; warehouse systems feature ad hoc queries and reports that access a much larger amount of data. High availability and real-time updates are critical to the success of the operational system, but not to the data warehouse.

Transformation of Operational Data

Why are most companies building data warehouses? Because they turn data into information. Most companies are trapped under the data deluge. Tons of data is captured by operational systems, but accessing the data and gleaning useful information can be difficult, if not impossible. To break out of this logjam, business people demand ease of access to data, business intelligence, and useful information. Results from the initial implementation of a data warehouse often show a respectable return on investment. The competitive advantage gained from using data gainfully will be far more valuable.

You must demonstrate business solutions from a data warehouse to secure users and sponsors. To lock in critical business buy-in, find the business pain and use the data warehouse to alleviate the pain. Real business pain does not have to be life-threatening to be annoying. Automate the production of manually scheduled reports. Reduce error rates from operational systems by *scrubbing* data before queries. Organize data from the business users' perspective, with summarized views and drill down queries for variance analysis.

Data warehouses organize business data to answer questions about *why* things happen, not just *what* things happened. The real value of the data warehouse architecture is not answering questions but formulating questions. Focus the data warehouse architecture on getting from *what* to *why* as quickly as possible.

Once the analysts are given the tools and taught to formulate real questions, they will be able to feed themselves information. They will be able to validate what is happening and, more importantly, why it is happening and determine how they can influence outcomes in the future. User empowerment can be rewarded.

Good data warehouse architecture can force a company to organize and summarize information from production systems and still not solve their integrity problems. The data warehouse should accept only *scrubbed* data that has integrity. Data redundancies should be removed. If you allow just anything to be thrown into the data warehouse, it will become as useless.

Operational Systems versus Data Warehouses

The architecture of a data warehouse differs considerably from the design and structure of an operational system. Designing a data warehouse can be more difficult than building an operational system because the requirements of the warehouse are often ambiguous. In designing a data warehouse, an organization must understand current information needs as well as likely future needs. This requires a flexible design that ensures the data warehouse can adapt to a changing environment.

Operational systems are typically developed first by working with users to determine and define business processes. Then application code is written and databases are designed. These systems are defined by how the business operates. The primary goal of an organization's operational systems is efficient performance. The design of both applications and databases is driven by online transaction processing (OLTP) performance. These systems need the capacity to handle thousands of transactions and return information in acceptable user-response timeframes, often measured in fractions of a second.

By contrast, data warehouses start with predefined data and vague or unknown usage requirements. Data warehouse users do not know the specifics of their queries. Indeed, ongoing queries lead to constant refinement of the data warehouse, as users learn more about the available data and how to use it for decision making. Typically a user does not know the second question he or she will ask until the first question has been answered. In the area of data mining, which looks for statistical trends and anomalies, users do not even know what the question is until they get the answer.

Both operational and warehouse systems play an important role in an organization's success and need to coexist as valuable assets. This can be done by carefully designing and architecting the data warehouse so that it takes advantage of the power of operational data while also meeting the unique needs of the organization's knowledge workers. As discussed earlier, a successful data warehouse must be able to deliver both the data and the associated metadata to users. A data warehousing architecture must account for both. Metadata provides a bridge between the parallel universes of operational systems and data warehousing.

Enterprise Data Warehousing

The data warehouse emerged as the solution to disparate data problems. The data warehousing effort has been primarily directed toward building an enterprise data warehouse that is organized into categories or subjects that are meaningful to business end users. The data is defined in a single, integrated model that attempts to meet the needs of the entire enterprise. (See Figure 2.1) In most data warehouses, data is extracted from operational files and stored in target databases that cannot be updated or deleted. The data is time-stamped and organized as a historical file. An information directory is provided to manage the metadata, or the data about the data. Metadata gives the description of and meaning to the data in the warehouse so the user can understand what data to use and where to locate it. The data is then integrated into common subject areas and provided to the business analysts and executives in a read-only environment.

The data warehouse so created is a combination of operational and historical data, packaged to accommodate knowledge workers who want to report, analyze, or drill down without having to access operational files directly. Thus far, the industry has not been totally successful in this quest because of the vast resources required.

A data warehouse has four major architectural components:

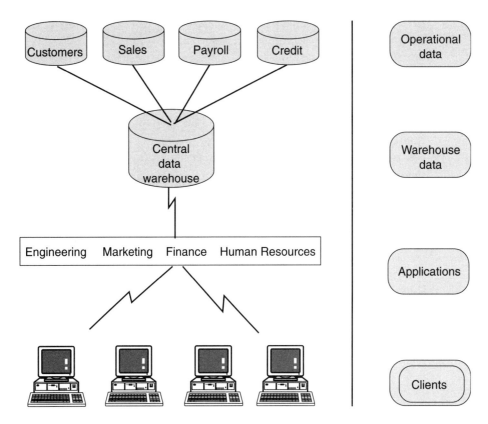

Figure 2.1 Enterprise Data Warehouse

1. Decision-support and analysis tools<I tools><I analysis tools>
2. Data extraction and transformation facilities
3. Data movement and triggering facilities<I triggering facilities>
4. Database management systems

Types of Data Warehouses

Data warehouses or data marts (used interchangeably in this book) are important strategic initiatives by corporations. These warehouses consolidate data from a number of different application sources for use in decision-support systems by the business lines. These business lines are seeking information to help them improve their competitive position in the marketplace as well as better manage their revenues and costs. Business lines want easy access to this information in a short time frame as well as the flexibility to change their data requirements cost-effectively and quickly.

A scalable architecture goes well beyond performance issues. Maintenance, security, and flexibility are equally important. The system architecture must support background processing of agents and information sharing. The Internet is a model of how *unstructured* text and image information can be accessed. The enterprise must adopt a similar model for providing *structured* data access and information sharing.

As you design your warehouse, it is important to put together an architecture that accommodates the ongoing maintenance and extensions of the warehouse efforts as well as the initial requirements of the project. The majority of the effort in a data warehouse revolves around the process of data integration—the components that are involved in making sure that the data has the quality and the structure necessary for inclusion in the warehouse. Several steps are involved in this effort:

- Data extraction from the production systems
- Data transformation
- Data matching, consolidation, and elimination of redundancies
- Data validation and cleansing
- Database loading
- Metadata management
- Data warehouse access via the web

These steps are critical in ensuring that the data populating the warehouses has the reliability and business logic that the business units demand.

Data Warehousing Solutions

Re-engineering data for warehouses requires careful planning and design to ensure that the business lines get meaningful information. This planning not only requires that data architects understand the business line information requirements—they must also understand the structure of the data elements in the source production systems. Source data must be *transformed*, *integrated* and *cleansed* so that the warehouse has reliable data for the business lines to use.

A data integration tool can reduce the time, complexity, and costs involved with the initial population and ongoing maintenance requirements of data warehouse and data mart applications. Through its filtering capabilities and business line rules-driven approach, it can populate both the warehouse and the data marts, ensuring consistency of data across multiple systems.

Data Marts

In today's environment, data marts have evolved to more cost effectively meet the unique needs of business lines. These marts can be built more quickly and contain only the data relevant to the specific business unit. For example, data marts may be divided based on departmental lines or by product type. These marts challenge the systems group in terms of managing the ongoing changes along with ensuring data consistency across the different marts. The architecture must provide for simplifying and reducing the costs in this multiple data mart management process (**Figure 2.2**), as follows:

- Administration through a single point
- Data consistency across data marts through sharing of business rules
- Metadata repository to help manage the changes in requirements

Traditional Data Warehouse Approaches

Information systems have evolved into their present state via a tortuous and convoluted path. The systems, far from having a global or enterprise-wide

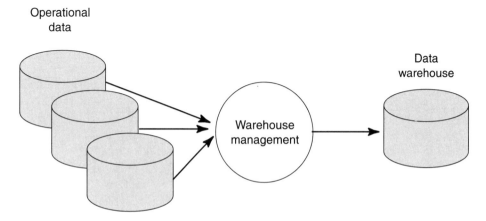

Figure 2.2 Enterprise Integrator

dimension, are rather turned inward, almost as if the guiding design principle had been parochial. This works well for individual departments, who typically have well-defined, well-bounded charters and whose motivation is simply to fulfill that charter.

For example, the payroll department does not need to worry about development; sales does not need to worry about manufacturing; engineering does not need to worry about human resources. However, senior management needs to see a broader picture to make effective decisions, and today's systems provide only a fractured jigsaw puzzle whose individual pieces conflict with each other in terms of contradictory data or overlap each other with inconsistent data definitions.

To get a cross-functional look at the company's vital statistics, one is first faced with finding out which of the individual systems contain which pieces of the desired information and reconciling discrepancies among them to get a single view. What they get with today's systems is a kaleidoscopic view of the enterprise, making effective management nearly impossible. Often, managers and executives turn to MIS to help them untangle the knot. Industry estimates are that a majority of the MIS budget is dedicated to creating reports for users (digging data out of the system) and responding to ad hoc end user requests for information (digging more data out of the system).

The primary objective of data warehousing is to resolve this dilemma for managers and direction setters in today's organizations, while simultaneously lifting the burden from MIS. It seems a simple enough concept: gather all the data needed for decision making from all the operational systems and arrange it in a single repository (or warehouse) in a consistent manner so that we can answer the questions we need answered. We have to make sure that the individual systems from which we extract the data are not impeded in their daily tasks by this process.

Architectural Constructs

Like many seemingly simple tasks, the actual construction and implementation of a system which meets the objectives defined above is more difficult than it first appears. The Figure 2.3 demonstrates the basic architectural constructs required to develop a Data Warehouse System.

The systems on the left, titled "Financial," "Inventory Control," and "Sales," represent standard, individual OLTP systems, which are designed to capture transactions in each department. In this configuration, data from each of these systems is uploaded into a data warehouse, which will then include all the information available from each department. Along with the data itself,

Data sources   Warehouse data metadata   Clients

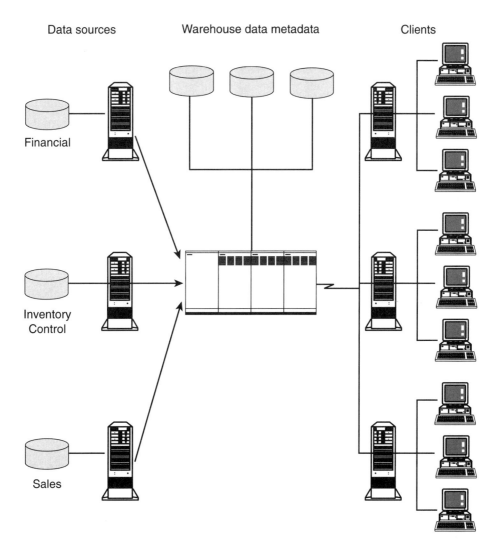

Financial

Inventory
Control

Sales

Figure 2.3   Data Warehouse System

there is information about the data, or metadata. These data warehouse systems are available throughout the enterprise and are used to manage and analyze the data in the warehouse for decision support applications. The following sections delve deeper into these architectural components.

Enterprise Data Model

The enterprise data model attempts to define the data requirements for the enterprise as a whole, from manufacturing and engineering through human resources and finance to sales and marketing. The enterprise data model then becomes the underpinnings of the data warehouse, since its constructs will control what information is available to end users as well as what level of detail or aggregation is available.

Scrubbing/Upload

Large organizations today can be characterized as an information Tower of Babel, with systems of every color and hue distributed across the multiple departments of the organization. The data warehouse, in providing a single point of consolidation for these divergent data, will need to transfer, or upload the salient data elements on a regular basis in order to have the warehouse reflect the latest information available to the organization.

Information contained in these disparate systems is often redundant, and since the systems were likely designed without a master enterprise data model in mind, the redundant data is usually maintained according to different data dictionaries. This means that even though engineering and finance both keep the name of employee Eric Quigley in their databases, they likely will have differing data definitions. The duplications and differences in individual data definitions will have to be *rationalized,* or *cleansed,* or *scrubbed* during the uploads. Often, small differences in seemingly innocuous data can lead to a significant amount of work in achieving this goal.

Metadata

Since the data warehouse will aggregate data from a multiplicity of sources within the organization, there is often a need to gather information about the data being stored in order to understand the significance of the data more fully. For example, is this data sourced from only one place in the organization, or is it a composite from multiple areas? How current is the data? Is it refreshed daily, weekly, monthly, quarterly, or annually? If the data is summarized data, where can I find the atomic transactions that were used, and what formulas were used in calculating the summaries?

Warehouse (Database)

The collective data must be stored in a central repository. From an architectural perspective, data warehouse developers have to determine the physical storage dimensions of the warehouse (how big is it, how should we partition it, etc.) as well as the logical dimensions of the warehouse (what database technology should we use). To date, most warehouses have been built on parallel or traditional relational technology.

OLAP

On-Line Analytical Processing refers to the ability of the system to support decision-making. This technology allows users to view information from many angles, "drill down" to atomic data, or "roll up" into aggregations to see trends and historical information. It is the final and arguably the most important piece of the data warehouse architecture.

Management

Managing and coordinating the successful integration of disparate databases into a consistent data model, which containing current and accurate data, requires a significant management component. Operational management also involves ensuring the availability of the system, which means managing the scalability of the hardware and software as the dimensions of the system (size of database, number of users, number and complexity of queries) grow.

The Challenges of Centralized Data Warehouses

So far, centralized data warehouses have failed to meet users' needs. A major part of the problem is the sheer size of the project and the attendant challenges brought on by tackling something as gargantuan as an enterprise-wide consolidation warehouse. This section will focus on how these challenges impact the architectural results.

Design Challenges

The thought of undertaking a single data model for the entire enterprise is enough to make the most battle-scarred veterans of data modeling faint. The road to a single model is tortuous and demanding. It starts with an understanding of the combined information needs of all users who might access the warehouse for decision support, whether they are in finance, marketing, sales, or senior management. This is followed by a thorough analysis of all existing data models (and some which are non-existent except as embodied in working systems). Finally, after running these two gauntlets, designers are faced with the task of rationalizing all of the existing models into a single model, which

houses, to knowledge workers. We call this a template because, in our experience, no two data warehouse architectures are the same. A full-blown architecture such as the one presented below would evolve to this mature state over time and with effort, as dictated by necessity.

The data flow has been the main focus of the data warehousing industry to date. **Figure 2.4** depicts an implementation of a data warehouse architecture. The data is extracted from operational systems, *scrubbed*, *integrated*, and *transferred* to a target data warehouse. Along with operational systems, external data and databases from packaged applications may be the sources of data. A data warehouse of this sort usually resides in a relational database. In this case the physical data warehouse acts as an archive and staging area for delivery of the data through focused channels depicted as data marts.

Subsets of the data are usually extracted by subject area and stored in *data marts* specifically designed to provide departmental users with fast access to large amounts of topical data. These data marts often provide several levels of aggregation and employ physical dimensional design techniques for OLAP.

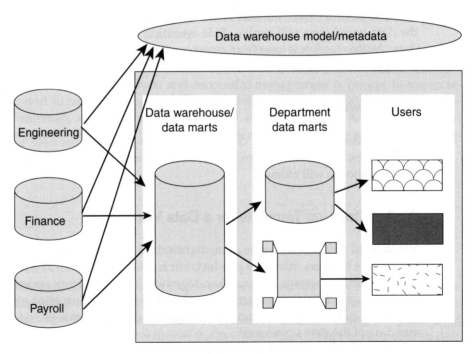

Figure 2.4   Operational Systems and Metadata

A corporate data warehouse architecture may have many data marts. Using sophisticated tools, users can extract information from departmental data marts and easily manipulate the data to perform specific analyses.

The operational systems are the source of metadata as well as operational data. Metadata is extracted from individual operational systems. This set of metadata forms a model of the operational system. This metadata includes, for example, the entities/records/tables and associated attributes of the data source.

The metadata from multiple operational data sources is integrated into a single model of the data warehouse. This logical model is not tied to any particular product or physical data storage implementation. The model provides data warehouse architects with a business model through which they can understand the type of data available in a warehouse, the origin of the data and the relationships between the data elements. They can also provide more suitable terms for naming data than are usually present in the operational systems.

From this business model, physical database design can be engineered and the actual data warehouse can be created. Additionally, the logical business model can serve as a basis for the physical design of multiple data marts that may flow from the data warehouse. The physical design of the data warehouse and data marts may be drastically different, with varying levels of data normalization and aggregation. But the logical model preserves business relationships, data origin and ties to the operational systems.

The metadata contained in the data warehouse and data mart models is available to specialized data warehousing tools for use in analyzing the data. In this way the data and metadata can be kept in sync as both flow through the data warehouse distribution channel from source to target to consumer.

Metadata

Metadata can be defined as "data about data." For example, a company's sales database contains both data and metadata. A customer's name, address and phone number is the data in the database. The names of the values stored for each customer record, i.e., "customer_name," "customer_address," and "customer_phone_number" are the metadata. Metadata is essential to bind together the database and application programs that access and update the data.

A helpful analogy is found in contrasting arithmetic and algebra. The expressions $3 + 6 = 9$, $2 + 7 = 9$, and $6 + 2 = 8$ are a family of arithmetic statements that are *data* to the algebraic formula $a + b = c$. They all respond to same rules. The data in a database, whether from an operational system or a data warehouse, is defined, controlled, and accessed through the *formula* of metadata.

In the most advanced forms of the data warehouse architecture, there are multiple operational databases, multiple extract and load utility programs, a single data warehouse database, and many more extract and load utility programs to move the data from the data warehouse database to the many data marts.

Managing these multiple sets of metadata is a real challenge that can require assistance. In addition, while the database metadata and the extract and load utility programs metadata are mainly of interest to data processing professionals, business professionals using decision support systems are also interested in metadata to help them express queries and establish data mining activities.

In Figure 2.3, metadata exists for each specific stage of the data warehouse: operational, physical data warehouse, data marts, and user tools. In fact each stage may have multiple sets of metadata (models) if the architecture provides for many data sources integrating into one physical data warehouse with many data marts and many tools. Although this is an unusual example, representing advanced forms of data warehousing, data warehouse architectures need to accommodate multiple sets of metadata (models) and the mappings between them.

The Process of Building a Data Warehouse

Recognizing that OLTP data is the basis for decision support, copies are made (to other subsystems or RDBMS platforms). Refreshed regularly, the data may be a subset of the OLTP elements, and might have summary tables, but actually is mapped one-to-one to the OLTP data. Although some would not classify this as data warehousing because of the absence *of data warehousing process*, it is a common mechanism for providing users with access to operational data.

Let us consider a large chip manufacturing company. Established databases support a mix of custom and packaged applications. Selected data is copied weekly from one system to another. Users with contemporary query tools use the data for ad hoc queries. Termed a *data mart*, no attempt is made to query data across the systems. Metadata is viewed via textual reports and facilities of the query tool.

The next step in the process is the recognition that OLTP issues are not applicable to the data warehouse. Data warehouse data is time-dependent, aggregated, summarized, and tuned and named differently. This is the origin of the movement in data warehousing to have separate, dedicated delivery systems.

Queries occasionally span application boundaries of the OLTP systems, placing more emphasis on standard names and representations of replicated data. Initial data quality assessments are made and occasionally quality controls are implemented prior to loading the data warehouse. The architects might need to get some data from a non-OLTP source.

Let us examine another manufacturing company. Recognizing the inherent differences between the OLTP data and what the knowledge workers need, this manufacturer employs a reuse approach. Using an existing corporate data model (built from and synchronized with the OLTP systems), they engineer the model to a new DBMS environment. The database administrator (DBA) indexes and tunes the design based on anticipated usage.

The idea of source-to-target is now very important, and therefore the metadata itself and mapping become very important. More emphasis is placed on metadata and it is used for pragmatic activities (unload and transform and load). Data sources that are non-OLTP are recognized and used.

As the differences between the data warehouse and OLTP metadata become greater, it becomes imperative to maintain the relationship between the two. The complexity of the programs that manage this relationship is increasing, and must be maintained via metadata mappings. To abandon mapping between OLTP and the data warehouse (source-to-target) as represented in the models would leave the logic in proprietary application programs with little chance for reuse.

The metadata serves at least three roles: automated transforms, aiding the developer in navigation and tuning, and helping users understand what they have to work with. Each user accesses metadata differently, and typically uses very sophisticated delivery platforms such as corporate intranets or local databases.

While the key modeling techniques—metadata synchronization and visibility of the metadata—were tackled, data may still have been implemented in standard RDBMS technology, query tools, and networks. The warehouse data has achieved some measure of uniqueness (volume, performance expectations, query complexity, or availability) that warrants specialized hardware, database, or query technology that is specially defined.

In all stages of the data warehouse architecture, companies that design with updates and changes in mind build better systems. In this environment, the role of a repository of metadata and records of changes and transformations is vital to the success of the data warehouse.

Common Enterprise Data Architecture

The idea of *starting small* makes a lot of sense from the perspective of minimizing risk and simultaneously deriving benefit from the system as early as possible. However, as the project is launched in its reduced scale, it is important to have a vision and plan in place as to how to propagate this technology to other departments in an orderly and integrated fashion. Doing so not only will help to reduce further the time and expense of successive installations, but it will also help reduce costs and increase productivity in the operation of the aggregation of data marts.

An integrated architecture should be developed to tie the data marts together to facilitate cross-functional analysis and maintenance. This is, after all, only common sense: it would be wasteful and foolhardy not to adopt as many elements of the initial successful implementation into subsequent implementations in other departments. Some of the elements to be considered in an overall architecture include common extraction tools, transformation tools, processes, data dictionary, metadata repository, and OLAP tools.

This raises the thorny question of the enterprise data model. Are we not proposing here the very same technique that we described earlier as being one of the downfalls of the centralized data warehouse? The answer is yes and no. Certainly a comprehensive effort at a complete and total data warehouse prior to the advent of any development would present the same issues for the data mart architecture as it does to the centralized data warehouse.

By agreeing on a strategy of data marts designed specifically for business area applications, we lay down an architectural principle that says the individual application is more important than the centralized data warehouse concept. This puts us in a position where the business application drives the technology, rather than having the technology drive the business application.

Economics

If data marts are indeed tools for management, then the economics of the technology must be a primary factor in the decision to deploy them. The success of data warehousing projects depends on a number of factors: the technology, the internal acceptance of the warehouse, and business strategy.

1. Technology choices are a major factor in the decision to deploy full-scale global warehouses or application-specific data marts. For example, roughly one-third of the initial cost is spent on hardware and another third on internal development services.

2. A second factor in achieving payback is the internal acceptance of the data mart. An organization's return is measured in productivity and market gains which accrue from the use of the warehouse. Therefore, organizations whose warehouses are unused have the same denominator (costs) as those whose products are well used, but have a much smaller, or nonexistent numerator (benefits).

3. Slow adoption can be an economic death knell for a data mart/data warehouse project. This makes it imperative that the initial design be usable and that its availability and utility be well publicized. Prudent use of pilot/prototypes where the target area is well chosen, the tools are well suited for the application, and the results are well communicated to the rest of the organization can go a long way here in ensuring the success of the overall project.

4. The most important factor is the impact of the warehouse on business strategy. The true, and most far-reaching, benefit of a warehouse lies in the solid decision making it enables.

5. The economics of data marts versus data warehouses is the almost too-obvious point that in most organizations it is far easier to fund at departmental level than it is at the enterprise level. This is especially true given the fact that there is no guarantee that the project will succeed, and thus a smaller risk is easier to sell.

Implementation Options

Corporate data represents a strategic asset for any firm, but its value becomes tangible only by turning that data into actionable information. The Information Technology industry has been talking about delivering data to knowledge workers and providing them with decision-support systems for two decades.

RDBMSs are very easily queried directly, opening a completely new marketplace for vendors who were providing easy-to-use SQL query and reporting tools. The SQL query products allowed the business user to go directly to the RDBMS production systems and retrieve the exact data they needed, when they needed it. Users were no longer willing to settle for MIS deciding what data they would get and what export schedule would be used.

The drawback arose as business users queried production data in an ad hoc fashion, resulting in tremendous performance and availability problems. If a user was not well trained, it was possible to submit a query that would tie up the entire system for hours, locking out mission-critical production applications. The MIS answer to this problem was to curtail, or in some cases forbid, ad hoc queries to production data.

To answer the surging demand for information within corporations, businesses began to invest resources in building databases, separate from the production databases, for housing and retrieving query data. The concept of a separate database just to support the knowledge worker was new and took the name of "information warehouse" from IBM and "data warehouse" from Bill Inmon.

Typically, major technology trends have a long life cycle with three main stages: introduction, deployment, and maturity. Today, we are entering the technology deployment phase of the data warehouse life cycle. Many leading practitioners are seeing a roadblock to data warehousing reaching another stage, when a technology is universally adopted.

The problem is that most of the software tools on the market today require a large system integration effort from the customer. The size of the typical data warehouses is growing rapidly, so that 100-gigabyte data warehouses are becoming commonplace in larger organizations. The warehouse size trend is particularly worrisome because the building, maintenance, and administration of such large data warehouses becomes very complicated. If there is no change in the current trend, a large segment of the market will not be able to afford the data warehouse, and the technology may never fully reach the maturity stage.

Multi-tiered Data Warehouses

A multi-tiered data warehouse is built to suit the customers' needs and economics, spanning the spectrum from an enterprise-wide data warehouse to a small group's data mart. Multi-tiered implies a hierarchy, but does not exclude a networked data mart layer within the hierarchy. In order to build a hierarchy of data warehouses, a sound data plan must be in place for a strong foundation. It makes no difference whether a corporation starts at the bottom of the hierarchy or the top—they must have a goal in mind and a plan for relating the various levels and networks. The data plan cannot be constructed or managed without an active metadata catalog.

If a corporation begins their information architecture with an enterprise data warehouse, they will quickly realize the need for subsets of the data and levels of summary. The easiest way to meet these needs is to spawn data marts, subject area and summary, from the enterprise data warehouse. This is top-down development and is the approach recommended by most warehouse gurus.

The other approach is where a data mart is built first to meet specific user group requirements, but is built according to a data plan and with roll-up as a goal (see Figures 2.5 and 2.6). The need will arise for the marts to participate in a hierarchy in which detailed information from several subject-area data marts is summarized and consolidated into an enterprise data warehouse. This method of construction requires thought but is probably faster method of arriving at an enterprise view than starting with the enterprise data warehouse.

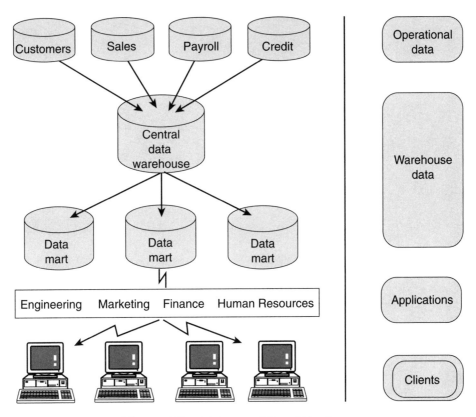

Figure 2.5 Multi-tiered Data Warehouse

Along with a robust metadata catalog, a tool that reverse-engineers the various data marts' metadata into a logical unit would be of tremendous value. Reliable algorithms can be used to scan the catalog and group the related items from each data mart, suggesting how they should be combined in a higher level data warehouse.

Since multi-tiered data warehouses can encompass the best of both worlds, enterprise data warehouses and data marts, they are more than just a solution to a decision-support problem. They are an important part of an information world (architecture or strategy). However, there are other components that are just as necessary as the Metadata store. This information world exists today in every corporation, just like the operational world has existed for some

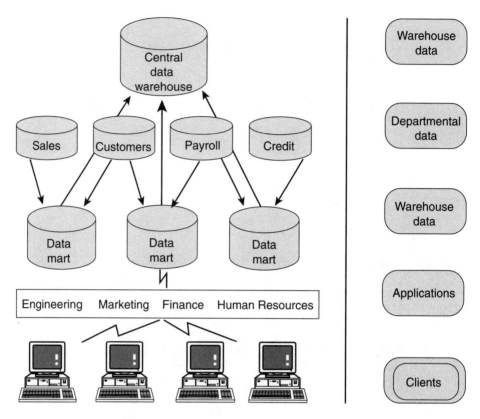

Figure 2.6   Multi-tiered Data Warehouse

time. The information side has some of the same requirements as the operational, such as data transfer mechanisms, and some different ones such as automated data type conversions.

A peer-to-peer, secure transport system is required to move large amounts of data safely between the warehouses. Scheduling becomes paramount in the information world to automate the loading, extracting, moving and delivering of data anywhere. Interfaces must be browsers so that the Internet/intranet can be used for inexpensive, global access.

As an infrastructure for the information world, there must be a management engine that is able to deploy the work to multiple servers, execute the tasks concurrently, automate the execution of multiple dependent tasks, and log, audit, and perform recovery and alerts. Key features of multi-tiered data warehouse architecture are:

- Bottom-up or top-down information strategy
- Robust, single catalog that not only holds the metadata about the contents but manages the spawning and roll-up
- Groupware capabilities for sharing information
- Client/server model with servers located in the business units or departments
- Distribution and deployment across Internet and intranet
- Catalog with construction, location, dimension, where user and mart relationship metadata is stored
- Data distributed to the user in the desired format on a user-defined schedule
- Subscription service allowing users to request information from any of the data warehouses
- Action scheduling by calendar and event
- Transformation engine that can be run concurrently and on multiple servers
- Management engine for deployment of tasks, recovery/restart, logging, and load balancing

After trying out these different architectures to meet varied information strategies, many corporations may come to the conclusion they need an enterprise-wide view of corporate data as well as a focused, single application view. An option is to consider building a total information infrastructure: a top-down data warehouse architecture with an enterprise data warehouse first and then the data marts, or a bottom-up solution, where the data marts are built first and rolled up to the warehouse. In either scenario, the corporation will eventually settle into a framework of multi-tiered data warehouses.

Conclusions

The advent of new technologies, the prevalence of the web, and the experience of those who pioneered the concept of data warehousing have brought us to a new and better way to build data warehouse architectures and implementations for enterprises today. That is the concept of starting with a limited scope data warehouse which will simultaneously prove the concept, introduce the technology to the organization, and produce a return on the investment. In parallel with the initial implementations, the organization can be building enterprise architecture to ensure that subsequent data warehouse implementations will be compatible with previous ones.

To build a successful data warehouse, planners and implementers must remember the key issues of fast, flexible access and scalability. Database technologies such as compression, vertical data storage, and bit-mapped indexing are essential ingredients which will contribute significantly to the initial success, which is in turn essential to the long-term success of any data warehousing strategy. As we have watched the data warehouse market develop, many different philosophies and methodologies have evolved, some requiring extensive resources and some with quick-fix solutions. Moving forward, it is apparent that no single architecture is right for every application. To move the data warehouse technology into the next stage of its life cycle, universal deployment, a corporation must be allowed to examine its information needs, its data source structures, and its timelines and requirements. Some organizations will chose to select the enterprise data warehouse; some will select smaller data mart solutions. Many will come to the conclusion that a multi-tiered architecture will bring the best results and the most flexibility for the future.

Once requirements are gathered and a strategy is outlined, the organization should build an information infrastructure data map. Although data mapping is time consuming, if the process starts with one subject area at a time, adding mapping and planning as more areas are added, the payoff will be many times the effort in the end.

The shortest, quickest solution may be to build from a bottom-up approach, creating data marts to meet specific departmental needs, but with the forethought to remain in line with the corporate information strategy. This will allow for some early, quick successes to provide departmental information to end users without derailing the enterprise-wide information effort. The multi-tiered architecture has the flexibility and scalability to support short-term and long-term objectives. An organization can now deliver better information to its end users and enable informed decisions based on accurate, timely and precise corporate data.

The data warehouse is a continuous flow of data and metadata, requiring continuously updated models, both logical and physical. A data warehouse at any level of maturity needs to provide not only data but also metadata to be successful. In data warehousing, success is not defined by the quantity of data, but by a user's ability to understand the data and act on it. Metadata is the key to this understanding.

A large variety of tools are available that have the flexibility to adapt to this changing environment. The logical model gives organizations the tool they need to maintain the architecture of the data warehouse. Changes in data warehouse content, physical implementations, available technologies, user requirements and the business environment can all be addressed in the data warehouse through the logical model.

Introduction

Corporations recognize that information placed in the hands of decision-makers is a powerful tool. To meet decision makers' nearly insatiable appetite for information, data is being extracted from operational systems and placed in data warehouses.

Delivery of data warehouse information to decision makers throughout the enterprise and around the world has been an expensive challenge. Once data has been extracted and organized for user access, analytic software must be loaded on each user's PC. User requirements and even the users themselves change constantly, resulting in a significant support burden. The World Wide Web offers a solution. In addition to simplifying the deployment of data warehouse access, the Internet and specifically the intranets can introduce a new level of collaborative interactive analysis and information sharing among decision-makers.

Two technologies that became commercially popular in the early 1990s are in the process of converging. These technologies are the World Wide Web, which is making information on computers linked to the Internet easily accessible, and business intelligence tools that facilitate making database contents accessible to non-technical users.

The way we obtain and analyze information to support our decisions has drastically changed the processes. This analysis promises to make data published on the World Wide Web easily accessible to non-technical decision makers for query, reporting, and analysis tasks. For corporations, this has introduced an alternative, low-cost mechanism for making data available to individuals who need it. For users, the end result is a much richer pool of easily-accessible information.

The Internet Phenomenon

Driving this transformation is the Internet, an almost chaotic arrangement of computers, network connections, and telecommunication lines. The Internet was initially designed to meet the needs of the US Department of Defense for secure communications. Consequently, certain aspects of the design of the network, such as the packet-oriented communication protocol, TCP/IP, were intended to prevent the interruption of communications during a military confrontation.

During the first 20 years of the Internet, only a select few *power* users in the military or educational centers had access to the system. In the meantime, several key technologies evolved, which gradually increased the number of people who had connections to the Internet. These technologies include:

- Powerful and affordable personal computers (PCs) and workstations
- Graphical user interfaces such as MS Windows, Macintosh, and Motif
- Improved network bandwidth and cheaper transmission rates
- Digital telephony
- Web TV

Factors That Sparked the Explosive Growth

Hyperlinks: The now much friendlier Internet became host to the *World Wide Web* (WWW), where users could easily and transparently navigate across documents from one network site to another via hyperlinks. Hyperlinks freed users from having to know the exact location of each document and the network path that leads to that site. Now the users can click on highlighted text or images to navigate to another set of information which may reside thousands of miles away, all transparently.

The User Interface: The *plumbing* slowly came into place over the span of 20 years, with only a gradual increase in users. What sparked the incredible growth of Internet usage for business as well as recreation in the mid-1990s was the appearance and commercial success of a friendly user interface to the Internet. This new interface, known as Mosaic, was originally developed at the University of Illinois. The interface was commercialized by Netscape, Microsoft Internet Explorer, and others, and quickly became popular.

While the *plumbing* had been in place, and while users could theoretically access vast amounts of information across the Internet via arcane operating system commands such as telnet, ftp, ping, rlogin, talk, finger, rwho, etc., it has been the ease of use that sparked the explosion of the Internet use.

Emerging Trends on the Internet

With millions of users on the Internet, the demand to enhance all aspects of the system, including usability, manageability, performance, and security has grown exponentially.

The web-standard HyperText Markup Language (HTML), which is the most common way to access the web today, while easy to use, limits the interaction between the user and the application. Users are limited to sending and receiving information as document forms, without the capability to drag and drop or to manipulate objects on the screen. The protocol used for HTML communication is the hypertext transfer protocol (HTTP).

Extensions or enhancements to HTML are quickly appearing which promise to make the user interface come alive with reusable application components that run on the user's PC. These extensions include Java from Sun Microsystems, LiveMedia from Netscape, VRML (Virtual Reality Modeling Language) from Silicon Graphics, ActiveX from Microsoft, and many others.

Decision Support for Data Warehouse

While the Internet was in its initial limited-growth phase, several new technologies emerged that brought data stored in corporate databases closer to decision makers.

The User Interface Factors

In the 1990s, enhanced user-friendly environments via newer technologies, such as OMG's CORBA-based Object Request Brokers, Internet Inter-ORB Protocol (IIOP), and the Internet made data available to non-technical users for decision support.

Relational Database Factors

Relational database management systems (RDBMS), which appeared in the late 1970s, simplified access to data for programmers with the Structured Query Language (or SQL). RDBMSs allowed application developers to build data access tools independent of the structure of the database. Before the emergence of the mathematically elegant relational model, data access mechanisms were database-specific.

The functional separation of data access mechanisms from the database itself, along with the proliferation of low-cost processing power on desktop PCs and workstations, led to another commercially successful technology trend, *client/server computing*. Client/server computing, introduced in the mid-1980s, de-coupled the processing of the database access tool from the processing activity of the database engine itself. Database client tools and database servers communicated across corporate networks using vendor- specific middleware and network protocols such as TCP/IP, Novell SPX/IPX, and others. By the end of the 1980s all relational database vendors had migrated to the client/server model.

Tied to the proliferation of RDBMS and client/server systems was the concept of open systems, where customers were in principle free to mix and match multi-vendor (or heterogeneous) components such as hardware, operating systems, network protocols, database systems, database middleware, and data access tools. Industry standards evolved to ensure interoperability between components.

By 1990, the infrastructure, which made corporate data more easily accessible to end users from their desktops, was thus in place. However, access to data was still limited in the following ways:

1. Forms and reports gave access to a static *window* of information—users had no flexibility to customize their forms. Hence, from the perspective of a decision maker, online access to databases via forms was not very different from legacy business reports on paper.

2. The useful lifetime of a corporate application decreased due to frequent reorganizations, to the point were Information Technology (IT) had trouble keeping up (application development time was frequently greater than the time during which the application was relevant to the organization).

3. Custom tools for specialized users appeared, such as executive information system (EIS) tools. These tools were limited either in scope or in capacity and demanded extensive IT resources to set up and maintain.

Emerging Decision Support System Trends

As the business-intelligent decision-support tool industry matures, the following technologies are emerging:

Integrated Query, Reporting, and Analysis

Database query and reporting was originally treated as an activity separate from data analysis. Hence, two different sets of tools evolved, one set of tools for query and reporting and a second, separate set of tools for data analysis. With an ever increasing number of people involved in decision-making and with more corporate data available for analysis in data warehouses, this artificial division has become outdated. Currently, most tools have integrated query, reporting, and analysis.

Analysis Using OLAP

The availability of data analysis tools are designed for everyone who needs to examine data from different perspectives. Multidimensional views of data for on-line analytical processing (OLAP) are thus becoming available through user friendly front-end tools.

Two Technologies Converge—Decision Support Over the Internet

The emergence of internetworking and object-oriented development tools, along with increased accessibility to information stored in large databases, has made decision-support data available via the Internet to everyone authorized to receive it. Accessing the World Wide Web during their analysis, users are able to navigate transparently to the data sources which contain the information they need.

Examples of decision support across the Internet include:

- A wine maker uses a web-based data mart to search for customers who may like his specific wines or gifts.
- A teenager who is about to buy (via the Internet) a new stereo system uses the home computer to analyze the prices, features, and availability of various offerings as well at the status of his or her finances. In the course of the analysis, the teenager *surfs* multiple locations on the Internet to obtain, combine, and analyze the information.
- A store manager who uses the web from a PC at the store to connect to corporate headquarters and to view reports such as price sheets, financial reports, etc.
- A business person at a remote island resort (on vacation, in theory) can use the corporate intranet to locate and download key corporate reports to analyze the information on his or her PC.

On the other hand, some view the Web simply as an alternative communication mechanism between clients and servers. However, the availability of information across the web makes application resources potentially available to an unprecedented number of users worldwide. This explosion in resource use has led to the emergence of the following architectures for decision support on the Internet:

Fat Clients

Fat client configurations are designed to take advantage of the low-cost processing power available on desktop PCs. They are essentially client/server applications which have been enhanced to take advantage of the World Wide Web. For corporate sites, fat client configurations offer the benefit of using the

Internet (or in this case, an intranet) as an alternative to corporate wide area networks (or WANs).

Thin Clients

For environments where it is difficult to manage application software distributed across large numbers of user sites, proponents of the *thin* client approach argue that application processing should be separated from presentation activities at the user's desktop.

Under this model, the software on users' desktops (which may be diskless systems) is limited to the (lightweight, down-loadable, and platform-independent) components that relate to the presentation of information. The majority of the processing of the application logic takes place on the back-end system. The *thin* client can thus be viewed as a terminal to the network, similar in concept to, though more intelligent than, the *dumb* terminals that are used to access multi-user legacy systems.

Multi-tier Systems

Performance, that is the speed with which a user's request is processed, is another important issue. Performance concerns in the multi-user Internet environment are driving toward further modularization of the current two tier (front-end browser, back-end HTTP server) environment.

Apart from infrastructure issues, such as the bandwidth of the user's connection to the network, or the hardware used, the architecture of the system can also be a factor. Under the multi-tier architecture, HTTP server activity is separated from application- related processing.

The three models described above are not mutually exclusive. A particular system could consist of a combination of *fat* clients and *thin clients*, as well as *multiple tiers*.

Key Requirements for Decision Support Over the Internet

To make the *dream* of decision support for everyone across the Internet a reality, the first generation of Internet decision-support tools must meet these four key requirements:

- Support interactive analysis
- Keep pace with the infrastructure
- Ensure security
- Keep options open for customers

Support Interactive Analysis

Decision support is an iterative process consisting of query, analysis, and reporting tasks. **Figure 3.1** illustrates a typical decision support workflow. The decision support task begins with the user submitting a query to a data source. When the query result set is returned to the user's PC in the form of a report, the user analyzes the data by viewing it in different levels of detail and from different perspectives. In the course of the analysis, the user may decide that additional information is necessary and may thus request additional data from the database. When the analysis is concluded, the user may add some finishing touches to the report format before distributing it.

An Internet-enabled decision-support tool must allow users to carry out these iterative steps efficiently.

Keeping Pace with the Infrastructure

The World Wide Web promises to change drastically the way people make decisions. However, it is important to understand the current constraints of the Internet, to use the existing infrastructure for what it is best at, and to *implement systems that play to the strengths of Internet/intranet technology.*

The web is best suited today for the publication of HTML documents, the navigation of users across documents (*surfing*), and the downloading of files across the network.

In the very near future, network performance delays may limit certain interactive decision-support activities such as performing data drills. While analyzing data, a decision-maker will not be willing to wait 20 seconds to a minute (*the typical response time on the web today*) for data to be returned after a drill.

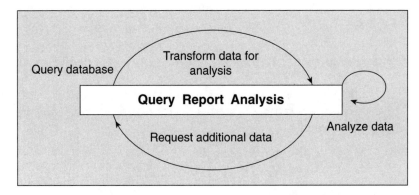

Figure 3.1   Typical Iterative Workflow in a Decision-Support Scenario

Security

The World Wide Web promises to make information available to an unprecedented number of users. The new decision-support environment must maintain the security of sensitive corporate and personal information. Security requirements include the ability to:

- Control publication rights for users who wish to post information on the Web.
- Control user access rights to information published on the Web.

For IT departments, a key requirement is that existing security information be reused. IT departments should not have to re-engineer existing user security information when a decision-support application becomes Internet-enabled.

Keeping Options Open

The web is a dynamic and changing environment with an infrastructure that is evolving rapidly. Organizations that deploy Internet-enabled decision-support applications need to ensure that the Internet application that they choose does not lock them into an Internet technology that becomes a dead end down the road.

Web-Distributed Environments

An intranet is far more than a place to manage e-mail and text files; it is the infrastructure for a comprehensive decision-support system where knowledge is placed in the hands of decision makers.

The network computer era allows users to evolve into *knowledge sharers* and emphasizes the powerful advantage of collaborative problem resolution. Knowledge sharing requires the free flow of all types of information among users, not just text file transfers, but an interactive data analysis capability that encourages the exchange of experiences and ideas.

By putting a data warehouse on an intranet (see **Figure 3.2**) and deploying structured content web servers, organizations gain economic and rapid application deployment benefits. More important in the long term is that users will collaborate more freely on an intranet, hopefully resulting in thorough analysis of business issues, free exchange of experience and ideas, and faster competitive response. An intranet could be the basis for rethinking the enterprise information infrastructure.

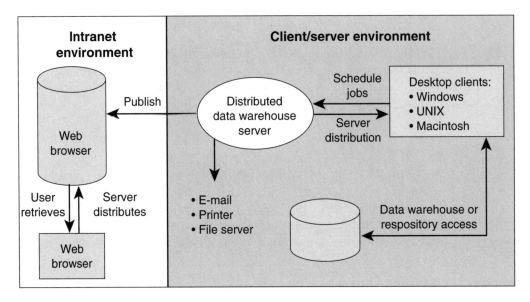

Figure 3.2   Web-distributed Environments

What Are Intranets?

Business computer systems are basically all about reports. All the information that is put into a system is there only to get it back out again, albeit in different forms. The people that need these reports are often decision makers without technical training.

Users communicate with an intranet through a web browser, which is a single, simple point of contact. The point-and-click paradigm of the browser is that anyone who can operate a mouse can deal with it easily. With a careful web page design and proper security, the users can point and click their way to the exact information they need regardless of its location on the system.

Using clients running a windowing system, the interface can be simplified even further. A web page link can be dropped directly on the desktop, as a *shortcut*. With a double-click on this *shortcut*, the browser executes automatically and loads the page selected. In this manner, intranets make getting to data easier, so that users can spend more time acting on a report, rather than looking for it.

In essence, intranets are a form of next-generation client/server, with a number of standardized characteristics. Like a traditional client/server, intranets have three essential elements: the *client*, the *communication protocol*, and the *server*. Each of these makes a distinct contribution to the data warehouse information delivery, as shown in Figure 3.3.

The Client

The client side of the intranet is the web browser. The browser receives web pages from the web server and formats that at the client for *presentation*. The presentation aspect of a web page is controlled completely by the browser—most settings, such as font usage, can be altered to the viewer's requirements. This is the part of the cooperative client/server intranet architecture. While basic page information is delivered by the server, the browser determines how it will be presented, based on the client hardware/software characteristics.

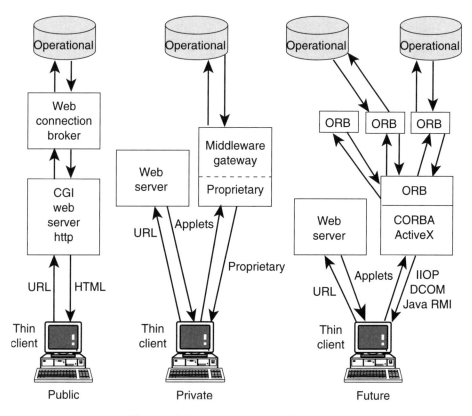

Figure 3.3   Web-enabled Computing

The Communication Protocol

The method of communication for an Internet is via TCP/IP. The latest editions of TCP/IP that are provided with most platform systems, such as Windows NT, Windows 95, and Microsoft BackOffice, make TCP/IP easy to deploy.

Working on top of the communication protocol is the transport language, or *middleware*, which is used by the client and the server to communicate. In a traditional client/server system, middleware is often the complicated piece for the user. While TCP/IP is the communication protocol, in an intranet, the transport language is HyperText Transport Protocol (HTTP).

The Server

The server component of an intranet is the web Server. An intranet web server is much like a file server, which responds to requests from its clients and the web browsers. It has the additional responsibility of being able to pass requests to other application servers.

Influence of the Intranets

Companies are hurrying to leverage the Internet's infrastructure to extend their corporate networks. The reasons are clear: intranets are easy to use, fast to implement, cost-effective, and an efficient way to make information available to the people who need it. The fact is that any authorized user can get to information on an intranet with nothing more than a standard web browser, and web browsers are now in widespread use in most organizations.

Intranets are quickly becoming stores of large volumes of information, much of which is static "corporate communications" materials such as telephone listings, internal memos, corporate communiqués and similar documents. However, as intranets become more pervasive, the kinds of information on them is changing and expanding. New technologies, such as object-oriented programming, are needed to keep up with the changing requirements. Corporations are now looking for ways to give users dynamic access to the information in their databases and data warehouses—tools to provide real-time information that people can use to improve the speed and quality of their decisions. Web-enabled data warehousing meets this need.

Why Intranets?

If you are an MIS professional and you have never set up an intranet before, you may be wondering why they have become all the rage. If your existing client/server system is working well, you probably believe that there is nothing that an intranet can provide that is not already available. Intranets are not as much about new functionality as they are about accessibility, standardization, and ease of deployment. Then why not implement data warehousing as intranets and extranets?

Most intranets currently manage unstructured content—text, image, and audio data types—as *static* HTML documents. A data warehouse stores structured content—raw alphanumeric data. With the right tools and the right architecture, a data warehouse can be made accessible over an enterprise intranet, forming the basis for a comprehensive enterprise information infrastructure. There are three important advantages of such an infrastructure:

1. Intranet economics
2. Information integration
3. User collaboration

Intranet Economics

The cost of client/server computing is high when communications, support, and other hidden costs are considered. In fact, numerous studies suggest that *client/server computing is more costly than mainframe computing*. Certainly the personal computer has become bloated with processing power, memory, software, and user-managed files of considerable proportions. The result is a *fat* client architecture.

Intranets are changing the economics of supporting a large population of knowledge workers. An intranet is usually a *thin* client architecture (**Figure 3.3**). Not only does an intranet reduce communications costs, but also some speculate that the personal computer may be replaced with a low-cost intranet device. Whether corporations will indeed replace existing PCs is debatable; at a minimum an intranet will increase the life expectancy of the latest round of PC upgrades.

The *thin* client model requires server distribution of applications software. Java allows software to be served to an intranet browser in code fragments or *applets*. The only portion of the application software that needs to be installed on the client is a browser such as Netscape Navigator or Microsoft Internet Explorer. And application software is acquired only when needed for a

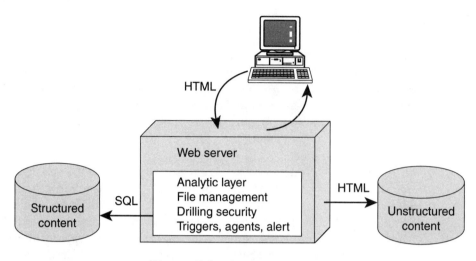

Figure 3.4   Application Layers

specific application. One possibility is the metering that tracks the number of users that download an applet or some other measure of usage.

Server software is distributed and a single copy of each such tier is easier to maintain and administer. The economics of an intranet, therefore, result in lower communications costs, less expensive thin client hardware, and, in some cases, reduced application software costs.

Information Integration

One of the most valuable assets of the enterprise is the operational data used in managing day-to-day business activities. This numeric data provides frequent measures of performance. By developing a data warehouse, corporations are organizing the data in a way that makes it useful to decision-makers. When a data warehouse is put on an intranet, users can toggle between structured data analysis (producing reports in columns and rows) and unstructured browsing (**Figure 3.4**). One software application can be used to view data both ways.

User Collaboration

A web-enabled data warehouse is as much about communicating at an interactive level as it is about making the needed information easily accessible. Few people would disagree with the view that decision making improves with timely, accurate, and complete information. An intranet influences how the ideas and experience of a workgroup are exchanged as part of knowledge sharing. This is the analysis and problem resolution process.

The key benefits of a web-enabled data warehouse are information-enriched communications and collaborative problem resolution. An intranet facilitates these capabilities on both a workgroup and an enterprise scale that is not possible under the communication constraints of a regular LAN-based application.

Types of Information on an Intranet

Today, most users can communicate via a corporate e-mail system. While an e-mail system allows text files to be exchanged, it does not facilitate true collaboration. An Excel spreadsheet or Lotus Notes is one step closer to a collaborative method of exchanging valuable information, but the focus is still textual file sharing.

A prudent business solution requires interactive sharing of information in such a way that the recipient can continue an analysis or branch off in an entirely new direction without assistance. For example, if I receive a report from another intranet user, I should immediately be able to drill down or drill up on any report dimension, pivot and rotate the results, add additional calculations as part of my analysis, and then pass my work to others in the organization. This requires dynamic report creation based on data stored in a warehouse.

True collaboration for business decision making requires a higher level of interactive analysis and knowledge sharing than exists today in most text-oriented groupware products. Users need to dynamically explore the data warehouse and freely build on each other's analysis of a business issue, jumping to structured content searches at any point in the analysis process.

Intranets and Data Warehousing

Intranets provide a powerful solution for data warehousing environments.

Benefits of Intranets

Intranet technologies represent the next major step in the evolution of computing and hold the promise of increasing returns on investment. A key benefit of the Intranet technology is the ability to provide up-to-date information quickly and cost effectively.

- An intranet can put vital information and decision-support reports on each desktop regardless of their location or the location of the information.

- Information disseminated on an intranet enables a high degree of coherence for the entire enterprise (whether the data content comes from data marts or a central data warehouse) because the communications, report formats, and interfaces are consistent.

- By giving each desktop the ability to architect, extract, and mine corporate data and generate reports and other time-critical information, intranets improve the decision-making process by empowering individuals with the knowledge necessary for faster and better-informed business decisions.

- Intranets allow the centralization of information, making it easier to maintain and update.

- An intranet provides a flexible and scalable non-proprietary solution for a data warehouse implementation. It enables the integration of a diverse computing environment into a cohesive information network.

- The Internet can be easily extended into Wide Area Networks (WANs) or extranets that serve remote company locations, business partners, and customers. External users can access internal data, drill through, or print reports through secure proxy servers that reside outside the firewall.

- Contrary to some beliefs, the web can actually improve the security for data warehouse deployment, because the databases can be centralized, allowing access to be more centrally controlled.

- Web browsers can provide a universal application delivery platform for any data mart or data warehouse user. As a result, the enterprise can create, integrate, or deploy new, more robust applications quickly and economically.

- The intuitive nature of the browser interface reduces user support and training requirements.

Requirements for Putting a Data Warehouse on an Intranet

Data warehouses employ relational database management systems that use SQL to retrieve rows and columns of numeric data, while unstructured content is managed as HyperText Markup Language (HTML) documents. The challenge in putting a data warehouse on an Intranet is in properly enabling SQL data warehouse access from HTML browsers. At least four application software layers (depicted in **Figure 3.4**) are needed:

- Analytic layer
- Security
- File management
- Agents

Analytic Layer

Putting data content on the intranet requires a server-resident analytic layer to generate SQL on the fly, perform computations, and format reports based on user requests. In essence, a specialized web server is required to support data warehouse access from an HTML browser client-initiated request. Often, this web server will be the same hardware platform used to manage all or a portion of the database.

The web server must be configured to support the higher processing loads. The analytic layer typically makes heavy demands on a relational database and the number of queries and results communicated are large. Therefore, there should be a high-speed network connection between the analytic and database layers or they should reside on the same machine.

The analytic layer shares some capabilities with spreadsheet software. The power of a spreadsheet is derived from a user's ability to author custom calculations based on facts stored in cells in a spreadsheet. For example, facts (numeric data) are stored in two dimensions: letters A, B, C, D, etc., and numbers 1, 2, 3, 4, and so on. Combining the two dimensions, A1, provides a unique address. This unique address can be used to create a formula for a required calculation, A1-B1. The number of calculated rows and columns in a spreadsheet application often far exceeds the number of stored facts.

A data warehouse has multiple dimensions—product, market, customer, outlet, vendor, period, and so on—as opposed to a two-dimensional spreadsheet. The combination of values for each of the multiple data warehouse dimensions provides a unique address. The analytic layer on the structured content web server allows users to apply calculations based on database dimensions to create more useful reports. Furthermore, once authored, calculations can be shared with other users much as calculation formulas are replicated within a spreadsheet. And, the calculation logic is maintained as the data warehouse is updated each day, week, or month.

Like a spreadsheet, reports that users request from a data warehouse often contain more calculated rows and columns than raw data. Without a robust analytic layer in front of a data warehouse, the user is limited to a simple listing of stored data elements. The analytic layer is key to addressing business questions that users must answer.

File Management

Decision support requires interactive analysis and knowledge sharing. A report requested by one user is valuable when it is shared with other users to gain their insight and ideas. The recipients should be able to continue the analysis initiated by the original author. In this way, the analysis process becomes an interactive exchange. Many users can pursue different analysis paths from a common starting point.

To meet the challenge of providing interactive analysis of a data warehouse, users must have access and be able to change their copy of the logic used to create the report. Users must be able to access public files and manage their personal files over an Internet connection. A sophisticated server-based file management system is required to support user collaboration and maintain security at this level.

Security

Accessibility is the web's greatest promise and its greatest threat. Enterprises welcome the opportunity to transform their operations by opening databases and other information repositories to customers and suppliers, yet they fear that such access will leave them vulnerable to security breaches. The challenge for anyone building a business web site is to achieve a reasonable level of security without impeding opportunity.

The liberal sharing of information and collaboration among users on an intranet immediately raises severe data security issues. A data warehouse contains highly confidential proprietary data for the entire enterprise. Only a few users should have security authorization to view data anywhere in a warehouse. Most users must be provided access to only a relevant portion of a warehouse. Data must be secure, but if it is too tightly controlled, the value of the warehouse will never be fully realized.

The security issues are indeed complex. To illustrate the point, a sales director has authorization to view financial data at a national, regional, and sales territory level. At the territory level, the financial data would include all salary data for sales representatives. If the sales director creates a report and decides to share it, the regional managers should have access to only territory information for their region and be blocked from accessing territory information for other regions. In other words, if a user is not authorized to receive and access a report, then that user must not be able to view the report or drill into areas where the user does not have authorization.

Reports that are created from data stored in the warehouse may not simply be shared as text files. All reports may include the underlying logic, giving the recipient the ability to immediately analyze and modify the report, as well as the logic and assumptions supporting the analyses. Before a recipient can view the report or build upon the analysis, the authorization level for that user needs to be verified. For effective decision support, reports must be shared throughout the workgroup and enterprise. If the recipients are not authorized, their access to report logic can be denied.

Encryption of data can provide a higher level of security than is generally available for business applications. Utilizing the Netscape Secure Socket Layer (SSL), data passing between the client and server can be encrypted. This enables business users to run important applications over unsecured communication lines without worrying about an intruder tapping into the network and viewing the transmitted information.

A multi-tier architecture, with the gateway server behind a firewall, can ensure that security demands are met. In addition, the server may be able to monitor the identity of users, access information, and other usage habits. Any server solution may be to extended previously existing host security to provide effective user authentication.

Agents

One of the common complaints about e-mail and even voice mail is that a mailbox fills up faster than a user has time to isolate and address the really important issues. Agents are intended to work on behalf of users to isolate important information sought by a user. An agent can be triggered by some predefined event or at a specified time interval. The agent sends an alert to notify specific users on a *need-to-know basis*. Agents must have the ability to run continually as background processes on an intranet logic server because each user is almost always disconnected, a result of the stateless nature of Web servers. This provides a means of automating the routine analysis process. And, when users sign on to the network, the agents must be smart enough to notify users of conditions that occurred while they were disconnected.

Because data warehouses tend to grow exponentially, it is critical that agents proactively monitor and manage activities, alerting decision makers only when specific conditions exist. It is unrealistic to believe that decision makers could be productive by aimlessly data surfing through potentially hundreds of gigabytes of data looking for valuable insight. The decision maker should be free to concentrate on the immediate and critical issues while the system ensures that developing conditions will not go undetected.

The Common Gateway Interfaces

Common Gateway Interface (CGI)

CGI is the original standard for creating plug-in enhancements for web servers. Its most frequent use is to process HTML forms. CGI works by using the operating system's standard input/output and environment variable mechanisms to pass information between the form, the server, and the plug-in.

While binary programs can be used as CGI plug-ins, scripting languages such as PERL are commonly used for CGI. Such scripting languages are portable, easy to modify remotely, and require no compilation or interruption of the server.

The downside to using CGI is that CGI scripts typically need to be loaded and unloaded from memory each time they are executed. This, combined with the use of standard input/output and environment variables, drastically impacts the performance of servers.

The Common Gateway Interface (CGI) facility of web server software (**Figure 3.5**) provides a method to execute server-resident software. Building secure applications for an intranet requires a well-thought-out security strategy as well as the appropriate application architecture. Most web applications provide all users with the same access permissions to the reachable files on the server. It is certainly possible to send a DBMS query from a web browser and enforce any DBMS security just as if the query came from a traditional LAN-based client application. The maintenance of security for each report application and user creates a significant burden. This approach is best suited to simple requests such as a query to determine a user's current credit card balance.

Business users require a system that maps them to their server account by verifying user names and passwords. When server applications are run, they will have access to their files secured by user, group, and permission levels. The same issue exists with database security. Users must be mapped to the appropriate database user or group in the relational database in order to control the data that a user can access. And, because the number of users may be large, the administration of the security system should be centralized at the server and minimized to the extent possible.

Another issue with the CGI interface is that it does not offer a continuous connection to the database. As a result, it is impossible to support an application requiring multiple interactive queries—*a data warehousing requirement*. One

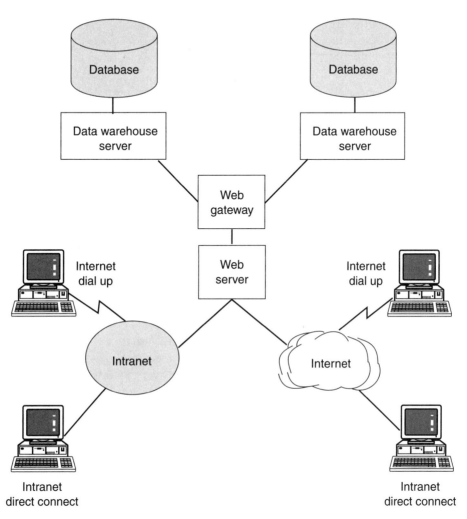

Figure 3.5 Web Gateway

approach to solving this problem is to employ a message-based protocol (such as IIOP) between the client browser and the server-resident analytic layer using the CGI.

By mapping a user to a server account and starting a process that executes as that user, a continuous connection is maintained between the logic layer and database during iterative queries over the lifetime of that process. This facilitates the execution of efficient SQL queries and computational routines to meet the user requirements for analysis. For example, an HTML form can request that the user enter their user-name and password and database user-name and password. Using Netscape's SSL facilities, the passwords are then encrypted before being transmitted over the network.

This information is then passed as parameters or through environment variables to a CGI program, which could be a C, C++, ActiveX, Perl, or Visual Basic program. That software then verifies the user-name and password via operating system security features and starts a process that executes as that user. This process could then connect to the relational database management system (RDBMS) using its API and the supplied user-name and password. Once this connection to the RDBMS is established, many queries and result sets can be processed. A final output report can be generated, converted to an HTML document, and sent back to the client browser for display to the user.

A set of replacements for CGI is being adopted on some platforms that allow the plug-in to remain in memory, and use more direct methods of interfacing—providing far better performance on web servers. ISAPI on MS Windows is one such alternative, and NSAPI is another.

Microsoft Internet Server API (ISAPI)

Microsoft Internet Server API (ISAPI) is an alternative to the Common Gateway Interface (CGI), optimized for Windows-based Web servers. The ISAPI provides an interface to back-end applications running on your web server. ISAPI is easy to use, well documented, and does not require complex programming.

This API, available on web servers from an increasing number of vendors, is quickly becoming the industry standard for web server application development. The Internet Server API is being endorsed by an increasing number of server developers, allowing application developers to write for a single specification and to deliver on multiple platforms.

Netscape API (NSAPI)

NSAPI is more universal (works on multiple platforms). It provides better control and power to programmers by exposing the server architecture and allowing functions to work on various levels, e.g., authentication, processing forms, manipulating errors, and log files. NSAPI provides capabilities for add-on objects and templates. These objects can then respond to a variety of situations (processing tasks such as path check, authentication, and delivering HTML pages from a database). NSAPI provides built-in functions to deal with a variety of existing needs of a programmer, such as dealing with name=value parameters, URI parsing, changing directory to path, redirecting the server to a new location, etc.

Web-Enabling Warehouse Solutions

There are three fundamental components of a web-enabled integration solution:

- Internet-to-server connectivity
- Web-enabling legacy applications
- Application integration

Efficiently linking older technologies with the newer web-based innovations must be at the heart of any integration solution and as such can be accomplished with the first two components. An intelligent hub that permits organizations to easily add new enterprise applications without creating time-consuming links to every other system is the third and final component.

Internet-to-Server Connectivity

Over 2.5 billion lines of legacy code are in use today, at least 90 percent of which will still be operational into the next century. As a result, the ability to connect to mainframe or AS/400 systems is mandatory in order to provide efficient, easy data access. A number of software applications now support integration of the Internet/intranets with the mainframe, but few meet the criteria set forth above for an effective enterprise solution.

Legacy data access represents only a partial integration solution. Delivering access to business application logic via a web browser comprises the second and more innovative half of the legacy equation. Rather than just provide data access, organizations themselves should be able to rapidly extend mission-critical applications to the web.

Application Integration

As the demand for new applications accelerates, organizations are faced with the growing task of managing the exchange of data and transactions between diverse systems. But new hub technology, such as *message brokering*, provides a new way to integrate these systems.

Application integration provides an efficient way to integrate legacy and other third party applications without extensive code rewriting to build web-like connections. Instead of creating *inter-application spaghetti*, companies use a *hub-and-spoke* system, similar to the airline industry. The enterprise only needs to build one connection to an intelligent hub when a new system is added, rather than a connection to every application.

Scalability

Solutions from a number of major companies and a handful of smaller ones have demonstrated the ability to scale up to a few hundred concurrent users. In a typical data warehouse environment at a company with perhaps 50,000 employees—never mind the supply chain or customers—a few hundred is clearly inadequate. Typically, a three-tier architecture and innovative gateway/server efficiency is required to scale beyond this number. By dynamically distributing incoming users across multiple systems, overall server load is reduced and performance is enhanced.

To scale to thousands of users, back-end host resources must be used extremely efficiently. A legacy application access solution should allow the creation of pools of back-end connections that can be shared across a large base of clients.

Ease of Implementation

For a distributed data warehouse environment, an Internet-to-mainframe server-based solution virtually eliminates client support problems. Utilizing Java or equivalent technology, application code is automatically downloaded each time a user requires access instead of manually loading and storing software on every possible user PC. Ongoing support costs are minimized because software installations and updates are loaded from centralized web servers.
A server for web-enabling legacy applications should be a straightforward one, enabling access through a message queue system, client/server network, or a web server.

Reliability

A system utilizing fault-resilient load balancing software can help to guarantee uninterrupted access. By soliciting the operational status of all servers and isolating any failures without user or operator intervention, it is possible to ensure resource availability.

Examples

The enterprise that leverages open TCP/IP protocols while supporting the parallel existence of enterprise client/server and legacy systems, as well as messaging networks, can realize a number of strategic business benefits, most centered on improved access to information. Those benefits are demonstrated by the following examples:

- A major retail company is improving connectivity and reducing costs in its 40 regional distribution centers with the deployment of a data warehouse solution. The company adopted web browsers as its *universal clients*, and web servers as the software distribution mechanisms of choice, thus reducing distribution and administration costs.

- A major credit card company has given 14 million credit card holders real-time access to their account information on-line through the web software.

- A large life insurance holding company provides customer service representatives with a total integrated picture of each customer, regardless of the number of business units involved, by enabling Windows users to access legacy data and create views in another RDBMS.

In each example, the end user need not know that the data ultimately resides on a corporate legacy system. Access is seamless and transparent. Yet each company is handling sensitive financial information with high security demands. In short, these companies have successfully provided access to mission-critical data and business logic on a large scale and are reaping the rewards of the interactive data warehouse implementation. With careful selection of proven, scalable, and secure connectivity solutions, any company can deliver this kind of access to a data warehouse. And this kind of access now spells enhanced opportunity.

The Web Gateway

The web gateway acts as a translator between the HTML language used by web browsers and servers and the data warehouse application API/CGI. The user first views a web page that contains standard HTML and application-specific tags (optional in some cases) created for data warehouse web applications. These tags guide the web gateway (**Figure 3.5**) in what buttons, dialogs, or objects to present to the user. Such tags can be treated like comments and ignored by the browser.

When a user issues a request to query, drill down, or update the database, the request first goes to the web server. The web server then passes the request (along with the tags) to the web gateway (see **Figure 3.6**), which translates them into data warehouse application commands.

The request comes back from the data warehouse server through the web gateway where it is translated into an HTML table and hidden HTML form controls that contain data for each of the cells. These form controls are important because they can interact with VBScript or JavaScript. These scripts can, in

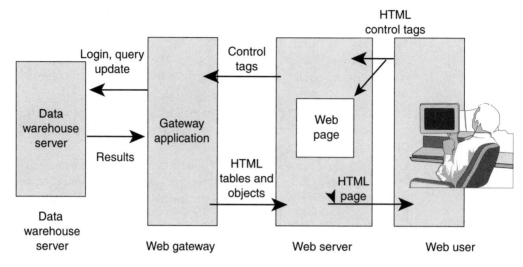

Figure 3.6   Web Gateway Information Flow

turn, interrogate and manipulate these controls to perform client-side processing such as data entry (query) validation.

The web gateway must support both the Internet and intranet through direct or dial-up links, as shown in Figure 3.6. Since the web gateway sends only small amounts of data over the network, performance is excellent, even for dial-up users.

The Developing Architectures

At first we only had one simple thin-client two-tier architecture, where a web client would make a request to a web server, which would serve up HTML and graphics. Pretty simple—although this provided a means of serving up static content, there was no means of becoming interactive with the end user.

The use of CGI, NSAPI, or ISAPI, has changed all this. Using a three-tier architecture, developers could create a process on the Web server that was able to pump custom dynamic HTML down to the web client, responding to the requests of the user (**Figure 3.7**). Search engines are the best example of three-tier Internet applications. This was a step in the right direction, but developers were still dependent on the stateless development environments of HTTP and CGI.

Java and ActiveX brought true interactive application development to the web by supporting the fat-client two-tier architecture. An applet is down-

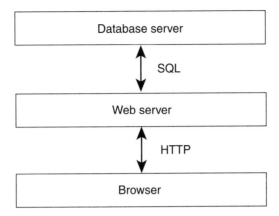

Figure 3.7.   The Three-Tier Architecture

loaded to the client, where it runs within the browser as an interactive application. The applet can then in turn link back to a database server using a native API—JDBC in the case of Java, or ODBC in the case of ActiveX.

If you think that is enough to worry about, you are wrong. In the past year, we have seen a rise in the use of additional web application architectures such as four-tier and n-tier web application development.

When using four-tier, developers employ the traditional three-tier Web architecture but place a TP monitor between the CGI process (the Web server) and the database server. This provides all of the benefits of using a TP monitor, including load balancing and database multiplexing.

When using an *n-tier* architecture, developers generally layer a set of distributed objects between the CGI or Java processes and the database. With the advent of IIOP, distributed objects can even run on the browser, the web server, the application server, or the database server (**Figure 3.8**). There are also Web architectures that use applets at the browser to communicate with Java running on the web server (servlets). The applets interact with the servlets, which interact with the database server and the web server using the native API of the web server.

Of course, one can mix and match all of the architectures and create one's own exciting combination of enabling technology that is even more complex.

Importance of the Object Technologies

The benefits of object technology in software development are well known. By abstracting software behavior into software pieces or components with well-

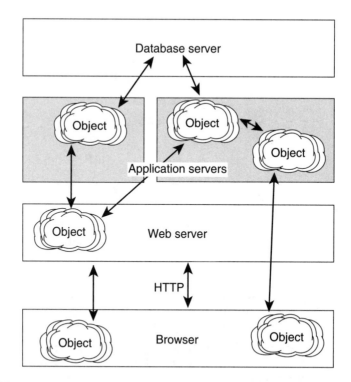

Figure 3.8.   The Distributed Objects in the Web Environments

defined interfaces, software developers can handle far more complex projects, reuse code, easily add new behaviors without breaking already-written code, and more accurately reflect business processes in data warehousing applications. Several of these benefits mirror the layered architecture of TCP/IP, and for the same reasons it is not surprising that object technology is rapidly finding a home on the Internet and intranets, especially in the realms of scripting languages, intelligent agents, and data warehousing applications.

Scripting languages can be used to automate common activities on the desktop, or by network administrators to automate many tasks such as software distribution, installation, desktop configuration, and control. An important consideration in the design of a scripting language is the amount of access to critical system internals it allows: too much and it can easily be used to craft viruses or other destructive software entities, too little and it is of limited use.

Intelligent agents are software modules that automate complex user or administrator tasks; often they are written in scripting languages such as Visual Basic. They exhibit many levels of intelligence, ranging from pre-programmed modules whose behavior must be defined in detail by the user, to adaptive intelligent agents that can detect patterns of use, thereby automatically adapting to a user's needs and modes of work. A major benefit of intelligent agents is their ability to perform useful work anytime the desktop computer sits idle, or when network usage is at a minimum.

An exciting new frontier in internetworking is the development of mobile agents: code, often called *applets* or *mini-applications*, that travel across the network to perform user tasks. This is especially compelling in the arena of mobile computing and remote access, and enables remote users to work off-line and then dispatch a mobile agent to do its work on a distant server with only a brief network connection. This technology can greatly reduce a user's impact on network resources. Additionally, it can be used to automatically add new behaviors to software on the fly, enabling clients to handle a new data type, for example, by downloading the code needed to process it transparently to the user.

Applets and mini-applications can also be viewed as a terrifying technology in some respects, because they basically could be considered domesticated viruses. The same security considerations that apply to scripting languages apply here, with even more importance: a mobile agent that can perform useful work is also capable of performing destructive work. Software development in this area is just beginning to evolve; it is far too early to tell what role this technology will play in Intranets and the Internet.

Summary

The data warehouse should not be seen as just a product, or a collection of products, or an individual technology, or a simple solution to a standard end-user information access problem. Data warehousing is properly an architected solution in which individual items such as extraction of data from production applications, delivery and consolidation of data into a usable structure, and browsing capabilities are handled in the method most conducive to the characteristics of a specific environment.

Data Warehousing Taxonomy

A three-tiered taxonomy presents major classes of data warehousing architectures. This includes a relatively simple reporting system intended primarily for end user computing, a moderately complex environment encompassing data from multiple applications, highly complex uses of distributed servers, relational data mixed with text-and-image documents, and complicated on-line analytical processing (OLAP) client engines.

Data warehousing is not new. All large organizations already have data warehouses, but they are just not managing them. Over the next few years, the growth of data warehousing is going to be enormous with new products and technologies coming out frequently, especially when these are webenabled.

In order to get the most out of this period, it is going to be important that data warehouse planners and developers have a clear idea of what they are looking for and then choose strategies and methods that will provide them with performance for today and flexibility for tomorrow.

In short, the data warehouse concept has received much attention recently by both the database industry and the database research community in general. Data warehouses will provide a means for querying huge amounts of data that was accumulated in the past, but never put to any productive use. Until recently, it was impossible to provide a system that could support efficient use of the vast amount of data that companies had collected for the purpose of analysis or exploitation.

Data warehouses will provide corporate users with a means to perform such tasks as data mining to find valuable tidbits of information in their seas of data, from their desktops. With this technology, decision makers in companies may now have a vehicle to process in a meaningful way the possibly terabytes of data that are the byproduct of the automation era of the past decade and a half. The need for this technology is evident in the demand by companies to deploy data warehouses for information discovery purposes. Data mining is what most organizations aspire to when they build a data warehouse. All companies will build a data warehouse in the next few years, if they have not already done so.

Future of the Web-Enabled Data Warehouse

So what is the future of web-enabled data warehouse development? More complexity? More proprietary solutions? That is about the size of it for now— that is, until the industry begins to normalize itself and a few architectures and enabling technology become commonplace. We also need to reconsider the use of standards—the CGI versus NSAPI versus ISAPI, two-tier versus n-tier, or the Java versus ActiveX conflict are some of the good examples.

The process is one of tradeoff. It's disturbing to see developers move away from the standards that made the Internet great, but they are doing so to get around many of the limitations that traditional web technology places on them. We are once again moving toward the same *quick fix* for application development as we did with client/server, and this time with more complexity. History always seems to repeat itself.

The convergence of two technologies, the Internet and decision-support systems, promises to change the way we make decisions by making information easily accessible to an unprecedented number of users.

In the following sections, we will build, step-by-step, a case to exploit the technologies needed to address the issues and requirements discussed. We will also explore building, maintaining, managing, and using the web-enabled data warehouses.

4

DATA WAREHOUSE TECHNOLOGIES

Introduction

The data explosion began with the advent of distributed systems capable of capturing a variety of useful business information. Today, even cash registers are nothing more than networked computers which record every detail of what is sold, who bought it, where they bought it, and how they paid for it. In the same way, banking transactions, telephone sales, applications for credit, even product inquires are dutifully recorded with the assumption that the data, properly processed, can reveal important secrets about how to deliver products and services better than the competition.

Today, enterprises have adopted the technique of data warehousing to organize and secure data so that it is available to those who require ready access to it. Properly implemented, data warehouses allow businesses to cope with narrowing market windows, reduced product cycles, demands for greater profitability, and the need to differentiate customer service. Data warehouses also promise concrete benefits to Information Technology managers by consolidating data from diverse operational systems, off-loading processes from overburdened mainframes, and promoting the use of powerful, commercially-available analysis tools.

Most data warehouses are hundreds of gigabytes in size, with some nearing terabytes. By its nature, data accumulates, resulting in requirements for scalable solutions that can accommodate explosive growth. Some foresee a day when terabyte data warehouses will be the norm, with capacities of hundreds of terabytes being common.

With the explosion of corporate databases, and the stockpiling of more and more kinds of business data, corporations worldwide are turning to parallel processing technologies.

Data Warehousing as an Enabling Technology

Many organizations have moved to data warehousing as a technology that addresses the business need to acquire and retain customers. However, data warehousing alone cannot provide all the information needed to understand one's customers. There are three primary components to a data warehouse architecture: data acquisition, data storage, and data analysis.

Data Acquisition

Data acquisition consists of identifying the data required for the application as well as the existing systems upon which it resides. Almost always, it is the detailed atomic data at the transaction level. The nature of information systems in organizations today is one where *multiple heterogeneous systems* are developed and used in various departments for multiple applications, usually with little accommodation for other applications that may use similar data.

The disparate data elements are often contradictory, not standardized, and kept in multiple disparate formats. This leads to a requirement to *cleanse* the data prior to moving it into the storage phase. During this cleansing, data redundancies are eliminated, contradictions are reconciled, and data is transformed into a standard, understood, and accepted format. *Cleansing* the data is a key step in data mining as well, and therefore enables data mining to build nicely on data warehousing initiatives.

The final data acquisition step in most warehousing applications is the *summarizing* of the data to some predetermined level of detail. Data is summarized for several reasons. First, most data warehousing applications are interested in trend analysis and historical performance, which lends itself to looking for aggregate numbers such as total sales by product by region.

Data Storage

The nature of storage technology is such that it would be prohibitively expensive to store all of the data in its atomic detail, plus all of the indexing and other navigational aids required to make that data useful to the end user. Depending on the ultimate use of data in the warehouse, the summarization can be characterized as lightly summarized to heavily summarized data.

Data Extraction and Analysis

Finally, access, extraction, and analysis tools are used to help users and management answer business questions from the stored data. Answering business questions involves a number of technologies that span a range of sophistication.

At one end of the range are standard database reports, issued at regular intervals or upon demand, which show different views of the data according to predetermined requirements. Quarterly profitability reports, monthly sales reports, and annual general ledger reports are examples of this type of a tool.

Slightly more sophisticated tools exist in the form of structured queries that can generate different views of existing relationships of the data within the data store. Structured Query Language (SQL) is one example of the kinds of tools that can be used for ad hoc views of the data.

While this data is absolutely important to the management of a company, note that none of these techniques allow companies to ask the kinds of questions that will lead them to determine profiles or motivators for buying habits or what to do to retain customers.

The problem is that OLAP is limited by the fact that it is a technique and a technology that must be driven by the user. The individual has to structure the request, and often there are implicit assumptions in the query that are based on the user's observations. What companies would like to do is make requests that are even more open-ended than those allowed by OLAP technology. For example, companies want to know the profile of the customers who bought the most profitable product last year. To obtain such a profile, the system is not looking for data, but rather using the data to build associations, cause-and-effect relationships, and ultimately build a model for the user that can be employed for predictive purposes.

Data Extraction and Analysis

Everywhere today, enterprises are drowning in their data. Managers know that this data, collected as part of the hundreds of millions of business transactions conducted daily, has value. For this reason, they are committed to extracting from it every bit of information that can give them a competitive edge.

The traditional techniques of database query languages, decision-support systems, and on-line analytical processing, while valuable, do not provide a way to find the unsuspected relationships in warehoused data. For this reason, we are turning to the powerful technique of data mining. Because unsifted data represents a huge untapped investment, vendors of systems and software are rapidly moving to provide the tools that enterprises need to turn their mountains of data into valuable information. One of those tools is *data mining*.

To process this information, we need powerful platforms capable of hosting large data warehouses and sophisticated data mining applications. In order to make these applications more accessible to a larger number of users, we have to turn to highly scalable Symmetric Multi-Processing (SMP) systems that can effectively and economically address the largest data mining problems. With their ability to host powerful data warehousing, decision-support system, and data mining software, SMP systems are a potent tool for the enterprise wishing to glean the maximum benefit from its hard-won data.

Several technologies are used to extract information from data warehouses. Many users begin by making educated guesses about relationships in the data and create simple database queries to confirm or deny their suspicions. As relationships and questions become more sophisticated, simple query languages become inadequate, and Decision Support Systems (DSS) or

Executive Information Systems (EIS) must be used to cope with the increased complexity.

On-line analytical processing (OLAP) technologies add sophisticated multidimensional analysis and statistical techniques to help uncover even more complicated relationships. Because data warehouses inevitably grow over time, we find that a scalable family of computing solutions is the only way to ensure adequate future capacity.

One assumption common to all of these approaches, however, is that the individuals sifting through the data know what they are looking for. Most EIS and OLAP tools organize their data in predefined ways, which can have the effect of prejudging the data. What troubles users today is the hidden relationships that no one has thought to ask about. In order to get the maximum benefit from data warehouses, a tool is needed to reveal the unobvious.

Data Mining

Data mining is the process of extracting meaningful, yet unobvious, information from large databases. This information, in turn, enables companies to solve business problems efficiently which gives them a competitive edge. With data mining, users find patterns in the data through extensive model building and predictive tests, uncovering unknown business models (e.g. credit risk) from data that is known (income, marital status, age).

Employing techniques like neural networks, set theory, fuzzy logic, genetic algorithms, and decision trees, data mining applications can help enterprises implement more sophisticated and informed business strategies.

Data mining output generally takes the form of a model which can be used to predict future behavior. This model can be built into new business applications (such as programs that might analyze and decide on a loan application), or it can be employed by users deploying DSS or OLAP systems as they conduct more focused examinations of new or existing business data. In either case, the key to data mining is uncovering unsuspected relationships useful to the business.

Data Mining Overview

Data mining is the use of an appropriate set of technologies to exploit patterns of information from massive customer-focused databases. Data mining technologies use a variety of algorithms and mathematical techniques to identify potential relationships and associations between and among the elephantine set of data elements stored for analysis. Users are still very much involved and very much in control, but at a different point in the process.

Data mining is an iterative process that begins with the specification of a business objective. Once a business objective, like customer retention or acquisition is identified, the next steps are to determine what data is available for use with the mining activity and to begin collecting the data. Identifying and collecting data often involves the use of a data warehouse or data mart to facilitate the cleansing of the detail level data required. After the data has been assembled, the actual mining takes place.

Using Data Mining Tools

Data mining is a powerful tool for finding strategic advantages in data already in the possession of many enterprises. Properly applied, data mining can address a multitude of important, and costly, business problems. Today, data mining is providing answers to fundamental questions in a diverse range of businesses, including telecommunications, financial services and insurance, health care, wine making, retail merchandising, and others.

Using Databases Effectively

A key issue in modern data analysis is the ability to work with database sample sizes large enough to provide highly accurate results. Users have often been forced to work with samples that represent less than 1% of their customer database, simply because anything larger will not fit onto a PC. At the same time, increasing competition is forcing businesses to look for well-defined niche –markets—markets which can be lost if sample sizes are too small.

Data Mining Versus OLAP

A common point of confusion for those new to the subject is the difference between On-Line Analytical Processing (OLAP) and data mining. We can trace some of the differences as follows:

1. OLAP tools tend to focus on interactive sessions, which circumscribe limits on the size of problems that can be practically approached and the type of questions that can be asked.

2. OLAP employs different algorithms than are typically used in data mining, relying on relational technology, multidimensional databases, and agents. Data mining uses sophisticated algorithms that are resource-hungry and can take a considerable amount of time to com-

plete. Data for OLAP systems is also stored and formatted according to the type of questions being asked, whereas data for data mining applications generally comes unprocessed directly from the corporate data warehouse.

3. Most importantly, users of OLAP tools know in advance the questions they want to ask of the data, e.g., *what are sales by product by store by month?* Data mining users may know what datasets they want to examine, but frequently have no predisposition to the results they may obtain. As a result, OLAP yields mostly numeric values, while data mining findings are most often expressed as relationships between different types of business data.

Because of these differences, there is a role for both OLAP and data mining in modern enterprises.

Platforms for Data Mining

A complex data mining algorithm running against a terabyte data warehouse presents some daunting challenges for even the fastest computing platforms. Finding ways to shorten runtimes and expand datasets can yield some valuable rewards. Shortened runtimes means the faster generation of models critical to meeting tight market windows, or time to investigate data more carefully. A system's ability to handle larger datasets allows the creation of more accurate models, and the examination of additional components of the business. The following key issues stand out when selecting a data mining platform:

Parallel Processing Power

The complex nature of data mining algorithms and the size of enterprise data sets demand performance that can only come from powerful parallel computing platforms and multitasking and multithreaded operating environments. Parallel processing yields bottom-line benefits by increasing the flow of useful business intelligence.

Storage Capacity

As companies continue to embrace data warehousing and data mining as a business computing strategy, the demands for more storage capacity, performance, and reliability will grow as well.

Balanced System Design

Processor performance simply is not enough for data warehouses. To avoid bottlenecks, systems must be designed with a balanced approach that ensures that CPU, I/O, storage, and networking performance are carefully matched to one another.

Scalability

As the need for processing power grows, companies must have cost-effective strategies for adding capacity. Incremental additions of performance and capacity are essential to swap entire systems on a regular basis. We can mine very large data warehouses without committing ourselves to hugely expensive, specialized architectures which take years to justify. Today, data mining is no longer just for the largest firms. Data mining is for any company committed to continuous innovation and industry leadership.

Architectures for Data Mining

For many years, a central thrust in the development of commercial systems has been the creation of faster processors. This emphasis paid off handsomely as increasingly sophisticated technology allowed the introduction of faster and faster systems. In the eighties, however, fundamental physical limitations, and the resultant costs of overcoming them, became roadblocks to continuing advances in single processor system performance.

Single processor systems, often in the form of PCs, bring a level of performance needed by many of the personal productivity tasks performed by millions of companies everyday around the world. Today, by employing special techniques (like sampling) to limit the size of datasets, even some data mining projects are hosted on personal computers.

Data mining has recently become more sophisticated, which requires faster processors to get the job done. Once available only on expensive, proprietary systems, data mining is an accepted application that is best hosted on scalable, symmetric multiprocessing systems. Single and multi-processor systems allow the creation of architectures that offer the most cost-effective resources to be quickly and easily applied to modern data mining problems.

Data Mining Technology

Data mining is not a single technology. It is a collection of tools that are used to extract information from data. Each tool has a range of utility for different kinds of problems. Specific data mining tools consist of existing statistical models for traditional statistical methods, neural networks, and tree-based models such as CHAID (chi-square automatic interaction detection) analysis.

The art of data mining is in determining which of the variables in the database are truly significant in determining the desired outcome. Organizations today are swamped with raw data, much of it meaningless from the standpoint of predictive utility. What data mining technology provides is a toolkit by which users can separate out the handful of predictive variables that will give the organization the highest probability of success.

Different tools work well on different kinds of problems. For example, neural network algorithms quantify but cannot precisely qualify data, so they do not work as well on non-numeric data. Data that identifies people, such as eye or hair color, for example, would be difficult for a neural net algorithm to classify. Some users, therefore, will use rule induction for this kind of data to generate a hypothesis, then test it against the data.

Statistical Methods

Data mining includes a variety of traditional statistical methods, such as cluster analysis, discriminant analysis, logistic regression, time series forecasting, and more. Also included are the more general methods for model fitting and validation that conduct automated searches for complicated relationships and apply fresh data to tentative relationships. The SAS System provides a unique multiplicity of tools for performing such tasks.

Cluster Analysis

In a data mining environment, the system discovers its own associations. Clustering/segmentation in databases are the processes of separating a data set into components that reflect a consistent pattern. Once the patterns have been established they can then be used to *decompose* data into more understandable subsets. Patterns also provide subgroups of a population for further analysis or action. For example, in target marketing, the previous response to mailing campaigns can be used to generate a profile of people who responded; this in turn can be used to predict response and filter mailing lists to achieve the best response.

Induction

One of the more powerful functions within data mining is the use of mathematical induction for the purpose of developing associations. The associations come in strange ways. Recently, Wall-Mart discovered that most often, if a new father went to a store to buy diapers, he also picked a six-pack of beer. Similarly, through data mining, businesses can develop associations and then increase their sales by rearranging shelf space. Tools can identify affinities or patterns that exist within a database and then can derive rules to express these relationships. The specific percentage of occurrences is called the confidence factor of the rule. Induction is obviously an excellent tool for applications such as market-basket analysis, as well as cross-selling analysis, where we can tell by historical data which kinds of products are typically bought in conjunction with each other.

An example of the use of associations is the analysis of the claim forms submitted by patients to a medical insurance company. Every claim form contains a set of medical procedures that were performed on a given patient during one visit. By defining the set of items to be the collection of all medical procedures that can be performed on a patient and the records to correspond to each claim form, the application can find, using the association function, relationships among medical procedures that are often performed together.

These facts can be used in fraud analysis, looking for doctors or institutions that demonstrate unusual couplings of procedures. They can also be used to test efficacy of treatment, comparing outcomes of different combinations of procedures to help do a better job in managed-care situations.

Inductive techniques often use the concept of tree-based models, which include classification and regression trees. Two very common tree-based structures are CART (Classification and Regression Trees) and CHAID (Chi squared Automatic Interaction Detection). These techniques build *decision trees* based on found patterns. Decision trees represent a simple technique to depict the knowledge inherent in the data by classifying examples into a finite number of classes. We want to know where people of different income levels go for vacations both in the winter and summer. By constructing a tree of different classification nodes, we can get a good representation of what vacation packages should be offered at which times of the year and how they should be promoted to different people at various income levels.

Neural Networks

Neural networks are an approach to computing that involves developing mathematical structures that have the ability to learn, or to adapt their behavior based on previous results. These methods are the result of research that enables software or hardware to mimic the neurophysiology of the human brain. Neural networks have the remarkable ability to derive meaning from complicated, incomplete, or imprecise data and can be used to extract patterns and detect trends that are too complex to be noticed by either humans or other computer techniques.

Neural networks use a set of processing elements (or nodes) analogous to neurons in the brain. These processing elements are interconnected in a network such that their influence on adjacent nodes can be increased or decreased. These linkages cause the nodes to *fire* or not *fire* in response to the data fed to them. The combination of nodes that fire under given conditions can then identify patterns in data once the network is exposed to the data.

Neural networks and tree-based models are both effective data mining tools. However, they each have their own unique strengths. Both are able to detect non-linear relationships automatically, a great advantage over linear models. But they have different virtues when it comes to making predictions from a large number of predictor variables. Tree-based models are good at selecting important variables and therefore work well when many of the predictors are irrelevant. Neural networks are good at combining information from many input parameters and therefore work well when many of the predictors are partially redundant.

Data Visualization

Data visualization makes it possible for the user to gain a deeper and more intuitive understanding of the data. As a result, data visualization is a key component of any data mining application. Data mining enables the user to focus on certain patterns and trends and explore them in depth using visualization. Rendering the data into a pictorial scenario, where variations in color, depth, and dimension can be used to provide differentiation, greatly aids users in identifying the patterns and relationships among a clutter of numbers and tables.

OLAP and ROLAP Technologies

On-Line Analytical Processing (OLAP) allows users to cut and slice data by posing queries with several attributes. OLAP uses an intermediate server to store pre-calculations of multidimensional data. This allows OLAP to deliver very fast results on smaller relatively static data sets that Do not require the power of ROLAP.

Relational On-Line Analytical Processing (ROLAP) is a data-querying tool that generates SQL commands against relational databases. It allows for ad hoc queries and aggregates the data at a faster rate than conventional OLAP. Because it does not use an intermediate server, ROLAP can work much faster with timely, constantly changing data. It can also work with much larger data sets.

Data warehousing, like any technology, evolved from a need. Companies use databases to keep accurate records and track transactions such as sales, inventory, purchases, or shipments. Databases are set up to handle transactions for which they are designed in the most efficient way. If a company uses an inventory management system and a sales/billing system, they are often kept in separate databases and systems.

The problem with this setup is the difficulty in relating what is happening in one system with what occurs in another. This leads to the use of Relational Database Management Systems (RDBMS). In a simplified view, an RDBMS is a series of databases built so that an item, such as a product code in a sales record, is found easily in another database, such as inventory. The items that tie the databases together are "callkey" fields. Using these keys allows easier transaction tracking throughout a system.

While RDBMS is a huge step forward, companies still find a void in having the information they need for business decisions. The problem is that RDBMS is used for online transactional processing (OLTP). Because OLTP is the backbone of daily operations, companies are reluctant to halt billing procedures so that someone in market planning can access data to evaluate sales trends.

How can companies keep critical transaction processes running while providing access to information critical for business decision making? The solution is a repository of information fed by the OLTP systems—a data warehouse. A data warehouse contains current information and historical data across all of a company's databases. A data warehouse often is supplemented with outside data to augment company information and becomes the central repository of a company's history, available to be reviewed, analyzed, mined, and reported.

To describe this in another way, OLTP systems are operational in nature. They are oriented toward the process they support—inventory management, sales processing or shipping—and their databases are highly structured and repetitive in nature. Data warehouses are designed to support company-wide decisions. As such, a data warehouse is designed not only to store and retrieve data records, but to facilitate the manipulation and cross-fertilization of that data in decision making.

A data warehouse contains four important characteristics: subject orientation, integration, time variation, and non-volatility. Being subject-oriented, the data warehouse presents data in a format that is easy to understand and manipulate. For example, a marketing person no longer is challenged to learn a shipping system to obtain information on where the specific product is being placed.

By integrating all of a company's databases, the data warehouse provides a view of data that is not available elsewhere. This means someone does not have to go to several different data sources to get a complete picture of what is happening. A data warehouse provides a view of a company's data over time, freeing analysts to look at trends and changes. Finally, a data warehouse is constructed so that once information is entered, it does not change, providing a constant view to examine and compare against.

For example, a company could implement a data warehouse that draws from three primary sources: an order management system, a sales contact management system, and a customer service system. By bringing these elements together into one database, the company can easily answer questions that otherwise would be difficult to answer. Marketing can examine people who previously responded to particular ads and did not make a purchase. Product development can look at customer service usage by product ownership to identify patterns. Finance can look at the purchase history of repeat customers to establish trends and forecasts. A data warehouse greatly simplifies generating the data needed to answer these questions.

Inside a Data Warehouse

Data warehousing by itself, however, is not the answer. It provides a doorway into a company's data. Once inside, additional tools that work with a data warehouse are needed to analyze data. Several approaches are available. On-line analytical processing (OLAP) is one technique. Using OLAP, information within a data warehouse is processed and summarized in various ways. Summarized data is placed into its own OLAP database. Users then can query this OLAP database and retrieve analysis, summary information, and information from the data warehouse. Because OLAP slices the data in specific ways, it is best suited for smaller datasets that are defined more narrowly and contained.

An alternative is relational online analytical processing (ROLAP). With ROLAP, requests for information are made directly into the data warehouse. By eliminating OLAP's intermediate step, ROLAP can extract information from the data warehouse more quickly. ROLAP is best suited for large datasets that change often. For example, OLAP is better suited for financial applications in which the data is often broken into smaller pieces, whereas ROLAP is better suited for marketing-based applications that often use large databases, such as point-of-sale, which are updated constantly.

Data mining techniques are coming into vogue also. Data mining differs from OLAP and ROLAP significantly because it is designed to find patterns and infer rules. Whereas OLAP and ROLAP simply quantify relationships, data mining identifies and quantifies them.

Another way to view the difference is that OLAP and ROLAP are based on deductive reasoning, whereas data mining is based on inductive reasoning.

For OLAP or ROLAP, you must know what you are looking for, then ask a specific question. Data mining provides a way to explore and identify relationships. Data mining typically uses techniques such as neural networks, genetic algorithms, and statistical pattern recognition to explore and identify relationships.

Spatial Data Warehousing

Data warehousing technology is evolving to fit a wider variety of data types. The next generation of programs will be able to accommodate a variety of objects ranging from traditional data to audio, video, and spatial data.

Current data warehousing technologies treat all data as tabular data. This treatment has some key implications for business geographics data. For example, a retailer has many decisions to make on a data warehouse implementation. Data relating to customers, store locations, trade areas, and markets, and competitive sites all contain a business geographic component.

The issues with customer data are fairly straightforward. These data are tabular in nature and easily fit within a data warehouse structure. In this situation, data such as a geodemographic segmentation code, latitude and longitude, ZIP+4, or other attributes can be added as additional fields in the data warehouse structure.

This data needs to be generated and stored for the location. Every year, when the demographic data changes, more data should be added to the warehouse. Given the extent of the data available, the data warehouse could grow rapidly and become larger than most companies want. An alternative is to house all the raw data in the data warehouse and let a ROLAP system calculate the needed data items. Again, the underlying dataset is larger than most companies desire.

One solution is a data mart. Think of a data mart as a small, specialized data warehouse. In this case, a data mart could be trade area and market demographics. A data mart and the data warehouse can be linked whenever needed.

Data warehousing and its associated tools provide unprecedented access to corporate information. The related technologies allow business managers to go through corporate databases in search of useful aggregated data. In actuality, the argument between OLAP and ROLAP is not hypothetical and there are real differences in functionality and performance between OLAP and ROLAP products.

Both OLAP and ROLAP support multidimensional views against a large number of attributes using graphical front ends, which are usually referred to as executive information systems. For example, an end user working for a retail chain using either technology can drill down into financial data to discover why a particular region's sales are flagging.

The basic difference between the technologies is an architectural one. It is the different ways that OLAP and ROLAP retrieve and aggregate information in a relational database. Because OLAP uses an intermediate server and ROLAP goes directly to the database, ROLAP software often is able to access more timely data than OLAP. For this reason, certain applications are more suited for OLAP engines than ROLAP.

Choosing one technology over the other requires an understanding of the type of data you want to query, such as the size of the data warehouse and how often the data changes, as well as the types of queries you want to do.

Although OLAP can offer a relatively inexpensive decision-support environment, ROLAP boasts advantages when employed at the departmental or enterprise level. ROLAP allows users to query against much larger data warehouses. OLAP products usually tap out when processing more than 50GB of back-end data.

OLAP and ROLAP technologies are likely to converge. More important, the Internet is likely to significantly transform the role of OLAP and ROLAP in business, something already evidenced by the large number of web applications already rolling out. Both OLAP and ROLAP tools provide similar decision support functions.

It is the Internet that looms as the most significant new development in the decision support arena. ROLAP has been on the market for a number of years. The Internet is going to provide a major shift into new data types. On the Internet or intranet level, URL and HTML technology is equivalent to SQL on relational databases. Using an OLAP engine to parse the World Wide Web for information is something of a new frontier. Drill down is a poor substitution for hypertext.

OLAP/ROLAP Is Not Data Mining

At first glance, OLAP and ROLAP tools would seem to offer many of the same types of business applications that data mining tools offer. In fact, many people make the mistake of lumping all of these tools together. But data mining tools use natural language tools, neural networks, and fuzzy logic to perform feats that OLAP and ROLAP do not even attempt.

Data mining, like OLAP and ROLAP, provides users with aggregated information. For example, using data mining tools, a supermarket executive with a database of nightly sales can send a query for the most frequently bought item among customers who also purchase breakfast cereal.

Data mining is similar in function to OLAP and ROLAP tools but differs in that users do not have to specify an output. Using the above example, OLAP requires a user to ask for cereal and toothpaste sales, whereas data mining users only need to ask for the item most often purchased with cereal.

Using OLAP and ROLAP

Data warehousing is a best-in-class corporate strategy that addresses a broad range of decision-support requirements served by a variety of personal productivity, query, reporting, and OLAP tools. OLAP fulfills a set of user-driven functional requirements for reporting, analysis, and planning applications. The inherent organizational requirement for planning and analysis is to help drive improved business performance. Successfully meeting this need requires that the company understands its past performance and prepares for its future.

OLAP technology is suitable for use with a data warehouse when analytical navigation of the data is required. Using OLAP, the data can be presented in a multi-dimensional view which can be further analyzed by drilling down or up through the hierarchy levels and slicing the data into two-dimensional tables. In analyzing the data, some computations are normally required which may slow down the response time of a user's analytical request. This is avoided in OLAP by executing some computations before accepting any request from the user. Thus, OLAP technology can be used to enhance the response time to a user's request.

MOLAP

MOLAP (Multidimensional OLAP) databases usually hold summarized data such as total sales by region and quarter, while relational data warehouses hold very detailed data, such as sales by product or salesperson.

Multidimensional analysis requires both foreknowledge of impending queries and complex, large matrices of information. When you slice and dice for multidimensional indexes, you have to take a guess at how you will cut the data beforehand. More cuts require more indexes and aggregates. A multidimensional database can quickly grow to many times the size of an equivalent RDBMS (relational DBMS). With such overhead, it can be difficult to justify MOLAP for all but the most critical applications.

The worlds of ROLAP and MOLAP are beginning to collide as vendors create hybrid servers that offer the best of both analysis methods.

Database Technologies

RDBMS (Relational Database Management System)

An RDBMS is a program that lets you create, update, and administer a relational database. An RDBMS takes Structured Query Language (SQL) statements entered by a user or contained in an application program and creates, updates, or provides access to the database and responds to queries.

The majority of new corporate, small business, and personal databases are being created for use with an RDBMS. However, a new database model based on object-orientation, ODBMS, is beginning to contend with the RDBMS as the database management system of the future.

MDBMS (Multidimensional Database Management System)

A multidimensional database is designed to allow for the efficient and convenient storage and retrieval of large volumes of data that is (1) intimately related and (2) stored, viewed, and analyzed from different perspectives. These perspectives are called dimensions. It is a group of data cells arranged by the dimensions of the data.

For example, a spreadsheet exemplifies a two-dimensional array with the data cells arranged in rows and columns, each being a dimension. A three-dimensional array can be visualized as a cube with each dimension forming a side of the cube, including any slice parallel with that side. Higher dimensional arrays have no physical metaphor, but they organize the data in the way users think of their enterprise.

Typical enterprise dimensions are time, measures, products, geographical regions, sales channels. Multidimensional data structures are intended to compliment existing transaction systems including relational technology by providing:

- A staging point for the integration of data extracted from a company's existing data storage systems
- A data structure that maps to end users' understanding of business issues
- An environment optimized for analysis-intensive applications
- An easily maintained analysis environment

Multidimensional technology is not designed to take the place of relational and other database technologies employed for transaction-intensive applications. In fact, by providing a staging point for data integration, manipulation and analysis, multidimensional database technology can be seen as a compliment to relational database technology.

Uses of Multidimensional Database

Both data warehousing and multidimensional database technologies are the systems developed to promote better data delivery to end users. In most cases, a data warehousing strategy can be complimented by implementing a multidimensional database as a data retailer. Likewise, a multidimensional database acting as a data retailer can benefit from a well-implemented data warehouse. By working together, multidimensional database technology and data warehousing can enhance the quality, speed and efficiency of delivering corporate data to end users.

It should be understood that as a database format, multidimensional technology can be used in theory for any stage in the data delivery pipeline. In practice, however, multidimensional database technology is rarely appropriate for OLTP and is only sometimes appropriate for data warehousing. A multidimensional database's primary strength is in data retailing. This is because multidimensional databases are explicitly designed to deliver data the way end users want it.

There are two scalability issues that are relevant in evaluating multidimensional database (MDBMS) technology. One has to do with the number of *logical* cells that the MDBMS can address, and the other, with the amount of *actual data* it can store. Given the inherent sparsity of multidimensional datasets, these two figures can vary dramatically.

In terms of *logical cells*, high-end MDBMSs are capable of addressing over 100 trillion cells. In terms of actual data, depending on the MDBMS architecture, some products are capable of handling up to 100 gigabytes. These capabilities make the MDBMS a good choice as an analytical front end to a corporate data warehouse, or for functional or departmental analytical applications. In either case, the MDBMS typically *stores summarized data from source databases, and should provide live drill down* to more detailed data if needed.

Most multidimensional database products provide SQL links to relational databases. They also provide various methods for accessing flat files.

Need for Multidimensional Database Technology

If your data structure is likely to be complex, if data accessing and retrieval speed is critical, or if the amount of analytical functionality the users will require is higher than average, think seriously about a natively multidimensional database solution. Similarly, if your company has requirements to deliver complex reports or perform intensive data browsing—for example, an application that requires extensive drilling down, rolling up, or rotating the data set—a natively multidimensional solution is an important option to consider.

Aside from its inherent ability to integrate and analyze large volumes of enterprise data, the multidimensional database also offers a good conceptual fit with the way end users visualize business data. Most business people already think about their businesses in multidimensional terms. Managers tend to ask questions about product sales in different markets over specific time periods, for example; and financial officers think about revenues and expenses in different business units for different accounting periods.

Analyzing data with complicated hierarchical structures is possible in the relational database environment. The difficulty, however, is in presenting that data in a timely fashion and in an intuitive format. Multidimensional database products, and more generally, On-Line Analytical Processing (OLAP) tools are designed to be a compliment to relational database technology. The latest step in the evolution of databases is the multidimensional database. This application category is widely recognized today as OLAP. The central reason for the multidimensional database's rise to corporate necessity is that it facilitates flexible, high-performance access and analysis of large volumes of complex and interrelated data.

Aside from its inherent ability to integrate and analyze large volumes of enterprise data, the multidimensional database offers a good conceptual fit with the way end users visualize business data. Most business people already think about their businesses in multidimensional terms.

ODBMS (Object Database Management System)

An ODBMS schema is created with an ODL (object data language) specification. The ODL is used to define objects and create interfaces to them. The ODBMS furnishes an ODL pre-compiler that translates this specification into source code (either C++ or Smalltalk) for subsequent compilation by the platform compiler. The ODL pre-compiler also generates an 'include' specification that lists data structures, class definitions, and method signatures identified by the input ODL specification.

Distributed Architectures

Many organizations are moving to a Three- or a Four-Tiered Web-based distributed architecture. The architecture uses a thin HTML- or Java-based client (Tier 1) accessing a Web server via HTTP (Tier 2), which accesses a business object layer, or Tier 3 (also called an application server) via CORBA (Common Object Request Broker Architecture) or message-oriented middleware. This in turn accesses Tier 4, which is either an RDBMS accessed via SQL-based middleware or mainframe legacy systems. These, in turn, can be accessed via message-oriented middleware or via distributed TP monitors.

In the Three-Tier version, transactions are served directly from the business object layer via IIOP (Internet inter-ORB protocol). The Third Tier would then be either legacy systems or a database, as in the Four-Tier example. Today, most of the parts of such an architecture can be secured, but it requires several different products.

For simple client-to-Web server encryption, SSL (secure sockets layer) is generally used. User authentication generally uses simple password-checking software running on the Web server. The security of the business-rules layer is usually vendor-specific. For DCE-based distributed systems, the security mechanism is based on Kerberos. Currently, there are few options for securing CORBA/IIOP traffic between the client and the transaction server. Although for those versions of CORBA that use DCE as a transport layer, DCE security can generally be used. OMG has proposed a standard for secure IIOP.

There are a new generation of Web security facilities becoming available that go beyond simple password protection of Web pages. These security facilities fall into two classes. One approach works somewhat like a firewall—a security server sits in front of the Web server. The others use the security exits from the major Web servers to authenticate and authorize users.

Multi-Tier Security

As corporations begin to rely more and more on the Internet and distributed systems, the need for increased security is becoming more important than ever. Every week, it seems, we hear about another security breach. Sometimes the amount of money/information lost through fraud related to a security breach is staggering. In other situations, the results are merely embarrassing or disruptive. These situations can occur in a traditional system as well, but the potential risk is multiplied in a distributed environment.

The Internet is especially vulnerable to security risks. These risks result from confusion about security issues and products. Often, managers do not know what they need and which types of products will address those needs. When they do implement a security product, it is often the wrong product for the task.

For example, organizations may try to implement an authentication product to manage user accounts and user access. However, authentication products only ensure that the users are who they say they are. We need a different tool to administer end-user security. To understand the security market better and which products solve specific problems, we can divide the distributed security environment into the following areas:

- Network integrity for firewall and communication security,
- Application/data integrity for access control and authorization, user account integrity for user group administration, single sign-on, and authentication,
- System integrity for virus detection and prevention, risk assessment, intrusion detection, and centralized auditing, and
- Data confidentiality and privacy for encryption.

Today, no one puts up a gateway to the Internet or any other external network without a firewall. Similarly, any organization that is considering electronic commerce is already planning its communication security with some level of encryption. Customers are not willing to pass information about themselves or their credit cards over the network without encryption.

Security is a complex issue for organizations to comprehend. Without sufficient attention to security, you will invariably put your organization at risk. The investment you make in a security policy and practice will protect your organization and your job.

What Is Security?

Different people mean different things when they talk about security, so it is probably good to start by setting some basic definitions. Some people talk about security in terms of computer viruses or hackers making a denial-of-service attack over the Internet. Others refer to privacy and encryption or authentication and authorization. Securing systems requires addressing all these areas. The primary elements of security are:

- Authentication
- Authorization
- Encryption

System Protection

This category groups all protection against system damage. This includes virus protection, firewalls and proxies, protection against denial-of-service attacks, and steps taken to minimize accidental system failures.

This protection can be partially addressed by applying authentication, authorization, and encryption techniques. A number of other facilities, such as virus-detection and removal software and virus-resistant systems environments (like Java) help with this. For interactive data warehousing purposes, we will concentrate on authorization, authentication, and encryption in a distributed environment, including the problem of single sign-on.

Today, there are point solutions that cover all these areas, but they provide very few provisions for building a complete security architecture. For example, current Secure Sockets Layer (SSL) implementations provide Internet server authentication and encryption but not user authentication, although the latest SSL standards address this. Various Kerberos-based private key mechanisms provide all three capabilities, but they are only viable when up to a few thousand user keys need to be administered.

Security Architectures

Securing a distributed environment will always require a combination of physical security and logical security (authentication, authorization, and encryption). Providing adequate security also goes beyond technical matters to security protocols and human behavior. All the physical and logical security in the world may not help you if some authorized person gives the information away. Technical security must always be part of a complete security system that incorporates proven protocols and manual procedures.

It is often forgotten that logical security only works if certain parts of the system are physically secured.

Security Protocols

There are a vast number of security protocols to protect against various scenarios, including eavesdropping, man-in-the-middle attacks, repudiation, and message alteration. Here we will concentrate on mechanisms for authentication, authorization, and encryption.

Private key encryption requires much less computing power than public key techniques and is usually faster, but it requires a shared secret that must be distributed in some other manner (out of band). For a small number of users, keys can be physically distributed, for example, using secure printing techniques. Often private keys are distributed using a public key technique.

Kerberos is a private key encryption approach developed at the Massachusetts Institute of Technology. It is based upon a central (possibly replicated) security server that is trusted by everyone. Every user has his or her own private key that is shared only with the security server. This setup keeps them from having private keys for each user/server pair.

The Kerberos protocol involves the issuing of tickets that grant a user access to a machine. To avoid interception of the tickets, Kerberos uses encrypted time stamps and an expiry time on each ticket. The default for Kerberos is to reject time stamps more than five minutes off. This gives up to five minutes for a ticket to arrive at the server after leaving the client machine. Unfortunately this requires that the clocks on all the client and server machines be accurately synchronized, which can be difficult when there are many users or when the users are in different time zones, which require special techniques. Kerberos is quite a useful approach for securing server-to-server communications within a business, and one can use it to provide single sign-on at the expense of complex key management.

Public key techniques are currently fashionable. The most popular of these use the RSA algorithm, although other algorithms, such as elliptic curve algorithms, are promising. Public key algorithms are very compute-intensive as compared to private key algorithms, so they are often used only for key exchange, after which private key techniques are used for message encryption. SSL key exchange is based upon the RSA algorithm.

Other techniques and algorithms include Diffie-Hellman, which uses a public key technique to negotiate a generated private key, rather than having one party generate the private key and send it to the other. The standard Diffie-Hellman protocol is vulnerable to man in the middle attacks, but this can be addressed by signing the messages digitally.

Most attention in the commercial world has been directed to securing messages. This is understandable in a distributed environment, especially given the open nature of the Internet. One area that has had very limited attention is securing databases. Most commercial implementations use simple password protection for access with no encryption and no single sign-on. Also, most database security routines with commercial DBMS are stand-alone and cannot integrate easily with other security mechanisms.

Messages are short-lived, but data in databases can be around for many years. Today, assuming that steps have been taken to secure the transaction messages, the easiest way to do damage or act fraudulently would be to access the relatively unprotected databases and alter the data.

Probably the biggest problem in securing distributed systems is the integration of disparate security systems. Your Web site may use SSL, your mainframe may use ACF2 password protection, and your internal servers may use Kerberos. There is no general solution to this problem today, although there are some proprietary solutions that cover a wide range of environments.

Securing Inter/Intra/Extranet Applications

The Internet is perceived as a hostile place, and as such it is a great proving ground for intranet and extranet security. If security technology works on the Internet, it will work anywhere. Right now, the emphasis on the Internet is providing secure financial transactions. The state of the art requires very careful coding of applications, firewalls, and servers and browsers that support the Secure Sockets Layer (SSL).

SSL is a flexible protocol that supports various encryption algorithms, including RSA and DES. Unfortunately, it only addresses the securing of HTTP traffic today, namely regular Web pages. This is not currently a problem because most Internet transactions are forms-based and as such, use SSL. As used in the standard versions of the popular browsers, SSL only provides server authentication based on public key technology and not public key-based user authentication. Although the software to have password protection for certain Web pages is available on many Web servers, the software uses passwords stored on the server, making them vulnerable to interception if someone uses the same password on many sites.

Increasingly, in a distributed environment, Web servers are not the source of data but provide access to legacy systems and databases located on other machines. With firewalls, this communication between the Web server and the source systems is isolated from the Internet and is less vulnerable to outside interference. On the other hand, users behind the firewall with inside knowledge are a major source of fraud, so protection needs to be end-to-end. The key is to secure the middleware, especially in server-to-server communications.

With the introduction of CORBA/IIOP as an Internet transaction protocol, there is another channel to secure. This is critical to the use of secure IIOP for transactions over the Internet.

Securing Middleware

Beyond physical security and the provision of dedicated connections between machines, the simplest—but probably least flexible and most expensive—way to secure middleware communications is to use hardware. Assuming the servers are in a secure environment, encryption boxes can be used to communicate securely over public connections. This could be an intranet or even the Internet. This approach provides solid point-to-point security.

The more flexible approach is to secure the middleware communications at a software level. This is potentially more vulnerable than the hardware approach, but it is cheaper and more flexible when new connections are needed. The potential extra vulnerability is a result of the software running on relatively insecure operating systems environments such as commercial Unix implementations or Windows NT.

Authentication and Single Sign-on

Public key mechanisms (such as RSA) are good for authenticating software and hardware elements of a distributed system. So long as the private key of the private/public key pair is physically secure, the identity of the hardware or application can be assured. To be truly secure, the private key has to be physically secured and packaged with the encryption engine so that it never leaves the physically secure environment. Today there are PCMCIA- and SmartCard-based hardware encryption devices that provide such capabilities.

The problem of authenticating people is much more difficult. Passwords, which are just secrets shared between the authenticator and authenticated, can become a big management dilemma.

The use of public/private key pairs can greatly simplify the key maintenance problem by reducing many private key pairs to a single private/public key pair. This approach has two problems. First, people do not have a cryptographic engine in their heads. This means that the private key has to be entered into a cryptographic engine for it to be used for authentication. The key becomes vulnerable to interception at this point. The second problem with this approach is that private keys are long and meaningless, making them very difficult to remember.

Tokens, such as the SmartCards, make authentication a matter of possessing of something physical and unique. One great advantage of token-based security is that it becomes relatively easy to know if you are vulnerable. The card must be missing because it can not be copied without great difficulty. Pure token-based security does leave open a window of opportunity if the token is lost or stolen.

Supplementing the token with a password can address this shortcoming. Ideally, the password should be entered directly into the token (some have keypads) for maximum security, but in most cases entering the password into the card-reading device is adequate if you are sure of the integrity of the card reader. There are, however, tales of passwords being intercepted using dummy card readers.

Biometric techniques are even better, so long as the biometric sensor is secure and encrypts its output. Unlike retinal scan, iris scan is non-intrusive. The front of the eyes are scanned from a distance of a foot or so using a high-definition camera. Current research indicates that the iris is a significantly better biometric than fingerprints, thus offering a substantially lower number of false accepts and rejects. With biometrics, there is no need for a user to remember or enter a password that can potentially be intercepted.

Conclusions

Beyond simple SQL-like queries, Data Warehousing has introduced a concept of On Line Analytical Processing (OLAP), which enables users to formulate unstructured queries into the data warehouse. OLAP differs from SQL queries in the level of abstraction, or *open ended-ness* that can be included in the query. For example, a SQL query might be constructed to show the sales of certain products in certain regions over a particular timeframe. OLAP enables users to ask questions like, which employee is paid the highest, in which department, at what level of education, over a certain timeframe.

In today's marketplace, those who get information the fastest and act on it the soonest are the winners. By extension, those who never even get a chance to get the information, because it is lost in a sea of data, are bound to be the losers.

Data mining, provides a set of technological tools, when combined with a practical methodology, represents an opportunity to organizations today to find that hidden wealth of information buried in their legacy databases. Most data mining applications are highly computationally intensive, and operate on data extracts from data warehouses. Today, companies everywhere are clearly reaping the benefits of data mining through better decision making, and the ability to mount a faster response to changing business conditions. A successful data mining application means selecting the right software and hardware.

Modern symmetric multiprocessing architectures offer the performance, economy, flexibility, and scalability necessary to a credible data mining effort.

A multidimensional database stores data elements in an array that can have dozens of dimensions, making it possible to directly query applications for answers to questions such as sales by month, product, and region, without creating relationships between tables of information. Because a multidimensional database (MDD) can group related information in a way that is not limited to a two-dimensional, row/column table within a relational system, it is able to perform complex computations on that data without incurring the overhead of managing multiple table relationships and indexes

These technologies are being tuned to adapt to the World Wide Web. However, some MIS managers do express concern about relying on the Internet as a data warehouse when their businesses consider decision support a vital competitive advantage, and they cite the continuing security limitations and technical immaturity of the Internet.

5

OBJECT TECHNOLOGIES

Introduction

Today's business is under assault from multiple, simultaneous revolutions in both the business and the technology arenas. Implementation of data warehousing, like most large applications, has to cope with many concurrent business issues, such as:

- Increased global competition
- Pressures to reduce costs, increase productivity, and increase responsiveness
- Pressure to achieve continuous improvements in core business processes and technological revolutions
- A breakdown in the centralized hierarchical management concepts
- The PC and the user empowerment
- The client/server paradigms allowing distribution of resources
- The distributed systems revolution (LANS and WANS)
- The graphical user interface (GUI) revolution

The introduction of decision support applications on the web has created an urgency to exploit improved development techniques. Data warehouse applications that will thrive in the next millennium will have overcome the chaos introduced by these conflicting innovations.

As with most major endeavors, the task of business redesign in the interactive web environment is increasing in complexity. The objective of taming complexity and bringing order to chaos requires new approaches to problem-solving and new ways of thinking about business processes and information systems.

Business processes must be designed for constant change. As business processes change, the underlying information systems must also change. Rapid change requires that both business processes and their underlying information systems be modeled and evolved together. Data warehousing applications are not any different.

Object-Oriented Technology

Object-oriented technology is based on simulation and modeling. Instead of deploying the traditional application development life cycle, models of a business or business area are constructed. These models are shared by individual computer applications.

The quality of the model is a key determinate of *reuse*. The model itself must be designed for change. Business processes change and their change is based on using the business model to simulate proposed processes.

A Brief Overview

Object orientation, as a way of thinking and problem solving, applies to a broad spectrum of technology disciplines and tools including:

- Analysis and design methods
- Programming languages
- Operating systems
- Development tools
- Databases
- Code-libraries/frameworks

Business people think in terms of people, places, things, and events. Examples of business objects include people and the roles they play (policeman, dispatcher), places (office, boathouse, beach), things (desk, alley, car), and events (auction, marathon, wedding).

An object contains both data and logic in a single software entity or package. An object consists of its own private information (data), its own private procedures (private methods) that manipulate the object's private data, and a public interface (public methods) for communicating with other objects. Objects provide properties representing a coherent concept and a set of operations to manage these properties. The fusion of process logic with data is the distinguishing characteristic of objects.

Each object is capable of acting in much the same way as the real object behaves in the real world. Objects are assigned roles and responsibilities, and they contain all of the information they need to carry out their activities. The only way to use an object is to send it a message that requests a service be performed. The receiving object acts on the message and sends the results back as a message to the requesting object.

When a service is requested of an object, the object is sent a message, much like a traditional function call. However, the difference is that the rest of the system does not see how the object is implemented and cannot suffer any integration problems if the object's internal implementation (code) is changed. This means programming without assumptions, where functionality is well-defined and programmers do not make assumptions about how the shared routines or systems work on an internal level.

Additionally, object orientation inherently supports and extends the concepts of modularity. *Chunking* is a mechanism used to build larger components from smaller components. This approach to modularity results in object-based systems being very granular or being formed by simple components that can be reused in other systems. Such *reuse* is the key to many of the benefits of object technology: productivity, quality, and consistency. Another important benefit is that modifications tend to be local to a single object. Thus, maintenance is simplified and less costly. Changes are automatically propagated throughout all the systems of the enterprise.

From a technical perspective, an object may be more precisely defined. The first principles include polymorphism, inheritance, and encapsulation. Let us explore these concepts to deepen our understanding of objects.

Polymorphism

Polymorphism when applied to objects allows the developer to use one name for similar kinds of operations or functions. Rather than create unique names such as drawLine, drawSquare or drawCircle, a single method named *draw* may be used. The polymorphism mechanism of the receiving class, depending on the kind of object sending a message, will implement the appropriate method such as draw a square.

Classes and Inheritance

The concept of *classes* brings order to the world of objects. Classes are templates used to define the data and methods of similar types of objects. An object created from a class is referred to as an instance to distinguish the object from the mold from which it was created (the *class*). Object-oriented programming languages and analysis and design methods both use classes to provide a means to share common characteristics among objects.

Inheritance, as a core feature of object-oriented systems, will provide the developer with some important advantages. First, inheritance introduces support for *code reuse* at a language level. If a developer needs to change the way several classes of objects perform a certain task, the modified behavior is applied to each of the classes via inheritance. The developer needs to perform the change in only one place. Inheritance makes it very easy to modify information systems. Second, inheritance reduces redundancy. Making it easy to reuse existing code discourages duplicating code.

Encapsulation

All, or at least many, of the descriptions of operations (behavior) and data (attributes) within an object-oriented model or system reside within objects. The only way to use or manipulate an object is to send it a message. The hiding of internal information within objects is called *encapsulation.* To use an object, the developer needs only to be aware of what services or operations it offers (to which messages the object responds).

A system comprised of objects is constructed in a modular fashion, in which each module (object) is engaged only through its defined interface (its messages). Objects do not become interdependent on their internal code or structure. The advantage of encapsulation is that the implementation of objects can change (being improved or extended) without having to change the way the object is used by the rest of the system. The result is that changes tend to be local to an object and maintenance is simplified.

Furthermore, as object-oriented information systems are implemented, additional reusable components (objects) become available so that programming becomes more a matter of *assembly* rather than coding. As an object-oriented infrastructure matures, programming is reduced to *exception* programming based upon modifications of existing objects. Such assembly and exception concepts are demonstrated by the new graphical programming environments where objects are simply *wired* together to create applications.

What's an Object?

We can think of objects as individuals. Each individual has special knowledge (*attributes*) and special skills (*methods*), some of which it gains from its ancestors (*inheritance*). By communicating with each other (messaging), individuals are able to work together to accomplish very complex tasks—much like a society. Different individuals may react to the same request by performing different steps as long as the results are consistent with the intent of the request (*polymorphism*).

Objects encapsulate their knowledge and behavior, inherit common functionality, communicate entirely via messages, and respond appropriately based on their individual capabilities when messaged by other objects, often determining the exact response at run-time. Various object-oriented languages support these features to differing degrees, but the essentials of the technology arc the same, regardless.

The Object Advantage

Object technology brings the following advantages to modern computing:

- The quantity of code needed to support a business is reduced.
- The time required to develop the code is reduced.
- All applications behave consistently (since they reuse the same objects).
- The quality of information systems is improved.

Object-Orientation

As discussed earlier, object-orientation has been applied to a number of technology areas. These areas include object-oriented programming languages, analysis and design methods, databases, and operating systems. In the discussion that follows, we build on the fundamentals presented in the last section and progress from definitions to discovery of how object orientation applies to each technology area.

Object Database Management Systems (ODBMS)

Relational database management systems (RDBMS) were the first systems to make it possible to decouple application issues from the design of a shared database. Before the era of the relational model, the imbedded pointers and links in hierarchical and CODASYL databases required that the developer focus on computer data storage models or data structures with cumbersome pointers and links.

The new relational focus is shifting to logical modeling of the application domain and away from the Direct Access Storage Device (DASD) physical data structure or other implementation issues, with data being truly independent from process. The relational data model represents the third stage in the evolution of data warehousing systems:

- Early file systems
- Hierarchical and network database management systems
- Relational database management systems

Data within a relational database is broken down and stored in two-dimensional tables in which each item exists as a row within a table. Complex (hierarchical) data items are arranged by joining rows from different tables and building artificial constructs such as foreign keys to facilitate reconstruction of the *real world* information. Languages such as Structured Query Language (SQL) provide a means for expressing how such data may be joined.

Objects in the real world often involve hierarchical arrangements of data. Object-oriented programming languages accommodate, and in fact simplify, the management and manipulation of such hierarchical data objects. Storing and retrieving those complex structures using a two-dimensional relational database forces the programmer to implement the composition and decomposition required for storing and retrieving data.

Object databases (ODB) have emerged as a means of providing a storage mechanism for hierarchical arrangements of data. In contrast, relational databases require programmers to translate data between their in-memory representation and their storage representation. An analogy would be the commuter who must take apart his car to park in his garage, then reassemble it when it is needed again. Object databases, on the other hand, store and manage data in the same way a program does—as objects.

The advantages of an object database are threefold. First, there is no semantic difference between data stored within a database and data in memory. Composition and decomposition programming is not required. ODBMSs are unique in their absence of a data manipulation language. Second, because of the way data is stored (maintaining its hierarchical relations), retrieving complex arrangements of data is often much faster than in a relational system.

A side benefit is that such an arrangement makes it possible to build information systems that span a network as though it were one large machine. Third, the encapsulated models produced during analysis and design are the same as the database models. In a traditional development lifecycle, the analysis model is different from the design model, which in turn is different from the programming model, which is also different from the database model.

The strategic reason to begin implementing an ODBMS is the ability to create true information management systems. Today, some object database management systems have (and eventually all will have) the capability to query processes (methods) of objects as well as the data (attributes). This means a user will be able to query for past-due *customers* without knowing the business rules defining *past due* or having to structure those rules in the query language.

By introducing access to object methods, even greater detail hiding is achieved. In such an environment, business process and rule changes do not disrupt existing applications or queries. Furthermore, such a capability ensures the consistency and integrity of information presented by all applications, queries, ad hoc programs, analysis, and reports across the enterprise.

Although object databases represent the next generation, relational databases offer continuing advantages to corporations with heavy investments in relational technology. The two models will coexist for years to come. Relational data structures are used within object databases, and bridges to existing relational databases (wrappers) play an important role in preserving existing assets while incrementally migrating to objects.

Distributed Object Computing

Data warehouse applications of the future will need to be spread across multiple, and sometimes specialized, hardware that will cooperate with other hardware, as well as the legacy computer systems we have today. To meet the demands of business, the data warehouse systems we build today and tomorrow must be based upon distributed object computing technologies and paradigms.

New types of information systems are needed that place the focus on the computer system to correctly convey information in a form that humans can process naturally. The information must reflect reality as perceived and understood by humans, not the artificial constructs of transactions, tables and spreadsheets characteristic of today's systems. Where it once stood on the sidelines, cognitive science plays a central role in new era information systems.

Systems rooted in human cognition can enable instant use (no training required), correct assimilation, confirmation of user intentions and error-free communication between man and machine. Such systems are required by the extended enterprise.

The Challenge of Enterprise Computing

Today's popular development tools and techniques suffer a number of problems concerning application scalability, modularity, granularity, and maintainability. In addition, they overwhelm the ability of users to assimilate diverse information. As such, these tools and techniques will not advance us much past our current position with respect to our ability to develop the necessary information systems in a timely and cost-effective manner.

Client/server technology is essential, but not sufficient. The issues limiting systems development today are not just technical. In our quest for supreme technology, business concepts have remained second-class citizens, standing in the shadow of a high-performance infrastructure. Clients and servers continue to evolve technically but, in these implementations, the business itself is not visible. Client/server technology, by itself, does not supply a uniform cognitive model for sharing information among systems and people.

Other limitations of the current client/server models promise to make them tomorrow's legacy systems. Even as *tiers* are added to decouple business logic, user presentation, network operations, and database processing, fundamental design methods center on user screens and forms. Forms or screen-based designs do not promote reuse nor do they support workflow or other applications that are identified as a result of business reengineering. What are conspicuously missing from most client/server models are the key abstractions of the business. Again, the issue is assimilation of information by people. This is where object orientation adds significant value to current client/server models.

Client/server design and development needs to incorporate the power of object-oriented technology. The graphical user interface (GUI) portion of client applications may appear object-oriented but, contrary to vendor claims, client/server development needs to make much more extensive use of object technology at both the client and server level. Thus, many *object-based* tools do not allow developers to leverage object technology. Object-orientation in this context is much more than attaching procedural scripting language to graphical interface objects.

The blending of the cognitive and semantic integrity of objects with the distribution potential of client/server architectures holds great promise for meeting the challenge of enterprise computing. This new computing paradigm, distributed object computing, is explained in the next section.

Distributed Object Computing

Distributed object computing is a breakthrough framework for computing that has resulted from the convergence of object-oriented and client/server technologies. When radio and motion picture technologies converged, something completely new happened. Unlike the radio and the movies, television pervaded and fundamentally changed society. Television combined the distribution advantages of radio with the richness of real-world information contained in moving pictures.

The result was far more than the sum of the two technologies. Distributed object computing blends the distribution advantages of client/server technologies with the richness of real-world information contained in object-oriented models. Distributed object computing has fundamentally changed the information landscape of business, and something totally new has started to happen. The way business software is developed will change forever.

Distributed object computing is a computing paradigm that allows objects to be distributed across a heterogeneous network, and allows each of the components to interoperate as a unified whole. To a data warehouse application built in a distributed object environment, the network is the computer.

Objects interact by passing messages to each other. These messages represent requests for information or services. During any given interaction, objects will dynamically assume the roles of clients and servers.

The physical glue that ties the distributed objects together is an object request broker. The object request broker (ORB) provides the means for objects to locate and activate other objects on a network, regardless of the processor or programming language used to develop either client or server objects. The ORB makes these things happen transparently to the developer. Thus, the ORB is the middleware of distributed object computing that allows interoperability in heterogeneous networks of objects.

ORBs provide a means for locating, activating, and communicating with objects while hiding their implementation details from the developer. The significant benefit of ORBs is that they remove the network messaging complexity from the mind's eye of the developer. The view of the developer is refocused from technical issues to the business objects and the services they provide.

When objects are distributed across a network, clients can be servers and conversely, servers can be clients. That really does not matter since we are talking about cooperating objects: the client requests services of another object, the server object fulfills the request. Clients and servers can be physically anywhere on the network and written in any object-oriented programming language.

Although universal clients and servers live in their own dynamic worlds outside of an application, the objects appear as though they are local within the application since the network is the computer. In essence, the whole concept of distributed object computing can be viewed as simply a global network of heterogeneous clients and servers or, more precisely, cooperative business objects.

Furthermore, valuable legacy systems can be *wrapped* and appear to the developer to be objects. Once wrapped, the legacy code can participate in a distributed object environment. Wrapping is a technique of creating an object-oriented interface that can access specific functionality contained in one or more existing (legacy) computer applications.

Each set of wrappers carves out a slice of legacy code and represents it as a real world object (person, container, and shipment). Corporations have significant investments in computer systems that were developed prior to the advent of object-oriented technology. Even though a corporation may want to migrate to object-oriented technology to derive its benefits, millions or billions of dollars of existing computing resources cannot be scrapped just because a new technology comes along.

There is not a solid business case for *converting* legacy assets to the object paradigm. However, a strong business case can be made for an evolutionary approach to building new generation applications that incorporate and leverage existing assets.

Several approaches to wrapping legacy systems can be taken from simple *screen scraping* to direct function calls to existing code. Approaches depend on what legacy asset is being wrapped: a mainframe COBOL application, an Excel spreadsheet on a microcomputer, or a relational database server in an existing client/server application all require different approaches. Regardless of the means used to wrap legacy applications, the result is that existing assets can become full participants in a distributed object application.

In a distributed object environment, an application supports a business process or task by combining active business objects. Component assembly is becoming the dominant theme for developing distributed object applications. Object interaction is accomplished through a sophisticated messaging system that allows objects to request services of other objects regardless of the machine or machines on which they physically reside.

Objects only know what services other objects provide (their interfaces); not how they provide those services (their implementation). The hiding of implementation details within objects is one of the key contributions of object-oriented technology to managing complexity in distributed computing. In a distributed object environment, the application developer does not even have to consider what machine or programming language is used to implement the server objects.

Customers, products, orders, employees, trades, financial instruments, shipping containers and vehicles are all examples of real-world concepts or things that could be represented as business objects. Business objects add value over other representations by providing a way of managing complexity, giving a higher-level perspective, and packaging the essential characteristics of business concepts more completely. We can think of business objects as actors, role-players, or surrogates for the real world things or concepts that they represent.

In summary, distributed object computing is an extension of client/server technology. However, there is a difference in its working process and its implementation. With client/server, there is generally an application running on a client computer while another application runs on a server computer. These two applications communicate across a network and relay data to one another, usually via some middleware provided in the form of an application program interface (API) or function call library.

In a sense, client/server is a restrictive version of distributed object computing. A distributed application is made up of objects, just as any other object-oriented application. However, the objects of a distributed object application may be split up and run on multiple computers throughout a network.

Distributed object computing is not magic. It is a very complex computing environment and requires a very sophisticated and robust technology infrastructure. The information technology infrastructures of the future must be based on very sound architectures, as we will discuss next.

The Technical Advantage of Distributed Objects

Object orientation can radically simplify applications development. Distributed object models and tools extend an object-oriented programming system. The objects may be distributed on different computers throughout a network, living within their own dynamic library outside of an application, and yet appear as though they were local within the application. This is the essence of plug-and-play software. Several technical advantages result from a distributed object environment.

1. Legacy assets can be leveraged. Object wrappers (object-oriented interfaces to legacy code) may be applied to various computing resources throughout a network to simplify the means of communicating with these resources. All communication between distributed objects occurs in the form of messages, just as local objects within an application communicate, rather than applying different middleware and network interfaces to each legacy system.

   Today's legacy systems can be encapsulated with multiple object wrappers to become full participants in new era information systems. Further, a single object may represent information derived from multiple legacy systems. In this way, the massive investment corporations have made in these assets, and the associated intellectual capital, can be leveraged.

2. Since all objects—both local and remote—communicate in the same fashion (via messages), programmers have the ability to distribute

components of an application to computers that best fit the task of each object without having to change the rest of the application using these objects.

For example, an object that performs intense computations, such as three-dimensional renderings, might be placed on a more powerful computer, rather than on an average desktop computer, where the user interacts with the presentation objects. Such partitioning provides businesses with a new approach to manage their investment in computing resources and to match the changing needs to change resources. Thus, hardware investments can be optimized.

3. Since objects appear to be local to their clients, a client does not know what machine or even what kind of machine an object resides on. As a result, migration of implementation objects from platform to platform is made easier. These migrations can be accomplished in steps without affecting the clients.

4. Systems integration can be performed to a higher degree. Software and hardware resources available on disparate platforms can be tied together into a single application. The goal of creating a single system image is achieved when applications can be assembled from distributed objects.

The overall technical goal of distributed object computing is clear: to advance client/server technology so that it may be more efficient and flexible, yet less complex. The benefits of distributed objects are indeed solutions to the problems with existing client/server paradigms.

The Business Impact of Distributed Object Computing

Distributed object computing, plus business objects, equals the next generation of business computing. Business pioneers who understand this technology are already developing new era systems. They understand that the ultimate next-generation methods and tools are still in the laboratory, but they know that sufficient standards and development resources are already in place. With a head start in their respective industries, these professionals intend to become well-armed for 21st century business warfare. Time waits for no one.

Distributed object technology is creating a new generation of client/server systems. Objects encapsulate data and business logic, allowing them to be located anywhere within a distributed network. Users need not know where these objects are stored or in what language they are written. The objects may reside on the user's desktop computer, on a corporate intranet host, or on a web server that sits on the other side of the world.

Distributed Objects and the World Wide Web

The objective of OMG (object management group) is to provide a CORBA-based environment from which the web appears to consist of a world of distributed CORBA objects. Also OMG wants to exploit CORBA's integration capability to integrate existing information systems into WWW.

This work uses the CORBA Internet Inter-ORB Protocol (IIOP) which will be mandatory for all CORBA compliant platforms. The initial phase of the project is to build an infrastructure consisting of:

- An IIOP to HTTP gateway which allows CORBA clients to access web resources
- An HTTP to IIOP gateway which allows WWW clients to access CORBA resources
- A web server which makes its resource available by both IIOP and HTTP
- Web browsers which can use IIOP as their native protocol

Within CCORBA, clients will be able to invoke CORBA services and the ORB (Object Request Broker) will locate and invoke the right service. If the service is outside the CORBA world, access will take place via the IIOP-to-HTTP gateway (this gateway will also convert from IIOP to other protocols such as FTP); the remote object will look like a CORBA object to the CORBA client.

Clients outside the CORBA world will see CORBA objects as web objects and will be able to direct HTTP requests to these objects through the HTTP-to-IIOP gateway.

The Benefits of Distributed Objects

If object technology promised to bring a new level of programming productivity to the IS world by allowing developers to package software into more manageable and useful components, then distributed objects, by bringing network facilities into the picture, make good on that promise by operating across different operating systems, networks, languages, and hardware.

With distributed objects, tens of millions of computers, all using different programs and operating systems are capable of communication. Information

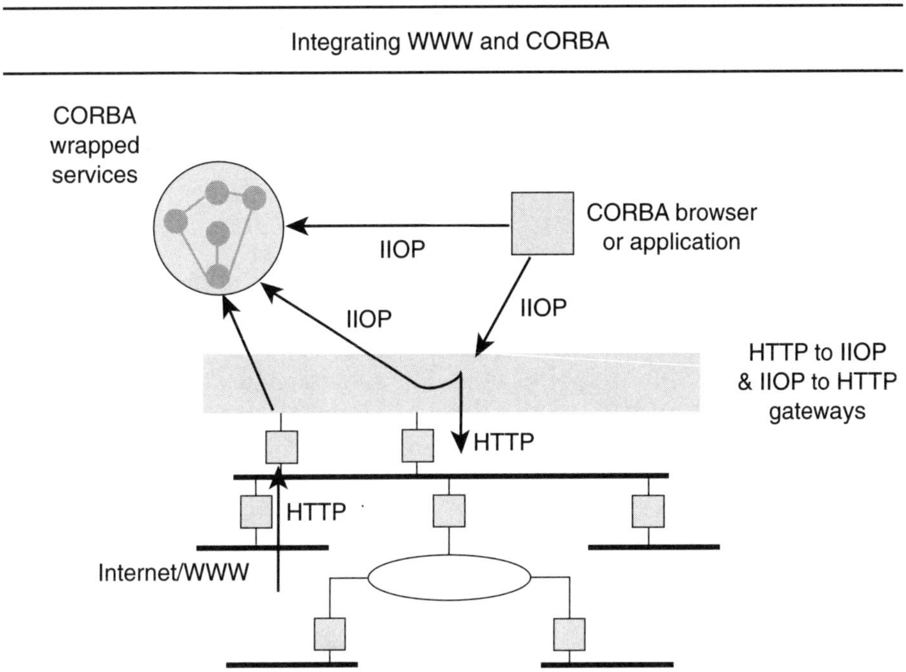

Integrating WWW and CORBA

Figure 5.1 Integrating WWW and CORBA (Gateway)

can easily be transferred between different software programs and brands of computers.

Like the client/server approach, distributed objects permit computing and network resources to be applied efficiently across an organization. For example, an application might be implemented as a set of objects, some running on a corporate server and others running on a departmental server or on end user PCs (see **Figure 5.1**).

Some of the benefits of using distributed objects are:

- Ease of programming, where the underlying object model, the Interface Definition Language (IDL), and the supporting tools combine to simplify the task of writing distributed applications.
- Encapsulation and systems integration where distributed object technology has proved very effective in encapsulating *legacy systems* as objects. These objects offer interfaces that can then be used to implement an integrated system.

- Extensibility and manageability where systems built from interacting objects are inherently extensible since objects can be easily added or replaced. Extensibility allows customized management interfaces to be added to the system.

Object Request Broker (ORB) Architecture

The Object Request Broker (ORB) manages interaction between clients and servers. This includes the distributed computing responsibilities of location, referencing of parameters, and results.

The CORBA specification defines an architecture of interfaces and services that must be provided by the ORB, with no implementation details. These are modular components so different implementations could be used, satisfying the needs of different platforms.

The Common Object Request Broker (CORBA)

CORBA specifies a system which provides interoperability between objects in a heterogeneous, distributed environment and in a way transparent to the programmer. Its design is based on the *OMG Object Model.*

The object-oriented software industry actually presents a variety of architectural object models that together provide important capabilities, yet may have somewhat contradictory goals. Vendors merge these different goals to provide customers the best tools and infrastructure for building and deploying enterprise systems that achieve standards compliance and also maximum performance and manageability.

The client-side architecture provides clients with interfaces to the ORB and object implementations. In consists of the following interfaces:

- Dynamic invocation interface allows for the specification of requests at runtime. This is necessary when the object interface is not known at run-time. Dynamic invocation works in conjunction with the interface repository.
- IDL stub consists of functions generated by the IDL interface definitions and linked into the program. The functions are a mapping between the client and the ORB implementation. Therefore ORB capabilities can be made available for any client implementation for which there is a language mapping. Functions are called just as if it was a local object.

- Either the client or the object implementation may call the ORB interface. This interface provides functions of the ORB which may be directly accessed by the client (such as retrieving a reference to an object) or by the object implementations. This interface is mapped to the host programming language. Any ORB must support the ORB interface.
- The ORB core is the underlying mechanism used as the transport level. It provides basic communication of requests to other subcomponents.
- The implementation-side interface consists of the ORB interface and an ORB core.
- IDL skeleton interface called by ORB to invoke the methods that were requested from clients.
- Object adapters (OA) provide the means by which object implementations access most ORB services. This includes the generation and interpretation of object references, method invocation, security, and activation. The object adapter actually exports three different interfaces: a private interface to skeletons, a private interface to the ORB core, and a public interface used by implementations. The OA isolates the object implementation from the ORB core. The CORBA specification envisions a variety of adapters, each providing a specific service. The Basic Object Adapter (BOA) is the most generic of the Object adapters.

The ORB manages the interactions between clients and object implementations. Clients issue requests and invoke methods of object implementations.

Request

The client requests a service from the object implementation. The ORB transports the request, which invokes the method using object adapters and the IDL skeleton.

The client has an object reference, an operation name and a set of parameters for the object and activates operations on this object. The Object Management Group/Object Model defines each operation to be associated with a controlling parameter, implemented in CORBA as an object reference. The client does not know the location of the object or any of the implementation details. The request is handled by the ORB, which must locate the target object and route the request to that object. It is also responsible for getting results back to the client.

The request makes use of either the dynamic invocation (dynamic link) or the IDL Stubs (static link) interface. Static links use the IDL stubs (as local function calls) and dynamic requests use the dynamic invocation interface (DII).. The object implementation is not aware of the difference. If the interface was defined in the IDL and the client has an interface for the target object, the IDL stub is used. This stub is specific to the target object. The DII is used when the interface is not known at runtime. The DII uses information stored in the interface repository to establish the request. The request is passed from the ORB to the object implementation through the IDL skeleton. The object implementation is made available by using information stored in the implementation repository. The object implementations encapsulate state and behavior of the object. CORBA only defines the mechanisms to invoke operation, it does not define how activated or stopped, made to persist, etc.

Object References

A request is issued upon object references. Object references are opaque references only, uniform within an ORB implementation. Since both clients and servers use object references as opaque references, different representation will not affect them. CORBA does have an object reference that is used to denote no object. It is guaranteed to be different from any other object reference, and usually maps to the null or nil object.

Object Adapters

Object adapters (OA) are the primary ORB service providers to object implementations. OAs have a public interface, which is used by the object implementation, and a private interface, used by the IDL skeleton.

Example services provided by OAs are:

- Method invocation (in conjunction with skeleton)
- Object implementation activation and deactivation
- Mapping of object reference to object implementations
- Generation of object references
- Registering object implementations, used in locating object implementations when a request comes in

OAs may be specialized. They are a major player in delivery of requests and are the primary service provider for object implementations. CORBA only defines the Basic Object Adapter (BOA) and any CORBA implementation must provide a BOA. CORBA assumes the definition of additional object adapters. There should not be a large number of adapters since one adapter can service more than one implementation.

Object Services

Object services refer to fundamental services provided by their own objects that support common interactions between other objects. The services follow the OMG Common Object Services Specification (COSS) guidelines. Current object services include:

- Event management services, which refer to the asynchronous communication of different CORBA objects with one another.
- Naming object services that map a human-readable name (string) to an object relative to its context.
- Persistent services assure that an object (CORBA developed) outlives its creator. They allow an object's state to be retained at a given point in time. This feature is used when a host crashes or is rebooted.
- Life-cycle services determine the methods for object creation and termination.
- Concurrency services provide for distributed locks on a given object.
- Externalization services collect objects and transport them as serial objects.
- Relationship objects are used for CORBA object modeling and graphing.
- Transaction object services allow the sharing of a transaction among multiple objects.

Common Facilities

This is one of the newer areas of OMG standardization. These are higher level specifications for supporting interoperability, the level most application developers will use. The specifications call for higher-level services and vertical market specialty areas. Some examples of common facilities would include system management and compound documents. Specialty areas would be more specialized such as geospatial data processing and financial services.

ORB Interface Operations

The ORBs provide operations on references and strings. There are two operations for converting an object reference to strings and back again: An is_nil operation for testing whether an object references is referencing no object and a duplicate operation for allowing a duplicate reference to the same object to be created. A release operation is provided to reclaim the memory used by an object reference.

In addition, the ORB provides two operations used for returning meta-information from the interface and implementation repositories. The get_interface operation is used to extract information regarding the object type. The get_implementation operation returns an object that describes the object implementation from the implementation repository.

OOPs (Object-Oriented Programs)

Most application programs are written for specific hardware and operating systems. Often, software written by different companies (or even different programmers within the same organization) will not communicate effectively because the information must be carefully organized and formatted to be transferred. As a result, programmers at many companies, as well as software manufacturers, have created large, monolithic programs to ensure compatibility with existing hardware and operating systems. Since hardware and operating systems are quickly outdated, this programming philosophy requires that you replace your applications within a few years, or spend a lot of money maintaining older systems.

Object technology is widely seen as the next-generation approach for application development, providing the mechanism for more efficient programming and rapid responses to business needs and opportunities. An object is a self-contained package comprising both code and data. Object design contributes to safety and product quality, since an object is able to do only a limited number of well-defined tasks (known as methods) to the data it contains. Use of objects speeds development time while reducing the cost of building an application because the capabilities of an object may be embraced and extended, through inheritance, to build yet another, different object.

Objects also allow an open environment in which the pieces of an implementation can be developed, at different times, by different IS departments, project teams, or independent software vendors.

Enticing as this sounds, and is, classical objects only live within a single program, on a single machine. In contrast, distributed objects, with the assistance of Object Request Brokers (ORBs), can live anywhere, yet inter-operate as effectively as when bound to a single machine.

Standards

With the advent of distributed computing environments, the number of tools and technologies available to developers has increased exponentially. Many technologies are competing to provide the infrastructure for distributing large-scale applications, the underpinnings of the emerging networked economy. Some of these technologies come from standards activities, and some from hardware and software vendors.

Each technology, including Java, ActiveX, HTTP/HTML, CORBA, IIOP, ActiveX, and DCOM (distributed component object model), offers unique possibilities for enhancing development productivity or providing a new capability to the user. However, as an application developer commits to a tool or technology, that commitment has the potential to limit the ability to retarget or adapt the core capabilities of the system. And that limits the ability to respond to change.

Each tool, distribution technology, or API a developer chooses represents a significant investment in software, training, and operational infrastructure. What the developer ideally wants is to leverage the best of each environment with relatively little compromise. For example, an application developer might like to write web-based data warehouse applications that are able to perform transactions against a DB2 database in a two-tier client/server environment, or write a three-tier client/server application that has a PC running MS Windows for the client, an NT or UNIX middle tier containing their organization's business logic, and a mainframe running CICS on the third tier.

Internet Inter-Orb Protocol (IIOP), OMG's widely popular Internet protocol, is being used as the infrastructure. These specifications are used worldwide to develop and deploy distributed applications for manufacturing, finance, telecommunications, electronic commerce, real-time systems, and health care, among other applications.

ORBs

Object Request Brokers (ORBs) are the middleware that conform to OMG's CORBA specification. ORBs allow companies to build scalable, reusable software that can change as the business changes. The features and benefits of object technology have attracted the attention of business leaders as well as corporate technologists; who wouldn't be pleased with a technology that allows a business to write software once and use it repeatedly in a myriad of applications?

ORB technology is used to build three-tier applications, update enterprise code, and create web-based information systems. It provides a means for interoperability between various types of object-oriented software. ORBs are a form of middleware used in distributed computing environments. They embody the methods that objects use to locate and activate other objects across a network, regardless of the processor type or programming language used to develop and implement the objects.

Like other kinds of middleware, ORBs are part of the *plumbing* in a distributed client/server environment. ORBs work behind the scenes, facilitating communications between distributed objects that run on clients and servers. Most ORBs are written in C++ and support binding of C++, Smalltalk, and, increasingly, Java objects.

At the heart of multi-vendor interoperability is IIOP, which was introduced by OMG's CORBA 2.0 specification. IIOP lets companies mix and match best-of-breed ORBs, which means an end to dependence on any single vendor in meeting your requirements for distributed computing.

DCOM

Distributed Component Object Model (DCOM) has its roots in Microsoft's object technology, which has evolved over the last decade from Dynamic Data Exchange (DDE), a form of messaging between Windows programs; Object Linking and Embedding (OLE), embedding visual links between programs within an application; the Component Object Model (COM), used as the basis for all object binding; and ActiveX, COM enabled for the Internet.

COM in a distributed environment (DCOM) extends COM to support communication between objects regardless of their physical location. Basically, Microsoft's starting premise is that communication between objects on different physical machines is virtually identical to interprocess communication between objects that reside on the same computer.

Basically, DCOM is competitive to CORBA. Even though CORBA has a large head start over DCOM, with Microsoft's installed base and marketing muscle, you will probably see both thrive and even interoperate. But both distributed object models are quite dissimilar, and may never be able to fully interoperate across platforms, so those writing component software will probably have to choose between the two models unless they can afford to support both.

WWW and Object Technologies

WWW and CORBA

A large number of toolkits offer a similar approach to web/CORBA integration. A Java applet that is retrieved from a web server can include a client-side stub generated from IDL, providing a client-side interface back to an object that is implemented in an ORB server. Alternatively, a subset of Java called JavaScript can be included inline in HTML page instead of in a separate file. In either case, a runtime layer is available on the client side to establish a connection from the Java code to objects available through the ORB.

WWW and Microsoft OLE/COM

Microsoft has chosen to provide an evolutionary path to integrate OLE/COM objects into web pages just as they can be integrated into compound documents today. These objects take the form of OLE controls (also called active controls) that have additional support for Internet access. Active controls can be referenced in HTML and looked up on a client's machine in the Windows registry or retrieved from a web server before being executed. Data to initialize the control may be contained in the HTML page or retrieved asynchronously from the server. Active controls can be developed in Microsoft Visual C++, or any environment that supports the creation of OLE controls.

Additionally, Microsoft intends to support the inclusion of code inline in a web page. Their language of choice is a subset of Visual Basic entitled Visual Basic Script. A Visual Basic Script program can be downloaded from a web server and executed. To further its adoption, Microsoft intends to make free licenses available for the Visual Basic Script source code to be incorporated in browsers and other tools. The advantage of the Microsoft approach is that it provides a clear path for the small army of OLE control developers and vendors to immediately leverage the distribution capabilities of the WWW.

Smoothing out the Edges

The combination of the Web with CORBA and COM offers great promise and flexibility to developers, as well as a clear path to widespread deployment for distributed object vendors. As with any combination of technologies, there are some rough edges that need to be smoothed. One is how best to retrieve both an object's state and its methods in a seamless fashion. Right now, it will be up to developers to standardize the underlying framework offered by CORBA or COM. Despite shortcomings, the technology deserves serious consideration for any organization embarking on distributed application development.

Data Warehouse and Object Technologies

Data warehousing involves extracting data from various operational systems, and transforming, integrating, and summarizing it into a relational database management system residing over a span of World Wide Web dedicated servers. Typically part of the client/server architecture, such data warehouse servers may be connected to application servers which improve the performance of query and analysis tools running on desktop systems.

Successful implementation of a data warehouse on the World Wide Web requires a high-performance, scalable combination of hardware and software, which can integrate easily with existing systems.

Conclusions

Object technologies, client/server, and the World Wide Web have greatly improved companies' abilities to organize and access historical data. Taking advantage of these newer technologies, data warehousing provides many improvements over traditional decision-support systems including easier and faster data access and analysis.

One of the benefits of object orientation in data warehousing applications is to provide interoperability between the World Wide Web and CORBA-based distributed object systems. The key elements of the design are the representation of HTTP in IDL and gateways that translate between HTTP and the IIOP encoding of the interfaces.

The gateways allow HTTP to be carried over IIOP and provide full interoperability between web and CORBA clients and servers.

Object technology can be used to provide interoperability between the web and distributed objects, such as diverse databases and data warehouses. IIOP can be seamlessly integrated into the web via servers and proxies. In this way, the data warehousing applications can already reap the benefits of distributed object technology and the Web such as:

- Ease of programming
- Extensibility and manageability
- Encapsulation and systems integration

Distributed object technology will help the data warehousing applications to evolve into an information environment of the kind demanded by its users and by commercial interests. At the same time, distributed object technology now has the potential to be used and tested in the biggest distributed system ever built.

Ultimately, the data warehouse can be used as an integrator for distributed object systems, and those object technologies will benefit from having the web client architectures provide them with a globally uniform front end.

6

DATA MARTS

Introduction

Unfortunately, centralized data warehousing has not lived up to its promise. It has instead proven to be filled with risks, long to implement, and costly. The lifeblood of an organization is the ability to develop applications which rapidly deliver valuable information to business decision-makers. However, centralized data warehouses tend to become architecture-bound and unable to adapt and change as new applications are needed.

Many organizations report *data explosions* of considerable magnitude from the original volumes of data, due to the constant need for new reports and summary tables. This results in significant additional expense and added management burden. Centralized warehouses are designed to accommodate predetermined queries for which they are tuned. Data warehousing, however, "is a process of discovery," as Bill Inmon has pointed out, and "users rarely know what information they need in advance."

Much of the expense of traditional centralized data warehousing is due to the brute force approach, built upon parallel processing concepts. Parallel processing, however, is very expensive but does nothing to provide rapid response to ad hoc queries. Therefore, we must resort to new approaches to satisfy this demand.

We will examine in depth the enterprise-scalable data mart architecture, a technology poised to drastically reshape the economics and application of data warehousing. Included is a contrasting view of the features and benefits of a data mart architecture with those of a legacy data warehouse for building, deploying, and managing enterprise-scalable data mart solutions.

The Corporate Data Warehouse

In the past, corporate data warehouse implementations have been mainframe-centric, enterprise-wide in scope, and top-down-driven by MIS management. Under this architecture, everything is built at the enterprise level. This usually results in one common data warehouse holding all of the decision-support information for all user requirements. A separate database is maintained for the company's operational systems.

These data warehouse implementations must deal with enormously complex issues mandated by their enterprise-wide nature. Everything must go through multiple levels of agreements because the data warehouse is designed for everyone's use. The impact of a single change may be enormous, because changing one thing changes everything.

An Alternative View of the Data Warehouse Solution

The result of such challenges to the centralized data warehouse has been the development of a new architectural construct, still aimed at the primary objective of delivering decision-support data to end users.

Fortunately a new, more pragmatic approach is now available. This can be viewed as *distributed data warehousing*. The focus in this approach is on applications and data marts, built rapidly with new cost-effective, scalable database technology. Now data marts can provide dramatic returns on investment, without the high cost and risk of centralized enterprise data warehouse projects. This enables organizations to rapidly develop decision-support applications, which can grow and change as their business needs evolve.

A data mart is a decision-support application system, which focuses on solving a specific business problem in a single department or subject area. A data mart must be built with an enterprise data model in mind to prevent non-integratable decision-support systems, inconsistent business information, and an inability to grow. But an enterprise data warehouse is not a prerequisite for a data mart.

Data marts are characterized by the rapid response they provide to ad hoc and multi-dimensional queries and their low cost to build and maintain. In many cases the cost is less than half that of a large centralized warehouse. There are a number of key components to a successful data mart implementation.

The Data Mart Solution

Clearly, data marts alone can not solve all business needs for enterprise wide decision support. As businesses build data marts and meet users' application needs, they learn what data elements are most valuable, what data elements need to be most current, and where additional detailed data or external data is needed. Over time, MIS may determine areas to centralize data, which can be shared among multiple data marts. This is the true role of a corporate data warehouse. Data marts, over time, become a place to centralize information that is needed by multiple users.

The corporate data warehouse is being built slowly, in steps, depending on the business needs. As their needs grow, companies build multiple data marts and eventually, over time, many businesses will have developed a multi-tiered decision-support architecture.

In many organizations, decision-making is decentralized and multiple data marts may never be consolidated. In others, where top-down decision making is strong, an enterprise warehouse can be built sooner. The key to success is to start with a pragmatic, application-focused approach. This allows MIS to deliver quick results.

This concept derives from the fact that any single user has limited data and information needs. Even though there are requirements for cross-functional analysis, the scope of the data requirements is materially reduced if we limit the scope of the warehouse itself to a single application. If we can build this reduced scope warehouse, we can solve the problems in a more focused and targeted approach, using fewer resources, reaching our goals quicker, and being able to respond to changing conditions easier. This concept is depicted in **Figure 6.1** and shows two application-specific implementations, each deriving their warehouse

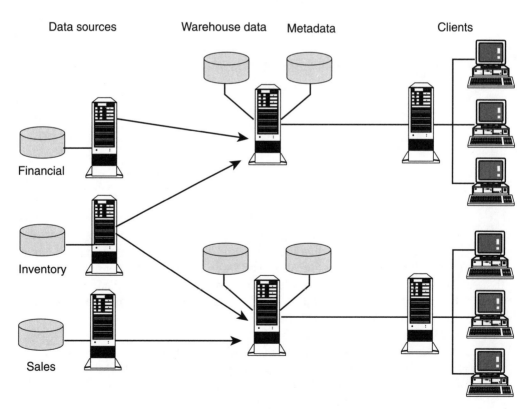

Figure 6.1 Shared Data Marts

data from some subset of the enterprise systems, and each serving an individual application or department.

What Is a Data Mart?

A data mart is an application-focused data warehouse, built rapidly to support a single line-of-business application. Data marts still have all of the other characteristics of data warehouses, which are *subject-oriented data that is non-volatile, time-variant, and integrated.* However, rather than representing a picture of the enterprise data, it contains a subset of that data which is specifically of interest to one department or division of that enterprise.

The data warehouse is the center of the decision-support universe. The data warehouse contains integrated, historical data that is common to the entire corporation. The data warehouse contains both summarized and detailed information. The data warehouse contains metadata that describes the contents and source of data that flows into the data warehouse.

From the data warehouse, data flows to various departments for their customized decision-support usage. These departmental decision-support databases are called data marts. A data mart is a body of data for a department that has an architectural foundation of a data warehouse.

The data that resides in the data warehouse is at a very granular level and the data in the data mart is at a refined level. The different data marts contain different combinations and selections of the same detailed data found at the data warehouse. In some cases data warehouse detailed data is added differently across the different data marts. Yet in other cases a specific data mart may structure detailed data differently from other data marts.

In every case the data warehouse provides the granular foundation for all of the data found in all of the data marts. Because of the singular data warehouse foundation that all data marts have, all of the data marts have a common heritage and are able to be reconciled at the most basic level.

There are several factors that lead to the popularity of the data mart. As long as the data warehouse doesn't contain much data, then the data warehouse may serve the needs of different departments as a basis for decision-support processing. But data warehouses do not stay small very long. For a variety of reasons, data warehouses quickly grow large. And as data warehouses grow large, the motivation for data marts increases.

As data warehouses grow large, the competition to get inside a warehouse grows fierce. More and more departmental decision-support processing is done inside the data warehouse, to the point that resource consumption becomes a real problem. Data becomes harder to customize. As long as the data in the data warehouse is small, the users can afford to customize and summarize data every time a decision support analysis is done. But with the increase in magnitude, the user does not have the time or resources to summarize and customize the data.

The cost of doing processing in the data warehouse increases as the volume of data increases. The software that is available for the access and analysis of large amounts of data is not nearly as elegant as the software that can process smaller amounts of data.

Data marts have become a natural extension of the data warehouse. Data marts are attractive for the following reasons:

- When a department has its own data mart, it can customize the data as the data flows into the data mart from the data warehouse. There is no need for the data in the data mart to have to serve the entire corporation. Therefore the department can summarize, sort, select, and structure their own department's data with no consideration of any other department.
- The amount of historical data that is needed is a function of the department, not the corporation. In almost every case, the department can select a much smaller amount of historical data than that which is found in the data warehouse.
- The department can do whatever decision-support processing they want whenever they want with no impact for resource utilization on other departments.
- The department can select software for their data mart that is tailored to fit their needs.
- The unit cost of processing and storage on the size of machine that is appropriate to the data mart is significantly less than the unit cost of processing and storage for the machine that houses the data warehouse.

There are many such reasons then why the data mart becomes attractive as the data warehouse grows in volume. There are organizational, technological, and economic reasons why the data mart is so beguiling and is a natural outgrowth of the data warehouse.

Under normal conditions the source of data that flows into the data mart is the current level detail, or the data warehouse level. Detailed data is customized, selected, and summarized as it is placed into the data mart. In addition, the data mart can be fed data from external sources.

Types of Data Marts

The data mart is a powerful and natural extension of the data warehouse. The data mart extends DSS to the departmental environment. The data warehouse provides the granular data and the different data marts interpret and structure that granular data to suit their needs. There are different types of data marts. Each of these plays a different role. **Figure 6.2** shows two distinct types of data marts.

Multidimensional Data Mart

One type of data mart is the *multidimensional* data mart. The *multidimensional* data mart is one that is used for slicing and dicing numeric data in a free form fashion. Some of the characteristics of the *multidimensional* data mart are that they:

- Contain sparsely populated matrices
- Contain numeric data
- Maintain rigid structure as the data enters the multidimensional framework

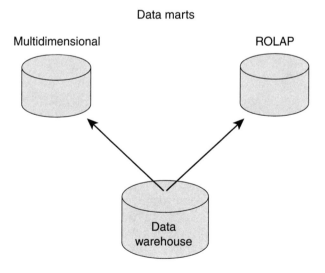

Figure 6.2   Types of Data Marts

ROLAP Data Marts

Another type of data mart is one that can be called for relational OLAP or *ROLAP* processing. ROLAP data marts are general-purpose data marts that contain both numeric and textual data. ROLAP data marts serve a much wider purpose than their *multidimensional* counterparts. Unlike *multidimensional* data marts, which are supported by specialized data base management systems, ROLAP DBMSs are supported by relational technology. Some of the characteristics of ROLAP DBMSs are that they:

- Contain numeric and textual data
- Are used for general purpose DSS analysis
- Maintain structured data
- Employ numerous indexes
- Support star schemes.

ROLAP data marts can have both disciplined and ad hoc usage. The ROLAP data mart environment contains both detailed and summarized data.

Networked Data Marts

Data marts rarely exist in isolation. Increasingly, multiple data mart systems cooperate in a larger network creating a virtual data warehouse. A large enterprise may have many subject-area marts as well as marts in different divisions and geographic locations. Users or workgroups may have local data marts to address local needs. Advanced applications, such as the web, extend data mart networks across enterprise boundaries (see **Figure 6.3**).

In the network data mart world, users must be able to look at and work with multiple warehouses from a single client workstation, requiring location transparency across the network. Similarly, data mart administrators must be able to manage and administer a network of data marts from a single location.

Implementation and management of data mart networks not only imposes new requirements on the mart RDBMS, but more importantly requires tools to define, extract, move and update batches of information as self-consistent units on demand. It also requires a whole new generation of data warehouse management software to support subset, catalog, schedule, and publish/subscribe functions in a distributed environment.

Sharing data across divisional and departmental data marts brings together information from throughout the corporation. To pull from two or more data marts, the data must still be cleaned up and standardized. Without data cleansing and standardization, data from one department may be meaningless to a user in another division. In addition, users that share data from various

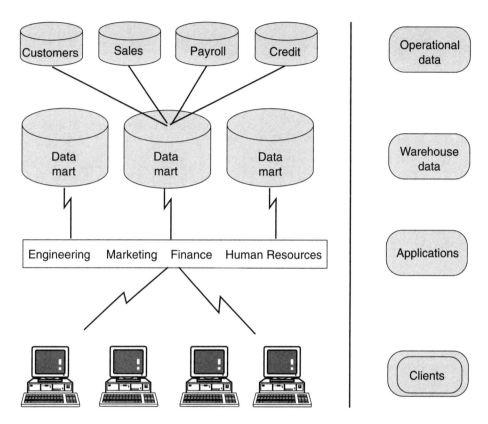

Figure 6.3 Networked Data Marts

data marts throughout the organization will need a standard metadata directory to clarify terms and business definitions of the departmental data. The lack of a shared metadata directory leaves data elements open for interpretation, and without a road map for definitions.

Data Mart Benefits

The data mart architecture offers several benefits due to its scalability and incremental approach. For example, an ad hoc data mart can be quickly built to address a pressing business need. This flexibility and simplicity stand in sharp contrast to the complexity inherent in attempting to address a wide range of often conflicting user needs in building a corporate data warehouse. Business problems and needs change faster than corporate data warehouses can react to them. Two years of development are too late in fast-moving competitive situations.

End users benefit from data that is customized and focused toward their needs. Data marts enable development and administration at a departmental level and reduce the support burden on the corporate staff.

Data marts can be very cost effective as a business tool, giving management the ability to start small. At the same time, this approach gives management the option to expand the concept incrementally to other departments. Over time, this can yield an enterprise approach which is responsive to changing business conditions, cost effective, and manageable.

Data Mart Implementation Requirements

Once an organization has decided on a strategy of defining and developing application-specific data marts, it must define the requirements which need to be met in implementing this strategy. Such requirements should include the following.

Source Data

The data mart contains whatever data is needed for departmental DSS processing. Contrary to common belief, there is a diversity of data in the data mart. The data mart contains both summary data and detailed data. In addition, the data mart contains prepared data and ad hoc data.

As a rule, the data mart mostly contains lots of ad hoc summary data and lots of prepared detailed data. While other data can be found in the data mart, these two categories comprise the bulk of the data.

Types of DBMS

The two types of DBMSs that are commonly used in the data marts are relational and multidimensional. Multidimensional technology is at the heart of numeric slice-and-dice processing. Relational technology forms the basis for all other standard data mart processing. The kinds of tables and the numbers of tables that are found in the data mart are many and varied. However, over time the numbers and the types of tables grow. The types of tables found in the data mart include:

- Historical tables
- Summary tables

- Detailed tables
- Ad hoc tables
- Reference tables
- Spread sheet analytical tables

As time passes, the number of tables and the number of types of tables grow. In addition, the data that comes from external sources grows as well.

The data is structured in the data mart along the lines of star joins and normalized tables. Star joins are created where there is a predictable pattern of usage and where there is a significant amount of data. Relational tables are used as a basis for design where there is not a predictable pattern of usage. Both forms of structure are able to reside in the data mart with no conflict of interest.

External Data

External data holds great promise for inclusion in the data mart. There are several important issues that relate to the use of external data in the data mart. The first issue is that of *redundancy*. When the external data needs to be used in more than one data mart, it is best to place the external data inside the data warehouse, then move the data to the data mart. This practice assures that redundancy can be controlled.

A second issue is that of *storage of secondary data* along with the external data. When external data is acquired, the history of the data needs to be stored as well as the data. The history of external data includes:

- Source of the external data
- Date the external data was acquired
- Quantity of the external data acquired
- Descriptions of the external data
- Editing and filtering criteria applied to the external data

Reference tables play an important role in the data mart environment. Data marts allow the data mart end user to relate data back to the expanded version of the data. The reference data is typically copied from the data warehouse. When reference tables are stored and managed in the DSS environment, there is a need to manage their contents over time. Time management of reference data is a complex task, and is best managed from the data warehouse.

Metadata

One of the most important components of the data mart is metadata. Metadata in the data mart environment serves the same purpose as metadata in the data warehouse. Data mart metadata allows the user to find out where data is in the process of discovery and exploration. Data mart metadata contains the following components:

- A description of the customization that has occurred as the data passes from the data warehouse to the data mart
- Identification of the source of data
- Descriptive information about the data mart, including tables, attributes, and relationships

There should be linkage between the metadata found in the data mart and the metadata found in the data warehouse. The metadata linkage between the two environments needs to describe how the data in the two environments is related. This description is necessary if there is to be drill down capability between the two environments. With the linkage, the data mart metadata user can easily find the heritage of the data in the data warehouse.

The metadata found in the data mart must be available to the end user at the workstation in order to be effective. Metadata is an integral part of the data mart environment. The metadata allows the end user to access data in the data mart efficiently.

Rapid Access to Data

Performance associated with data marts is an important consideration in the overall approach. Performance can include:

- The load performance (how smoothly and rapidly data can be loaded)
- Data management, quality, and maintenance,
- Query performance

Effective interactive query applications require near real-time performance. End users need to be able to fluidly ask questions, get answers, and ask follow-up questions at a pace matching their own thought processes. Users should be able to pursue different lines of inquiry, to look at information from different perspectives, and to drill up and down through different levels of detail.

Interactive query applications require response times measured in seconds. Independent of the level of detail and the size of the database, this performance level must be maintained in multi-user environments. Query response times measured in minutes or hours are unacceptable.

These application performance requirements translate directly onto the data warehouse server. The data warehouse RDBMS must include query performance optimizations analogous to those that have yielded OLTP performance of thousands of transactions per second. In the warehouse environment, performance optimizations must also address the aspects of query processing such as joins, sorting, and grouping.

Scalability

Data marts come in all sizes. While the idea is to start small, the inevitable outcome is that the demand for the data collected, the reports generated, and the relationships presented in the data grow as users become familiar and proficient with the system

Data marts may start small, but as users explore information, they start to ask for more history, more external data, and more detail. Many data mart architectures store only summarized data (e.g., salary by length of service or sex), and then expect the user to drill down to operational systems to get detail. The problem with this approach is that users naturally want to explore data in different dimensions. If the data mart does not hold the detailed data, these queries are impossible.

To support analysis of detailed data, the database engine and platform must support dynamic aggregation and fast, flexible queries against tens to hundreds of gigabytes of detailed data. In addition, the initial single departmental data mart may eventually be required to support multiple departments. The system will need to allow cross-functional analysis, for problems that involve more than one department.

Flexibility

Flexibility refers to responsiveness to user queries and changing conditions. Ideally, since many of the requests for data may be ad hoc, the database should be capable of being built without advance knowledge of what queries are going to be requested. Users should be able to drill down and surf through their data to find the information required.

The platform, RDBMS, and design must support a rapid and iterative implementation. Data marts must deliver results fast. The database engine must support a wide range of queries and not lock the designer into a fixed *star schema* design. Many data marts are built from large mainframe normalized databases, and it may not always be cost-effective to implement a full star schema.

A flexible system is also easier to change to accommodate changing business conditions. Managing the processes for automating downloads of data, transformations of data, and indexing allows for multiple options to enhance flexibility.

Performance

The issue of performance in the DSS environment is entirely different from the OLTP environment. In the DSS environment, response time requirements are relaxed. The issue of performance is especially relaxed for the data warehouse, where there is an abundance of data and where there is a lot of exploration occurring. Performance is achieved in several ways in the data mart environment, such as:

- Limiting the volume of data that is found in the data mart
- Making extensive use of indexes
- Creating arrays of data
- Using star joins
- Creating pre-joined tables
- Creating profile records

Management

Like the data warehouse environment, the data mart environment requires periodic monitoring. The monitors for the data mart grow in importance in relation to the volume of data in the data mart and the amount of query activity that passes through the mart. When the data mart is new and small there may be no need for monitoring the environment. But when the data mart grows in volume of data and/or usage of the data, then a monitor facility makes sense.

Security

The data mart needs to be secure, just as other components of the DSS environment need security. When the data mart contains sensitive information, there is a need to secure that information, especially over the Internet. Typical sensitive information may include:

- Medical record information
- Financial information
- Human resources information

There are many different forms of security. The level of security that is needed is dependent on the sensitivity of the data. If the security exposure is not large, then a casual approach to security may suffice. If the security exposure is large, then a much more rigorous approach to security will be required. Some of the approaches to security in the data mart environment include:

- Logon/logoff security
- Firewalls
- Encryption/decryption
- Application based security
- DBMS security

Fast, Flexible Query Response

Data marts are user- and application-driven. Users need to *drill down* and *surf* through their data to find the information they need. Often the users are using ad hoc and OLAP query tools, which generate complex SQL statements rapidly. If it is to succeed, the data mart must respond to any query rapidly.

Support for Multiple Databases

Enterprises today are heterogeneous in terms of their existing databases. Therefore, it is likely that data marts need to access data from a multiplicity of systems and databases, which makes it essential for a data mart to support a broad spectrum of data types and database systems.

Data Consistency, Transformation, and Refresh Architecture

Data marts cannot be built in a vacuum. Each data mart must use common data elements, share common data transformation programs, and use common data movement tools to maintain enterprise data consistency and quality. A Payroll data mart, for example, must share employee information with a management data mart to make sure that both are analyzing the same view of employees. And both data marts must be refreshed in a consistent way, as employees are added or deleted.

Architectural Constructs and Technologies for Data Marts

One of the architectural approaches is called the "enterprise scalable data mart," which is a highly focused line-of-business data warehouse that puts targeted information into the hands of decision makers. Data marts are data warehouses but, unlike the highly centralized, multiple line-of-business warehouses developed in the past, data marts are single subject (e.g. salaries, productivity), fast, and easy to implement. They offer organizations greater flexibility without sacrificing the all-important requirement of enterprise scalability.

In contrast to the COBOL code-generation approach required by many of the traditional data warehousing solutions, today's *second-generation* data mart technology propagates data from either centralized data stores or operational transaction databases using a real-time extract/transform/load engine. This is combined with features such as highly graphical client/server tools, integrated metadata, and innovative centralized management capabilities.

The results are nothing short of astounding. This has resulted in data warehousing systems built and managed at a fraction of the cost of centralized implementations. These are completed in months, instead of years.

Scalability

The scalability of a data mart has several dimensions. First of all, we need to consider the scalability of the size of the database. Different technologies may considerably impact the size of the required database for a given application. For example, raw data stored in a multidimensional database could easily explode by a factor of ten to one hundred times. On the other hand, using bit-mapped indexes and data compression techniques could shrink the database by a factor of two to three.

History tells us that no matter where we start, the trend is to continue to grow over time. This is certainly true in any warehousing application, as more data is gathered in the organization's OLTP systems and is uploaded into the data marts, and as users become more sophisticated and decide they need more information upon which to base their decisions. It is only logical to deduce that techniques which compress data are to be preferred to techniques which expand data in order to allow for maximum scalability, all other things being equal.

Scalability also applies to the number of users a system will need to support. A successful warehousing project can draw many users as the word spreads of the capabilities of the system. More users mean more simultaneous queries, and this could lead to frustrated and disenchanted users if their ranks overload the capacity of the system. For this reason, it is wise to develop a system whose response time scales linearly with user demands, and whose architecture can support increases in user population. Bit-mapped indexing and data compression help in this regard by keeping response times very low.

Queuing theory tells us that shorter response times mean the ability to service more users simultaneously without saturating the system. Another technique is the use of parallel processing and parallel databases as a means to achieve scalability, particularly in user load. In multidimensional database schema, where the size of the database is great, parallel processing is used to churn through the vast quantities of data available in responding to ad hoc queries.

Other techniques, such as data compression and bit-mapped indexes, can free the parallel processors from the *data crunching*. This means that the multiple processors can be used to support more users, rather than crunch more data, again helping the scalability of the system.

Finally, we have the scalability of the number of data marts which comprise the enterprise system. In the ideal extension of the data mart architecture, cross-functional analysis is possible by allowing, for example, HR personnel to access payroll and employee information. This form of scalability is only made possible by the development of and the adherence to an overall enterprise architecture and standards by which the full complement of data marts are constructed and operated.

Flexibility

Warehousing projects must be implemented so as to allow the maximum flexibility for both users and management. Users need flexibility in designing their queries. OLAP represents a discovery process where initial results may lead to further queries not considered when the system was first designed. Management needs flexibility in responding to user requests, in managing the expansion of the systems into other areas, and in coordinating the interactions of data marts.

Organizations want to be in a position to react quickly. Therefore, any warehousing project must be easily and quickly deployable to allow the organization to reap its benefits quickly. A major factor in the speed to deployment is rapid and simple integration with the existing OLTP legacy data sources. Systems must be able to accept flat files, RDBMS files, and other data sources which are used by the enterprise to contain operational data.

Once deployed, data marts must be easily modifiable to respond to user needs, organizational restructuring, and the myriad other changes which are likely in business today. They must also be capable of integration with other data marts, which implies adherence to standards and the support of a variety of vendors whose products include extraction and transformation tools and OLAP.

Parallel Processing

Advances in hardware and software architectures have significantly contributed to the rapid growth and exploitation of the data warehouse or data mart market. The price/performance and acceptance of multiprocessor machines, coupled with the attendant software rewrites of existing applications and tools to take advantage of the new hardware architectures have made it possible to work with very large databases, from tens of gigabytes to multiple terabytes.

SMP Technologies

Technologies such as SMP (symmetric multiprocessing) and MPP (massively parallel processing) as well as hybrids of these two approaches are the predominant hardware architectures used in data warehousing applications. In a symmetric multiprocessing environment, a number of processors operate cooperatively using a common memory pool. Sometimes the SMP architecture is known as a Shared Memory Processing architecture because of this fact. MPP systems have large numbers of processors working in parallel each with their own system resources. These systems are sometimes known as *shared nothing systems.*

Innovations in database systems and hardware architectures are blurring the lines as to when one architecture outperforms the other in cost and speed. The notion of scalability in hardware refers to the ability to add processors and not lose a significant portion of the additional processing power to system coordinating activities such as handing a job from one processor to another.

Traditionally, SMP machines do not scale as well as MPP machines, and at some point (16-32 processors), the overhead associated with coordinating the processors became so onerous that the increases in processing power becomes insignificant. However, newer hardware techniques have now obviated this argument, and we find SMP machines scaling linearly up beyond 64 processors.

SMP advocates point to this fact along with the fact that with a shared memory architecture it is far easier to add memory to a common pool than to add memory to individual processors, because we do not know which processor will need more memory at any given time. They insist that SMP systems are cheaper and if initial system requirements are modest and need to scale up, SMP will be there when the time comes.

MPP Technologies

MPP advocates take the position that once the applications are in an MPP environment, the upside potential of the system far and away exceeds the capability of SMP systems. Further, the inherent latency (the time taken to coordinate processors) is still far lower for MPP systems than for SMP, the advances in scalability of SMP systems notwithstanding. Finally, a new architecture known as NUMA (Non Uniform Memory Access) promises to allow MPP architectures to share common memory so as to take advantage of the flexibility of shared memory while at the same time maintaining the low latency of MPP. This addition of shared memory also helps eliminate another of the negatives of MPP—the hot spot.

If a processor is dedicated to a particular portion of a query and that portion requires much more processing than others (toy sales for December as opposed to other months of the year for example), that processor may run out of memory or other system resources while the others are idle and waiting for it to complete. In a NUMA architecture, additional resources can be made available to that processor, balancing the load more equitably.

All the major relational database vendors are attempting to improve query performance by adding parallel query capabilities that spread the work of a single query over a number of processors. It is certainly true that parallel processing can reduce response times for large bulk processing operations that scan all the data. Examples include report generation, list management, and data maintenance.

Adding processors also enables a system to scale up to maintain performance as the amount of data increases. However, as noted before, when used in combination with bit-mapped indexes, data compression, and vertical partitioning, the power of parallelism can be used to handle a greater number of users. These can lead to significant benefits to your data mart implementation increasing its overall longevity, utility, and return on investment.

Schema Considerations

Star Schemas

Star schema is a technique used to improve the decision-support performance of RDBMS products. Star schema designs produce a large fact table and many, smaller *dimension* tables which extend the different aspects of the facts. By processing the dimension tables first, fewer of the detailed records in the fact table need to be scanned to complete the query.

Because of the pre-built tables, this schema is very effective in systems where the queries are well understood and well defined. The approach, however, has major limitations when it comes to delivering ad hoc query performance.

Star schemas lose detail in some instances. For instance, if transactions have both multiple line items and multiple methods of payment (coupon or cash), then these details must be collapsed to avoid an explosion in the size of the fact table. Combining these elements is impractical because of the many-to-many relationship between the tables.

Star schema fact tables are expensive to query. If the query does not include a highly selective dimension table (e.g., if one tries to aggregate sales for all transactions over a long period of time), then the system must scan a significant portion of the large fact table.

Star schemas require considerable dimensional constraints. Because it is only practical to store a limited number of dimensions with a limited number of values, effective tuning requires limiting the scope of the queries that can be supported with fast performance.

Multidimensional Schemas

Multidimensional database schemas *pre-aggregate* values in *hypercubes*. As the number of dimensions or the cardinality of each dimension increases, there is a significant increase in the size of the hypercubes generated, often an order of magnitude greater than the raw data in the database. One documented case had a raw transaction database of .5GB with a set of multidimensional tables approaching 18GB. Pre-aggregation limits the flexibility and the raw atomic data is not available for users to drill down.

Ideally, users want the option of looking at segments of their data in a multi-dimensional fashion without incurring the overhead of having the DBA set up a customized database each time. With this in mind, more and more client tools are adding multidimensional viewing capability as an option for analyzing relational data. To do this, they require fast data aggregation on the fly from the relational data store as and when the user needs it.

Column/Row Partitioning

Horizontal table partitioning is used by RDBMS (Relational Database Management Systems) and allows organizations to store large tables in pieces. Queries, which would otherwise involve full table scans, could involve a table scan of only the particular piece.

One can similarly partition by department or region. This can create a problem of hot spots within the database, where one piece becomes of particular interest to many users at once. Some operational/organizational issues can also create particular problems if we have a database partition by department and then departments are reorganized. The severity of these issues could require restructuring of the database.

Vertical data storage takes columns and indexes them, which has the effect of lining up disk I/O pages by column, and is therefore more consistent with query demands. This significantly speeds response times because the system only has to read the columns of interest and therefore is not burdened with reading the unwanted remainder of the records.

Indexing Considerations

Traditional RDBMSs have improved data retrieval performance by using balanced-tree (B-tree) indexes. An index provides a shortcut to finding data records by keeping track of the values of selected fields and pointing directly to the data pages that contain them. Irrelevant data is automatically screened out. To find the records for a particular customer, the system simply reads the customer index, then goes directly to the pages of data with information about that customer. Indexes eliminate costly table scans by pointing directly to the relevant information

Indexing techniques intended for traditional OLTP databases are not as efficient in a warehousing/decision support application, and therefore new and innovative techniques have been developed, which, in combination with traditional techniques can offer tremendous advantages in decision support.

B-tree Indexes

Balanced tree indexes keep track of the values of selected fields and point to the rows which contain them. B-tree indexes maintain a constant *depth* in terms of levels of access so that all indexes are reachable with approximately the same number of disk accesses.

B-tree indexes are well-suited to finding and retrieving a small number of rows. Examples of this type of high-cardinality data include fields such as order number or customer ID. Unfortunately, B-tree indexes have three characteristics that make them a poor choice for the complex, interactive query applications typical of data warehousing.

First, B-tree indexes are of little or no value on data with few unique values such as male/female, or cash/check/credit, because using the index eliminates very little of the data. This is similar to using the index in a book to find all the pages with the word *don't*. It is easier just to start at the front of the book and scan all the pages sequentially.

The second limitation of B-tree indexes for data warehousing is the cost of building and maintaining indexes. Because B-tree indexes contain actual data values and additional information, the indexes become larger as more data is indexed and the data warehouse can balloon to many times the size of the raw data. B-tree indexes are also sensitive to bulk inserts and updates that may unbalance them and degrade performance. A small percentage change in the data can frequently require the entire index to be rebuilt.

Finally, B-tree indexes are designed for environments where queries are relatively simple and access paths are known in advance. Typically, the database will evaluate B-tree indexes sequentially, which works well if one index is designed to be very selective, such as returning all open orders for a particular customer. This approach is less appropriate for data warehousing applications that combine many less-selective conditions. Moreover, as the index becomes less selective, the amount of data that must be scanned to yield the required aggregates and groupings can become very significant.

Overall, B-tree indexes have limited applicability for data warehouse applications, but are of value in data marts if the sizes are kept small. They are primarily useful in speeding predetermined queries and generally do not aid much in ad hoc queries, which make up nearly 50% of the warehouse activity. B-tree indexes usually result in poor performance. They need resource-intensive tuning, such as building clustered indexes for known queries, to overcome their inadequacies.

Bit-mapped Indexes

Bit-mapped indexes have actually been resurrected from the past in response to increased demand for complex queries in decision-support systems. The basic concept behind this technique is to save space and time by using a single bit to indicate a specific value of data, rather than cumbersome ASCII characters. Bit-mapped indexes are generally used against low cardinality data. This is data, which has very few possible values, such as male/female, or marital status (married, divorced, separated, and widowed).

Bit-mapped indexes address some of the limitations of B-tree indexes. Unlike B-tree indexes, bit-mapped indexes efficiently represent low-cardinality data, are much smaller and easier to maintain, and can be processed simultaneously. But while bit-mapped indexes are efficient for low-cardinality data, they are unsuitable for high-cardinality data because, as implemented in most database products, they require a separate array of *True or False* bits to be created for every unique value. This is clearly impractical for continuous data, such as sales or customer name and address, which can have many possible values.

In most cases the system must still process the detailed records, and often the entire table, to complete any query that combines low- and high-cardinality data. This effectively eliminates most of the performance benefits. Bit-mapped indexes are also limited in their ability to aggregate data, implement relational joins, and retrieve the actual raw data values.

Until recently, it has not been practical to use bitmaps to index high cardinality data.

Data Compression

Data compression provides benefits to warehousing applications in a number of ways. First of all, it saves space on the disk, which in turn speeds disk accesses. Second, the compressed data can be held in memory cache more efficiently, and since more data can be held in memory, the chances of a *hit* in the cache are higher, which means more times when immediate access to data is possible.

Remember that typical disk access speeds are measured in milliseconds, while memory access times are measured in nanoseconds, so that any technologies which reduce the amount of time spent retrieving from the slower devices and increase the availability of access to the faster medium will necessarily be beneficial for system performance.

Replication/Transformation

Most data warehousing applications require the mass movement of data at predefined times, a process known as *uploading* or *refreshing* the data mart. The frequency of the data movement can vary according to the degree of need for currency of information by the application and user community. In some cases, the need can be for immediate updates, while in others a quarterly update will suffice. Data replication can automate the process of uploading all or parts of a transactional database to the data mart at specified times, and ensuring the integrity of the upload end-to-end.

In addition to being replicated from a content perspective, the data must be transformed into the structures defined in the data mart. Aggregations, precomputations, partitioning, and metadata updates must be accomplished if the data is to integrate with the structure of the existing data mart. Replication and transformation technologies provide key services in these areas.

Conclusions

Data mart is more focused than the all-encompassing centralized data warehouse. Because it is targeted at a single application or business problem, it typically requires a narrower scope of data to be collected and rationalized than the larger enterprise model. This in turn makes the data model simpler, more stable, and easier to identify, design, implement, and maintain.

Targeted to a Specific Application/Business Problem

The simple fact that the target of the system is a known business application makes it easier to align the system to the business problem. Compromises may be necessary to address a larger expanse of business problems, which in turn may make the *fit* between the application of the technology and the business need less customized.

Easier to Modify with Changing Conditions

Any data warehousing application has to continue to relate to the business goals even if those goals change over time. Despite changing market conditions, financial conditions, reorganizations, mergers, and takeovers, the data warehouse applications must continue to deliver their benefits. The smaller and simpler data models tend to be easier to modify to meet changing business conditions.

Often, the need for change comes from user experience. As users become more familiar with the capabilities presented to them by this technology, they begin to demand new reporting formats and may want to see new relationships which were not initially built into the model. In a smaller data mart environment, the impact of change is not as severe as in a centralized data warehousing environment.

Easier to Navigate, Better Decisions

A simpler data model is also more user friendly in that the navigation of the tables is more easily comprehensible by end users, who tend to be relatively unsophisticated about the technology. A byproduct of this ease of navigation is also better information quality, which leads to better decisions.

A user who has difficulty understanding the schema of a large data warehouse is prone to making errors in structuring queries, and even more important, in interpreting the results of the queries. Since mission-critical business decisions may be made on the interpreted results of these queries, the case can easily be made that simpler schema, which are easier for a user to understand, can lead to better interpretation of the resultant queries, and therefore lead to better business decisions.

Empowerment of End Users

Today's organizations are running leaner. More and more, management direction is towards user empowerment. Decision making is moving down the organization chart, closer to the users whose departments are directly involved in specific issues. Application-specific data marts facilitate this management model by providing access to the decision-support systems to those users directly affected.

7

OLAP AND THE WEB

Introduction

Data warehousing is not a product, but a best-in-class strategy—one that accommodates the need to consolidate and store data in information systems dedicated to improving the performance of the corporation by providing end users with timely access to critical information.

User requirements and even the users themselves change constantly, resulting in a significant requirements changes. The World Wide Web offers a solution. In addition to simplifying the deployment of data warehouse access, an Intranet can introduce a new level of collaborative interactive analysis and information sharing among decision-makers.

It sounds almost romantic, but the World Wide Web and the data warehouse seem made for each other. The data warehouse, with its underlying support for OLAP technology, enables users to slice and dice through reams of corporate data to present meaningful information for decision making.

The OLAP-enabled web, with its robust and far-reaching Internet backbone, is the technology that allows widely distributed users affordable, reliable, and uncomplicated access to information sites all over the world. OLAP can create the underlying technological framework to extend astonishing analytical power to a worldwide electronic audience of millions to provide decision support in the age of the web.

OLAP and the Web

For several reasons, the logical platform for broader deployment of OLAP is the Internet/intranet/World Wide Web because:

- The web provides complete platform independence. Businesses can deploy any web browser on any platform, which provides cross-platform application access.
- Administration is a critical requirement for OLAP. The web provides much easier maintenance. Unlike client/server architectures, everything can be installed and maintained on the server. When the application changes, only the server needs to be updated, not the potentially thousands of clients.
- The skills and techniques used to navigate and select information are the same as for all other web-based applications.
- The browser interface, with hyperlinks and buttons, is immediately recognized by the millions of computer users who already use the web.

- With proper security—such as the Secure Sockets Layer protocol (SSL) and already available sophisticated database security—the Internet can be used as an inexpensive Wide Area Network for decision support and OLAP applications.

The Intranet Link

Web browsers are becoming a popular user interface to many kinds of data and information stores. Corporate developers are planning to evaluate and build intranets using browser-based interfaces and tools instead of using traditional client/server development tools to build customized GUI applications. Vendors, including those who sell On-line Analytical Processing (OLAP) tools, are fueling this trend by enabling their products to work with web browsers and servers.

Today, most OLAP solutions provide some level of web browser access to their OLAP engines, often referred to as web OLAP or WOLAP. A closer look at how analytical reporting is used in corporate environments reveals that the browser can provide an effective complement to more functional client/server OLAP applications.

What Is OLAP?

OLAP is a specialized form of analysis. Many of the same issues pertain to data warehouses and data marts, which store data to be analyzed using a variety of querying, analysis, and reporting tools and techniques.

OLAP is a category of business software that gives users access to analytical content such as time series and trend analysis views and summary-level information, as well as insight into data organized into multiple dimensions. There are three ways to deploy OLAP applications.

1. A multidimensional database server is used to store data. Data is stored as a cube, which lets the user peel off pieces of it while keeping certain dimensions of the data constant.

2. Data from relational database engines is retrieved in a multidimensional fashion. Metadata defines where the data resides in the relational database. The OLAP server uses this metadata dynamically to generate the SQL statements necessary to retrieve the data as the user requests it. Users see a multidimensional view of data that is stored in relational tables.

3. Less common and somewhat of a hybrid, the third approach uses a multidimensional database server as middleware to access data stored

in a relational database. This process lets a multidimensional server provide users with the detailed transaction data that contributes to the summary totals stored in the multidimensional server.

Because users seem comfortable with browser navigation, the web can deliver a single interface for client/server applications. As more information providers and data warehouse managers support HTML, it becomes easier to share corporate information and mix and match it with related information residing elsewhere on the Internet. Likewise, the internal plumbing of the web, particularly the web server, provides a platform-independent mechanism to support remote users, groupware applications, and client maintenance.

Ironically, a few of the driving factors for the web are also issues of concern. HTML, CGI, and HTTP, the fundamental technologies of the web, are limited when compared to those used in building client/server applications. It is difficult to deliver the same interface and functionality users like and need in the applications they work on today. Technologies such as Java and ActiveX, which are being evaluated to deliver more functional web-based systems, are for the most part new and still unproved. XML, a new marking language, based on ActiveX and Java, is poised to succeed HTML for industrial-strength applications in the next few years.

The task of the web server is to build processes that can speak HTTP and HTML on one end and communicate with the OLAP application or database server on the other. The web server manages communication between the browser and application or database server, usually through a combination of CGI scripts, web server APIs, application APIs, and database APIs. On the client side, a combination of HTML, ActiveX controls, Java applets, JavaScript, and VBScript concoct the functionality and interface (see **Figure 7.1**). (Another alternative being evaluated today lets multiple client applications, both traditional client/server and web-based, use the same protocols to access the same business processes installed on networks as application servers. This capability lets a single architecture deliver systems across multiple delivery mediums.)

OLAP works in this mix by being installed on the network as an application server. You can access the application server via any client application, including one delivered through a web browser. The developer can thus use the best technology for each part of the job in delivering web-based applications.

As **Figure 7.2** shows, the web server delivers the interface components in HTML files to be loaded by the browser. Once in the browser, the application's components communicate directly with the application server, effectively bypassing the web server. Protocols such as Distributed Component Object Model (DCOM, formerly Network OLE), Distributed System Object Model (DSOM), or Common Object Request Broker Architecture (CORBA) are used with HTTP to accomplish the communication. Under this design, tighter com-

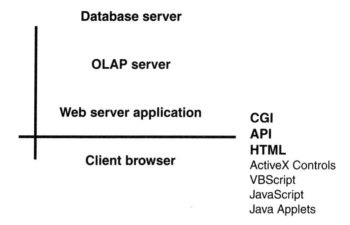

Figure 7.1. Web-based OLAP Delivery System

munications between the client and server improve performance, provide better functionality, and address security issues (through the process of exchanging information in memory).

The Technical Issues for OLAP

We face multiple technical and functional design issues in moving OLAP into the web browser. In implementing OLAP for the web, a top-down design philosophy is necessary. First, vendors decide how users will move through re-

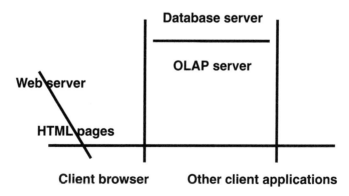

Figure 7.2. HTML Files Loaded by the Browser

port information in a browser. Then they map out the series of processes necessary to provide browser-based access to the OLAP engine. These processes include providing HTTP access to the database or application server for live data and functionality, and designing interfaces that support the analytical functionality.

Publishing encompasses the steps necessary to prepare or create information to be viewed in a browser. Administrators must somehow generate the reports and graphs to be presented. They can accomplish this task by using publishing utilities. Some of these utilities are being positioned as programmer tools. An assortment of proprietary HTML tags, for instance, may be used to tell web server processes which data to pull from the database. However, such tools make the implementation browser-dependent. Similarly, programs can use a toolkit that provides HTML functions to customize what gets delivered to the browser.

Other publishing utilities may be extensions of existing products. For example, a development environment or scheduler could include a *Save as Web Report* option for administrators who want to build reports using the applications they already know.

Some new products can be positioned as the vehicle for publishing reports that can run against their OLAP servers. In any case, a static approach to providing information almost always offers user-friendly dialogs to create reports as HTML files.

OLAP on the Browser Side

There are several different levels of functionality in browser-based OLAP reporting. These levels range from static reporting with no analytical capability to paging report views, rotating dimensions, and drilling through data. An interface that uses standard HTML looks plain and provides rigid functionality. In order to rotate two dimensions of data in a report using an HTML interface, a user must make three or four selections before seeing the new report layout.

As a result, we have to look to *Java applets* and *ActiveX controls* to improve the user's experience with the browser. These technologies can be used to provide functionality and a look and feel comparable to those in traditional client/server applications. In this scenario, a user could switch the layout of a report by dragging a *product* panel onto a *time* panel. However, portability across server platforms and web browsers may be sacrificed, as we embrace technologies that may be neither standard nor widely supported.

Approaches to Web-Enabling OLAP

The approaches for providing access to OLAP functionality over the web fit into one of three categories:

- Through *static HTML reports, created off-line,* schedulers can pull data from off-line OLAP engines, creating static HTML reports from HTML templates. The HTML templates are used so that all reports maintain a consistent look. The reports are then managed and delivered to the browser by web server processes. These static HTML reports rate high in portability, and they move to the browser quickly. However, the user can not really interact with the data. Some static approaches simulate dimension drilling through report navigation. A scheduler can create a number of reports linked together by hypertext links in the data.

- The OLAP server *populates HTML templates with data on the fly*, as users request information from the browser. In this approach, only report templates and metadata exist on the web server. This metadata tells the web server which data to put in the HTML file before sending it to the browser. The metadata exists on the server in two formats. It may reside inside custom HTML tags in the templates on the server. Alternatively, it may be stored in binary format such as fields in a database.

   Independently of how templates and report metadata are stored on the server, the web server based on a report code sent from the browser gathers the information. The web server software uses the report metadata to pull the appropriate data from the database. The database that houses this data may or may not be on the same machine as the web server application.

   This information merges with the template, and the whole package is sent to the browser as an HTML response file. The default report usually offers some level of OLAP functionality. As the user interacts with the report, a user code is sent with other information to the web server, which uses the code to keep track of what information a user is looking at in the browser.

- The Java or ActiveX components feeding the browser use Java applets and ActiveX controls to minimize communication between browser and web server and to enhance the user experience through improvements to the interface. Two approaches in using these components can be deployed:

- The web server populates a binary file with the data for the reports, and the interface controls are sent to the browser along with the HTML response file. On the client, a property of the control tells the browser the name of the corresponding data file. The browser downloads this file and the component loads the data. In this design, the components provide functionality such as drilling and layout rotation with a slick interface, without going back to the server. Also, because data is passed in binary format between client and server, this approach is more secure.
- The interface component communicates directly with the server, interactively bringing data to the client as the user requests it. Here, an interface component requests data from the web server by opening an HTTP stream. When the component receives the results from the server, it parses the results and moves the data into an object for displaying the information.

    This approach has similar advantages to the first. But to achieve the same security as the first method, a protocol such as Netscape's Secure Socket Layer (SSL) must be used with HTTP. For example, a web server might use SSL to encrypt HTML being sent to the browser; an SSL-compliant browser can then decrypt this information on the client. Of course, security protocols are not entirely a function of the application. Any HTML-compliant application can take advantage of these protocols, as long as the application's web environment supports them. The component approach also entails several hazards. Even though Java is fast becoming an Internet standard, it is not as portable as HTML. Vendors who choose to use ActiveX risk making the wrong choice.

The next generation of browser-based reporting may see web-based applications mixing other network protocols with HTTP to communicate directly with the same server processes used by traditional client/server applications. These more generic network transport protocols can be used with HTTP to facilitate this communication. Again, these protocols include DCOM, DSOM, and one based on CORBA. This design can enhance the user experience when using a browser and enable corporate IS to develop a single architecture to deliver systems across multiple delivery mediums.

Whenever you evaluate systems to move to the web, you should apply two general assumptions:

- Information-centric applications migrate nicely to the web and stand to gain much value from its architecture. That is, systems that present information with a low-level of functionality, in multiple formats, to a broad audience are the success stories.

- Conversely, using a browser to deliver specialized, functionally-intensive applications with a small number of users will create headaches for users and developers alike. Developers must administer additional software on the server, and users get a less capable interface if only HTML is used. The largest headaches will come from the attempt at duplicating functionality on the client and managing the larger demand for information between the browser and the web server.

Reports distributed over the web that provide basic analytical functionality, including drilling, paging, and rotating dimensions, complement the more functional client/server OLAP application very well. One can use the advanced selection criteria, such as exception queries, in these traditional applications to prepare default reports for widespread distribution over an intranet or the Internet.

Looking to the future, the largest hurdles faced by OLAP technologies in delivering functionality over the web will be the browser's procedural environment and the volumes of data that could potentially be needed on the client. Much like a DOS application, users usually move through information in a browser one page at a time, navigating back and forth in a procedural fashion. Although newer browsers offer some support for a window object, implementing a multiple document interface (MDI) application with multiple windows or forms is not easy.

Information passed between the browser and web server is text that must be parsed before it can be manipulated. As a result, moving large amounts of data between the two platforms is inefficient. As client/server technology begins to adapt to browser-based applications, developers will have the tools they need to address some of these issues. For example, Java or ActiveX could be used to pop up a form over a web page to prompt a user for information, an efficient alternative to moving the user to a totally different page in the browser.

Now that OLAP vendors have web-enabled their engines, they have begun focusing on the authoring and improved delivery of information in the browser. Today, some approaches require that administrators know how to write HTML in order to provide web-based access to OLAP engines. In most cases, applications with more user-friendly dialogs are needed to create and manage browser access to data and functionality.

Core Components of a Data Warehouse Solution

The role of the OLAP server is best understood in the context of the five key components of a data warehousing or data mart development strategy:

- *Policy:* Rules governing business issues such as goals and scope of the data warehouse; operational issues such as loading and maintenance frequency; and organizational issues such as information security are as critical to successful data warehouse and data mart implementations as are product and technology choices.
- *Transformation:* Before raw data can be stored in a data warehouse, it must be transformed and cleansed so that it has consistent meaning to users who access it. This transformation may involve restructuring, redefining, filtering, combining, recalculating and summarizing data fields from a range of disparate transaction systems.
- *Storage:* As data is moved from various transaction systems into the warehouse, it must be stored so as to maximize system flexibility, manageability, and overall accessibility. The information stored in the warehouse is historical in nature and includes detailed summarized transaction data and detail. The technology best suited to serve the role of historical data repository in the data warehouse is the relational database.
- *Presentation and Access:* This refers to the ability to select, view, and manipulate data. Desktop tools such as spreadsheets, query tools, web browsers, and report writers meet this need by presenting a graphical interface for navigating warehouse data.
- *Analysis:* This is the component of a data warehousing solution which addresses the corporate need to understand what is driving business performance. The analytical component must support sophisticated, autonomous end user queries, rapid calculation of key business metrics, planning and forecasting functions, and what-if analyses on large data volumes (see **Figure 7.3**). Unlike the data warehouse storage component, the analytical solution must encompass historical, derived, and projected information. The technology best suited to serve this role as the analytical engine in the data warehouse is the OLAP server.

Data Warehouse Access

Both data warehouses (comprehensive, enterprise-wide) and data marts (subject- or application-specific) must be accessible to a wide variety of users with

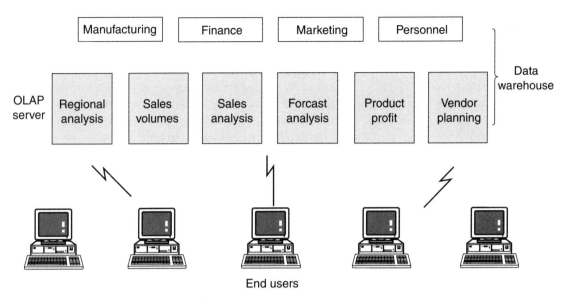

Figure 7.3. OLAP Server

an equally wide variety of application and information needs if they are to provide a high return on investment. In general, the user tools for accessing data warehouses and data marts can be placed in one of two main categories:

- Personal productivity tools (such as spreadsheets, word processors, statistical packages, and graphics tools) are characterized by the requirement to manipulate and present data on individual PCs. Developed for stand-alone environments, personal productivity tools address applications requiring desktop manipulation of small volumes of warehouse data.

- Data query and reporting tools deliver warehouse-wide data access through simple interfaces that hide the SQL language from end users. These tools are designed for list-oriented queries, basic drill-down analysis, and generation of reports. These tools provide a view of simple historical data but do not address the need for multidimensional reporting, analysis, and planning, nor are they capable of computing sophisticated metrics.

Analysis—The Role of the OLAP Server

By combining standard access tools with a powerful analytical engine, users are able to gain real insight from the data in the warehouse. OLAP servers address warehouse applications such as performance reporting, sales forecasting, product line and customer profitability, sales analysis, marketing analysis, what-if analysis, and manufacturing mix analysis—applications that require historical, projected and derived data. A key characteristic of OLAP servers is a robust calculation engine. Historical data is made vastly more useful to the business user by transforming it through OLAP calculation into derived and projected data.

OLAP applications share a set of user and functional requirements that cannot be met by applying query tools or personal productivity tools directly against the historical data maintained in the warehouse relational database. An OLAP server is designed to provide the functionality and performance to meet the needs of planning and analysis in the data warehouse. The planning and analysis function mandates that the organization look not only at past performance but, more importantly, at the future performance of the business. It is essential to create operational scenarios that are shaped by the past, yet also include planned and potential changes that will impact tomorrow's corporate performance. The combined analysis of historical data with future projections is critical to the success of today's corporation.

Requirements

Requirements for OLAP applications in a data warehouse or data mart strategy include:

- The ability to scale to large volumes of data and large numbers of concurrent users
- Consistent fast query response times that allow for iterative, speed-of-thought analyses
- A calculation engine that includes robust mathematical functions for computing derived data (aggregations, matrix calculations, cross-dimensional calculations, OLAP-aware formulas, and procedural calculations)
- Seamless presentation of historical, projected, and derived data
- A multi-user read/write environment to support what-if analysis and planning
- The ability to be deployed quickly, adopted easily and maintained cost-effectively

- Robust data access security and user management
- Availability of a wide variety of viewing and analysis tools to support different user communities

Neither personal productivity tools nor query and reporting tools by themselves are designed to meet these requirements. To deliver planning and analysis applications within a data warehousing strategy, an OLAP server must be implemented.

Table 7.1. OLTP servers handle mission-critical production data accessed through simple queries, while OLAP servers handle management-critical data accessed through an iterative analytical investigation. This table shows the evolution of data as it moves over three server platforms, how they differ in purpose, means of access, and the data they store, and how they are implemented.

OLAP and Data Warehouse Architecture

Creating a successful business intelligence environment means finding a middle ground between two extremes: independent implementations driven by business units and the integrated data warehouse architecture defined by IT departments. On one hand, IT departments must accept the fact that they cannot give their customers intuitive, free-form access to information and query response times without incorporating OLAP technology into their data warehouse designs. IT is never going to satisfy the needs of the typical business manager simply by enabling a limited group of business analysts to execute canned queries directly against the data warehouse using fat-client, managed query environment (MQE) tools that generate SQL directly from client workstations.

ROLAP servers also generate SQL to an RDBMS, but they do so from a middle tier server that sits right on top of the RDBMS, thereby taking most of the load off both the client workstation and the network. Both analytical flexibility and query response times will always suffer. On the other hand, business managers must learn to recognize the value of having a common method so that all the numbers and all the terminology match on all reports across all departments. This ensures that managers won't waste their time arguing about whose numbers are right. Only a central data warehouse data source can provide this consistency.

In *Building the Data Warehouse* (John Wiley & Sons, 1996), W.H. Inmon says, "There are four levels in the architected environment—the operational, the atomic or the data warehouse, the departmental, and the individual."

Table 7.1. OLTP versus Data Warehouse RDBMS versus OLAP Server

Purpose	OLTP Server	RDBMS Repository	OLAP Server
Access			
Type:	Read/write	Read only	Read/write
Mode:	Singular, Simple Update	Singular, detail, List-oriented queries	Iterative and analytical
Process:	Is-supported queries	Pre-planned queries and reports	ad hoc queries, drill-down
Response:	Fast update/response	Very slow response	Fast/consistent query/response
Data Storage			
Scope:	Application specific	Cross-subject	Many cubes
	Actual	Data Mart; single subject	Summarized; aggregated
	Limited historical	Historical	Projected; historical
Data detail:	Transaction detail	cleansed and summarized	Summarized and sophisticated
Data structure:	Normalized	Normalized or denormalized	Dimensional or hierarchical
Design goal:	Update	List-oriented query	Analysis
Volumes:	Gigabytes	Gigabytes/terabytes	Gigabytes
Implementation			
Deployment:	Slow (months)	Slow (months)	Fast (weeks)
Adaptability:	Limited	Low—significant resource	High—easily modified
Investment:	Moderate to expensive	Moderate to very expensive	Minimal to moderate

The Operational Layer

Operational systems are the source of the raw, transaction-level data that populates the data warehouse. Operational data is current, volatile, transaction-level data stored in normalized or proprietary form in an OLTP system.

The Atomic Data Warehouse Layer

The atomic data warehouse layer is a read-only archive that contains subject-oriented historical snapshots of the same transaction-level data scrubbed and rearranged into a multidimensional format more suitable for decision support.

At the data warehouse layer, a single fact table may have a record for every transaction, and each record will contain a full range of statistics (such as orders, revenues, and costs) and as many as two dozen or more descriptive fields representing the entire potential universe of qualifying business dimensions (such as time, location, customer, and product) covering a broad *content* subject area (such as product sales data or general ledger cost data). However, once such a database grows to a size of any consequence, it becomes dangerous (from an IT resources perspective) to provide typical users with direct access to it, and it becomes impossible to provide speed-of-thought response times to queries posed against it. This is why there is the need for the departmental level.

The Departmental, Data Mart, or OLAP Layer

In his same book, W. H. Inmon writes, "The departmental level is sometimes called the 'data mart' level, the 'OLAP' level, or the 'multidimensional DBMS' level." OLAP technology should be employed at this layer in the architecture. An OLAP data mart will be limited in scope to the relatively small subset of available statistical measures and dimensions needed to study a specific, well-bounded business problem. Limiting a data mart's scope ensures that the resulting data mart will fit within the scalability limits of an OLAP database server and permits the analysis at hand to be conducted without the distractions presented by extraneous data. Using an OLAP database server, in turn, allows the use of OLAP indexing and pre-summarization techniques to deliver rapid response times and intuitive access.

The OLAP layer of the architecture should bear the brunt of the query load. In a well-designed business intelligence environment, 80 percent or more of the queries will be posed to the data marts and the OLAP servers—thin clients should be the rule. The remaining queries that demand access to transaction-level data will generally be limited to sales analysis queries.

When the data arrives in the warehouse it must be ready (cleansed and transformed) for immediate redistribution to subscribing data marts. Its basic dimensional structure must already be defined and reflected in the warehouse's star-schema relational database design. It should also have a central metadata repository that catalogs the contents and status of the warehouse. The OLAP server should be able to read, directly from the warehouse tables, both the data and the metadata required to restructure and update each data mart with its required subset of measures, dimensions, and records.

Furthermore, the architecture must be comprehensive and flexible enough that new marts can be quickly created and existing marts can be quickly redefined, simply by selecting new combinations of measures and dimensions from those already existing in the warehouse "library" in response to new or redefined business requirements. When OLAP databases fail to scale up, it is usually because the architect tried to anticipate every possible business requirement for every possible subject area and then tried to stuff the contents of the entire warehouse into a single, fully pre-summarized OLAP "data mart."

Battle-scarred business analysts often demand such a solution because they're afraid that if they don't ask for it now, they'll never be able to get it in the future. Data warehousing is necessarily a process of continual, iterative development. It is impossible to anticipate all analytical requirements up front, and you shouldn't even try. What you *must* do is give yourself the ability to adjust your data mart designs rapidly in response to fluid perceptions of business needs.

In any case, all successfully designed architectures will include both a relational data warehouse layer and an OLAP data mart layer.

MOLAP versus ROLAP

At this point it is worthwhile to touch briefly on the MOLAP versus ROLAP debate. MOLAP servers (also known as MDDBs) store data in multidimensional array-like data structures. ROLAP servers use metadata to map star-schema relational databases into multidimensional views.

Just as organizations use a variety of desktop query and analysis tools, most companies will also need different kinds of OLAP servers at the data mart layer of their architectures. Interactive planning applications such as demand forecasting, financial analysis, and resource allocation will typically require an MDDB database server that offers uniform speed-of-thought query response times and read-write capabilities. Read-write is a key distinction in favor of MDDBs. On the other hand, applications such as retail sales analysis or customer loyalty marketing that require databases with hundreds of thousands of continually changing products or customers and numerous attributes such as customer demographic fields or product characteristics will demand a ROLAP server.

The Presentation Layer

Graphical ad hoc query tools (both OLAP and MQE), EIS presentations, report writers, web browsers, data visualization tools, and spreadsheets, all reside at this level of the architecture.

Custom decision-support applications that create new information such as budgets, forecasts, recommended resource allocations, and the like also reside above the data marts at this level of the architecture, as do tools such as statistical analysis packages and data mining tools. The new information created by these processes should be written back to OLAP data marts. The *target* data marts for these outputs can thereby serve as information clearing houses for derived information, such as customer demand forecasts, that is useful across the entire enterprise.

OLAP in the Middle

OLAP sits in the middle of the business intelligence architecture, bridging the gap between the atomic data warehouse layer and the presentation layer. Deploying OLAP technology effectively requires seamless integration with both adjoining layers. Building a successful business intelligence environment requires integrating a variety of OLAP servers and front-end tools. In an ideal solution, users should be able to perform their analysis without having to be aware of the physical form of the underlying database.

OLAP Platforms: New Choices for New Deployment Objectives

For many forward-thinking, leading enterprises, OLAP has been a strategic contributor to business performance. These companies have made large investments in underlying client/server architectures, servers, client operating systems, and other infrastructure.

Historically, client/server architectures have not been known for their low costs. Increased hardware costs (RAM, processor, disk), increased communications costs (e.g., modems and network adapters), and increased management and maintenance (numerous platforms, vendors, and interoperability issues) have historically precluded a wider deployment of OLAP.

Although the client/server cost profile has constrained its deployment, OLAP is ideally suited to a broader audience. The rich analysis functionality of OLAP is well-suited to a larger community of users who can use it to perform their jobs more productively. The challenge for software professionals is to alter the cost dynamics found in client/server OLAP to deliver it economically to that wider potential user base.

Client/Server OLAP has traditionally been available only to executives, managers, and analysts. Companies are seeking ways to deploy the benefits of OLAP across the enterprise.

Implementing OLAP

The goal of a data warehouse project is not to warehouse data, but to enable business managers to become self-sufficient analysts. In a successful business intelligence environment, even non-technical business managers compose their own requests for information as they conceive of them, without programmer assistance, and they retrieve results at the speed of thought. Their follow-up questions are immediately answered through instantaneous drilling down and slicing and dicing of the data. Managers must be able to maintain their trains of thought as they conduct an analysis through free-form exploration of a database.

Online analytical processing (OLAP) technology has gained popularity because of its use of multidimensional structures, special database indexing schemes, and summarization have enabled intuitive access and rapid response times for complex analytical queries. But the ultimate success of OLAP depends not strictly on its capabilities but rather on how well OLAP fits into broader data warehouse architectures.

Islands of OLAP

To date, most OLAP technology purchases have been application-specific decisions made at the departmental level. OLAP tools tend to be relatively easy to learn and deploy. Hence, business unit managers frustrated by the slow pace of enterprise data warehouse projects frequently purchase them directly and implement them over the objections of—and with minimal assistance from—corporate IT departments. Consequently, it is not unusual to find companies in which three different departments have purchased three different OLAP tools, totally unaware of each other's activities and making no effort whatsoever at cross-departmental integration.

It would be fair to say that most businesses have introduced standalone OLAP products in ways that have aggravated the *islands of information* problem. Isolated departments are able to satisfy their immediate information needs in this manner, but information compiled by one business unit remains beyond the reach of analysts in other departments. There can be no assurance that the numbers presented by one department on one set of reports will match the numbers on a seemingly equivalent set of reports produced by a second business unit.

On the other hand, in those cases where IT departments have successfully thwarted the introduction of OLAP technology into the enterprise, business managers remain virtual prisoners in the data jailhouse.

OLAP is not a panacea for decision support. Like other hot decision-support technologies such as data mining, data visualization, and data warehousing, OLAP is just one key component of the overall business intelligence framework. As is the case with these other technologies, OLAP must be woven into the larger fabric of a company's business intelligence architecture to realize its full potential.

Connecting OLAP Clients to OLAP Servers

OLAP clients communicate with OLAP servers using multidimensional APIs, not SQL. All OLAP servers, both multidimensional OLAP (MOLAP, multidimensional databases, or MDDB) and relational OLAP (ROLAP, front ends to relational databases) are proprietary insofar as each product publishes its own API for communicating with client front ends. Likewise, a majority of OLAP servers, both MOLAP and ROLAP, still communicate only with their own proprietary front ends using their own APIs. An industry-standard OLAP API would enable customers to mix and match freely among best-of-breed OLAP clients and OLAP servers, just as ODBC has obviated the need for point-to-point native driver connections between client tools and database servers. To date, two non-product-specific OLAP APIs have emerged.

Microsoft's OLE DB for OLAP API

To assure the instant success of this product, Microsoft undertook its own OLAP API initiative, called OLE DB for OLAP. The OLE DB for OLAP API is a set of communications interfaces designed to extend Microsoft's OLE DB for efficient access to multidimensional data. Designed to be generic enough so that they can be employed by any relational or multidimensional data provider, these extensions allow for representing, expressing, transporting, and efficiently navigating multidimensional data within the Microsoft operating system environment. They are designed to link multidimensional data providers and consumers of such data, regardless of the data storage environment.

Hybrid OLAP

An alternative would be to employ an internally integrated *hybrid* OLAP solution, with both three-tier ROLAP and MDDB data storage options within the same product line. Oracle provides a similar capability to draw a subset of a star- schema relational database into an Express MDDB. While such options let you easily extract data from a star-schema relational database into a new MDDB hypercube, DB2/OLAP allows you to build a hypercube and physically store the data in a special star-schema relational database.

Desktop or Portable OLAP

Another segment of the OLAP market is composed of desktop, or portable OLAP products that create small OLAP cubes that fit on a client workstation. Although products such as Cognos Corporation's PowerPlay or Andyne's PaBLO are widely deployed on a standalone basis to solve small-scale business analysis problems, another potential use of these products is to carve a small subset cube out of a larger OLAP database for portable analysis.

For example, field salespeople might dial into the corporate sales data mart, carve out the latest data for the piece of the database that corresponds to their territory, and take it with them on their laptops to analyze at their leisure.

Web OLAP

Much has been written about web-enabled OLAP lately. Vendors are now offering outstanding third-party web servers that can be used as graphical front ends for a variety of OLAP and relational database servers. Several OLAP client vendors are also offering web server versions of their OLAP front ends.

Enterprises are increasingly looking at Java-based OLAP web application servers as an alternative to portable OLAP for field access to corporate databases because of both reduced client hardware requirements and the virtual absence of remote client software maintenance hassles.

Data Mining

Data mining and OLAP are complementary technologies. In fact, many data mining techniques would be most efficiently run against databases that are organized multi-dimensionally. However, there has been relatively little integration between OLAP and data mining products to date. For the most part, data mining tools read flat files and, at best, provide outputs that can easily be imported into OLAP databases for review.

Other Decision-Support Tools

Many other complementary decision-support technologies should be integrated with OLAP database technology, including statistical analysis packages, geographic information systems (GIS), and data visualization tools. A majority of OLAP server vendors now offer spreadsheet add-ins as front-end options.

Custom Development Toolkits

Most OLAP APIs allow you to develop custom applications that tap directly into the OLAP database using popular object-oriented programming languages such as C++ and Visual Basic.

OLTP to Warehouse to Data Marts

At least as important as integration between OLAP client and OLAP database server is the integration of the operational data store, data warehouse, and data mart layers of the architecture. In any business intelligence project, the lion's share of the work goes into extracting, scrubbing, and transforming the data from OLTP to OLAP format. This has been a tedious, multistage process with little synergy between the steps of extracting the data from OLTP systems to the warehouse and the process of populating the data marts from the warehouse.

A large number of OLAP database servers offer graphical administration tools for mapping data from warehouse databases to OLAP data structures.

Opening Up OLAP

Although there is still much progress to be made, OLAP software is poised to enter the mainstream of enterprise decision-support software and take its place in a well-integrated business intelligence architecture. The market for OLAP software continues to grow, which has postponed what is seen as an inevitable shake-out in the OLAP server marketplace.

The Case for Enterprise-Wide OLAP

Since their rise to prominence in the early 90s, OLAP systems have become indispensable ingredients of the information architecture for the world's largest enterprises. No longer is OLAP an early adopter technology. Quite simply,

OLAP has enabled large- and medium-sized companies to quickly implement flexible operations, faster cycle times, and opportunistic marketing campaigns that are all driven by decisions based on sound analyses, rather than hunches and anecdotes.

Many companies around the world have implemented OLAP systems because they provide a strategic platform for delivering timely and accurate information to executives, analysts, decision makers, and knowledge workers.

Prior to the growth of the web-enabled OLAP market, decision-support operations were typically limited to fairly narrow bands of users. Using a variety of niche packages, perhaps mainframe statistical packages or internally developed analysis routines, a few key employees performed time-consuming analyses of corporate data. Often that analysis was subject to data delay, diminishing its value to the company.

Today, OLAP systems are widely respected for their ability to deliver fresh views of management information quickly. Current OLAP systems help enterprises with business-critical functions such as:

- Customer segmentation
- Customer and product profitability analysis
- Geographic and channel analysis
- Sales forecasting
- Financial consolidations
- Budgeting and financial planning
- Enterprise information systems
- Manufacturing mix analysis

Multidimensional Data Model Driving OLAP's Success

The key behind the growing success of these systems lies in the ability of OLAP technology to present data in an intuitive multidimensional view. With OLAP, data is presented along dimensions such as time, products, regions, channels, and packages.

Multidimensional views display data the way a user needs to see it, in a summarized cross-tabular format, not in volumes of detail that lack context. Multidimensional data is structured the way people think. With this intuitive presentation of business information, users can easily navigate through gigabytes of information. And since the value of timely information continues to grow, web-enabled OLAP will grow in its use as a strategic tool for a much wider audience.

Conclusions

Expanding the OLAP environment from its traditional client/server platform to the web implies key OLAP and web requirements for successful deployment:

- *Complete OLAP functionality:* Feature subsets or restricted implementations will not do. For wide scale adoption, web-enabled OLAP must give users all OLAP features, including drill-down/up/across, pivot, and slice-and-dice capabilities.

- *Read and write access:* OLAP is not simply passive analysis of a data warehouse. It is dynamic and active. Key OLAP applications such as budgeting, forecasting, and planning require updates. Read-only access severely limits the usefulness of web OLAP applications.

- *Support for Open Web Standards:* HTML-based web pages that do not overly rely on non-standard extensions or proprietary interfaces and communications are a requirement. Standard web-authoring and administration tools must integrate with the web OLAP application development environment.

- *Security:* OLAP information often deals with business-critical data. Security is essential, even in an intranet environment.

- *Integration with other information:* This is important for certain classes of applications such as EIS, where users need to retrieve different types of information into a single application.

WEB SECURITY
AND DATA WAREHOUSE

Introduction

Most likely, you have heard or read about security on the World Wide Web. With security, you can safely send the credit card number and buy something right on the web, without faxing information or talking to someone on the phone. You can also use the web to transfer money between bank accounts, or even sell stock. But why you should trust the World Wide Web?

Consider the Internet as a new postal service. This new service operates at a blinding speed, sorting and routing messages through various post offices in seconds. In fact, the Internet was not really designed to protect information.

Unfortunately, this new postal service has a strange drawback to it. Anyone and everyone can be a postmaster, and there is nothing to prevent a postmaster from reading, copying, and even altering the mail as it passes through the post office. Another drawback is that there are no registered letters requiring signatures or return receipts. As a result, you can not be sure that the person to whom you sent something actually received it.

Because the Internet was designed to be an open system, any computer on the network can see the messages passing through (Figure 8.1). When you surf to a URL or submit a form to a server, that information passes through anywhere from one to hundreds of computers and users.

Data Warehouse Security

On the other hand, secure business environment via the web requires the following four features:

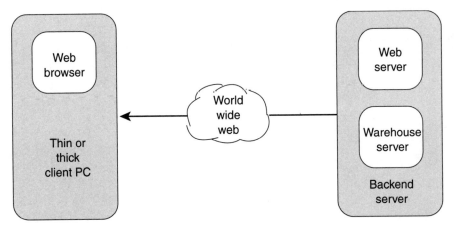

Figure 8.1   Web-enabled Data Warehouse

- Authenticity
- Confidentiality
- Integrity
- Accountability

There are a couple of different ways that you can secure the transactions for safe surfing.

1. If you wish to send your credit card number so that you can order a case of wine, you will probably use a protocol named **SSL** (also known as **Secure Sockets Layer**).
2. If you are doing something more involved, like banking, buying airline tickets as part of a frequent buyer club, or some other transaction where the business needs to verify who you are, then you will probably use **HTTPS or SHTTP** (Secure HyperText Transport Protocol). The server offering these transactions determines which protocol you will be using.

This conceptual information is nice, but you probably want to know how it applies to the data warehouse. Companies today are looking to expand the access to business-critical data-warehouse information to an even greater number of knowledge workers and decision-makers. Yet deployment of data-warehousing user applications today entails significant costs—costs that could potentially be slashed by using web-based applications. For example, a web-enabled application could be accessed by every networked desktop in a corporation with no additional client software installed. The corporation would only need to install the server application that the existing web browsers could access directly.

Many companies are opening up their data warehouses to designated users outside of their companies. In particular, companies are interested in making warehoused data available to companies in their supply chains. For example, a manufacturer might want to share warehouse data with original equipment manufacturer (OEM) partners, or a credit-card handler might want to share data with its merchant banks. Most important, the data warehouse needs to be available to both inside and outside users with tight security controls.

A data warehouse implementation via the web requires security over the connected networks as well as "data" security and authorizations. True Internet/Network security can only be achieved when the information is isolated, locked in a safe, and rendered inaccessible. Some would argue that even then, there is not absolute security. It is just not possible to make a network system completely secure.

The reason is in the motivations for the development of networks. Networks were created as a remedy to the problem of data isolation in the early days of computing. *Islands of automation* were a hindrance to conducting business successfully because critical information required by one island could not be accessed by others. Networks became the communication bridges by which these islands could be integrated.

This does not imply that network security is unnecessary, or that management should ignore it. However, the explosion of information across the internetworks has raised the specter of corporate espionage to new heights. Corporations today know that information is power and those organizations which control their information appropriately can gain competitive advantage.

This section is intended to help management successfully navigate this course by providing an overview of security principles and the technologies that are appropriate for securing the internetworks which empower the user to successfully garner the benefits of the warehouse.

Web Security Issues

Some Basic Security Concepts

The key words in the security terminology are *vulnerability, threat, attack,* and *countermeasure.*

- *Vulnerability* is the susceptibility of a situation to being compromised. It is a potential, a possibility, or a weakness. A vulnerability in and of itself may or may not pose a serious problem, depending on what tools are available to exploit that weakness.

- A *threat* is an action or tool which can exploit and expose a vulnerability and therefore compromise the integrity of a given system. Not all threats are equal in terms of their ability to expose and exploit the vulnerability. Some viruses could do a lot of damage.

- An *attack* defines the details of how a particular threat could be used to exploit a vulnerability. An example of an attack is a Trojan horse attack, where a destructive tool such as a virus is packaged within a seemingly desirable object, like a piece of free or downloadable software.

- *Countermeasures* are those actions taken to protect systems from attacks which threaten specific vulnerabilities. In the network security world, countermeasures consist of tools such as virus detection and cleansing, packet filtering, password authentication, and encryption.

These countermeasures are the essential ingredients of an data warehousing application deployment.

Any security scheme for data warehousing must identify *vulnerabilities* and *threats*, anticipate potential *attacks*, assess whether they are likely to succeed or not, assess what the potential damage might be from successful attacks, and then implement countermeasures against those defined attacks which are deemed to be significant enough to counter. Therefore, we can see that security is all about identifying and managing risk, and that security is a very relative concept, which must be tailored to the needs of the data warehousing applications.

For example, a Trojan horse attack on one organization could succeed easily and compromise extremely important information. The same attack on another organization would only result in minimal damage, perhaps because there is no sensitive data available on that particular system. In each of these organizations, different security schemes will be employed with different countermeasures to suit their specific situations.

Management must consider all of these factors in defining a security strategy. Management must also consider the cost of protecting against all possible attacks. Security costs money and/or system performance, and each enterprise must determine how much it will cost to institute appropriate countermeasures. Only then can an enterprise truly determine which of the possible spectrum of attacks should be defended against and which should be ignored.

Generic Security Threats

One of the major threats which companies are dealing with is the introduction of malicious programs over the network. The term *computer virus* has been used loosely to categorize these attacks which come in Trojan horses, worms, and logic bombs as well as true viruses. Some of these are:

1. A *Trojan* horse is a program that conceals harmful code. It usually disguises itself as an attractive or useful program, which lures users to execute it, and in doing so, damages the user's system. The program hidden in the Trojan horse can be one which causes malicious damage, or one which performs some espionage for the attacker, such as stealing the password file from the computer it invades.

2. A *logic bomb* is code that checks for certain conditions and, when these conditions are met, it starts to do its damage. Sometimes, like the Magellan virus, the trigger logic is a date, but it can be any given set of parameters, including a person's name, a bank account number, or some combination of events and parameters.

3. A *worm* is a self-contained program which replicates itself across the network and therefore multiplies its damage by infecting many different nodes.

4. A *virus* is code which plants a version of itself in any program it can modify. The Microsoft Concept virus is a good example: once it has *infected* Microsoft Word, all subsequent documents which are opened by the user may only be saved as template files. In all other respects, Microsoft Word continues to operate normally.

It should be noted that these are not mutually exclusive threats. A logic bomb could plant a virus under the specified conditions, as could a Trojan horse deliver a worm. Furthermore, each of these threats could have different or multiple missions, such as the theft of data, the compromising of confidentiality, integrity, or availability, or the disruption of service to the organization.

In addition to planting computer programs which could create these effects, there are also threats which involve the theft or compromise of information while it is in transit between endpoints of a network. One such example is called *snooping*, in which an attacker simply eavesdrops on electronic communications.

These are the classes of threats that today's network managers must deal with, and that senior management must be aware of, since they play a major part in determining the appropriate and tolerable cost of security to counteract these potential threats.

Security Countermeasures

Given the above scenario, a reasonable question at this point might be "what tools are available today to help mitigate the consequences of these security threats on the network?" The good news is that there are multiple technologies which can be brought to bear on the issues and they are impressively effective.

Security Policy

The bad news is that no amount of technology can overcome a poorly planned, poorly implemented, or nonexistent security policy. A customer being waited on at a public place (say a doctor's office) requires some information from the clerk who in turn needs to access that information from a workstation centrally located in the area behind the window. Sitting at the workstation, the clerk yells to a co-worker *his password*.

Again, the security of any information in any organization today is primarily dependent on the quality of the security policy and the processes by which that organization imposes the policies on itself. If the security procedures are lax, are not enforced uniformly, and allow gaping security holes to exist, no amount of technology will restore the security breaches. Organizations that are concerned about security on the Internet should ask themselves a few of the following questions before worrying about encryption, packet filtering, proxy servers, and other related technology solutions.

1. Does the corporate policy allow passwords such as name of the application "order" or "password," employee initials, or names or initials of employees' immediate family members?
2. Is there a process in place to change passwords periodically?
3. Do employees keep their password written on paper under their mousepads, keyboards, monitors, etc.?
4. Is there a program in place to make employees aware of the need for security and to disseminate security procedures to the employees to facilitate its implementation?
5. Do employees understand the different levels of security of information and what techniques to apply to each to ensure an appropriate level of protection?
6. Is the responsibility for information security assigned to a senior member of the management team, who is held accountable for maintaining appropriate security?
7. Is there a set of guidelines to identify the security classification of different documents and information generated by the employees; is there a process in place to classify or categorize these documents and information and secure them appropriately?

It should be evident at this point that the primary need for any organization is to get its own house in order, identify its security needs based on the types of information with which it deals, and develop a security policy and plan before committing to technology.

Following are some elements of a good security plan.

- Remember that security is not only technology, physical security and procedural security are as important as the technology used.
- Develop security requirements based on an analysis of the organization's mission, the information at risk, the threats to that information, and the implications of any successful attacks.

- Define appropriate security services and mechanisms and allocate them to components of the company's IT systems.
- Identify different measures of security appropriate for each level.
- Identify users who should have access to each level of security.

Authentication

A primary tool in securing data warehouse applications is the ability to recognize and verify the identity of users. This security feature is known as authentication. Traditionally, special names and secret passwords have been used to authenticate users, but as the anecdote above demonstrates, the password is only as good as the users' ability to keep it secret and protect it from being abused by unauthorized users. There are three generally accepted techniques for authenticating users to host machines.

1. *Authentication by something the user knows.* This is the password/username concept described above. There are two common approaches to password authentication, known as PAP and CHAP. PAP, which stands for Password Authentication Protocol, simply asks the requester to provide a password, and if the password provided is included in the user profiles, the requester is given access. CHAP (Challenge Handshake Authentication Protocol) takes the concept one step further by challenging the requester to encrypt a response to the challenge message. This, in effect, acts as a different password for each entry. Often, the CHAP mechanism is combined with an encrypting smart card, which uses an encryption key to encode the challenge message. Only if the challenge message is correct will the requester be granted access to the system.

2. *Authentication by something the user has.* In this technique, the user is given some kind of token, such as a magnetic stripe card, key, or, in sophisticated cases such as the remote access standard RADIUS discussed later, the user has a smart card equipped with a computer chip which can generate an encrypted code back to the computer system.

3. *Authentication by physical characteristics.* Here, the mechanism is to recognize some measure of the individual, which ostensibly cannot be duplicated. Biometrics techniques such as fingerprint ID, palm print ID, retinal scan, manual and digital signature, or voice recognition are used to validate the identity of the potential user.

Authentication is also necessary when two computers communicate with each other. For example, what should my host computer do when another computer asks to have a disk mounted which contains all of my organization's personnel data? How do I know that the requesting computer has a legitimate reason to access that information, and that it is not some external network hacker trying to steal information from my organization?

In addition, there are a number of *de facto* standards—those which are developed by companies rather than by official standards committees, but which enjoy widespread acceptance.

Network Security

The Internet community is constantly seeking new and better mechanisms to secure the Internet. Today, there are several other relevant proposals for standards under review by the Internet Engineering Task Force (IETF). One, which is generating some potential interest, is the Level 2 Tunneling Protocol (L2TP). These would ensure that even though the traffic is being transmitted over the public Internet, individual sessions can be established which are private to those members allowed to work within that channel.

The technology is known as *tunneling* because the correspondents are creating a tunnel of sorts through the public packets inhabiting the Internet, and exchanging very private communications within them. The concept comes from medieval times, where tunnels were built between fortified towns and castles to allow their inhabitants to move safely between them away from the dangers of the bands of marauders outside their gates.

The use of tunneling technology allows another concept to be implemented: the Virtual Private Network or VPN. Companies who want a less expensive alternative to private Wide Area Networks can use tunneling within the Internet and develop their own virtual WANs, safe from unwanted intrusions, yet riding on the cost benefits of the Internet mass volumes.

Non-Repudiation

This security concept protects against the sender or receiver denying that they sent or received certain communications. For example, when a person sends a certified or registered letter via the United States Postal Service (USPS), the recipient is supposed to prove his or her identity to the delivery person, and then confirm their receipt by signing a form.

The signed form is then returned to the sender, which proves to the sender that their correspondence was delivered. This prevents recipient (for example, debtors) from claiming that they never received the correspondence (for example a demand note), using that as an excuse for their actions (not paying the debt). In computer networks, these kinds of services are also available and are becoming increasingly valuable as commerce on the Internet continues to gain in popularity.

There are two different types of non-repudiation services that are applicable in computer network messaging:

- Non-repudiation of delivery service
- Non-repudiation of submission service

Non-repudiation of delivery service is similar to the USPS certified mail example above. This provides the sender with proof that a message was successfully delivered to the intended recipient. Many e-mail packages offer senders the option to request a return receipt. This return receipt provides the sender with a non-repudiation of delivery service feature—the recipient can't legitimately claim they did not receive the message.

Non-repudiation of *submission service* is similar to the concept of non-repudiation of delivery. This service offers proof that a given message was in fact sent from a particular sender. If we go back to the USPS example, when we mail important papers such as legal documents, it is considered prudent to send them via registered mail. When we do so, we get a receipt from the Postal Service and a special identification number is affixed to the return. Thus, if the recipient does not receive the documents, or contends that it was not sent on time, we have evidence that our submission did occur at a particular time.

Integrity

Integrity refers to the completeness and fidelity of the message as it passes through the network. The key here is making sure that the data passes from the source to the destination without undetected alteration. We may not be able to thwart someone from tapping (copying and listening) our messages and attempting to modify them as they move through the network, but we will be able to detect any attempt at modification and therefore reject the message if such a modification attempt is detectable.

If the order of transmitted data also is ensured, the service is termed connection-oriented integrity. The term anti-replay refers to a minimal form of connection-oriented integrity designed to detect and reject duplicated or very old data units.

Confidentiality

Confidentiality is a security property that ensures that data is disclosed only to those authorized to use it, and that it is not disclosed to unauthorized parties. The key point behind ensuring the confidentiality of information on the network is to deny information to anyone who is not specifically authorized to see it or use it. Encryption is a frequently used mechanism for guaranteeing confidentiality, since only those recipients who have access to the decrypting key are able to decode the messages. Confidentiality therefore equates to privacy.

Access Control

Access control relates to the accepting or rejecting a particular user requesting access to some service or data in any given system. A service could be a program or a device such as a printer or a file system, and data could be a text file, an image, a collection of files, or any combination of the above. The real question is, what are the risks involved in allowing access to any of the system's services or information to individuals requesting such access?

In some cases, such as the advertising web page of an organization, the answer is that no damage could occur. The objective of such a page is precisely to spread the word about the organization, and therefore access control is not an issue. On the other hand, access control is a major issue if someone requests access to the file which contains the passwords for all of the users of the system.

It is therefore necessary to define a set of access rights, privileges, and authorizations, and assign these to appropriate people within the domain of the system under analysis.

An Overview of Internet Architecture

In order to understand better how these security principles can be applied, we need to understand the standard networking architecture and how the specific Internet Architecture fits this model. Then we can see how the security principles we have just discussed apply to that Internet model.

ISO 7 Layer Model

The International Standards Organization (ISO) published an architecture in the early 1980s whose primary philosophy is that different telecommunications functions should be handled by different standard and open "layers" of the architecture (see **Figure 8.2**).

The very lowest layer is the physical layer, which is responsible for the physical transmission of the data from the computer to the network. Here, there are the electronic circuits and mechanical connectors which define how transmissions are to occur over coaxial Ethernet, modems, FDDI, or any other medium for transmitting data.

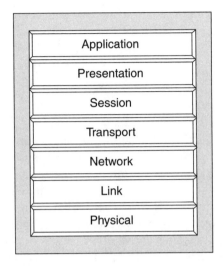

Figure 8.2   The ISO 7-Layer Model

Next is the *data-link* layer, which is responsible for the integrity of the bit-stream between any two points. Here, there are standards for redundancy checks, parity, retransmission protocols, etc., to ensure that the same sequence of bits sent from point A is received at point B.

The *network* layer extends the concepts of the link layer into multiple networks, which may or may not be compatible. Internetworking also implies that this layer must be aware of different routes available to connect the sender with the recipient.

The *transport layer* ensures that different transmissions, which may be part of a sequence and which may have traversed the network via different paths, are appropriately re-sequenced at the receiver's site.

The *session layer* manages the connecting and disconnecting of interactions between two computers and how the data is to be exchanged (duplex, simplex, etc.).

The *presentation layer* determines what code sets will be used (ASCII, EBCDIC, international character sets, etc.).

Finally, we come to the *applications layer* in which specific applications like FTP, Telnet, e-mail, X400, FTAM, and others reside.

The architecture of the OSI model is such that each layer uses services "below" it and provides services to those layers "above" it, giving the appearance of a stack. In fact, the model is known as a protocol stack and other architectures, such as TCP/IP, also follow the stack model.

Internet Layers

At this point, the vast majority of people interested in the Internet are familiar with the abbreviation TCP/IP (Transmission Control Protocol/Internet Protocol), which refers to the foundation of communications for the net. This section will cover the architectural constructs of the TCP/IP structure and their relationship to the Open Systems Interconnect (OSI) model (by ISO, The International Systems Organization)

Packet-Switching Networks

The Internet uses the concept of packets and packet switching to allow for simultaneous access by millions of people. Transmissions between any two points are broken into smaller transmissions known as packets. By doing this, everyone's messages can be sent in an interleaved fashion so that all users see nearly the same level of performance.

Each connection to the Internet is designated with a unique Internet Address, usually written as four numbers determined by a standard *Internet Protocol* (IP). Packets are shipped to Internet destinations through routers, which use Transmission Control Protocol, or TCP.

These fundamental layers of the Internet form the backbone upon which data can be sent from one point to another, with integrity.

Applications Layer

Getting data from point A to point B is essential, but it is not enough. It is the equivalent of finding a telephone number in a phone book and being able to establish a telephone connection between the US and a foreign country. The individuals will not be able to communicate unless there is a common language. Similarly, on the Internet, as specified in the OSI model (see **Figure 8.3**), there are other protocols and tools which are specific to the application layer and which correspond to these telephone analogies. Application layer is the top-most layer of the OSI model.

File Transfer Protocol (FTP) is the oldest commonly used method to allow files transfer from one location to another. Using an anonymous FTP, users can browse the files of a host, select appropriate files, and have those files transferred to their own system.

Telnet is an application and a set of protocols that allows a user's Internet-connected terminal to act as if it were directly connected to the host computer.

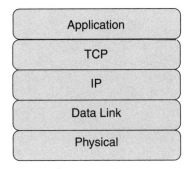

Figure 8.3   The Application Layer

E-mail applications use the Internet as an interconnecting infrastructure to allow messages to be transmitted among users. For example, AOL and CompuServe use the Internet to move e-mail traffic to and from each other.

We can see, therefore, that the Internet layers roughly correspond to the OSI layers, with the exception of session and presentation. This means that Internet applications must handle the tasks generally assigned to session and presentation in the OSI model.

Most PCs today also support a TCP/IP software protocol stack, and most likely use Netscape Navigator or Microsoft Internet Explorer as its application software. On the server end, all of the bottom layers are identical, and the application is the web server and any custom software, such as shopping or search engine applications. As mentioned earlier, each layer has its own set of dialogs and its own language in which to conduct those. For the application layer, for example, the language and protocol are contained within HTML commands and responses.

Internet Security Architecture

Given the architectures described earlier, where are the vulnerabilities and, specifically, what countermeasures can be taken to thwart potential attacks in this architecture? The placement of these security components constitutes a Security Architecture for Internet configurations. Note that, as in any architecture, the components are designed with a great deal of flexibility and depending on particular needs of specific situations, the selection of components and their interrelationships may vary significantly.

Two Approaches to Security

Over time, two distinct approaches have evolved to applying security counter-measures: *networked-coupled security* and *application-coupled security*. As the names imply, the first philosophy favors the use of securing the network infrastructure, while the second builds security into the applications themselves.

Network-Coupled Security

In a network-coupled scheme, the focus is to make the network itself a trusted and secure subsystem so that the applications can assume the data being transmitted is safe, comes from authorized users, and is being delivered to the appropriate recipients. If the network itself is secure, then the applications do not have to do anything special to operate in a secure environment—they simply assume that the network itself is performing all security functions.

Applications which operate in the OSI and Internet environments do not concern themselves with sequencing of packets, validation of IP addresses. The applications assume that the layers below in the supporting protocol stacks have done their job, and therefore the applications can concentrate on the data content. Similarly, in a secure network environment, applications can assume that the lower levels are handling the security.

The most significant advantage to network-coupled security is that applications do not have to be security aware. Applications which are not security aware can be moved into a secure environment without modification. Less obvious, but equally important, is that the use of a consistent security mechanism within the network allows applications to inter-operate from a security standpoint. There is no possibility that different applications will insist on different authentication schemes, key management schemes, etc.

Application-Coupled Security

Proponents of this scheme argue that the application knows best what kind of security is required for that application. Therefore, control of the security aspects should rest in the application layer. To these proponents, the need to create security aware applications is not a disadvantage, but rather a natural and reasonable consequence of the need to apply security at that level. Similarly, the potential for interoperability issues is seen as a flexibility advantage to the proponents of application-coupled security, who argue that a "one size fits all" approach in network security is insufficient for the broad range of security requirements.

Different Tools for Different Layers

There is no shortage of technology available to secure an organization's Internet connections. More appropriate questions have to do with which tools to use at which layers for effective secure communications.

Early on, router manufacturers recognized the key role they could play in this endeavor, and have placed filtering capabilities in their products to establish a primary front line of defense. A router's ability to examine and discriminate network traffic based on the IP packet addresses is known as a *screening router*. Some advanced routers provide the capability to screen packets based upon other criteria such as the type of protocol (http, ftp, udp), the source address, and the destination address fields for a particular type of protocol. This way, a communications manager can build "profiles" of users who are allowed access to different applications based on the protocols. Such a case is shown below.

The packet filtering of the screening router is enhanced with authentication software, which can add either password authentication or challenge authentication. In the scenario described above, simple filtering, even with profiles, cannot authenticate that the individual on the other end of the connection is in fact the individual who should have access to the applications and data residing on the server connected to the local LAN. Therefore, we need to add PAP/CHAP authentication to accomplish this, which provides another layer of security to the system.

The screening router either alone or in combination with authentication, is known as a *firewall*, because it keeps the "fire" of unsecured communications outside a protective "wall."

Protecting against unauthorized access to the data by controlling what is allowed to communicate with the protected servers will guard against many of the vulnerabilities of networks. However, these schemes do not prevent espionage and theft of the data, which may be captured en route between two validated correspondents. This is an area where the addition of encryption and key management, will provide effective countermeasures. By encrypting the data and properly managing the keys to the encryption and decryption, the data which is intercepted is rendered unusable, and at the same time unmodifiable, thereby adding a further layer of protection for the data.

Beyond this level, additional security is still available coupled to the applications, as mentioned earlier. For example, database systems also have authentication capabilities with user names and passwords as well as profiles, access control lists, and the like. It is possible to add yet more layers of security beyond those discussed so far by adding similar technologies to the application layer.

In these schemes, applications could also issue challenge passwords beyond those required to gain access to the network, thereby increasing the security of the data by decreasing the odds that a single error (lost password, etc.) could compromise the application or the data. One common form of application level security is the use of Secure Socket Layer (SSL) directly coupled with the application. In order for SSL to work, both the Browser client and the Server application must support its use, making the application security aware.

Managing the Risk

Network security is all about managing risks and using this risk management analysis to provide appropriate security at an affordable price. This section will explore a Risk Management tool, which can be used to analyze the risks in your organization and take appropriate countermeasures.

Risk Determination

Risks can be characterized by two criteria: the likelihood that a particular attack will be successful, and the consequences of the results if the attack is successful. Security costs money, and therefore we must use that money wisely and only spend it where there is a real likelihood of significant damage. Risk mitigation strategies, then, focus on either minimizing the likelihood of occurrence (by employing countermeasures), or by minimizing the consequences of the attack.

One way to depict this is to characterize the risks along two axes, one indicating increasing likelihood of an attack succeeding, and a second indicating increasingly dire consequences. The individual attacks are plotted according to the two axes, and depending on where they fall, they can be characterized as worthy of defending or not. If an attack is considered serious enough to defend against, countermeasures are developed to reposition the attack into the lower left-hand quadrant.

CGI

CGI (Common Gateway Interface) is the interface between the web site's HTTP (HyperText Transport Protocol) server and the other resources of the server's host computer.

CGI is not really a language or a protocol in the strictest senses of those terms. It is actually just a set of commonly-named variables and agreed-upon conventions for passing information back and forth between the client (your web browser) and the server (the computer that sends web pages to the client). When viewed in this admittedly simplistic light, CGI becomes much less intimidating.

The Common Gateway Interface (CGI) makes the World Wide Web interactive. CGI enables users to do more than simply read static files; it enables them to perform tasks such as searching for information, filling out and submitting forms, and more.

This capability makes the web a far more useful place and has been widely adopted by the Internet community. Throughout the universities, laboratories, companies, and other organizations that comprise the web, CGI scripts are developed, refined, shared—and sometimes compromised.

As always, whenever you allow somebody to execute tasks on your machine, you are opening a potential security hole and you need to make sure it is adequately plugged.

The Mechanism

Basically, there are two parts to a CGI "script":

1. An executable (the script itself)
2. An HTML page that drives the executable

    The executable can be just about anything that runs, including system calls, Perl scripts, shell scripts, and compiled programs (C, Pascal).

The HTML page is actually optional. CGI scripts can be used without user input to increment page counters, display the day and date. If the user is to enter any information, however, the HTML page is needed. When both parts are properly constructed, the CGI action is performed as follows, as shown in **Figure 8.4**.

- The user pulls the HTML form page from the server onto the client machine.
- The user fills out the form on the client machine.
- The user presses *Submit,* which then sends an execute request to the server. (The client-side browser interprets the form into an execute re-

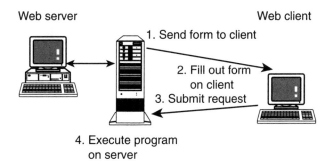

Figure 8.4 CGI Execution Cycle

quest, which identifies the server-side program and includes the information that was filled into the form.)

- The server executes the requested program.

The same basic process occurs for other CGI scripts that accept user input. A clickable imagemap, for example, sends the image to the client machine and issues an execute request that specifies which part of the image was clicked on.

The fundamental strength of CGI is its simplicity. Entering information on the form and all other manipulation is performed on the client machine, so the server doesn't have to worry about it. All that the server has to do is to execute the request when it is issued.

There also lies the fundamental security weakness within CGI. Because the HTML page itself is transferred to the client machine, the user has an unrestricted ability to edit the page at will and to enter whatever he/she pleases. The execute request might easily be a good deal different from what you expect.

A Simple Shell Breach

The most commonly cited examples of CGI security breaches involve cajoling the shell into performing something unexpected. Aside from capturing a password file, malicious users can also exploit poorly defended CGI to access other sensitive files; install and execute their own programs on your system (including *Trojan horses* that monitor system activity and report back to the user); install other viruses; or gain an overall map of the file system in order to search for potential weaknesses.

Not all of the weaknesses are at the system level (and UNIX is not the only vulnerable operating system). Other vulnerabilities that have been identified include the following:

- Certain mail programs allow a ~ to execute arbitrary programs.
- Server-side includes have been tricked into executing commands embedded within HTML comments in the input.
- C programs that misplace the array boundaries have been tricked into executing programs via very long input.
- Some early sendmail programs allowed any user to execute arbitrary programs.

This is by no means a complete list. More breaches have been identified; others have been invented but not yet identified; still others have not yet been invented. The basic point, however, remains the same. CGI should always be used with caution.

How to Make CGI Secure

As with other areas of computer security, the basic idea behind securing CGI is to understand the demonstrated and potential threats, to counter these threats, and to monitor system activity for unusual events.

Start with an adequately secured server. This includes appropriate screening at the router, turning off unneeded daemons, creating a non-privileged WWW user and group, and restricting the file system. Additional precautions may be required, depending upon the partition in which you are working, who the intended audience is, and the sensitivity level of the data on the machine. These precautions including monitoring who accesses the scripts and the other activities those users perform, and consulting with your computer security officer as needed. Beyond the basics, there are other methods of improving CGI security.

Always check for special characters such as ";" before you open a shell. You can do this either by restricting the input you accept or by escaping any dangerous characters. In Perl, for example, the following line escapes dangerous UNIX shell characters within a variable:

$var =~ s/([;<>*\ | `\$!#\(\)\[\]\{\}:'"]@)/\\$1/g;

Among the other things to check:

- For server-side includes, check for "<" and ">" in order to identify and validate any embedded HTML tags.

- For scripts that utilize e-mail, validate that the addresses are within an acceptable domain (e.g., make sure they're "@llnl.gov").
- Look for any occurrence of "/../" (which might indicate that the user is attempting to access higher levels of the directory structure).
- For selection lists, check to make sure that the value sent is a valid choice.
- Prefer compiled programs to interpreted scripts.

The last one is a very general guideline, by no means an ironclad "rule." The basic idea is that a compiled program (e.g., a binary executable from C) is more difficult to make sense of if a user is able to get a copy of it. This in turn makes it more difficult for the user to search for potential weaknesses within the program.

Counterbalancing this general preference are the facts that an interpreted program (e.g., Perl) is generally easier for the programmer to understand (including whoever has to support the program after it is written) and easier to test (no need to compile before each test). Hence, even though the compiled programs are generally preferred, there are many specific cases where the interpreted program is perfectly acceptable.

Again, this is a very general guideline—more of a caution than a rule. There is nothing inherently wrong with opening a shell, provided that the security implications are understood and addressed. Frequently, though, it is easier to sidestep the shell concerns and call a program directly.

In UNIX/Perl, for example, a new shell is opened by system, exec, eval, backticks, etc. Hence, the basic weakness of the following line (taken from the above example) stems from the fact that it is operating at the system level in its own shell:

```
system("/usr/lib/sendmail -t $send_to < $temp_file");
```

Keep in mind, however, that when you call a program directly you are in a sense trading the known security vulnerabilities of the shell for the potentially unknown vulnerabilities of the program. Users need to execute CGI scripts, but there is no reason for them to have read or write permissions. Similarly, users need to read the HTML driver files (and to read and execute their directory), but there is no need for them to have write or execute permission to the files (or write permission to their directory).

There are many CGI scripts freely available on the web. While these can often serve as a good starting point, many of them come from university environments that do not have the same security concerns as the laboratory. A number have been demonstrated to contain security holes, and some have even been found to contain Trojan horses.

Any time you *borrow* a free script as a starting point, make sure to validate it for security. Check it as outlined above, and modify it as needed. Above all, do not run anything that contains any lines you do not understand.

As CGI programming has become more popular, the amount of information about it and security has grown.

The Tools for Data Warehousing Web Security

Secure Sockets Layer (SSL)

The SSL is inserted between the TCP protocol and the application protocol. The SSL protocol operates in two phases. In the first phase, the sender and receiver agree on the read and write keys to be used, and then in the second phase data is encrypted using the keys chosen in the first phase. Authentication and secure key exchange is also achieved using the RSA public key encryption algorithm.

HyperText Transport Protocol Secure (HTTPS)

By layering a version of SSL between HTTP and TCP, Netscape has developed a secure version of HTTP as well.

Proxy Servers

A proxy server is a firewall implemented in a hardware unit such as a workstation on an NT server, rather than in a router. This device looks at all of the data in each packet, not just address and headers. In most cases, the proxy examines the content and replaces the network address in the packet with proxy destinations that are known to be secure. Besides hiding the network from the outside world, they provide more control over the actual data at the application level. However, because they inspect all of the data in each packet, there have been reports of some significant performance degradations in high traffic areas.

Encryption

Encryption is a technique as old as the Romans. It is simply the scrambling of the transmitted text using a set of rules (algorithms, which in today's world means mathematical manipulations) which is known to the recipient, but hopefully to no one else. The recipient can then use the same set of rules in reverse to unscramble the coded text and read the intended message. There are two classes of encryption algorithm. They are:

1. *Symmetric key.* A symmetric key algorithm is one where the same key is used both to encode and decode the message. The most popular symmetric key algorithm is the Data Encryption Standard (DES), whose major advantage is that it is fast and widely implemented. Its major limitations are its relatively small key size (56 bits), which weakens the security of the algorithm, and the need to exchange a secret key between the communicating parties, before secure communication can be established.

   A variant of DES, Triple-DES or 3DES is based on using DES three times (normally in an encrypt-decrypt-encrypt sequence with three different, unrelated keys). Many people consider Triple-DES to be much safer than plain DES.

2. *Asymmetric key.* It is a surprising fact that there are some algorithms which are difficult to reverse, even when the algorithm, the key, and the encrypted data are all available, unless some other piece of information is known. A public key encryption system is based on an algorithm of this type. Two keys are generated. One is kept private and the other can be made public. Two systems that want to hold a secure conversation can exchange their public keys. When one system sends to the other, it will encrypt the message using the other system's public key. Even though an attacker might observe the exchange of keys and an encrypted message, the irreversibility of the public key algorithm ensures that the data is secure.

Although public key algorithms solve the key distribution problem, they are much slower than symmetric key algorithms. When implemented in hardware, DES is up to 10,000 times faster than other known algorithms. If efficiency is required, a public key system can be used to securely exchange symmetric keys, which can then be used for the bulk of the data transfer.

Firewalls

The term *firewall* has become a generic term for a spectrum of technologies intended to provide protection from communications attacks on an organization. Screening routers, application gateways, proxy servers, authentication servers are all examples of firewalls in use today. It is possible, and often desirable, to combine these different technologies according to the needs of the organization and their budget limitations.

Application Gateways

All packets are addressed to an application on the gateway that relays the packets between the two communication points. In most application gateway implementations, additional packet filter machines are required to control and screen the traffic between the gateway and the networks. Typically, this is a use of bastion hosts. These are secure but inefficient, since they are not transparent to users and applications.

Screening Routers

One of the most cost efficient and ubiquitous techniques for securing a network, a screening router, sometimes known as a packet filtering router, will allow known users (known by their IP addresses) to connect to specified applications (determined by their port address), thereby limiting the connections of even those users allowed to enter through the firewall, and completely denying any connections to those not authorized to access any applications.

Authenticating Servers

Authenticating servers are often used in conjunction with screening routers to provide authentication services, thus verifying that those users who claim to be originating from valid addresses are in fact who they say they are.

Managing Security

Technical security alone cannot provide appropriate security at an acceptable cost. Before implementing technical solutions, you must resolve two areas of security management. One involves managing the risk during the design and implementation stage, and the other involves managing the risk during operations.

Risk assessment for a security architecture is technically complicated, especially in a distributed environment where many products and protocols may be used.

Technical security does not work unless it is supported by appropriate processes, the right control structure, and educated attitudes toward security. Operational security addresses these issues. As many organizations have well-established security operations departments, I will not discuss this topic in great detail.

Authentication capabilities, especially single sign-on, are limited today. It may be some time before there is widespread availability of single sign-on authentication implemented on the server side to cover many environments. In the short term, the most promising approach is the use of SmartCard or PC-Card technology to give the appearance of single sign-on by holding many keys.

Distributed systems security is an exciting and important area. Providing rock-solid security for the Inter/intra/extranet is essential for it to reach its enormous potential.

Conclusions

Currently, the vast majority of secure data warehouse sites on the web use the SSL security protocol. Very few enterprises, not even the Federal Government and the military, can afford "security at any price." Eventually, you will be forced to stop building security features and learn to live with the residual risks of the data warehouse system. Where you stop depends on how much you are willing to pay to get the amount of security appropriate to the applications.

One typical and common-sense approach is to develop a security infrastructure incrementally. Start inexpensively with packet filtering and authenticating routers as the beginning firewall. Many experts contend that integrated routers and firewalls can successfully defend a majority of attacks. Later, if you still need more, you can add encryption and key management for further enhancements. At each point, determine where the vulnerabilities are and what consequences would ensue from a successful attack.

METADATA AND WEB DISTRIBUTED SYSTEMS

Introduction

Not too long ago, raw information was extremely difficult to acquire and therefore highly prized. Today, you can get higher quality raw data, including satellite pictures if you wish, over the Internet.

Data has become an abundant commodity. We can get it anywhere and everywhere. However, just as with any other item which becomes a commodity, data by itself is losing value, in part simply because there is so much of it. Now that data is plentiful, we are faced with the problem of separating the significant facts from the rest.

Data Acquisition

We do know that in order to make good business decisions we need good data. The process which has been generally accepted as good business practice begins with:

1. Acquiring quality raw data
2. Combining and integrating the data to make useful information
3. Analyzing the information and making high quality decisions

The torrent of raw data has added more choices, and therefore complexity, to the process. In this section, we discuss the issues confronting management today as they grapple with the quantity of raw data and the need to know what the data assets are and how to achieve the goal of better decision making.

Data from Everywhere

As pointed out earlier, raw data is proliferating rapidly. Data is flowing into organizations from suppliers and customers. Corporations are coupling together with webs of suppliers, partners, and customers, exchanging myriad information through a spectrum of technologies such as Electronic Funds Transfer (EFT) systems, e-mail, Electronic Document Interchange (EDI) systems, and a host of other data acquisition and networking applications.

The existing legacy systems within enterprises continue to generate data on every parameter imaginable, such as orders, sales, revenues, employee information, manufacturing schedules, and inventory. As technology expands, the computer costs continue to fall; as user sophistication increases in the use of information technology, the proliferation of the technology adds to the exponential growth of the data it generates.

The information technology advances of the last many years have added significantly to the amount and depth of data produced, managed, and stored. The changes in achieving operating efficiencies by centralizing, decentralizing, and re-engineering has created the opportunity for the data used by one group to have a different meaning from the data used by another group in the same organization, despite the use of the same application development tools, applications, database products, spreadsheets, and other client-friendly products.

Recently, we have begun to recognize the value of using data as a corporate asset. The concept of a data warehouse has emerged as a technology by which management can get a single comprehensive view of the state of the organization. Data is extracted at regular intervals from existing systems and placed in the warehouse, summarized to allow management to look at trends, but also available in detail for drill-down data access and analysis.

However, the problem becomes complicated, when the same data element may be used by different divisions to mean different things. Different groups may have different standards and approaches. This is an everyday reality to most companies working with data warehousing systems.

The availability of data and the staggering proportions of the quantities available makes it difficult to deal with. When data was scarce, the amount available was consumable by users with fairly primitive tools. Now that data is plentiful, we are faced with the problem of separating the significant facts from the rest.

The acute issue is knowing which data to use to create useful information. The end goal is to make higher quality decisions than your predecessors could. The varieties of raw data has made the process complex. What we need to do is put the data in context, give the data meaning, relevance, and purpose, and make it complete and accurate. Data which is viewed in this light is called *information*, because we can use it for deductive and inductive insights which lead us to quality decisions.

Some Facts about Data

Data is by and large dispersed across the enterprise. Each department, division, subdivision, group, branch, or section is today capable of generating its own unique caches of data. The information technology advances have added significantly to the amount and depth of data produced, managed, and stored.

- The waves of centralizing/decentralizing/re-engineering along with the technological changes of mainframe to two-tier/multi-tier/web client/server architectures have created the opportunity for the data to be shared.

- Also, the data generated by each group belongs only to itself, and is intended only for its own uses.
- We also know the potential for integrating these disparate data elements across various departments is poor without some significant work.

The need of using all of the organization's data to get a complete picture of the enterprise is deemed essential. In addition, management is recognizing the need to view data from multiple departments to get some kind of combined view of operations.

Data as a Potential Resource

Faced with these dilemmas, management has realized that data is a resource but only if all its important attributes are known and understood. Data must be set in context, have meaning to its users, be relevant, and have purpose.

Data must also be complete and accurate. We must know the sources for a particular data element, which one is being used in the data warehouse, and why. We must know the business rules which impact how we view data. Only when these data characteristics are known, understood, and applied can data be fully utilized, and only then can we begin the reliable building of information from the data which ultimately leads to quality decision making.

The need to understand the data leads to a need for managing the data. This need is particularly acute in systems such as data warehouses whose primary purpose is to provide answers and supply a fertile ground for exploration and insight.

Having thus established a requirement to understand and manage the properties of the data, the question then becomes, what is the best mechanism for achieving this. What we are really talking about then is a store of attributes about the data, or data about data. Semanticists have termed this concept *metadata*, from the Greek word "meta," which means a later stage, transcending, or situated behind. Literally, then, we are talking about data that sits behind the operational data, and that describes its origin, meaning, and derivation. Metadata can range from a conceptual overview of the real world to detailed physical specifications for a particular database management system.

A data resource becomes useless without readily available high quality metadata. Its primary objective is to provide a comprehensive guide to the data resource.

Metadata Status in an Organization

One of the better definitions is that it is the *meaning* of data, in its narrowest sense, but also in its broadest, *relational* sense. The business users, to whom you want to deliver information, know their data.

If organizations today are having problems managing data, then how can they manage metadata? Most companies suffer from the syndrome, in that they are so rushed to implement systems that the planning and documentation aspects of most projects are the first to suffer. Pressure from management and users to gain the information or functions they need to do their work leads inevitably to a rushed implementation where there is little thought given to coordinating data elements with other groups who may use the same concept and few if any resources dedicated to a careful documentation of the properties of the attributes, the business rules used in their derivation, and so on.

In short, the problem continues. In most companies, the metadata situation is worse than the data situation. Along with the disparate data arriving from multiple sources from within and outside the corporation, there are multiple tools creating metadata in a variety of formats.

It is typical that companies want to rapidly implement data warehousing systems and then discover themselves in a metadata dilemma. That is, they have a critical need for readily available high-quality metadata to leverage their data resource, yet the organization has no system in place for maintaining adequate metadata. As a result, many data warehousing projects slow down as an organization grapples with these issues brought about by disparate data and poor quality metadata. In any given project, there is a need to include business experts, domain experts, and data experts so that the metadata that is formed is relevant and useful as applied to the project's purpose.

The Role of Metadata

The role of metadata is rapidly expanding as organizations develop a data warehousing strategy that creates operational databases, integrated data warehouses, and multiple data marts. The *data warehouse* increasingly utilizes multiple databases that have common elements but serve different functions. Metadata must describe the enterprise warehouse even if it is no longer a single database residing on one server.

The role of metadata is being redefined as providing data about distributed information resources. Metadata must isolate the user from the complexities of accessing distributed information resources, while facilitating the currency and synchronization of multiple databases. Failing this, users are confronted with precisely the problems that data warehousing was intended to solve—different answers to the same question and the resulting lack of confidence in the information obtained.

Every software product involved in loading, accessing, or analyzing the data warehouse requires metadata. In each case, metadata provides the unifying link between the data warehouse or data mart and the application processing layer of the software product. Application software vendors have each developed their own metadata to address the unique requirements and capabilities of their products. This creates a binding relationship between the data warehouse and each application software product.

The obvious problem with application-level metadata is that managing and synchronizing the metadata used by each application software product is a very difficult task, particularly if there is little commonality among vendors' metadata requirements. The focus is on synchronizing and sharing common application-level metadata that is needed to establish the bond between tools and the data warehouse. However, application-level metadata only addresses requirements for metadata that facilitates the linking of application code to the database. It does nothing to address a growing need for metadata that addresses the needs of users.

The largest and most complex data warehouse on earth is the World Wide Web. It consists of hundreds of thousands of information resources managed in the ultimate distributed architecture that is accessed by millions of users each day. The web serves as a useful model for what must be achieved inside the enterprise with respect to organizing information resources for easy user access. Of course, the web is composed mostly of static pages of text and images, generally referred to as "unstructured content." In contrast, the alphanumeric data contained within a data warehouse represents structured content. As Internet technologies grow to adopt intranets and extranets within the enterprise, adding this structured content from a data warehouse to the unstructured content information resources is essential.

Content and the Internet

The important lesson of the Internet is that content comes first. Content, unstructured or structured, is the user interface. For the first time, application logic is hidden beneath the content. Unlike application software developed for diskettes, the Internet user interacts with the application only via the content.

Finding information on the Internet is surprisingly easy because users are beginning to think in terms of content rather than the application code used to create the content. Users do not need to know if the information exists or where it is located. Search engines only require the user to ask for content without regard to an application. This important web-navigation tool has trained the user to focus on the items they need, not the application software that delivers it. By leveraging the web's native publishing and navigation capabilities, such as a search engine, users require minimal training whenever a new application is added to their intranet.

Intranets, which include structured content information resources, must also rely on search engines to provide metadata about the location of information resources contained within the data warehouse. The Internet and corporate intranets use the URL (Universal Resource Locator) as the common address for all information resources. From the user's perspective, this is the most useful form of metadata (user-level metadata) because it describes the location of all available information resources.

Metadata Levels

A data warehouse without adequate metadata is like a filing cabinet stuffed with papers, but without any folders or labels. Generally speaking, there are three main layers of metadata in a data warehouse:

- Application-level (or operational) metadata. This defines the structure of the data held in operational databases and used by operational applications. It is often quite complex, and tends to be application- or department-oriented.
- Core warehouse metadata. This is held in the catalog of the warehouse's database system. It is subject-oriented and is based on abstractions of real world entities like "project," "customer," or "organization." It defines the way in which the transformed data is to be interpreted, as well as any additional views that may have been created. This includes decision-support aggregates and computed fields, as well as cross-subject warehouse views and definitions.
- User-level metadata. Maps the core warehouse metadata to business concepts that are familiar and useful to end users.

As organizations begin to integrate data warehouses and data marts with the corporate intranets, users are provided with universal access to a wide range of structured and unstructured content. Decision support is extended beyond the confines of an elite group of power users to front-line decision makers throughout the enterprise. At one level, the difference is between the requirements of traditional and enterprise decision support.

Traditional decision support requires a robust set of data analysis tools for the users who often spend hours, days, or even weeks exploring a business issue from every perspective. Enterprise decision support responds to the users' needs for the content that will be employed immediately to make the hundreds of tactical decisions that are made every day throughout the organization.

The major contribution of the intranet and the integration of data warehousing technologies with the web technologies is that they focus more attention on the information needs of all users within the enterprise, making content available everywhere. In other words, the content of the data warehouse should be accessible from a browser, search engine, e-mail, or Lotus Notes. The user should arrive at the same content destination regardless of how they request the information. In addition to creating a metadata link between the application and the database, a link must also be established between the common tools of the intranet and the browser interface.

If URLs are to serve a metadata role to allow a user to invoke dynamic access and analysis of the data warehouse, the OLAP application processing layer must have some means of registering virtual reports to user-level metadata. This virtual document is essentially a reference to a program that, on demand, dynamically generates SQL queries, performs analytic processes, and formats final documents for display in a browser. In effect, this provides a means of registering virtual documents to an intranet search engine.

The virtual documents are dynamically generated and formatted for display in a browser (report or graphic representation) only when requested by the user via standard browser selection methods. The key is to dynamically generate the actual report based on the user's request. The virtual document is merely a template that is completed based on the selections that are presented to the user.

Data and Metadata

Metadata is an abstraction from data. It is high-level data that describes lower-level data. Software is full of metadata, for example,

- Record descriptions in a COBOL program
- Logical view descriptions in a data server's catalog.
- SQL Create statements
- Entity-relationship diagrams in a CASE tool's repository

Metadata as a Key to Data

Metadata is instrumental in transforming raw data into knowledge. For instance, it is metadata in the shape of a field definition that tells us that a given stream of bits is a customer's address, part of a photographic image, or a code fragment in a given computer's machine language. If the metadata gets mixed up or out of alignment, none of the data will make sense. The address will contain unrecognizable characters, the code will give unpredictable results and probably crash any process that runs it—even the photograph will not look quite the way it should, though our eyes may not detect the difference.

For example, a large multinational corporation is building a data warehouse and loading it with data and metadata from departmental and local databases. In one such case, it turns out that there are over a dozen different ways of encoding the unique badge number allocated to each employee. If one department uses a 32-bit integer for the purpose, while the others use binary coded decimal, the chances are that applications written to use these two representations would be unable to interpret each other's data. Organizations are increasingly turning to external sources of information, in search of both impartial data and the expertise of specialists in other fields of knowledge. There is still more scope for confusion and misunderstanding in the interpretation of external data. In fact, information from one source may flatly contradict another.

Without metadata, the data is meaningless. If you take away data definitions, it becomes impossible to query a database. We do not even know where the data is, or how much of it to take. All we could hope to recover would be a string of ones and zeroes. In the early days of commercial computing, each application created and handled its own data files. Because the files' metadata was embedded in the application's data definitions, no application could make sense of another application's files. When databases were introduced, one of the greatest advantages they brought was that the metadata was stored in the database catalog, not in the individual programs. There was one version of the truth, and that was held in the database.

When we describe *structured data* in a database, we are implying the presence of metadata. Relational databases can store information for which they have no corresponding predefined data types, but it is not a pretty sight. *Binary large objects* or BLOBs are a case in point. These are used to store large complex data items, such as maps, medical X-rays or scans, photographs, or CAD diagrams. Because relational databases lack the metadata to describe these items, we term them *unstructured* data, in relational terms. However object-oriented databases can store these items and many others in a structured format, even including the code routines needed to make sense of them.

Metadata in Operational and Warehouse Environments

In the operational environment, metadata is mostly valuable to software developers and database administrators. Operational databases are accessed only by transaction processing applications, which contain data definitions embedded within them. The end users—people like bank clerks, travel agents, and hospital staff—do not need to know how information is held in the database. They simply interact with the forms and screens provided by the applications they use in the course of their everyday work.

The decision-support environment is very different than the on-line transaction environment. Here, data users and executives are looking for useful facts and correlations which they will recognize when they find them. Routine applications are of no use to them. Since they need to interpret the data successfully, they need to understand its structure and meaning.

Metadata in the Data Mart

One of the most important components of the data mart is that of metadata. **Figure 9.1** depicts metadata in the data mart environment.

Metadata in the data mart environment serves the same purpose as metadata in the data warehouse. Data mart metadata allows the data mart decision-support user to find out where data is in the process of discovery and exploration. Data mart metadata contains the following components:

- Identification of the source of data
- Simple descriptive information about the data mart, including tables, attributes, and relationships
- Description of the customization that has occurred as the data passes from the data warehouse to the data mart
- Definitions

Data mart metadata is created by and updated from the load programs that move data into the data marts. There needs to be linkage between the metadata found in the data mart and the metadata found in the data warehouse. Among other things, the metadata linkage between the two environments needs to describe how the data in the two environments is related.

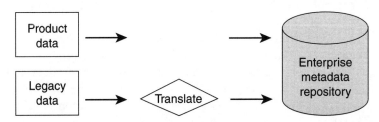

Figure 9.1 Metadata Representation

The Necessary Metadata

Unreliable or missing metadata leads to the familiar situation where one department tells that the corporate profits are up 10%, while another says they are down 15%. Each department is using its own figures, collected in accordance with its own procedures and interpreted by its own applications. The discrepancies produced in this way are sometimes referred to as the *algorithmic differential*. In the absence of hard facts, decision making lapses into a chaotic tug of war.

Most corporations have tried to implement a data dictionary of some kind and have come to consider the whole technology a failure. Developers and data administrators were supposed to keep the dictionary up to date at all times, but they saw this as an extra chore that stole time from their real work. Once a few changes are made to a system without corresponding updates to the dictionary, that dictionary is out of sync and is rendered unusable. It is no longer synchronized with the live system, and everyone can legitimately ignore it.

The data warehouse, on the other hand, is set up for the benefit of business users and executives. The personnel who create and administer the warehouse are there to help the end-users get their work done. If they need metadata, then the warehouse support staff makes sure they get it.

Planning for Change

In the data warehouse, not just the data but the metadata keeps on changing. The business users are continually looking for interesting new patterns, and this can lead them to compare information from the four corners of the enterprise. It can also lead them to keep asking for new sets of data, which have to be replicated from operational systems or imported from outside sources. The warehouse's metadata map has to be extended to embrace each new addition.

Besides, many business entities, such as product lines, organizational structures, markets, and plans, change regularly. Some of the factors to evaluate are:

- Different sources of data
- A different definition of the product line
- Different sales territories (perhaps with the same names)
- Different shipping structures

Once such factors have been considered, the various changes in the basis of measurement can be noted on the report. Not only must warehouse administrators keep up with ever-changing corporate definitions, they must also agree on a single version of the truth. An executive in one multinational was once heard to remark that if the revenues for which credit was claimed by all the product line managers were totaled, the resulting value would exceed the corporation's actual revenue by a factor of five. In another company, a marketing manager found that the product costs for which he was responsible were 15% under budget for the quarter.

In another situation, a strenuous scrutiny of various databases revealed that the manager of a systems integration unit had unilaterally created a set of new part numbers under which the products were sold as part of a systems integration contract. This resulted in diverting several million dollars worth of products from the marketing manager's top line to the systems integration manager's. Once these facts were ascertained, it took a matter of minutes to set things right. But only a manager who was on intimate terms with metadata would have been able to uncover the facts.

Metadata Components

Warehouse metadata is not very different from ordinary database metadata, although it is versioned in order to permit historical analysis. The following factors of warehouse metadata may be considered:

- *Extract history:* Whenever historical information is analyzed, meticulous update records have to be kept. The metadata history is a good place to start any time-based report, because the user has to know when the rules changed in order to apply the right rules to the right data. If sales territories were remapped in 2001, then it has to be noted that results from before that date may not be directly comparable with more recent results.

- *Aliases:* Aliases can make the warehouse much more user-friendly by allowing a table to be queried by a full product name. They also become useful when different departments wish to use their own names to refer to the same underlying data. Obviously, though, aliases could also cause a great deal of confusion if they are not carefully tracked.

- *Summary algorithms:* A typical data warehouse contains lightly and heavily summarized data as well as detailed records. The algorithms for summarizing the detail data are obviously of interest to anyone who takes responsibility for interpreting the meaning of the summaries. This metadata can also save time by making it easier to decide which level of summarization is most appropriate for a given purpose

- *Mapping:* The mapping information records how data from operational sources is transformed onto the warehouse. Often, parts of the same data warehouse may be in different stages of development. *Status information* can be used to keep information classifications.

- *Volumetric information:* The volumetric information lets users know how much data they are dealing with, so that they can have some idea how much their queries will cost in terms of time and resources. Volumetrics could usefully include such information as number of rows, growth rate, usage characteristics, indexing, and byte specifications.

- *Tools:* Many well-known software tools have long been used for generating metadata in other contexts. These include CASE tools, and, to a limited extent, compilers and 4GLs too. More recently, vendors have designed tools specifically to create data warehouse metadata.

- *Life expectancy:* It is also useful to publish the criteria and *timescale*s for purging old data.

- *Ownership:* Operational databases are often owned by particular departments or business groups. In the nature of an enterprise data warehouse, however, all data is stored in a common format and accessible to all. This makes it necessary to identify the originator of each set of data, so that inquiries and corrections can be made to the proper group. It is useful to distinguish between *ownership* of data in the operational environment and in the data warehouse.

- *Access patterns:* It is desirable to record patterns of access to the warehouse in order to optimize and tune performance. Less frequently used data can be migrated to cheaper storage media, while various methods can be employed to accelerate access to the data that is most in demand. Most databases do a good job of hiding such physical details, but specialized performance analysis tools are usually available for accelerated access. There are also some general-purpose tools.

Turning to consumers of metadata, the first obvious category of tools consists of data transfer tools that load data from operational systems into the warehouse. The simplest way is to keep metadata in the data warehouse's own catalog, but some transformation products keep metadata in a separate database while they are working on it.

Tools also provide a very useful extra layer of metadata between the end user and the raw database catalog. The data warehouse is only as good as its facilities for handling metadata. Every time data moves from one place to another, it is vital that it is correctly and appropriately labeled. Such essential activities as filtering, cleansing, summarizing, and consolidating all involve mapping from one metadata representation to another.

If there is to be any hope of setting up a fast and reliable system of bulk replication from the operational systems to the data warehouse, it follows that metadata checking and mapping must be carried out automatically.

Enterprise Repository

Some areas to focus on in reviewing repository functionality are discussed in the following sections.

Non-proprietary Relational Database Management System

A repository should ideally use an industry standard DBMS, which provides significant advantages over vendor-proprietary DBMSs. These advantages include advanced tools and utilities for database management (such as backups and performance tuning) as well as dramatically enhanced reporting capabilities. Furthermore, maintainability and accessibility are enhanced by an *open* system.

Using a standard database also allows the repository use to focus on the quality of the repository, not the features of the database management system. Non-proprietary DBMS also allows the user to take advantage of new features made available by any DBMS vendor.

Fully Extensible Meta Model

A repository should be completely self-defining and extensible, based on a common entity/relationship model. By using a model that reflects industry standards, it can provide users with the ability to easily customize the meta model to meet their specific needs. The repository should incorporate the following meta model features:

- Adding *user* views (with different screen layouts or validations) to entities or relationships
- Adding or modifying commands or user exits
- Adding or modifying an *entity type*
- Adding or modifying a linkage between entity types (associations or relationships)
- Adding, deleting, or modifying *attributes* of relationships or entities,
- Modifying the list of allowable values for an attribute type

- Adding custom command macros
- Adding or modifying help and *informational messages*.

Application Programming Interface (API) Access

An API access to the repository can provide an organization with the flexibility needed to create a metadata management system which suits their unique needs. Architecture can make the repository powerful by allowing users to create custom applications and programs.

In addition, the separation of metadata from the tools that access and manipulate it by the API is a flexible feature. The tools can manipulate metadata through the API, thereby allowing transparent access to the data. If the data structures change, the tools do not need to be changed. This allows for greater efficiency and flexibility in an organization's application development.

Central Point of Metadata Control

The repository serves as a central point of control for data, providing a single place of record about information assets across the enterprise. It documents where the data is located, who creates and maintains the data, what application processes it drives, what relationship it has with other data, and how it should be translated and transformed. This provides users with the ability to locate and utilize data that was previously inaccessible. Furthermore, a central location for the control of metadata ensures consistency and accuracy of information, providing users with repeatable, reliable results and the organizations with a competitive advantage.

Impact Analysis Capability

If the repository has an impact analysis facility it can provide virtually unlimited navigation of the repository definitions to provide the total impact of any change. Users easily determine where any entity is used or what it relates to by using impact analysis views.

An impact analysis facility answers the true questions in the analysis phases without forcing a user to sift through large quantities of unfocused information. Furthermore, sophisticated impact analysis capabilities allow better time estimates for system maintenance tasks. They also reduce the amount of rework resulting from faulty impact analysis (e.g., a program not being changed as a result of a change to a table that it queries).

Naming Standards Flexibility

A repository should provide a detailed map of data definitions and elements, thereby allowing an organization to evaluate redundant definitions and elements and decide which ones should be eliminated, translated, or converted. By enforcing naming standards, the repository assists in reducing data redundancies and increasing data sharing, by making the application development process more efficient and therefore less costly. In addition, an easily enforceable standard encourages organizations to define and use consistent data definitions, thereby increasing the reuse of standard definitions across disparate tools.

Versioning Capabilities

In repository discussions, *versioning* can have many different definitions. For example some version control capabilities are:

- Versions as unique occurrences
- Version control as in test versus production (lifecycle phasing)
- Versioning by department or business unit
- Version by aggregate or workstation ID

The repository's versioning capabilities facilitate the application lifecycle development process by allowing developers to work with the same object concurrently. Developers should be able to modify or change objects to meet their requirements without affecting other developers.

Robust Query and Reporting

The repository should provide business users with a vehicle for robust query and report generation. The end user tool should seamlessly pass queries to its own tool or third party products for automatic query generation and execution. Furthermore, business users should be able to create detailed reports from these tools, increasing the amount of valuable decision-support information they are able to receive from the repository.

Data Warehousing Support

The repository provides information about the location and nature of operational data which is critical in the construction of a data warehouse. It acts as a guide to the warehouse data, storing information necessary to define the migration environment, mappings of sources to targets, translation requirements, business rules, and selection criteria to build the warehouse.

Metadata Management

Metadata is a key resource for the warehouse during all phases of its life cycle, from the warehouse construction, through the user access, and into the maintenance and update of the data it holds.

During the past few years there has been a tremendous level of activity in the vendor metadata repository field, largely due to the rapid growth in the data warehouse and data mart markets. Syncing metadata between two products—different functions, different metadata stores (database), or different vendors—is a challenge. You need to get the right piece of metadata at the right level of detail from one product and map it to the right piece of metadata at the right level of detail in the other product. And repeat it for each of the hundreds of other points in metadata space that the two products share in common.

Syncing the metadata between two products is tough. Syncing metadata among each of the half dozen tools it could take to build, run, and access a data warehouse is an almost unthinkable task. But syncing is a necessity for a smooth, robust, efficient data warehouse operation. There are several possible approaches, and some vendors are propagating the concept of a single enterprise-level metadata repository to integrate the enterprise's disparate metadata However, the simplest approach is to have all vendors use the same semantics and collect all of the metadata in a single format in a single location.

Metadata Maintenance

After all the source data has been integrated into a unified whole, all the spelling variants discovered and reconciled, all the data homogenized, how and where do we document the rules used in the integration? The next time we reorganize, how do we get the warehouse to reallocate revenues, costs, and profits to the new set of regions. All of the information about the data gathered for the data warehouse or data mart must be documented and explained if the data is to be of use to the enterprise, and if the system is to be manageable in the future. The second half of the definition of integrated data therefore must include the documentation of the derived consistent and uniform structure, syntax, and semantic notation of the data so as to allow two important benefits:

- Users can understand what the data means, where it comes from, and how it is derived

- Planners and maintenance managers of the warehouse can adapt the definitions, derivations, and sources to accommodate changes in business conditions

All of this, of course, happens within the metadata repository. Management is a critical need for metadata management as part of the challenge of data integration.

Managing Across Data Warehouses

Most large organizations today have had some experience with data warehousing implementations. Today, these typically take the form of data-mart-style implementations in various departmental focus areas such as financial analysis or customer-focused systems assisting business units.

Many organizations have multiple warehousing initiatives underway simultaneously and these systems will most likely be based on products from multiple data warehousing vendors, in the typical decentralized approach of most corporations. This approach has allowed reasonably rapid implementation of these systems. This approach has also demonstrated to the organization the benefit and potential of data warehousing as a business tool at a fraction of the cost of the enterprise data warehouse model. However, as pointed out earlier, this is the typical approach to implementing data warehousing.

Data and metadata are spread across multiple data warehousing systems, and system managers are wondering how best to coordinate and manage the dispersed metadata mess they have today. We must maintain consistency when business rules change as a result of corporate reorganizations, regulatory changes, or other changes in business practices.

Changes are forcing businesses to take a larger view of metadata management systems. Coordinating metadata across multiple data warehouses is one significant step in the right direction, and a repository is just the tool to do that.

A Repository as an Integration Platform

Ideally, a corporation should adopt a repository as a metadata integration platform, making metadata available across the organization. This would serve to manage key metadata across all of the data warehouse and data mart implementations within an organization. This would allow all of the participants to share common data structures, business rule definitions, and data definitions from system to system across the enterprise.

The platform would accept and manage information from multiple sources. These would include systems from major vendor technology databases (e.g., IBM, Informix, Oracle, Microsoft, and Sybase) and across a broad spectrum of tools, from extraction tools to analysis tools. On the output side, the system should provide open access by multiple tools as well as APIs for custom needs.

The metadata repository also facilitates consistency and maintainability. It provides a common understanding across warehouse efforts, promoting sharing and reuse. If a new data element definition is required for a data mart implementation, the platform should permit versioning to support the need. With a shared metadata repository, the exchange of key information between business decision managers (facilitated by good solid end user access tools) becomes more feasible. When multiple data marts and data warehouses are involved, a central metadata platform can simplify and reduce the effort required to maintain them when viewed as a whole.

Factors For Success

To be successful in data warehousing applications, the critical success factors are:

- Deliver the solution quickly.
- Provide users with metadata to help them understand and work with warehouse metadata.
- Deliver high quality data consistent with user requirements.
- Implement a manageable infrastructure to keep costs down.

The above factors are essential, easy to understand, simple to enunciate, and extremely difficult to do well. To demonstrate, let us consider a very common data warehousing application and examine the process and tools used.

The example is the creation and maintenance of an integrated customer profile database. Many companies today are developing such a system to identify individual customers, analyze their buying patterns, support targeted marketing initiatives based on analysis of those buying patterns, and improve the coordination of sales and marketing activities. The coordination of activities is particularly important for companies that have different lines of business that target a common customer base.

The insurance industry provides an example where a typical company may be active in three lines of business (life insurance, health insurance, and fire and casualty insurance). It is not difficult to see how typical suburban homeowners with two cars and a family would be ideal prospects for all three lines of business. Each line of business has personal information on our typical customer, as well as information on policies that the customer purchased or expressed interest in, and premiums quoted or charged. The objective of a data warehouse is to integrate a set of customer profiles to look for cross-selling opportunities and to help target prospects who fit the profiles of the company's best and most profitable customers.

Lifecycle Issues

Repository systems need to contribute to and integrate with the existing legacy system environment and play an active role throughout the lifecycle of data warehousing systems to be truly considered enterprise metadata repositories.

Documenting database and legacy information are important capabilities in metadata repositories. Legacy models provide the information sourcing, data inventorying, and design that are key to developing an effective data warehouse. The metadata surrounding the acquisition, access, and distribution of warehouse data is the key to providing the business user with a complete map of the data warehouse.

The metadata should play an active role in the entire life cycle of the data warehouse and all the output attributes of system and business value. This includes existing legacy system as sources and third party tools. This then leverages the repository's role so it contributes in the development phases as well as the bulk cost of all. These would include systems management, database management, business intelligence, and application development tools and components such as:

- Database management tools that can help create and maintain the database management systems for operational systems, data warehouses, and data marts.

- Systems management tools that can be used to manage jobs, improve performance, and automate operations, not only in operational systems but also in data warehouse systems.

- Business intelligence tools that provide end user access and analysis for making business decisions.

- Application development solutions that help you build, test, deploy, and manage operational and warehouse applications throughout the enterprise.

- Repository-to-CASE interfaces that enable an organization to manage multiple CASE work-stations from the repository. These tools are designed to allow an organization to better utilize the data maintained in their CASE workstations by providing a central point of control and storage.

- CASE tools support that provides consistency and maintainability immediately by developing consistent terminology and structures.

- Data movement tools that transform and integrate disparate data types and move data reliably to the warehouse.

- Business applications that provide packaged warehouse solutions for specific markets.

- Data warehouse consulting that uses a methodology based on the experiences of hundreds of other companies, thereby reducing the risk associated with making uninformed business decisions.

Sophisticated version control, collision management, and bi-directional interfaces, enabling the sharing and reuse of metadata among programmers and users working independently.

Conclusions

Initially the Internet was used by a small number of technical people. The World Wide Web and Internet browsers expanded its use significantly. However, as the content expanded exponentially, search engines such as Infoseek and Infoseek, AltaVista, and Yahoo were needed to help people find information. But even the search engines are not enough, because inquiries returned thousands of choices. Users can also select data published through various information channels which are organized by content. Both approaches, regardless of their underlying technologies, are successful because they offer an organized information catalog for users to browse and select information from.

Organizations are becoming increasingly aware of the limitations of their own systems and internal data. The attempts to liberate and leverage data across the organization have been replete with frustrations and failures. These experiences, coupled with the need for flexibility in business processes, are moving towards the need for an enterprise level view of metadata. Database query tools have proliferated over the past few years. Despite allowing business users to access virtually any database, these tools have not gained the widespread usage that spreadsheets or word processors enjoy.

Data warehouses, implemented by a heavily data-reliant enterprise, are typically very large and centrally controlled. These are normally based on a central server, static in terms of the data provided, and constantly being added to and often only lightly used by the business user. With a strong metadata reliance, data marts tend to be individually small, distributed throughout the enterprise, constantly fluctuating in terms of content to meet changing market needs, and controlled by the business unit.

Search engines are increasingly being called upon to play a key role in providing metadata about the enterprise information resources. This has begun to integrate structured and unstructured content through a standard browser interface. Metadata requirements need to be understood in their expanding role of providing data about all information resources available to users. Whereas standards may be slow to be adopted by vendors at the application level, standards are already being established for user-level metadata as intranets are being deployed.

Metadata is one important key to unlocking the information door.

10

WEB-DISTRIBUTED DBMS (RELATIONAL TO ODBMS)

Introduction

Delivery of data warehouse information to decision makers throughout the enterprise and around the world has been an expensive challenge. The World Wide Web offers a solution. In addition to simplifying the deployment of data warehouse access, an intranet can introduce a new level of collaborative interactive analysis and information sharing among decision makers. This section discusses the concepts of information sharing through object databases.

The Use of a Flat File Database

A database is simply a collection of data or information which has been organized for ease of search and retrieval. A database is ideal for keeping track of information which might be contained in a card file, such as a customer list, inventory records, or a library card catalog. In many cases, a database can replace the need for paper files.

The flat file database module can create both simple and complex data relations. It can quickly search and sort large amounts of data and retrieve various data items according to selected criteria. The concept of a flat file database can best be illustrated by the example of a traditional card file. Each card contains information. Each item of data is called a field. Each physical card is called a record. When a number of cards are collected they become the foundation of a database of information.

A flat file database simply lets the computer do the work of organizing, sorting, and submitting the information to reports. The term *flat file database* comes from the physical organization of the information. Each screen of information constitutes a single record. As the user moves between screens, different records are revealed.

Database Management System

A database is a collection of data or information that is durable, shared, and accessible, and whose integrity is maintained. A database management system (DBMS) is a program that manages data in a database. A database could be as simple as a phone book or stock tables, or as sophisticated as a biological repository with terabytes of data.

Relational databases are those that follow the relational data model described by E. F. Codd. Object-oriented databases refer to those that store objects directly, or use mapping technology to store objects instead of simple data. The most important quality characteristics expected of a database are:

- *Usability:* Users and program developers must be able to access the information easily, efficiently, and effectively.

- *Performance:* The system must offer adequate response time, capacity, and throughput. Particularly, it must provide facilities for measuring, predicting, and performance tuning.

- *Availability:* The data must be available to users for a significant proportion of a day and must be maintained in the event of system failures and upgrades.

- *Change Management:* Information is often long-lived. The database systems must allow protection against changes in the business requirements and technology.

- *Security:* The system must protect the confidentiality, integrity, and availability of information against malicious attacks or negligence. It must enable proper auditing for management control.

Web Access from a User's Desktop

Modern organizations are constantly extending user access to more and more enterprise data stores (type of databases). User demand for GUI-based PC and UNIX applications, with all of their advantages, fuels this effort. Simple and reliable connectivity from shrink-wrapped, desktop productivity tools to legacy data sources has proven to be elusive. The ability to provide management and control features as part of the solution is still rare.

For example, a number of solutions are available that allow popular ODBC-compliant desktop applications, such as Powersoft's PowerBuilder, Microsoft's Visual Basic and Access, Borland's Delphi, and Cognos's Impromptu and Business Objects, to run seamlessly and transparently with data retrieved from a heterogeneous mix of databases. Every type of user at any level of the business hierarchy can gain a competitive edge when they have ready access to corporate-wide information. New advances extend the reach beyond legacy databases and into business transaction systems.

Relational Databases

Relational DBMS (RDBMS) is still the most popular database management system in use. Most large-scale commercial applications are built upon relational database systems, typically in client/server models.

Relational databases arose from theoretical considerations of data structures. RDBMSs use the Structured Query Language (SQL) to extract and update data and conform as closely as possible to the theoretical relational rules of normalization. Some typical implementation examples are Oracle, Sybase, and Informix. RDBMSs work best when the data structures have been *normalized* to eliminate data and field duplication. Data is organized within *tables* and relationships expressed between tables and data elements.

Note that just because a system uses an RDBMS, that does not mean that the data structures have been properly defined in the first place. You can build rotten data structures with a good tool. SQL is now the industry standard for data querying and updating of relational databases.

Advantages

There are many, many tools such as report writers tuned to work with the popular RDBMS via standards such as Open Database Connectivity (ODBC). RDBMSs offer distributed database and distributed processing options. They also offer extremely well-developed management tools and security with automatic data logging and recovery. They provide referential integrity controls, ensure data consistency, and have transactional integrity features to guarantee that incomplete transactions do not occur.

Disadvantages

In the early days they were slow. RDBMSs had to employ many tables to conform absolutely to the various normalization rules. This made them slow and resource-hungry compared to more flexible systems. Most RDBMSs today have been tuned for performance.

Field lengths are usually defined with a maximum. This can lead to occasional practical problems. SQL does not provide an efficient way to browse alphabetically through an index. Thus some systems cannot provide a simple A-Z browse.

Object Databases

Object orientation for a database means the capability of storing and retrieving objects in addition to mere data. As the name suggests, database management systems were designed to look after data—numbers or words. Objects are complex and not well handled by standard RDBMSs. Object-oriented DBMSs have been emerging over the last few years. Most systems can handle images, video, and other objects but do so in a non-standard way in many cases.

Object Orientation

While the current database market is centered around relational technology, most agree that the future for object database technology is tremendous because it allows us to better represent the real world. Traditional database technology is very good at handling classical data—small amounts of text, numbers, date and time values—organized in tabular structures. In the Internet web world, data needs behavior in the form of methods, to allow binary information to represent business processes, such as OLAP queries. We need to manage new data types, arranged in new structures. These new data types such as faxes, videos, and images, are increasingly used in business applications.

Different from Relational DBMS (RDBMS), Object-Oriented DBMS (ODBMS) stores objects rather than simple data types. Since it is capable of handling image, graphics, and audio/video data, the use of ODBMS has expanded beyond the engineering arena. More importantly, ODBMS provides transparent bindings to object-oriented languages such as C++ and Smalltalk, rather than forcing a single query language (i.e., SQL) as its interface. This helps in building reusable, component-based, mission-critical, decision-support software systems.

For some practical reasons, many available ODBMSs are hybrid systems, or object-relational DBMSs. These systems are able to handle complex data types equally well.

In short, an object database is simply a database that contains objects. The ideas of object technology were developed as a way of controlling system complexity. The most important idea is that objects are independent of each other. This means that there are clean interfaces between objects, maximizing the potential for change in the system as a whole. Some of the main features of objects are:

- An object has an identity that remains fixed, though its properties may change with time. It is therefore possible for one object to refer directly to another without resorting to primary keys. This fixed identifier is particularly useful for objects that have no natural primary key.
- Objects are classified into types which are organized in a type hierarchy.

  For example, employees can be categorized as salaried, casual, or contract staff. The hierarchy of types reduces system complexity because it makes it easier to handle variety. Some people are interested in the difference between different categories of employee while others are not.

Organizing objects in a type hierarchy makes it easier to design systems that can handle a variety of different kinds of account, or different kinds of airline ticket, or that can interface to different kinds of electronic mail systems. Variety, of course, goes hand-in-hand with change. A system that can cope with a variety of different ways of doing things is one that can also accommodate business process change.

- Objects have published interfaces that hide their internal implementations. Users do not need to know, for example, how the color and shape of a chair are represented internally. All they need to know is what questions they can ask about the chair, such as how big it is, how much did it cost, and straight back or folding in nature ?

These features explain why object database systems are useful for storing complex information.

The Need for Object Databases

Object databases are needed because not all information fits neatly into the rows and columns used by relational databases. The Web, in particular, means that users now expect all kinds of information to be linked so that they can browse through it, in a structure that suits their view of the world and not the machine's. Visual presentation of information is becoming the norm. Other trends that have led to the emergence of object databases are:

- *Multimedia integration:* To make all the information about a customer available in one place, regardless of whether it is structured data, text, or image.

- *Increased flexibility in human-computer interface design:* To deliver complex information to untrained users, perhaps members of the public, tabular presentation of data no longer gives the best solution. It is often better to present information in the form of diagrams, graphs, or maps.

- *New system architectures:* As organizations try to extend the availability of their information systems to reach far-flung communities of mobile employees, customers, and suppliers, the conventional client/server architecture of the relational era becomes unmanageable. The new thin-client architectures depend on object technology, making object databases a natural choice for information storage.

- *New development methodologies:* Almost all modern methods of analysis and process modeling use object-oriented concepts to describe systems. This leads naturally to a demand to implement these concepts directly in the database, avoiding the need to translate them artificially into a relational model.

Object Database Applications

The usual reason for using an object database is that the data is too complex to be stored efficiently in tabular form. For example, the data underlying a weather map consists of hundreds of different kinds of objects with many interrelationships. Extracting the information from hundreds of relational tables to assemble the weather map for any specified area would be inefficient and time consuming. Very often the data used in such complex applications is multimedia in form. Examples of such applications are:

- Computer-aided design systems, where hundreds of objects need to be accessed to assemble a single drawing.
- Document publishing systems, where the same material needs to be published by different routes using a fast production process.
- Engineering information systems, which handle complex interrelated information in a variety of media, with complex rules for version and configuration control.
- Scientific databases containing medical, biochemical, pharmaceutical, or meteorological data.
- Network modeling of telecommunications or power transmission networks, where there are many complex links between the items.
- Spatial information systems, for example land registry, vehicle scheduling, or equipment inventory management, which keep track of where items are within an area.

Traditionally, applications such as these have been developed with custom-written data management routines because relational database technology imposed excessive overheads. Object databases bring to these application areas the benefits that are now taken for granted in commercial data processing using relational databases for increased productivity, flexibility, and data integrity. These have direct uses for the data warehousing applications.

Object-Oriented Application Development

Once defined, objects can be assembled into components that are used and reused as the building blocks of many applications, and object application developers can realize enormous productivity gains.

Tools are being made available that capitalize on object database capabilities. For example, class definitions can be used to manipulate objects stored in the database via an object query interface. In addition, the ODBMS will need to support persistent binding for objects defined, accessed, or used in C++ applications.

We also are witnessing the emergence of high-level, GUI object-oriented tools, such as OLAP tools, for creating wrappers that turn existing COBOL and 4GL programs into object components and assemble the components into applications.

Object Database Standards

There are three recognized standards initiatives for object database technology:

- The Object Management Group (OMG) has defined a number of separate services and standards for object-oriented technologies.
- The ANSI and ISO committees are working on SQL3, which adds some object-oriented features to the relational model.
- *ODMG (Object Data Management Group)*, a consortium of object database suppliers, has defined a standard that resembles SQL more closely in its query facilities. It also provides a Java interface alongside C++ and SmallTalk.

There is a consensus in the industry on the functionality and terminology appropriate for an object database. However, the detailed syntax used by the various products and standards proposals varies widely. Genuine portability of applications between different object databases is thus some time off, although a high level of design portability is already possible.

Integration with Relational Processing

The most practical approach to object commercialization holds promise by integrating object technology with relational database management. Object database management systems must be created by marrying the best-of-breed object technology and superior relational technology with specialized SQL threads for relational requests and object query threads for object requests.

The resulting system can provide efficient techniques for all the essential operations of an object-oriented database and can exploit. custom indexing technologies optimized for object database interactions.

With the integration of object and relational, users benefit from both worlds in one DBMS, with extensive facilities to bridge the gap, including unprecedented facilities to access relational data via an SQL class or access object data via an object query. Because both database paths utilize the physical input/output (I/O) database layer, both have the advantages of advanced database management technology, including robust backup and recovery, transaction management, locking and logging, replication, distributed processing, and heterogeneous data access.

The benefit is that existing data warehousing applications will continue to operate unchanged as long as they are web-enabled, while developers enhance these applications to exploit the new object server capabilities.

Object Databases on the Web

From a database point of view, early web sites used a simple flat-file approach to data storage. That is, all of the information required to process requests was stored in the native file system with the web server as the query processor. However, the availability of the CGI provided access to any program or data storage networked to the web server. The opportunity to bring powerful database technology to the data warehousing arena has become irresistible.

Every system in an enterprise data warehouse can be exposed to the web for browser access, and every database flavor is pushing object-oriented technology as a core engine to deliver complex multimedia content and advanced transactions, such as OLAP queries. In fact, the web of the future, whether within or across enterprises, will likely be characterized by distributed and real-time transactions across multiple organizations. The questions that beg some answers are:

- How do we manage multiple versions of web pages as sites evolve and change?
- How should we track the user activity on our site?
- How do we effectively manage the multimedia content?
- What sorts of commercial transactions can we use to reduce transaction costs and provide greater organizational flexibility?

These are very real questions, especially as organizations require that their investments in the web provide more tangible and measurable benefits. And as we deploy more powerful web sites and web-based applications for data warehouses, object databases are an obvious enabling technology for building and managing these data warehouses.

Object/Relational Databases

Most commercial databases restrict the user to either a flat file or relational database model. Often, this involves the manipulation of master/transactional records. Recently, the object-oriented database has emerged as yet a third structure for organizing information. The object-oriented database model also establishes data relationships, but it is not rigidly structured, requiring a hierarchy of master records that governs transactional data.

This database provides the flexibility of utilizing all three of these models individually or in connection with one another. The term *object-oriented relational database* is a hybrid used to denote the flexibility available in structuring information. The three structures available include:

- *Flat file database structure:* In a flat file structure, records are organized in such a manner that all the information is self-contained without interdependencies on other data. Typically, a screen of data composed of input fields is defined as a single record. Each record or group of records can be manipulated, retrieved, sorted, or as desired by the user.
- *Master/transactional database structure:* This model establishes relationships between two or more databases by forming a hierarchy of information. The master database is the controlling structure that governs what information can be collected in transactional databases. This may be viewed as a parent-to-child relationship in which controls are placed on the activity of the child process. The transactions of the child, if they are within the master's guidelines, will be retained in that database.
- *Object-oriented linked database structure:* The object-oriented database model permits the user to inter-relate one or multiple fields from one or multiple databases. Information stored in one database can be dynamically linked to other databases. In addition, this database permits the inclusion of other information including word processing, spreadsheet and graphics files. The actual amount of information that can be stored within a record is limited only by the memory available on the computer system.

Object/relational database management systems (ORDBMSs) add new object storage capabilities to the relational systems. These new facilities integrate management of traditional fielded data, complex objects such as time-series, geo-spatial data, and diverse binary media such as audio, video, images, and applets. By encapsulating methods with data structures, an ORDBMS server can execute complex analytical and data manipulation operations to search and transform multimedia and other complex objects.

The object/relational approach has inherited the robust transaction-and performance-management features of relational and the flexibility of object-oriented structures. Database designers can work with familiar tabular structures and data definition languages (DDLs) while assimilating new object-management possibilities. Query and procedural languages and call interfaces in ORDBMSs are familiar (SQL3) vendor procedural languages, and ODBC, JDBC, and proprietary call interfaces are the extensions of RDBMS languages and interfaces.

Object/Relational Features

Object/relational databases organize information in the familiar relational tabular structures. In fact, object/relational implementations subsume the relational database model. ORDBMSs are an incremental upgrade to their RDBMS predecessors, and, unlike the move to object database systems, object/relational migration will not involve wholesale re-coding. Just as a C++ compiler will handle C code despite its lack of classes, once you accommodate the mostly syntactic changes in SQL, an ORDBMS should support relational schemas. Current ORDBMS implementations do have gaps, such as the lack of replication facilities and of inheritance.

User-defined types may be *distinct*, *opaque*, and *composite*. Distinct types, also known as value types, are derived from other types but have their own domains, operations, functions, and casts. ORDBMS applications can be strongly typed, helping assure application integrity.

System-defined types are more familiar. Most RDBMSs implement money as a numeric type with a defined number of decimal places. It is logical to add and subtract money values and to multiply them by scalars, but not by other money values.

Opaque types are not derived from source types, so their internal structures must be defined to the DBMS along with their operations, functions, and casts. Once properly defined, an opaque type can be used as a source type for defining distinct row types and can be used in tables. A row type is a collection of fields of other types. One row type can include another row type nested among its fields. Handling of the constituent fields is derived from their types; the operations, functions, and casts of the row type itself must therefore be defined.

Scalability of Object/Relational Databases

We have all come to the conclusion that the data warehouse world needs object/relational database technology. The premise behind being able to put objects into a database is very compelling. Even though standard relational databases are powerful, only a tiny fraction of the world's information actually lends itself to being stored in the row-and-column format of a relational database. Therefore, giving users the ability to store more complex objects of any format and any data type means that users can now put all the rest of their non-relational data on-line. This is an important feature to consider when designing data warehouses or data warehouse applications. Basically, with object/relational databases, if the information can be digitized, it can be put in a database.

While vendor corporations have been busy developing and marketing these products, we have been trying to put these new technologies to use in real-world situations. Since this technology gives us the ability to manage far more types of data, object/relational databases will inevitably be much larger and will grow much faster than standard relational databases ever did. This raises an important question as to whether this technology is scalable enough to meet these demands. From direct experience, the truthful answer is that object/relational technologies will definitely enhance the ability to build scalable systems, but some important unresolved issues still exist.

Scalable Performance for Complex Data Types

One of the more important requirements of a scalable solution is that it must maintain acceptable performance levels even when the database grows to a very large size. While there are certainly numerous operations that can be performed efficiently by relational databases, there are countless others that do not easily fit into the relational model and, therefore, are woefully inefficient to process using standard relational approaches. For these operations, achieving scalable performance in a relational database is either extremely difficult or outright impossible. However, object/relational databases solve this problem. By allowing users to define their data storage, data access and data processing methods, users can define operations that are optimized for a particular data type.

We know that relational databases are notoriously inefficient at processing *time series* data. Time series data is used to track the value of a particular entity over time. The classic example is tracking the value of stock market equities on a daily, hourly or even minute-by-minute basis. In a relational database, this time series data typically would be stored in a table that has at least the following three columns, such as equity name, time stamp, and equity price.

While this approach gives you a way to store the information you need, it is not an optimal solution. First, data for a single stock will usually end up being scattered across a possibly large number of non-contiguous disk blocks, completely intermingled with information about other stocks. Because the data is spread across a large number of disk blocks, the time it takes to access all the data associated with an individual stock is increased.

Also, relational technology just does not give you an efficient way to achieve the types of functionality that are needed for time series data. For example, a common request is to plot the *moving average* of a time series for a stock price, which for any given day returns the average of the most recent closing prices. Or, analysts might want to look at the spread between the maximum and minimum stock price for each week to see how the price volatility is changing on a week-by-week basis. Trying to generate these answers using standard SQL is extremely inefficient, often requiring a separate query for each data point desired. In these cases, performance is usually poor and as data sizes scale up, generating your results using relational technology is not feasible.

The solution in the object/relational world is very different. If your application requires storing and analyzing time series data or any other non-relational data type that you can imagine, you would simply purchase a database that supports the storage, manipulation and analysis of that data type. Or, if the extension you need is not available on the market, you can create your own. Either way, once the extension is plugged into your database engine, all the functionality you need would be available.

For example, a time series extension would treat all the time series data for a specific equity as a single object. Storage mechanisms would be included that know about these time series objects and which try to keep all the information for an individual time series object spread across as few disk blocks as possible. This greatly reduces the number of disk blocks that need to be read, thereby speeding up data access times and making performance acceptable even for large data sizes.

This extension would also contain intelligent functions that read a time series object and generate all the data points for a moving average graph or a volatility graph with only a single pass through the data, rather than requiring the execution of a separate query for each data point. Because of the dramatically increased efficiency of these functions, analyzing very large data sizes is feasible.

Scalable Functionality

By definition, scalable solutions must be able to handle not only increases in the amount of data managed and the number of users supported, but must also handle increases in functionality. As alluded to earlier, object/relational systems let you add to the database any functionality you want. Third parties will create extensions for many common non-relational objects, and you may be able to buy these extensions and plug them into your own system. You would be able to do such things as search through digitized pictures and return only those that contain a particular image, or perform complex statistical analysis on large data sets or search through unstructured text to find documents discussing a specified topic. The flexibility object/relational integration databases enable is enormous.

Unresolved Issues

By being able to efficiently handle complex data types and by being able to support arbitrarily complex functionality, object/relational technology promises to deliver scalable performance and scalable functionality. In this case, we use the word to imply that there are still some questions that need answers before we can fully leverage object/relational technology to build scalable applications. That is not to say that the answers can't be found. Rather, it just means that it is going to be up to the early users to discover the answers.

Performance Tuning

Most obvious to any early user is the fact that as an industry, we are not fully versed on how to tune object/relational database extensions. Many books exist on how to tune relational databases but not on how to tune object/relational databases. The tricks of the trade have yet to be discovered. And, it is likely that different extensions will require different tuning techniques. For example, some objects might be hierarchical in nature (meaning that a single object will be comprised of several sub-objects, each of which could, in turn, be comprised of several sub-sub-objects). Other objects might simply be very large, as is the case with digitized video. It is safe to assume that designing and tuning these very different objects for performance will require a very different skill set for each.

Taking Advantage of Parallelism

One of the most successful ways to achieve scalability is to use parallelism. The idea behind parallelism is simply to have multiple processors working on different portions of a problem "in parallel." Loosely speaking, if a problem gets twice as large (for example, the amount of data doubles or the number of users doubles), then by using parallelism you can double the number of processors and get your answer in the same amount of time.

But, this requires that the problem can be broken up into smaller portions and that the results from processing each of the portions can be meaningfully merged into a final result. For relational databases, we already understand how to run queries and other operations in a parallel environment. The same is not yet true for many of the data base extensions that are developing.

Take image processing as an example. We mentioned that we will be able to scan a digitized picture to look for specific images contained within the picture. But, the question is as to how do you take advantage of multiple processors to perform this scan.

Your initial guess might be to divide the image into pieces and have each piece scanned by a different processor. That is, if you had four processors, you could divide the image into quadrants. Unfortunately, that will not work. If the feature you are looking for spans the boundary between two or more quadrants, you may not find it using this approach because the entire image does not exist in any single quadrant. For an application to be truly scalable, we will have to learn how to make all database extensions work in a parallel environment.

In a parallel processing environment, databases and even tables can be transparently partitioned across multiple processing nodes. Complex queries are then divided into subtasks that execute in parallel on individual processors. In addition, an efficient parallel database can perform maintenance activities—including backups, index creations, updates, and re-partitioning—even as queries are taking place. On top of parallelism's intrinsic performance and scalability capabilities, new data access optimization techniques, index management methods, and joining technologies combine to accelerate the response times.

Modeling Methodologies

There are many reasons for creating a model—and for using a modeling and design tool—rather than just jumping in and directly programming a database and application code. Modeling can help bridge the gaps between business concepts, database designs, and physical database implementations.

A logical model created with a design tool is insulated from DBMS specifics, allowing a single design to be implemented in different DBMSs. Unlike logical models, schemas are tied to specific DBMS server products. For many years, modeling tools have had both reverse-engineering capabilities and forward-engineering capabilities.

Unified Modeling Language (UML)

UML development was spearheaded by Rational Software Corp. based on the unified model for software objects, or so-called enterprise component modeling (ECM). ECM is a complex approach that includes conceptualization and requirements analysis covering conceptual modeling with mappings into classes, components, and distribution in the system and detailed design phases. UML's classes and methods, however, are roughly equivalent to an ORDBMS types and methods.

ORDBMSs have not yet entered the mainstream. At this stage only very adept users seek to exploit object/relational features. Perhaps a hybrid solution is in order for those who need and can afford it.

Object versus Relational

We have learnt that object and relational databases are different beasts. Relational databases (RDBMSs), were designed to provide an incredible amount of flexibility in the way simple data is processed and made available to users. On the other hand, object databases (ODBMSs), were meant to handle the complexity of data and relationships required by the object model of development. Object databases initially took hold as repositories for CASE and CAD applications. Today, they are widely used in network-management systems across industries, in financial systems, in publishing systems, and in other application areas not well served by relational-database technology.

RDBMSs and ODBMSs are actually complementary technologies. If an application has relatively simple data, simple data relationships, and a static schema, a relational database engine is usually a good choice. If an application has relatively complex, interrelated data, or if the database schema may evolve rapidly over time, an object database is a more likely a better choice.

Relational databases can be given object front ends and extended to handle complex data types while object databases can provide standard ODBC interfaces to access stored objects. ODBMSs are normally intimately tied to a given application, given their direct linkage to the object programs.

Content Management and Object Databases

It would be difficult to store a Java applet in a relational database and maintain information about ownership, rental charges, and usage histories, but this is tailor-made for an object-database engine. Whether the information is complex video information, complex graphical and spatial layouts, or even time series data, an object database handles the complexity of the data types natively and with extremely high performance.

Object databases are commonly used as content-delivery repositories for HTML (SGML) publishing systems. The object database provides a set of valuable data-management functions, including versioning, distribution, and high-performance access. There is no mapping of object data to a relational engine. Thus, by eliminating the need to *join* data in order to deliver information from the RDBMS to the browser, the ODBMS can operate significantly faster on complex types of data.

This does not preclude the use of relational databases to vend important data. The natural move to increase the value of web interaction for users is to expose existing systems for web access. Within an intranet, this may be form-based access to financial information. On the Internet, this ranges from subscribing to catalog lists, to running OLAP reports, to vending content stored in a relational database based on a user login. In general, each access from a browser will require a separate access back to the database. Resource-wise, this can be very expensive, as each CGI request spawns a process of its own on top of the specific database access.

In a web environment with hundreds of simultaneous requests, this makes for large machine requirements. Moreover, the lack of intelligent caching within the browser limits the potential functionality. In this mode, it makes sense to use a three-tier architecture, where the object server provides an intermediate repository for existing systems.

This type of architecture helps the web browser handle more-complex interactions. The object database, caching the information from the relational database, provides a fast programmatic access for the web browser. In addition, if we build this application using Java, we can use the memory space provided by Java to cache this information. This functionality is much more difficult to build without the object database.

Object Databases in the Infrastructure

Netscape currently offers a file-system-based proxy server that caches frequently accessed information, eliminating the need to go across the network to get the information every time it is requested. An object database can easily provide the same functionality as the file system, but can likely perform at significantly higher levels, due to its innate caching capability. Moreover, management of these proxies can be simplified by using the standard management routines of the ODBMS rather than running against the file system directly.

The next area where object databases have a critical role is in managing the actual interactions and transactions that occur within a given session executed by a user. Session and profile management are becoming increasingly important both as companies try to provide the exact information required by their clients and as advertisers move to the Web in force.

By far the most important area for an object database is as a server for Java. The combination of Java, a CORBA-compliant Object Request Broker (ORB), and a powerful object database can create a potent application server that extends the capabilities of the web and the intranet beyond publishing and into the realm of on-line data warehousing, based on distributed transactioning.

The object database, as a repository for the ORB, not only provides extremely fast caching to handle requests from clients, but it can supplement the distribution capability provided by the ORB. Thus, where an object database fits the application requirements, the ORB provides a transparent and consistent interface to that application for standard browser access by users.

Object Data Management: Relational, Object, or Hybrid?

Today, organizations are faced with increasingly difficult choices about their current and future needs for data management. Primarily, these amount to one of the three alternatives.

Where Does the DBMS Fit?

Relational DBMSs are commonly used for high-volume on-line transaction processing (OLTP) systems such as airline reservation systems. Because the technology is more mature, they are able to provide 24x7x365 availability, and security levels certifiable to US DOD (Department of Defense) standards. In addition, a large number of good database administration tools are available, while using a standard language interface (SQL).

Object DBMSs have been proven for complex data operations and managing intricate graph and web structures. Because most of them have been strongly influenced by object-oriented programming languages, they are able to provide support for user-defined and abstract data types.

Currently, many ODBMS implementations are providing SQL capabilities, fault-tolerance, and high transaction throughputs which challenge the RDBMSs. Object-relational is becoming more popular since it provides the extensibility required to manage new data types with support for SQL and large databases with large numbers of concurrent users.

Hybrid Configurations

There are hybrid systems and hybrid databases. Basically, a hybrid system is one that uses two DBMSs for handling the complex requirements, such as a library system—complex searching where a free-form DBMS excels and a relational DBMS for structured data transaction processing.

Distributed Database Technology

Data warehouse servers use distributed database technology to share data in many different ways. This includes remote data access and replication which can be done on either a real-time or a deferred basis.

Servers use distributed database technology to share data in many different ways. When a local server needs to share data that resides on a remote server, the local server can use distributed database technology to access the data on the remote system directly. Alternatively, the two servers can use distributed database technology to maintain copies, or replicates, of the data on both servers so that both can access it locally.

Added to this is the dimension of time. The question is whether we need to access remote data in real-time or will deferred access suffice? Similarly, when replicated data is updated, do the updates need to be applied to other copies in real-time or can the updates be propagated on a deferred basis?

Real-time remote data access and real-time application of updates to replicated data is provided by synchronous distributed database technology. Deferred remote data access and deferred propagation of replicated data updates is provided by asynchronous distributed database technology. Understanding the tradeoffs between these two technologies is key to determining which to use to solve a particular business problem. Some business problems will require synchronous distributed technology. For others, asynchronous technology will be a better fit. In still other cases, both technologies will be needed to solve different aspects of the problem.

The tradeoffs between these two involve application integrity, complexity, performance, and availability. Synchronous technology ensures application integrity and minimizes complexity, but can be less available if the systems and networks involved are not reliable. It can also incur poor response time if network access between systems is slow. Asynchronous technology maximizes availability and response time, but can be more complex and requires careful planning and design to ensure application integrity.

Synchronous Database Technology

In an order entry system and a shipping system, the systems can share inventory data using synchronous distributed technology. Since we are using synchronous technology, both systems have access to the most current, up-to-date inventory information. You could, for example, store a single copy of the inventory data on the shipping system and access the data remotely from the order entry system in real time. Alternatively, you could use synchronous technology to maintain exact replicas of the inventory data on both systems. Any update to the data on either system would be applied synchronously, or in real time, to the copy on the other system.

Orders can now be placed knowing exactly what is in inventory. Inventory items can be reserved as an integral part of the order taking process. Shipments can be made knowing that the resulting decrements to inventory qualities will be immediately seen by the order entry system. In this way, synchronous technology provides simplicity and ensures application integrity.

To place orders or ship products, however, processing needs to take place across the network and on both systems, which may be slow. Also, the systems and network need to be reliable or availability can suffer. If the shipping system or network goes down, for example, orders can't be placed. If remote access is being used, the order entry system can not access the inventory data on the shipping system. Similarly, if the inventory data is replicated, it cannot be updated because the update cannot be applied to both systems.

Asynchronous Database Technology

Asynchronous technology maximizes availability and response time performance, but can be more complex and requires careful planning and design to ensure application integrity.

Now let us use asynchronous distributed technology to share inventory data between our order entry and shipping systems. We will place the inventory data on the shipping system. The order entry system has access to this data but on a deferred basis. If we are using asynchronous replication, updates to inventory data will be propagated and applied to a copy of the inventory data on the order entry system on a deferred basis. This copy will contain accurate information but will not always be current. It may, though, be current enough for many businesses. If inventory levels are high and/or are easily replenished, then slightly out-of-date information may suffice. The chances of ordering an item which is out of stock will be either very low or will only cause small shipment delays.

Ensuring that asynchronous distributed technology provides adequate application integrity requires careful consideration but it can be complex. The advantage of asynchronous technology, however, is availability and response-time performance. Transactions operate against local data only. They may initiate deferred operations which need to be propagated to other systems but if these other systems are not available the propagation will be deferred until the systems come back up. In our example, orders can be placed even when the network or shipping system is down.

Replication Concepts

Replication is a key element of an overall distributed computing solution, but also a demanding one. One particular challenge is understanding the range of potential uses for synchronous and asynchronous replication.

With synchronous replication all copies of data are kept exactly synchronized and consistent. If any copy is updated the update will be immediately applied to all other copies within the same transaction. Synchronous replication is appropriate when this exact consistency is important to the business application.

With asynchronous replication, copies or replicates of data will become temporarily out of sync with each other. If one copy is updated the change will be propagated and applied to the other copies as a second step, within separate transactions, that may occur seconds, minutes, hours, or even days later. Copies therefore can be temporarily out of sync, but over time the data should converge to the same values at all sites.

Ensuring convergence in asynchronous replication environments is critical for nearly every application. What happens, though, if the same data element, e.g., the same column in the same row, is updated at two sites at the same time, or to be more precise within the same replication interval? This is known as an update conflict. To ensure convergence, update conflicts must be detected and resolved, so that the data element has the same value at every site. Alternatively, update conflicts may be avoided by limiting the right to update a given data element to a single site.

Selecting Distributed Database Technology

Building successful distributed computing systems, such as web-based OLAP or other decision-support systems, are some of the great challenges of this decade. To ensure success, the distributed database technology that you select should be flexible, manageable, and integrated.

- *Manageable:* Functionality without the ability to manage it is not usable. To minimize complexity, distributed operations should be as automatic and transparent as possible. Implementations should be robust to handle real-world stresses. Powerful management tools must be available.

- *Integrated:* Distributed capability should be an integral component of the server. No additional, external components should be required that must be separately configured and administered. No performance penalty should be incurred requiring shared data to pass through extra components or *hops* before it reaches the database where it is needed. No incompatibilities between the server and the external components should limit functionality.

- *Flexible:* Distributed capability must fit your business, not the other way around. Whether an application requires remote access or replication, synchronous real-time operations or asynchronous deferred operations, the ability to query or update data, or use procedure calls, the capabilities need to be there.

Conclusions

The emergence of object/relational technologies is having a significant impact on data warehousing systems. It means that data bases will be storing more data coming from more sources and it will be accessed by more people. This, in turn, means that a premium will be put on scalability. A few issues still need to be resolved, but with a little more effort, we may be able to turn the promise into reality.

Databases of all types are critical to Internet computing. Since much existing corporate data is already stored within relational databases, they have an important role in providing content for web-based applications and sites. However, object databases are highly appropriate and can supplement the computing infrastructure. In fact, since the web is nothing if not dynamic, filled with complex relationships and multimedia content, and accessible from anywhere, an object database can easily provide a flexible front end for the enterprise.

The data warehouse is one of the most popular new application areas requiring the movement and synchronization of large volumes of data. There are many potential opportunities for data replication to automate and simplify the maintenance of a data warehouse. There are also many special requirements that replication products must address in order to support data warehousing. DBMSs must be continually extended to meet decision-support mission-critical application requirements.

Object databases are evolving quickly, from their current primary role managing textual and numeric data to becoming the cornerstone of distributed information technology. The addition of significant new capabilities such as the integration of complex data, object storage, and management; hardware exploitation; mobile node deployment; seamless heterogeneous data access; open data replication; and systems management integration will be the differentiators required for a DBMS to be a player in the new world.

11

CLIENT/SERVER ENVIRONMENTS

Introduction

It has become apparent that distributed interactive processing using client/server architectures is required for economical and complete web-enabled data warehousing services. Unfortunately, as this awareness has grown, the place for multi-tier client/server systems has not been clearly understood. Distributed client/server computing cannot always provide the necessary reliability, data integrity, and performance without implementation of multi-tier techniques.

As database servers have become the popular solution, their weaknesses and failings have become apparent. Most notably, the database server places a heavy load on the network. Potentially more important is the difficulty of changing the database configuration without changing the programs. A well-designed client/server system can provide full-service computing to data warehousing users.

Historically, transaction processing (TP) monitors have implemented a single- or two-tier client/server configuration. In a single-tier client/server architecture, the transaction server, business logic, and presentation services all run on a single hardware platform. Normally, dumb terminals display the presentation logic executed by the transaction application running on the server. IBM's IMS transaction monitor (TM) is an example of this type of architecture.

Web Client/Server Model

A client/server system is very common way of distributing information across information systems like a local area network (LAN), a wide area network (WAN), or the Internet. A client/server system works something like:

- A server sits somewhere in the network with a set of files that users (clients) might want to access.

- This server runs a software package that listens 24 hours a day to requests from the users, over the Internet. Typically, these requests are in a language and a format that the computer understands.

- The user (client) connection is possibly via a twisted pair network hooked into a local telephone company POP or a cable or fiber optics network hooked up to a corporate WAN or LAN that is also linked up to the global telecommunications/information infrastructure through a local telephone company.

- The *server software* can access the server hardware, find the requested file, send it back to the *client* who requested it, and then wait for another request from the same or another client.

Usually, the *client* is actually a software program, like Netscape Navigator. The client software deals with all the underlying client/server protocols and then displays the document (interpreting HTML, if needed) to the user. The client/server protocol used by the web is HTTP (HyperText Transport Protocol).

HTTP is a *request-response* communication protocol which specifies that a client can open a connection to a server and send a request using a very specific format. The server can then respond and close the connection.

The details of HTTP are less important for an HTML designer than for a web programmer. The primary thing the designer needs to know is that HTTP is a language spoken between the web browser (client software) and a web server (server software) so that they can communicate with each other and exchange files/information.

Two-Tier Client/Server Model

With the advent of the two-tier client/server architecture, presentation services, and sometimes portions of the business logic were pushed to the client (see **Figure 11.1**). Since most client/server applications were implemented for departmental use, they were built on a two-tier architecture. And most of these applications were built with tools that place the presentation services and busi-

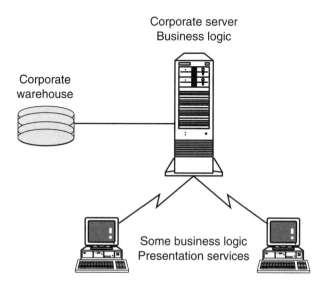

Figure 11.1   Two-tier Client/Server Model

ness logic on a *fat* client, which issues database calls across a local area network to a relational database to retrieve data for processing.

Regardless of the client/server architecture employed, TP monitors were built to leverage hardware sales by ensuring a robust and distributed transaction processing environment. However, many IT managers are concerned that distributed systems lack the security, reliability, and systems management capabilities that are found in enterprise systems.

As organizations come to know the advantages of client/server implementations, they quickly attempt to expand the scope and complexity of their applications. They are asked to increase the number of users, functions, and information sources. Nevertheless, it has become apparent that the two-tier architecture is not sufficient to support enterprise client/server applications that provide high performance, scalability, availability, and reliability.

To manage increasingly large, complex, and mission-critical applications, companies are beginning to rely on three-tier client/server architectures. As noted above, early client/server implementations were primarily two-tier architectures in which presentation and part of the application logic reside on the client whereas the data reside on the server.

Three-Tier Client/Server Model

A three-tier client/server architecture consists of presentation logic and possibly some business application logic located on the client, while data and most business application logic reside on separate servers, as illustrated in **Figure 11.2**.

Some of the key technical reasons to move to three-tier client/server architectures include:

1. Improving application and database management by isolating/distributing those functions
2. Reducing the process load on the database server, thus improving performance and application integrity
3. Reducing database and application costs by decreasing the number of clients that directly access the database server
4. Facilitating the creation and maintenance of business rules by isolating them from the data

At first glance, the three-tier environment appears more complex to developers than the two-tier environments, typical of early client/server implementations. However, three-tier environments enable a more effective modularity of development that can facilitate modification and expansion. By isolating the functional layers of applications, organizations and users can:

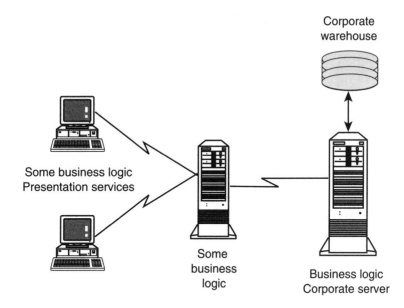

Figure 11.2 Three-tier Client/Server Model

- Smoothly deploy new applications that integrate with existing applications without major modifications
- Effectively create and disseminate standards for applications, such as a standard user interface
- Accommodate additional controls, such as security or transaction processing monitors, as applications become more widely distributed
- Easily modify any aspect of the system, such as business rules or user interfaces, as changes are made
- Effortlessly deploy and maintain application changes over time

Unfortunately, the architecture of a TP monitor does not allow developers to easily take advantage of features available when building object-oriented application programs. Also, most application developers with object-oriented skills do not have the background or training for a particular TP monitor.

Further, millions of dollars have been invested in TP monitors and client/server systems, yet they don't work together. TP monitor vendor offerings have been slower to adapt to client/server computing.

Multiple Computing Platforms

To use multiple computing platforms efficiently within the organization, it is necessary to spread the work, thus allowing several computing platforms to operate in parallel to service the needs of the organization. This method is called distributed processing, or sometimes distributed computing. Ideally, the distributed processing model provides a number of important advantages, including:

- Modularity, which allows separate functions to be placed into separate server processes
- Ease of distribution, which allows application processing to be distributed among various computing platforms
- Scalability, which supports expansion of computing resources to support additional users or to improve performance without changing programs or application system design
- Extensibility, which allows adding additional functions

Distributed Data and Distributed Processing

Data distribution is related to distributed processing. Data distribution, usually implemented with a distributed database, is effective in a two-tier architecture, where all application processing takes place on one computing platform, but the data is distributed on several platforms.

In a two-tier architecture using a distributed database, the application server process accesses data through a single data base management system (DBMS). The data in the database can be spread over one or more platforms. In this case, the database engine includes the necessary algorithms to access and update the data on any platform, transparent to the application process. Often, the client programs are developed using tools provided by the DBMS vendor.

Many situations demand that the application server processes be placed on multiple computing platforms and cooperate in some way to perform the operations necessary on independent servers. Distributed databases in a two-tier architecture provide little or no help in this case. The application server processes on the multiple platforms cooperate in completing the transactions, but only the application communicates directly with the database engine.

Distributed processing systems are generally built on a three-tier architecture to provide a number of required functions. This additional functionality includes:

- Transparent location of processes and data
- Improved system reliability

- Enhanced data integrity
- Better recoverability
- Load balancing and increased performance by using computing resources more efficiently

Distributed Client/Server Computing

Statically connected networks have evolved to dynamic networks of nomadic computers, where users *sync up* at irregular intervals. Client/server database applications are everywhere, connecting notebook, laptop, and desktop computers with servers located locally, remotely, and globally. Software agents roam the networks acting on behalf of clients.

This forces us to manage data distribution in the mixed environments commonly found in most enterprises, with multiple hardware platforms, operating systems, and DBMSs.

Database Stored Procedures

Some databases have a method to store program code in the database, providing a pseudo three-tier architecture. The client invokes the stored procedure to perform processing, which is oriented to accessing the database. The stored procedure includes application logic which processes the data contained in a message from the client, then returns the result. Stored procedures can increase the performance of the system by decreasing the amount of data sent over the network and by decreasing the number of times the client must access the database engine. The problems which have been encountered with stored procedures include:

- Scalability is limited, because the stored procedure requires the existence of the database engine which cannot be easily split among additional platforms.
- The stored procedure engine processes the procedure interpretively, thus increasing the load on the computing platform and decreasing throughput.
- It is difficult to change the location of databases without changing the client program.
- There is no standard language for stored procedures, and each database vendor has implemented a different language.

Distributed Processing in a Client/Server Environment

A modern three-tier distributed processing system adds a new dimension to client/server processing by adding the following constraints:

- Standard transaction management interface so that multiple databases can be accessed
- Transaction integrity, by assuring that all the work done on behalf of a distributed transaction is either completed or rolled back
- Transparent service request routing, assuring that the location of services is transparent to application programs
- Data-dependent routing of service requests, allowing an administrator to create horizontal data partitions and to move services and data transparently to the application programs
- Load-balancing of service requests among instantiations of servers
- Asynchronous service requests, allowing a transaction to be spread over a number of computing platforms working in parallel, while still guaranteeing transaction integrity

Standard Transaction Management Interface

Open systems distributed processing systems interface with DBMS systems using a standard ODBC interface. In this way, any DBMS that provides a standard interface can be used with the distributed processing system.

Transaction Integrity

Transaction integrity means that a transaction is either completed successfully or not at all. Both the local database and the centralized database must be updated for each order, regardless of where the order is entered. If anything should fail, such as communications, then neither database should be updated. Distributed processing systems guarantee this by centralizing control of the commit process.

For example, in an order entry system, if the order was entered at one location, then the application client program at this location will request that the distributed processing system commit the transaction when all data has been entered. If for any reason either the local order entry database or the centralized inventory database cannot commit the transaction, the distributed processing system will request that both databases rollback all changes for the transaction. This is accomplished by the use of a presumed-abort two-phase commit coordinated by the transaction manager within the distributed processing system.

Transparent Server Location

Distributed processing systems use named servers and named services to route service requests. The application client need only request the service without regard to where the service and its associated database are located. Thus, if for some reason, the administrator decides to change the location of the database and the service, the application client program will not be aware of the change.

Data-Dependent Routing

In the real world, each client location must be able to access any data in the database, irregard to the location. Data-dependent routing provided by the distributed processing system allows this to occur transparently to the application client program. An administrative function in the distributed processing system allows the administrator to specify, based on values passed with the request, as to which server will be used to service the request. If the administrator decides at any time to move the data from one location to the other, the application programs are not affected.

Load-Balancing of Service Requests

The distributed processing system can balance the load between the two platforms, depending on the number of service requests in the current queue on each platform. This action is usually transparent to both the application clients and the inventory server programs. This is usually accomplished by some combination of database software and common disk configuration.

Asynchronous Service Requests

The distributed processing system can manage the transaction such that transaction integrity is maintained in case of failures, even in an asynchronous environment. Since the distributed processing system will not allow the databases to be committed until all asynchronous operations are complete, this difficult programming technique can be used with confidence that should a program problem occur, there is no chance of getting the databases out of sync.

A good distributed processing system can be the foundation for a well-designed client/server system, providing full-service computing to every individual in the organization who has the need. Some organizations have attempted to support large numbers of users and high volumes of queries and transactions on a two-tier architecture and found that the cost was much higher than anticipated and the results did not meet expectations. A three-tier architecture based on a good distributed processing system can provide a large payback in both actual cost and end user satisfaction.

Recoverability

Many of us have spent long hours in the middle of the night attempting to reconstruct databases when the system crashed during heavy query/transaction activity. The problem has been that we could not determine the state of related files or tables at the point of the failure. Using presumed-abort two-phase commit protocols, managed over heterogeneous databases by a distributed processing system, can help alleviate the problem. Open Distributed Processing (ODP) Standards provide features for the recovery process that allow the distributed processing system to query all involved databases and decide which ones to commit and which ones to roll back.

A Tiered Data Warehouse

For most data warehouse projects, the design of a tiered data warehouse is a major architectural consideration. A tiered data warehouse is an architectural solution to the problem of managing a data warehouse in an Internet or unstructured data environment. Like other software engineering techniques that practice information hiding, segmenting a data warehouse into tiers hides the semantic complexities of source data systems from the warehouse. Furthermore, a tiered warehouse leverages the investments made in data cleanup and integration by saving the intermediate results in a generic data pool. Data from the generic data pool is subsequently recombined to form user-specific business views.

In the data warehousing community, strong opinions exist on the extent to which a warehouse should be layered. On one extreme, some argue that if the task of data modeling is done well, a data warehouse can be built with a minimum of layers (perhaps as little as two). At the other extreme, some architects argue that multiple layers are essential to any warehouse implementation.

The notion of a tiered data warehouse is not a new one. In the past, some organizations have used the metaphor of a consumer goods cycle to illustrate the tiered data warehouse. Others have described two layers of storage in the warehouse, with tables of normalized data arranged around subject areas and tables of combined, summarized and denormalized data.

Elements of a Tiered Data Warehouse

Although the nomenclature identifying the various layers of a tiered warehouse varies widely, the basic structure is:

1. The *source system(s)* from which the raw warehouse data is extracted. For the most part, these sources are either vertically integrated OLTP systems or third party data.

2. The *base warehouse* contains integrated and rationalized data extracted from the system of record. The data is aligned along data *subjects* rather than application semantics.

3. The *delivery layer*, where the warehouse meets the business users and their decision-support application tools. This data structure can range from strategic data stores for subject areas, such as star schemas, to project-specific multidimensional databases. The essential attributes at this level are presentation interfaces for ease of access.

Implementing a Tiered Data Warehouse

Typical data warehouse projects cost millions of dollars and last for several years. The following factors must be considered to justify the building of a tiered warehouse:

1. Because of the requirements for data cleanup and rationalization, it is exceedingly more expensive to re-extract data from the systems of record than it is to reconfigure data already integrated into a generic store.

2. Decision support is an iterative and heuristic process.

3. A majority of the structural changes to the warehouse normally require reconfiguring data that already exists in a generic data pool, rather than enlarging the warehouse's data domain.

4. It is advisable to build an intermediate data store of cleansed, normalized, rationalized, generic data from which to respond to user requests for new business views.

There are three basic factors to be considered when using the application of layering within a data warehouse:

- Project lifecycle risk
- Organizational independence of the user community
- The semantic volatility of the warehouse data domain

The foremost factor influencing the extent to which layering should be employed in data warehousing is the degree of semantic volatility of the underlying source data. The greater the degree of semantic volatility in the source data, the greater the need for data warehouse layering.

It is important to remember that the benefit of layering is not in the initial implementation of the warehouse, but occurs over time, as the semantics of the various contributing systems evolve independently. We hope that by investing in these layers we will be better able to manage the data warehouse even in an unstable data environment.

The factor to be weighed in considering implementing additional tiers in the data warehouse is the risk that it introduces into the project lifecycle. By investing in infrastructure we run the risk of extending the lifecycle beyond the tolerance of the business community. The 1990s have seen an almost fanatical emphasis on tactical IT projects. The tolerance for infrastructure *investments* has all but disappeared.

The prudent project manager would be well-advised to exercise caution when implementing additional infrastructure, especially early in the project lifecycle.

An Alternative to Full Implementation

In many projects, a sophisticated tiered data warehouse is envisioned for the production warehouse. However, it may be politically untenable to divert project resources to construct additional warehouse layers in the first phases of the project. A low-cost, safe alternative to constructing materialized tiers in the warehouse is to insert data indirection between data warehouse loading steps. The notion can be easily understood by focusing on the data extraction process in the warehouse.

Each extraction process expects its source data to be in a certain state (e.g., cleansed, rationalized, normalized, subject-oriented), even if that source is not materialized in physical data stores. This leaves room to introduce more sophisticated processes and intermediate data stores (i.e., tiers) in the future. Thus, a warehouse architect can create *virtual* tiers by defining the data semantics of each layer and enforcing these through software interfaces.

Obviously, more intricate warehouse designs would have more layers and interfaces.

Alternatives to Client/Server

One of the greatest challenges that IT management faces today is the task of replacing old legacy software systems with new client/server systems. The reasons to replace these systems can generally be classified into three categories:

1. The current system is not adequate for the current business conditions
2. It is too expensive to continue using legacy technology when other alternatives such as client/server are available
3. The current system requires a substantial investment to maintain

Of course the current system can be plagued by all three of the above categories, which leads to the obvious solution of buying a replacement system.

The Obvious Solution

Although a replacement system seems like a reasonable and logical solution, it is not nearly as simple as trading in the old house for a new one. The company has a huge investment in business processes that have been successful in running the business for the many years.

Most companies, large and small, do not have accurate documentation listing the required features contained in the current system. If all the required features of the current system are not known, there is a substantial risk associated with implementing a complete replacement system which may need major unforeseen modifications to provide the functionality of the current system.

Another Solution

The other solution is to migrate the current system to a client/server design. The first condition is that the current system should satisfy most of the business operating requirements. This is not as easy as it may seem. It involves three major components:

Database Interface

All requests for database information are in the database interface component. If the existing COBOL database interface is transportable (i.e., it is a SQL-based relational database), and there is no immediate need to redesign it, then the database interface migration is a minor task.

For the majority of legacy software, the database interface will probably require a redesign to take advantage of the SQL products currently available. Since all of the database access is already known from the existing application, all that is needed are modifications which present the same data to the existing logic. If the existing application is structured so all database access is in one area of the program, the task is even easier.

User Interface

The user interface component consists of the logic to transmit data to the user, primarily to character-based terminals. It is suggested that each character-based screen be redone manually using the screen design facility.

Application Logic

The application logic component contains the language statements that manipulate data presented to the user. Although this is usually the largest of all the components, it is also the easiest part of the migration, since virtually all of the logic can be converted electronically using client/server application language.

Putting It All Back Together

Once the three components have been migrated, all the pieces can be used to construct the program as a client/server application. Since the database logic is contained in the application logic component, the only task is to attach the translated application logic from the original program.

Another choice is to employ object-oriented design as well as middleware that hides the complexity of the old application from the web-based user interfaces.

A Web-Enabled Client/Server Migration Strategy

Throughout the 80s and into the 90s, businesses have identified the need to introduce more flexible work practices, to optimize efficiency in order to cope effectively with competitive pressures, and to promote an emphasis on high quality service. These demands have forced organizations to optimize work flows and to implement systems that more closely match the new business and workflow practices.

The high tech industry has responded to these business demands by delivering a number of interrelated technologies and architectures that assist developers in delivering the flexibility. Technologies such as client/sever and products such as personal computers and Microsoft Windows (and associated products and standards such as OLE2, Common Object Model [COM], Open Data Base Connectivity [ODBC]), have delivered the graphical user interface (GUI) ease of use, integration, and enhanced access to information that have been demanded. Such technologies are either server-based or client-based. We discuss some of their characteristics in the following sections.

Server-Based System Characteristics

Server-based systems have a number of characteristics, some positive and some negative. Given the strengths and weaknesses of server-based systems, we are confronted with a development dilemma. Current users demand more integrated and easy-to-use systems that more closely match the business practices, but the investment already made in technology and the prohibitive cost of totally redeveloping in a client/server environment demand that the existing systems remain in place.

An Option

That decision, up to now, has been a black-and-white one—either redevelop in client/server or continue to enhance the legacy applications and compound the difficulties associated with these systems. There is now another option available through the implementation of client/host technology, which facilitates the migration from legacy systems to client/server systems in a managed and controlled evolutionary fashion.

Migration Strategy

Managing the transition from legacy to client/server systems demands a migration strategy that protects the original investment in existing host systems while leaving the door open for full client/server evolution. This strategy can be described in the following three forms:

1. The *first form* involves using the existing server-based applications, without modification, and providing an intelligent GUI front end on the client (PC). The functions provided by the server are reengineered with a new front end that more closely matches the new business processes. This can involve integrating different host applications with the front end or offloading validation, document printing, integration with spreadsheets, and graphics to the front end.

2. In the *second form*, a more traditional view of client/server is implemented. This is where the client holds all of the logic and intelligence of the application and requests raw data from the server either via native API or ODBC calls to the database (i.e., Ingres, Oracle, Sybase, and Informix).

3. This client/server environment can be a database server environment where:
   - The client makes a request for data from the server.
   - SQL requests are usually issued via native API or ODBC.
   - The server sends raw data to client.
   - The client applies logic to the data received and presents it to the user.

   Alternatively, the client/server environment can be a transaction server environment where:
   - The client makes a request for the server.

- The client continues until the server completes the task.
- The server then sends the result to the client.

3. *The third form* involves a program-to-program client/server environment where any process on the network can operate as either a client or a server. Messages are sent between processes to request data or to initiate processing and the results are returned by messages. This type of operation is often termed cooperative processing.

All three forms of client/server can coexist in one client/server application, so the migration from one dimension to another can be seamless to the user. As the systems expand, the new functionality can be implemented in a different dimension of client/server as needs demand.

The Benefits of Client/Server Migration

The implementation of the first step in the migration to client/server can be a small cost of redeveloping the application in a client/server environment, while still providing all the benefits of that environment.

In many instances the source code for the host applications is very complex, little or no documentation is available, and the original developers are long gone. The risks associated with modifying the host applications can be great. With this migration process, no modifications are required to the host applications.

The migration can facilitate rapid delivery of vital systems in a fraction of the time previously envisioned. In addition, the 80/20 rule can be very successfully applied in this environment, whereby the most important and critical functions can be delivered without the need to develop the non-critical functions, thus substantially reducing the development effort.

The migration provides an effective and efficient method of delivering the user requirements in a client/server environment, especially with legacy source systems for data warehouses; it also provides a clear path for new client/server developments. Legacy systems can therefore be upgraded and expanded to a full client/server environment and the technology within the organization can evolve in a managed and controlled environment.

Managing the Client/Server World

Before client/server, administration was something taken care of by the operators. With the advent of client/server technology, life is not simple. Administration now has a variety of components, each of which is more complex than its mainframe counterpart. Three separate components need to be administered:

- *Client,* including client hardware, operating system software, application software and potentially a separate security subsystem
- *Server,* including hardware, operating system software, DBMS server software, and security subsystem
- *Network,* including hardware, operating system software, and a separate security subsystem

The single worst administrative headache is to get all of the individual components installed and communicating with one another. You need several layers of software on each of these three levels that are specific to platforms, operating systems and application/DBMS software. In the "open system world," you have to mix and match, since no single vendor produces all the pieces of the puzzle.

The first time you install each of the pieces and try to make all three interoperate, you will find that some sub-component is at a release level too early or late to inter-operate with the others. Administering each of the three components has its own special characteristics and nuances. However, the web makes the user's job a little simpler. *Client* administration has several components:

- Workstation, and a variety of software
- Hardware components
- Network card
- Network operating system interface software
- Application that can communicate with a Data Warehouse DBMS.

The data warehouse *server* has a variety of components that must be administered, such as:

- A server operating system (UNIX and NT are the most common flavors)
- The DBMS itself

The component that requires careful planning is network security, adding users and removing users. There is something mystical about network security. We seemingly are denied access to random objects at random moments, and there is not always a logical explanation.

In short, there are three separate and distinct components to manage in a client/server system, and each of them frequently have components that take more than one person to manage.

Supporting a Client/Server Implementation

With varying degrees of awareness, most companies are evolving toward distributed heterogeneous environments. Sometimes it is a strategic decision to migrate toward a client/server implementation so that application processing can be distributed, allowing divisions and departments—which were previously dependent upon the glass house—control over their own reports and applications. In other organizations, the decision is less conscious, but the effect is no less real. It started with PCs on desks, then networks of PCs, e-mail, local databases, shared databases, and eventually there's enough significant data in these environments that there is strong pressure to interface to operational systems.

In either case, the realities of maintaining distributed heterogeneous computing environments entail complexity. This depends on a number of factors.

Sources of Complexity

For years database technology and IT organizations were focused on tools and methodologies to assist organizations in minimizing the amount of replicated data which had to be maintained or providing mechanisms for insuring that modifications to replicated data could be synchronized. In the distributed heterogeneous computing environments, the percentage of replicated data can be expected to explode, as individuals not only download the results of querying data warehouses (or data marts), but exchange data across working groups.

Data Inflow

The person who uses the information from the data warehouse and from fellow PC users to create a forecast needs to have that information fed back to the operational systems in some form or another. Similarly, even control of word-processing documents becomes an issue. Keeping track of the electronic version which correlates with the final version can require significant discipline as electronic drafts are frequently circulated for input and revision across multiple people.

Security Systems

As distinct business entities increase the use of report and administration via the web, to exchange business information, the potential for inappropriate access to confidential information is greatly increased and not just by unauthorized access to networks. As users demand additional accesses to heterogeneous data, it becomes harder and harder to monitor the information being placed in data warehouses. Moreover, with the easy transfer of information across workstations, restricting access to the data warehouse to a limited set of users does not help.

Impact of Change

As an increasing number of users depend upon each other over the Internet, even the most trivial change can affect the ability of an organization to keep up with the demands. For example, consider the case where a company's development, sales, and marketing organizations have settled on a particular workstation standard and are accustomed to regularly exchanging memos for review and edit. A small change in software/hardware version can start a third world war between the parties.

As the rate of change in the business world increases and the window of what constitutes a timely response shrinks, the importance of minimizing these glitches in the smooth interchange of data across these distributed heterogeneous computing terrains becomes greater. To combat such problems, additional software monitors need to be developed and maintained.

Managing Change

Just as data administrators serve to coordinate and communicate the needs between database administrators, there are at least three other areas where a new corporate function could help to coordinate the efforts of the organizations maintaining distributed heterogeneous environments:

Enterprise-wide system administration

System administration requires knowledge not only of hardware, networking, and system utility costs, but also an awareness of how the systems are being used by the various business units.

Change management control

There are numerous sources which instigate change within IT:

- Technology advances, such as improved processors and software
- Internal changes within the business
- External changes affecting the business, such as mergers
- Changes in regulations and rules
- Software/hardware upgrades requiring changes

Regardless of the impetus for change, the nature of it, and the impact it has on system resources and applications, the tradeoffs, strategies, and coordination required to implement the change require a global perspective.

Choosing the Appropriate Client Tools

Much of the new software development that is occurring today is using client/server methodologies. There is a need for integrating data from several data sources and using tools on the server to achieve this integration. Therefore, we need to define criteria to help organizations make better choices in the tools used to develop applications. These criteria can be categorized as follows:

- Support for standard user interface deployment
- Graphical user interfaces (GUIs)
- Product robustness
- Development tools
- Primary and secondary database support for a multi-tier architecture

Common User Interface

Support for a common user interface with a consistent look and feel across the entire application suite is becoming an important factor to the success of the enterprise. One of the promises of a GUI environment is improved productivity through increased usability and a reduced learning curve. Consistency in the user interface plays a large role in the delivery of this promise.

A user interface that behaves the same way throughout the application environment,, follows a standard user interface, and makes the application easier to learn.

Graphical User Interfaces (GUIs)

If a standard user interface is important, the GUI development tool should be evaluated as to how it facilitates deployment. A robust tool should provide mechanisms for implementing a standard interface. These should include the ability to capture the standard user interface into reusable components.

These mechanisms should be easy to use. For a common interface, the choice of a standard is important as well. An organization must choose between implementing an industry standard interface or developing its own product.

Robustness

The robustness of a GUI development tool encompasses several areas. Some considerations in evaluating robustness of a GUI tool include:

- The features of the tool which facilitate the reduction of the development effort
- Ease of integration with the development platform
- Application portability from one platform to diverse deployment platforms

Reusable Component Tools

The development environment should make the reuse of components easy to implement. Language constructs such as included source code and compiler directives and deployment features such as libraries facilitate reusable components.

Software Tools

It has long been a dream of software developers to create systems that effectively hide heterogeneity. The history of DBMS research contains a number of efforts to build heterogeneous data managers. While many of these efforts already have made life easier in the software development arena, there are no near-term solutions, although one can expect to find great growth in the area of tools for managing distributed heterogeneous computing environments.

Software Tools in Data Warehousing

An increased rate of change, heterogeneity, more replicated data, and wider and wider geographic distribution of data are all hallmarks of the new information technology world.

Repository or metadata managers have been in use in many organizations for years. These are critical to both the data administrator and change management control groups since they represent the physical and logical relationships within and across databases. They also represent the business and transformation rules as well, which indicate differences in the semantics or representation of the data in different environments.

Maintaining this information in a central place can significantly reduce both the design cycle for new development and the cost of maintenance. Whether there is a single repository with all groups using the same product or different groups using different repositories that permit metadata exchange is less important than the fact that the organization builds the use of this type of tool into its infrastructure.

If these tools can exchange metadata with the repository, then not only can the impact of a proposed change be determined in a relatively short period of time, the actual code modification can be realized quickly as well. Note that change management needs information not only about the interrelationships between databases but also about the direction and timing of database feeds.

Object-oriented tools to record and track this information can help facilitate reuse of existing components and reduce the cost of new development over time. When compared to a complete replacement of the current software, software migration provides a viable alternative with the following benefits:

- Retraining of personnel costs much less since the new system functions are similar to the existing system, only with an easy-to-use graphical interface.
- The cost to migrate the existing system should be substantially less than replacing it with packaged software.
- Overall implementation time is shorter by using the migration approach, since the customizing of a generic package is eliminated.
- If a complete or partial migration of the current system appears to be a feasible option, the next step is to initiate a "proof of concept" project by selecting programs which model the current system for migration and evaluation.
- Software migration presents a cost-effective and low-risk solution for companies involved with changing legacy software systems.

Challenges in Client/Server Development

For any client/server data warehousing application to be successful, it must provide robust multi-user concurrency control and deliver good performance. Implementing these features is hard and the methods used to design and implement the distributed environments are critical.

How you implement performance and concurrency control in the OLAP application will have a big impact over the future of data warehousing applications. The assumption often made is that somehow performance and concurrency control will be automatically handled by the client and server working together.

Performance

Many advocates of client/server methodologies have the mistaken belief that performance is determined solely by the server-based database driver software being used. Similarly, data warehouse query design can have a dramatic impact upon server performance, while advanced coding methods on the client can also improve performance.

Stored procedures that are precompiled can run faster, resulting in a greater server yield and providing a major improvement in performance. They also provide the added benefit of centralizing program logic on the server, and simplifying coding for the client software. Again, in-depth knowledge of the server software is the prerequisite for this method.

Concurrency

In addition to performance and rapid query response, concurrency is of a major importance in data warehouse decision support. Concurrency refers to the simultaneous access of the same data in a database by more than one user and the operations the client/server system performs to accommodate it. If two users attempt to access the same record at the same time, both the database server engine and the client application must work together to help both users reconcile the conflicting operations they are trying to perform. Concurrency control doesn't magically happen—a specific method of concurrency control must be decided upon and specifically written into the application.

Typically, concurrency control is implemented in client/server databases through locking. A lock is a hold, placed on data being updated, which prevents other users from accessing the same data until the lock is released. Any user who tries to access locked data must wait until the lock is released.

Conclusions

The web is the largest client/server system implemented to date. It is also the most complex and heterogeneous and one that must deal with multitudes of operating systems, human languages, programming languages, software, hardware, and middleware.

The evolution in client/server computing has now provided data warehousing applications with a migration path from their existing technology platform to full client/server technology while protecting the existing investment and allowing them to respond effectively to the demand of the business and the marketplace.

12

IMPLEMENTING A WEB-ENABLED DATA WAREHOUSE

Introduction

Fifteen years ago, I could have told you how Coca-Cola was selling in the United States. Today, not only can I tell you how well Coca-Cola sells in the United States, I can also tell you how well they are selling in North Carolina, in Orange County, in the town of Chapel Hill, in the local Kroger's supermarket, with a special promotion, at the end of aisle nineteen, on Mondays.

The data warehouse gathers information from disparate sources, organizes it, and makes it available to the appropriate people within that organization. As discussed in earlier sections, the corporate data comprise a giant jigsaw puzzle, with each piece residing in a different area of the organization, perhaps scattered among multiple heterogeneous systems. All the pieces fit together correctly in the warehouse to allow the entire picture to be viewed and analyzed.

Information systems are truly *distributed* in the widest sense of the word when it comes to deriving any understanding of the corporation as a whole. Most systems are installed with a local or provincial view, and their sole purpose is to solve a singular isolated problem, such as accounts payable, employee tracking, manufacturing planning, or customer tracking.

While not necessarily incorrect, this approach does present problems when cross-functional views are required in order to understand the dynamics of a situation. Today's increasingly affordable technology now makes it possible to access huge amounts of data from a variety of sources, analyze it, and derive measurable results.

Implementing Data Warehouses

Operational systems and data warehousing systems possess fundamental differences in evolution, usage, system configuration, and performance. Rather than post operationally focused transactions, the ultimate purpose for data warehousing systems is to provide a tool to guide the business.

Data warehousing systems use separate computing resources with deeper historical archives. Data warehouses are tuned differently and process different applications than operational systems. However, a very fundamental requirement links the two systems (operational and decision support). They must use the same data source to be truly symbiotic. The data that is used by the data warehousing system must be pulled from the operational systems and verified.

Occasionally, the data must be transformed and consolidated in order to be useful. The data stored in the decision support system (DSS) is processed in a different way since it is not stored with the same schema as an OLTP system. In order to accommodate such variations, a number of architectural approaches are in use today to structure data warehouses.

Initial Thrust

Initially, data warehouse building and implementation followed an all-inclusive comprehensive approach. In this structure, enterprise data models were laboriously and meticulously planned. The data needs of the entire enterprise were then documented, and data was extracted from most if not all transactional systems in the organization. Several years ago, most major companies indicated that they were planning such data warehouses.

The Internet Phenomenon

Two technologies that became commercially popular in the early 1990s are in the process of converging. These technologies are the World Wide Web, which is making information on computers linked to the Internet easily accessible, and business intelligence tools, that facilitate making database contents accessible to non-technical users.

The way we obtain and analyze information to support our decisions has drastically changed the end result. This promises to make data published on the World Wide Web easily accessible to non-technical decision-makers for query, reporting, and analysis tasks. For corporations, this has introduced an alternative, low-cost mechanism for making data available to individuals who need it. For users, the end result is a much richer pool of easily-accessible information, from a wide variety of sources.

Driving this transformation is the Internet, an almost chaotic arrangement of computers, network connections, and telecommunication lines. The Internet was initially designed to meet the needs of the US Department of Defense for secure communications. Consequently, certain aspects of the design of the network, such as the packet-oriented communication protocol, TCP/IP, were intended to prevent the interruption of communications during a military confrontation.

During the first 20 years of the Internet, only a select few *power* users in the military or educational centers had access to the system. In the meantime, several key technologies evolved, which gradually increased the number of people who had connections to the Internet. These technologies included:

- Powerful and affordable personal computers (PCs) and workstations
- Improved network bandwidth and cheaper transmission rates
- Graphical user interfaces such as MS Windows, Macintosh
- Web TV

Data Marts

Organizations have realized that implementing an all-inclusive data warehouse is an uphill task with limited prospect of success. The concept of deriving smaller subsets of data for specific departmental applications has caught on, primarily as a way of controlling information and allowing for speedier deployment. This approach consists of offloading specific targeted applications down to the departmental level. Data is then drawn from the large warehouse so all users are working with the same version of the information.

There are three types of data mart implementations that are commonly employed. These are: independent data marts, integrated data marts, and point solution data marts.

Independent Data Marts

Independent data marts are those in which individual applications are architected for specific departments without the use of a data warehouse. Only the enterprise data required for that application is gathered from operational systems.

Such data marts are easy to fund, fast to build, and generally obtain user commitment. Industry statistics also confirm that most new plans for warehousing are for such data marts.

Integrated Data Marts

These depend on whether or not there is a unifying data architecture behind the independent marts. Those data marts which have a unified data architecture are said to be *integrated data marts,* also known as a *data mall*. The data mall, like a shopping mall, has a unifying theme, well-defined standards and rules for the participants. This is then carried over to the data and system architecture. In this approach, any new mart which comes on line has to comply with the rules of the mall. Otherwise, it does not get to participate in the traffic flow of customers (users) which the mall attracts.

In electronic commerce, this type of implementation is becoming quite prevalent. A large number of shopping carts have been designed to support such an architecture. The user is presented with a common user interface to peruse, drill down, and order from any shop on the mall.

Point Solution Data Marts

Another architectural construct is known as a *point solution* data mart. Here, each mart is built according to the specific needs of a particular department. No regard is given to adhering to any integrative architecture, standard, or other conformance with any other mart. This is obviously the cheapest and quickest to install, since no time is spent attempting to integrate the effort with any enterprise-wide architecture. It is also the one which will most likely have to be re-designed in the event that it proves successful. Any possibility of cross-functional analysis is at best difficult, if not impossible, due to the lack of standardization.

It also puts the greatest stress on the existing infrastructure. All of the point solution data marts are independently extracting data from the same operational systems. A great deal of redundancy of extracts may occur, causing more thrashing than necessary on the part of the existing systems. Such data marts are found to be internal to the organization and are usually based on intranets.

Factors for Consideration

There are obviously multiple approaches to constructing a decision-support data warehouse system for enterprises today. However, it should be clear that, regardless of the approach taken, the underlying technology issues must be addressed.

Performance is a key factor in the success or failure of a data warehouse system. It must deliver the results to the right people, in the right format, at the right time, and in a timely and responsive manner. Some symptoms of failing implementations include queries that run for hours on end, system-unavailable notifications, and data rendered obsolete by an infrequent load/refresh cycle in the data warehouse. These conditions will not be tolerated by the user community

Scalability comes right behind performance. The warehouse, if it is successful, will be subjected to increasing stresses as the amount of data grows, the number of users increases, and the level of sophistication of the users develops. As users get their feet wet, more complex joins, more variations in the models, and more demands for greater functionality, such as data mining, will inevitably follow the initial implementation. Implementations which cannot scale up with the increased demands will pay dearly in the long run.

Availability is another critical area. Users will want the system to be available when they need it, and the times they require it may not be very predictable. When a competitor surprises the market with an innovation or pricing move, the warehouse must be in a position to respond with the resources and analysis on demand.

Organizations today are typically large and complex with numerous systems developed over the last thirty years. They often possess many departments and use a variety of standards. These attributes make coalescing rational information a formidable undertaking. The following characteristics of most data warehousing installations are critical to the performance and success of any system.

Data Aggregation

To acquire information about an organization requires gathering data from many different systems. The aggregate of this data is large. Further, the nature of analytical processes requires the raw data of the operational systems. It also requires the derived data such as trends, averages, standard deviations. This supplemental data will increase the total amount of data to be stored, and it impacts systems in several different areas.

The first area is the time and the computing power required to scan such huge databases in response to specific queries. The second area is the time and the horsepower required to load and refresh the warehouse in order to maintain its currency and relevance to the organization.

Clearly, the larger the database, the more aggregations, summaries, trends, and averages will affect the amount of time required to refresh the existing tables with additional data. Time required to update all of the calculations based on the new data will also be affected. Many organizations underestimate the database requirements of their systems. Therefore, it is important to do the analysis up front to ensure that your system can expand to meet demand.

Cross-Functional Analysis

By definition, the need for a corporate-wide view of the information means that analyses will be cross-functional in nature. Users will need to combine information from one view of the data with information from other views. This will require the use of complex multi-way joins on the data tables. These operations are taxing on computer resources. When combined with large databases where the tables themselves are large, the problem is compounded. Data warehouse veterans share horror stories about queries which keep processors tied up for many hours attempting to execute a complex combination of commands.

Ad Hoc Queries

Unlike traditional reporting structures in operational systems where the database queries were defined prior to the system's construction, the data warehouse is constructed to satisfy an unstructured query model. When McDonald's announces that their cornerstone product, the Big Mac, drops in price from nearly one dollar to fifty cents, the analysts for Burger King and Jack-in-the-Box will be busy trying to figure out what such a price drop will mean in terms of their competitive response. Many models will be built to determine the results of each potential response, each built on assumptions regarding the behaviors of customers, supply chain markups, costs, distribution models, and so on.

Assuming these organizations have data warehouses in place to support this kind of decision, it is clear that there would be no way for the developers of such a warehouse to have known ahead of time that this would be a subject for analysis and research. Burger King and Jack-in-the-Box will want to look at several potential scenarios and multiple responses for each scenario. They will need to consider many iterations and permutations of queries into the demographics of consumers, the costs associated with producing competing products, the revenues and profits generated, and the trends in the marketplaces. Given this example, a data warehouse system will be subjected to significant stresses and will require significant computing and input/output resources.

Organizational Process

Today's management philosophies are much different than they were a decade ago when Executive Information Systems (EIS) first surfaced. In fact, the very name denoted the exclusivity of audience for these systems. It was assumed that only executives in an organization were involved in decisions which required ad hoc analysis and summary information from a cross-functional perspective.

Responsibility and decision making get pushed down the organizational pyramid into the hands of the professional staff. Thus, more and more people are demanding access to the information and the cross-functional analyses which decision making requires. As data warehousing implementations grow and expand into the organization it is important that the DSS (which will require more CPU and I/O performance) step up to the demand.

User Sophistication

Users will experience a learning curve in acclimating to the new technology. As they become more familiar with the data structures, query languages, and data analysis, they will build on previous experience and develop more and more sophisticated models for analyzing their particular problems. This will mean more complex joins, more full table scans, more sophisticated mathematical computations, and, in general, more demand on the system in terms of horsepower and I/O capacity. The hardware and software systems must have the capacity and capability to ensure performance.

Use of Multidimensional Databases

In an effort to improve response times for data warehousing systems, some organizations have opted to implement multidimensional databases or star schemas in relational databases. In these structures, the different parameters which describe the data are given as dimensions of the database, such as, time, number of products, number of stores, sales regions, and demographics of the target market. It is very easy for multidimensional databases to become quite large, simply because of the multiplicative effect of carrying multiple dimensions.

For example, we have 100 products being distributed by 50 stores, each of which is represented in six geographic sales regions. If we want to track the purchases over the last two years (24 months) by user demographics which include six age groups, six income levels, and five levels of education, then we have to track over 90 million facts. In fact, for each additional dimension added, the raw data for each table increased by a factor of almost two to one.

It is possible, as this scenario evolves, that the size of the raw data is exploded to many hundreds of times its original size as the number of dimensions increases to six, seven, eight, or more. This explosion in data can cause a data warehouse's I/O subsystem a great deal of stress in dealing with multiple users. More importantly, it also creates problems in refreshing the data and uploading both the required summaries and pre-calculated fields in a timely manner. In order to meet these demands, systems have to be exceedingly performant. They must be able to scale up to meet increased demands.

Pitfalls

In order to best understand how to achieve the results needed, it would be instructive to see where computer systems have potential pitfalls in the area of data warehousing. By identifying the areas where things could go wrong, the organization can better define countermeasures to avoid the pitfalls.

The primary technical issues are dependent upon the four elements of the computer system. These are the memory architecture, the I/O architecture, system tools, and the application software which utilize the other three elements in order to deliver a solution to the end user.

CPU Architecture

There is no better place to start any discussion of performance than the capability of the processing element of the system. Decision-support systems (DSS) are only as good as their ability to satisfy decision makers. The warehouse project is doomed to fail without a good, consistent computer architecture which can deliver performance and which will be stable and have the capacity to grow.

Significant attention needs to be paid to the ability of the selected computer to handle the demands placed by completely random searches into very large databases, as described earlier. While attempts are made to avoid full table scans and complex joins by providing star schema, indices, join indices and the like, the simple fact is that there is no way to avoid them completely. Therefore, there will be significant demands on the ability of the CPU itself.

Memory Architecture and Performance

The way a system's memory is architected contributes to its ability to respond to the demands of data warehousing. A significant aspect of this is the width of the memory. As the amount of information which can be transferred into and out of memory per clock cycle increases, the system's ability to deal with larger blocks of data in a timely fashion increases.

In a multiprocessing and a multithreading environment, some amount of time must be devoted to synchronizing and coordinating the activities of the various processors. In a shared-memory environment, there may be times when the memory is busy servicing other processors. Some processors must sit idle until the memory is free again. Minimizing latency, improving memory availability, and speeding up the access time to the memory will help keep more processors working at a higher utilization. In turn, this improves performance. Conversely, longer latency times, reduced availability, and slower access times will result in a poorer overall system performance.

Furthermore, the ability to load index tables and other database portions directly into memory can significantly improve overall performance times due to the much faster access times over disk memory. However, limitations on the size of memory could impede this process, which is becoming a significant problem for warehousing installations today.

I/O Capacity and Performance

When dealing with databases sized in the hundreds of gigabytes and well into the terabyte range, it is reasonable to be concerned about the performance of the input/output subsystems. A potential exists for operational problems related to the amount of time required to read and analyze large quantities of data and for problems from a maintenance standpoint. Bottlenecks in the I/O subsystem will cause longer load and refresh times and longer backup and recovery times. Each of these can cause reduced availability to the user community.

The amount of down time required can encroach on the users' work day. The alternative is to take fewer backups or to refresh the system less frequently. In the former case, the action is imprudent. In the latter, the user is forced to deal with *stale* data.

Scalability

A sure sign of the success of a data warehouse installation is the constant flood of users asking to gain access to the data for their own needs. Chances are that they are doing so because they heard how responsive, performant, and efficient the system was, and the success stories circulated by their peers intrigued them to the point of joining in.

A system which cannot gracefully scale with these growing demands runs the risk of not only alienating the new users who are enticed to join, but of disenfranchising the loyal ones who were spreading the good word to begin with. Clearly then, data warehousing implementers must seriously consider the implications of scalability for their projects-especially since the ultimate size of the system is often very difficult to predict.

Application Compatibility

A significant and often overlooked area of concern is the integration and architectural consistency of the applications and support software with the overall computer architecture. Although their marketers tout high performance and state-of-the-art technology, some systems in fact do not have all *the bells and whistles* needed to take advantage of today's technology. A good example of this is the situation which existed in symmetric multiprocessing computer architectures before databases and other applications were modified to take advantage of the multiple processors.

Today, all major database managers have been rewritten to take advantage of the performance improvements of parallel processing architectures. But, prior to those rewrites, there was little advantage to be gained by using symmetric multiprocessing in a database-intensive application. No architectural consistency existed between the processor and the attendant applications. It is important that you look under the covers of any proposed system and its many components. This ensures they have been written or updated to extract all the performance available from the technology.

System Availability

A final point of concern for managers of data warehousing systems is the availability of the system. The idea behind decision-support data is that it is available when you need to make a decision.

As warehousing systems become more accepted, end users begin to rely on them as necessary instruments to get their jobs done. Data warehousing applications are truly becoming mission-critical today as their role in strategic and tactical decision making grows. With increased stature comes a corresponding need to protect its availability for the user community.

Business Factors

Lets us focus on business and relationship issues which a manager must control in order to succeed. These issues have to do with other elements of the solution, such as selecting software applications which can take advantage of the technology or using methodology and support services to enhance the value of the technology and customizing it to suit the business needs of the enterprise. Integrating the correct set of components is key to a successful data warehouse.

Tools Required for a Data Warehouse

Tools and processes which are compatible with the enterprise's business needs are required in each phase pictured. Each of these sets of technology and applications needs to be compatible and integrated.

Data Extraction and Metadata Management

The operational cycle begins with the extraction of data and metadata from operational systems. There are many challenges here, including issues of multiple data sources from incompatible systems as well as from antiquated systems which utilize flat files, network, and hierarchical databases. In addition, metadata management must start at the very beginning of the cycle if the user is to have reasonable navigation through the tables in the warehouse and understand the nature and definitions of the data that is being analyzed. The tools must be comprehensive and adaptable to all the variety of systems and sources of data within the organization.

Data Quality Tools

Most legacy systems were built without the benefit of any enterprise data standards. This means that there is little or no data consistency across systems, and even sometimes within any one given system. For example, an office supply manufacturer has a decades-old database in which customer names are held in a single field. No data standards were ever imposed in terms of abbreviations, capitalization, and name order. In order to move this data into a warehouse, the data must be transformed and rebuilt into a consistent and well-defined system.

Of particular interest here is that, in order for users to have access to current data, data must be extracted and cleansed/transformed without impacting business processes. In the case of large databases, the extraction/transformation cycle can be lengthy and laborious.

Database Management

A good solid DBMS system is critical and must be compatible with the overall architecture. A number of good vendor choices employing a number of technology strategies are available in this class.

Information Access

In this phase, the need for users to build models, navigate tables, join tables, and in general build complex queries is of paramount importance.

Backup and Recovery

Refreshes must be scheduled so as to be timely but not disruptive, as mentioned earlier. Of equal importance is the need to develop a disaster recovery and backup scheme to allow minimal disruption to the business in case of a catastrophic failure. The use of 64-bit SMP with clustering may minimize the frequency of catastrophic failures. It may also facilitate the recovery via the improved I/O capacities of the architectures.

Implementation

Data warehousing is a technology which must be custom-fitted to the organization. Therefore, organizations must take a methodical and structured approach in defining and building them in order to take full advantage of the applications potential.

Some vendors offer services along with products, either in partnership with management consultants or through their own staff. Furthermore, some vendors also employ the services of software partners to aid users in successful integration of the products. Make sure that the technology implemented supports the business goals of the enterprise.

Prototyping techniques can be used to determine an information architecture. This is an area in which there is a legitimate dilemma. On the one hand, it is desirable to have a complete information architecture and data standards prior to commencing any work on a warehouse. This ensures that there can be consistent business rules for transforming data and for analyzing the data. However, given the size, political diversity, and time constraints on today's organizations, the likelihood of being able to produce a complete, agreed-to architecture is difficult at best, and often virtually impossible.

By starting small and building prototypes upon which to gain consensus, some organizations are able to gain enough of an architecture definition to build upon in later iterations. The thrashing of redoing a complete architecture is minimized while simultaneously achieving a timely implementation.

Piloting initial designs also serves to gain consensus, prove the concepts and increase the chances for success in any warehousing implementation. A successful pilot is more likely to ensure a successful installation, and will point out areas of concern in the pilot stage which are much more manageable than those caught in production.

As the organization learns of the abilities of the technology, new needs will arise, and they should be addressed within the architectural framework defined for the initial system.

Reducing the Risks

This section will delve into the issues uncovered and advance some techniques and technologies which address the primary areas of risk.

Performance

Recently, 64-bit architectures have emerged, allowing significant improvements in performance over their 32-bit ancestors. The benefits which accrue from the architectural change directly impact many of the issues surrounding data warehousing implementations. A 64-bit CPU can address a memory space over four billion times the size of the maximum memory space of a 32-bit machine. This feature can allow data warehousing applications to maintain frequently accessed areas of the database directly in memory.

The access times are orders of magnitude faster than they are for disk reads. The end user gains much faster response times, higher availability, and the capacity to do more work more quickly.

Memory Architecture

A 64-bit memory architecture also contributes to performance benefits. In addition to being able to address vastly greater quantities of data, each access results in the transfer of 64-bits of information as opposed to 32-bits. This offers several benefits in its own right. First of all, doubling the number of bits transferred in a single clock cycle feeds the CPU with that much more data, instructions, addresses and so forth. This makes each transfer from memory much more efficient. Secondly, it allows shared memories to service more processors, reducing the latency and minimizing wait times for processors. Finally, when combined with the increased clock times of today's CPU architectures, the three effects combine geometrically to produce staggering performance increases.

Single processors can only address some finite amount of memory attached to them. By clustering memory (with other processors) each individual processor now can have access to more memory that it could individually support. For example, if the memory limit for a single processor was 14 MB, by clustering with another processor, it could now access 28 MB. This increase in capability can significantly impact the performance of certain data warehousing implementations.

I/O Performance

As expected, a 64-bit architecture also provides substantive improvements in the I/O subsystems if the architecture is carried through. Again, the combination of faster clock cycles with the doubling of the width of the bus provides a multiplicative effect for much greater throughput. In data warehousing, the nature of the applications is such that there is likely to be heavy I/O traffic so it is vitally important that the architecture extend to the peripherals and I/O subsystem.

In data warehousing applications, data can be partitioned over multiple disks running in parallel. This kind of bandwidth makes it not only possible but practical to think of supporting large communities of users in a decision-support environment. Load and refresh times are drastically reduced, allowing more frequent refreshes of important current data, or even real-time updates if appropriate.

System Scalability

Scalability is another important area of focus. No one can precisely predict the demand and needs required of the system in its life cycle. The ability to scale up in size and performance when needed is critical.

Scalability and performance are related but are not the same. Scalability is the characteristic of a system to maintain a given rate of performance (response time per user) as the demand for the system increases. Therefore, in order to mitigate scalability risks we have to understand how systems can grow in total performance to maintain a relatively constant rate.

Today's computer architectures are capable of maintaining scalability via several different techniques. One technique to achieve scalability is to introduce multiple CPUs in parallel. While there are two techniques today to accomplish the paralleling of processing power (Symmetric Multiprocessing [SMP] and Massively Parallel Processing [MPP]), SMP architectures are dominating today's marketplace.

In Symmetric Multiprocessing systems, multiple processors share a single bus and a large shared memory. This means that any processor which becomes available (finishes a task) can work on either computing tasks or I/O tasks. A special version of an operating system is required to be able to manage the distribution of tasks and the breaking up of larger tasks into smaller parallel subtasks. Symmetric multiprocessing systems are also known as shared-everything architectures. The most critical characteristic of SMP systems is the degree to which they scale as more processors are added.

The amount of coordination and synchronization required to allocate tasks and recombine the outputs of the various subtasks into a main processing stream becomes more complex and more difficult as the number of processors increases. Therefore, the increase in performance as more processors are added is not perfectly linear, and, at some point, the curve will flatten out.

SMP technology, then, is a mechanism for providing scalability to data warehousing systems, and for protecting the manager from the ravages of success.

At this point, scalability is augmented by the use of clustering technology in which SMP configured systems are loosely coupled to share the load. Clustered systems can share disk drives and memory. They may also have a dedicated connection among them to monitor and synchronize activities. Again, there will be overhead associated with this coordination and synchronization of the systems. This is in addition to the overhead within each box of coordinating the individual processors, but the overall effect of SMP and clustering technology is to provide a graceful, affordable and responsive growth path for data warehousing managers.

System Availability

Clustering provides more than support for scalability, it also provides a hedge against hardware availability problems. As described earlier, hardware down time is inevitable in any computer system. It is especially nettlesome for mission-critical systems, which many data warehousing systems are becoming. Clustering configurations allow for CPUs to share disk drives and other peripherals. Should one computer fail, the other clustered machines will sense the loss of the failed unit and redistribute the work among the remaining clustered units. Therefore, even though performance may degrade due to fewer CPUs handling the demand, the system will continue to be available to the end users.

Availability problems due to load windows and other maintenance processes are adeptly handled by the increased throughput of the 64-bit I/O architecture as described above. Managers can be confident that reloads and maintenance will be handled during off hours and that the amount of time required for these functions will be minimized by the performance of the architecture.

Application Compatibility

64-bit computing is not limited to the CPU chip or its supporting hardware system. The DBMSs and applications must be adapted for 64-bit computing as well to achieve the performance and scaling benefit. In fact, the operating system, compilers, and runtime libraries must be developed, coordinated, and tuned in order for the overall system to be a success.

After the system hardware and the system software are designed and built, the next step in the development process is to work closely with the database vendors to take full advantage of the underlying 64-bit architecture. When this is completed, the potential for application growth in size and speed is enormous. For example, in a 64-bit architecture, the operating system could be set up to handle single files which span multiple disk volumes. This means all of the overhead associated with controlling file sizes with disk volumes can be simplified and will no longer be an issue for application programmers.

Applications written to a 64-bit architecture provide the ability to handle huge amounts of data without limitations of size, complexity, or performance. Gone is the 2 GB limit in terms of file size, which can be handy when dealing with terabyte-sized structures. It has been shown that 64-bit database response sometimes actually improves as the complexity of the query increases compared to 32-bit databases. As for performance, the most important area of all, 64-bit databases can exceed the performance of 32-bit databases by over 1000 times in some cases.

Applications in a 64-bit environment deliver the ability to solve larger problems. 64-bit RDBMS applications can respond in seconds instead of minutes or hours. This means that users can carry on a dialog with the system, rather than constantly waiting for the responses. As opposed to a series of disjointed questions posed hours or days apart, this constant interaction means that a faster, more organized analysis of the data can take place. Faster response time can also be used to run more iterations of a model for better quality of analysis.

The power of 64-bit computing is the next evolutionary step for data warehousing and large computing problems. 64-bit computing creates significant advantages in three areas:

- Larger data set capacity
- Increased performance as complexity increases
- Huge performance gains when used with larger system memories

The studies have shown that the least significant improvement over the 32-bit architecture was nearly an order of magnitude better. The full table scan was eight times faster in a 64-bit architecture. This means that for this type of application, a 64-bit system could service eight users in the time that a 32-bit system could handle a single user. Results for the other benchmarks were significantly better. For complex joins, such as the five-way table join, the 64-bit system performed 251 times faster. Again, this kind of power can be used either as a buffer to allow for scalability or as a performance feature for initial users.

For example, in the case of the five-way join, we can safely assume that the average user will wait five to ten seconds before becoming impatient. This means that if the results today come back in less than one second, we know we have a *cushion* of five to tenfold in demand before users become frustrated with the system. Therefore, today's lightning fast performance ensures a healthy safety margin in which the system can scale to a greater number of users.

Data Warehouse Implementation Plan

An objective for a data warehouse is to make all critical business data available in standard form for rapid inquiry, analysis and reporting. To achieve this, it is necessary to move data out of its non-standard form in existing applications by following a well-defined plan.

Implementation Steps

The more the existing applications adhere to some set of common data standards, the easier the implementation should be. For implementation, some of the major steps are:

1. Identify the *critical data subject* areas-accounts payable, general ledger, orders, inventory, customer, vendor, and employee.
2. Specify the *target performance* for creating extract files-the rate at which conversion must proceed to be acceptable. This is particularly important if the warehouse is to be for *near operational* data.
3. Set up *source data* for evaluation, field by field, character by character, to establish actual contents, mapping needed, and acceptable data standards for the organization. A variety of tools can assist in this analysis, and for value mapping, normalization.
4. Establish organization-wide *size and other standards* for various common field types-name, address, city, and postal code.
5. Establish *content and format* standards.

6. Incorporate standards into *conversion code* on servers to change sizes, map content and formats, and create fully mapped, standard versions of the data in the *source record layouts*.

7. Make clean, standard data accessible for analysis by *loading to SQL* or other warehouse-specific data server. This provides access to existing data in standard form, but may contain differing levels of normalization.

8. Define the *normalized content* of the required subject data sets.

9. Implement code to perform normalization of source files and create tables in normalized form with common content, at least within the same subject areas.

10. Develop a *common metadata* dictionary of elements and tables to define the new standard elements and support future data access by users.

11. *Evaluate results* and implement further changes needed to complete cross-subject integration.

Data Access Considerations

The result of completing this effort is that all applications data, organization-wide, is available in standard form. In addition to allowing access to historical data, the achievable performance targets for data transfer and conversion are such that, for most organizations, their current data can be moved daily.

Because of the daily transfer of all data, the effect is to provide consistent access to operational data, with the opportunity to replace existing applications reports by direct access to this consistent warehouse data. In addition, the standards and content defined for the normalized tables provides the basis for designing the replacement for the legacy, should that be a requirement.

Possible Constraints

The major problem areas encountered in implementation could be as follows:

1. Inadequate documentation of source data content is a significant problem. It usually requires character-by-character analysis of all data extracted so as to determine exact content and nature of the data.

2. Processing time to extract data from the source systems can prove a major constraint because of the need to use disparate tools from the vendor packages for the extracts. The more proprietary the package and internal data structures and representation, the more likely it is that this constraint will be encountered. It may need to be resolved by redoing the code, or by transferring much of the standardization load to the servers after extract from the source files.

3. To provide adequate processing speed for data mapping and loading, high speed servers may be required.

The Web-Enabled Warehouse

Although supporting the decision-making process with information technology is one of the hottest areas in computing these days, the focus is decidedly technical. Instead, we deal with data warehouses, data marts, web-enabled data warehouses/marts, and *push* technology.

Since the inception of the Internet, there has yet to be a topic as controversial as *web-managed push*. Web-managed push is a methodology that lets everyone in the information chain to have the tools, the access, and the security to obtain enterprise-wide data when, where, and how they need it. The information is pushed down to the client voluntarily, involuntarily, or by subscription. For example, users can subscribe to "selected financial" data about their favorite stocks or the same users can allow a news organization send information to the client without solicitation or the users can request information from a set of organizations to be sent but without any real control over the content. Similarly, we can subscribe to certain reports from a data warehouse, or allow certain enterprises to broadcast information or obtain unsolicited information without any real control over it. It is, in fact an extension of the client/server model. Push can be "indiscriminate," "selective," or "publish and subscribe."

Indiscriminate Push

Indiscriminate push is an on-going instance of updated information, used to distribute data from inside or outside the organization on a real-time basis. The recipient has no control over the inflow of information. Examples include stock quotes, news releases, and sports scores, mostly unsolicited once you subscribe to the service. It is distributed to the desktop, pager, cell phone, or fax. For single or small groups of subscribers, this is a very effective method for up-to-the minute information. The downside occurs when network bandwidth is clogged with information that may not be critical for the recipient.

Selective Push

Selective push gives the user, and the company, more control. Instead of a constant channel of information, subscriptions can be defined at the server level. A filter sorts and prioritizes data to be delivered to the desktop, funneling external and internal information to subscribers. This is effective for pushing predefined sets of information to classes of employees, say by job title. Examples include monthly or weekly sales reports to regional locations.

Decision-support summaries and reports can be sent to subscribers at given intervals from any part of the enterprise. These smaller packets of information place less stress on network traffic. The drawback is profile administration. Management tools are not yet available for large companies and the data warehouse requires intensive server administration.

Today, in data warehousing, there are two sides of information systems: operational or transactional, and informational. The operational side includes the systems familiar to most people. Examples are the finance or manufacturing systems, payroll, and human resources systems that run the daily operations of the business. Operational systems require data to be stored in a specific manner to achieve maximum performance from those systems processing day-to-day tasks.

The informational side was created to pull corporate information together. Informational systems support analysis and decision making and require the data to be stored in an entirely different manner for correctness and clarity. Data warehousing lies within the informational, or decision-support, side of the organization's information systems, and has its own unique requirements for information flow.

Data from multiple operational systems is collected, transformed, and integrated to a single platform for decision support. These warehouses can be *operational data stores, reporting databases,* or *query databases.* All have the same function, to provide a universal resource of information for *pushing* data to a warehouse or data mart for decision support. However, there must be a process to gather data from legacy, operational, and external databases, and *push* it to the warehouse.

Pushing data from operational systems through the warehouse out to the desktop is a process management opportunity. To effectively manage and distribute corporate data, a set of tools must be integrated into the data movement/push scenario. These tools include built-in scheduling mechanisms, and recovery/restart, to ensure job completion and data integrity.

The result is a tightly integrated *managed push* solution which gives corporations the tools and processes to actively leverage the wealth of information available from enterprise data. The data warehouse becomes a reservoir of mission-critical information to be shared across the organization. By combining scheduling, monitoring, movement, and recovery facilities, organizations can automate the information environment and directly contribute to the success of any warehouse project.

A data warehouse is a technical solution to a business problem. Decision makers who would most benefit from the warehouse are the least likely to use a query tool or run an SQL-based report writer to get information.

It is expected that the Internet is replacing client-oriented tools due to the low cost of deployment, easier administration, and distribution it enables. It is not a stretch of the imagination to see how the web has opened a whole new venue for accessing, reviewing, and sharing organizational data. The challenge is defining the process and having the tools to enable such an application.

Managed Push

A *managed push* moves the crucial business information out of operational systems to the desktop, with maximum control and flexibility. The universal interface, cost-effective deployment, and accessibility of the web browser have transformed the information in the warehouse into a resource available to any knowledge worker within the corporation.

It is only when these leading technologies, combined with the push methodology, are brought to bear that organizations can bridge the gap between knowledge workers and operational systems. The incorporation of a *managed push* methodology ensures that companies can leverage their data in a productive, measurable, and secure manner.

Publish and Subscribe

At its most fundamental level, the concept of *publish and subscribe*, of which push is a manifestation, is designed to provide three services: coordinating processes, replicating content, and informing people.

Publish and subscribe is not new, even in electronic terms. Such services have provided daily news summaries, based on each subscriber's predefined areas of interest, via fax and email for a few years. But this *feed* was limited, initially, to a point-to-point feed of static textual information. For example, In-foBeat provides a free service that includes not only content but the live hyper-text links to other web resources. Clients merely specify at what interval they desire an update (every hour, for example), and the messaging between client and server is automatic. In fact, one can even specify the stocks and stock prices that can be displayed on the user's desktop.

The implications of this technology are enormous, especially for expand-ing the reach of all types of applications, including data warehouses. Using this approach, clients can *tune in* to *broadcasts* that provide not only content but the application logic required to view or even manipulate it.

With an informational system infrastructure in place, the most effective method to push information to the knowledge workers is *publish and subscribe*. This *push* method extends *managed push* to the desktop by giving knowledge workers the power to schedule only the information they need, when they want it. These knowledge workers may require a stream of defined reports and infor-mation in a repeatable and consistent manner. Publish and subscribe is a perfect application to deliver integrated, enterprise-wide information to the desktop without burdening the recipient with additional training or systems knowledge.

Publish and subscribe can streamline the information delivery process. It is much more efficient to publish views of the data, and assign security to those views once, in the warehouse. Users may subscribe to views or subsets of views and determine the delivery format and schedule. By publishing data once to the server, the data is contained in a central location, reducing data re-dundancy. All users are now able to obtain and reference the same informa-tion, providing a common basis for decision making across the organization.

Publish and subscribe is a balance of subscriber control and administra-tor process management. Instead of pushing mass amounts of information to the desktop, data is published one time to the server.

Subscribers then determine when they want the information, and under what criteria. When the scheduled time or event arrives, the information is pushed to the users. Subscription is usually by time or event, requiring sched-uling and monitoring software. Users have the ability to discontinue a sub-scription or change the delivery schedule. Administrators need not worry that resources are being used to push information to a user who has changed their requirements, for the user is in control.

Push/Pull Paradigm

User control over information is known as the push/pull paradigm. The pull is as much an integral part of warehouse information distribution as push. Pull is the ad hoc side of access, whereas push is the pre-planned side. To achieve this flexibility in a warehouse, subscription interfaces and management tools must all be in place.

The object relational catalog provides optimum performance for a central repository of information about each data source, system users, and data maps detailing how data is mapped from one data source to another. Java servers use JDBC connections to the catalog to retrieve instructions for how and when data should be moved.

Java also plays a role in data movement. Native method calls from the Java server are made to the source database to extract the data. Native method calls are the most efficient way to extract data from DBMSs.

Impact on Data Warehousing

Push technology is having a major, positive impact on data warehousing. The impact is so positive, in fact, that need for data warehousing may begin to become transparent as content and process become unbundled.

The impact is vastly increasing the usage of the data warehouse. The increase is internal, reaching across the extended value chain of the organization (such as customers and suppliers) and external, as a source of *push* information for other users. By providing the mechanisms for publishing new information easily and subscribing to it by content, not contract, an unfathomable variety of services and products can emerge.

Push technology may change the way people interact with the data warehouse, perhaps even causing the whole concept to evolve into something else, such as an *information repository network*. Rather than being the repository of numeric data to serve spreadsheet transfer, reporting, OLAP, and data mining applications, it may become the focal point of a whole new set of web-enabled work processes for decision making, analysis, notification, exploration, and implementation. The entire decision-making process can be expanded to include customers and suppliers with off-the-shelf utilities instead of costly and time-consuming development efforts like EDI.

The enabling architecture, which can accommodate this technology, provides for adaptive networks of computing resources. This has broad implications for the data warehousing industry, too. Those tools that have not yet adapted to a network model may become obsolete. Traditional databases, such as RDBMS, MDBMS, ODBMS, tools, and methods may see a diminished significance.

Implementing Push

Granted, the manifestations described previously may sound just a little too good to be true, but the move to push technology is inevitable. Information

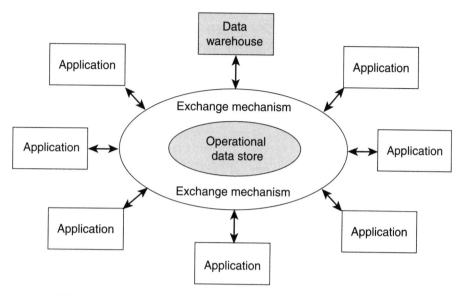

Figure 12.1   Publish and Subscribe Application Integration

technology, satisfied that it has finally begun to wrest control of computing re-sources back from the desktop, is going to be overwhelmed by what is bearing down on it if it does not get with the program.

Push and publish technologies are commonly used to integrate heteroge-neous applications. A logical by-product of this implementation can be a data warehouse or an operational data store (see **Figure 12.1**). A data warehouse is created if an application publishes events and keeps historical records.

Conclusions

Look at data warehousing as a means of improvement, not merely record-keeping. Simply to supply data is not enough. It must be packaged within a context of frameworks, analyses, and rules. To be effective, it must challenge people's thinking, not reinforce it, and lead to asking the right questions. Effec-tively deployed, data warehousing can be a rising-tide strategy, raising the level of everything in the process.

No decision-support system delivers sustainable improvement unless it fundamentally changes the nature of work. The best data-surfing program in the world will only have a temporary and localized effect if the analysis can not be shared with others. Data warehouse architectures miss this component completely by being overly focused on data and reporting issues instead of the broader issues of content and problem solving.

The primary design goal is flexibility, where the ability to continuously evolve to meet changing user needs is even more crucial than efficiency. Data warehousing is an application of computer technology which is demanding by virtue of its inherently large size and the need to integrate data from disparate, disjointed operational systems. Businesses today have taken a broad range of approaches to solving this problem, from creating monolithic centralized warehouses to distributing data marts or to implementing isolated point solution data marts with no integration attempted. Regardless of the approach taken, the fundamental characteristics of the problem are unchanged: large databases derived from many systems will still require I/O capacity to absorb the data in a timely fashion.

Complex analyses by end users will demand computational performance and increased penetration into multiple areas of the business will require scalability. More and increasingly sophisticated users will demand more sophisticated tools (e.g., data mining, data visualization). Acceptance of the technology will demand high levels of system availability and reliability.

Today's new enabling technology plays a large role in making data warehouses affordable and performant. The use of 64-bit computer technology will be invaluable, and even mandatory in addressing these issues in the months and years to come. The performance gains of 64-bit computing are well documented, and the move to this technology is as inevitable as was the move from 16-bit technology to 32-bit technology.

Organizations who make the move early will benefit in a number of areas. First and foremost, they will have a much easier time addressing the present needs of their constituency. However, beyond that, the inherent growth trajectory available through this technology ensures that their investment will be leveraged for some time to come.

The inevitable increases in demand from the user community will be addressable without the need for the proverbial forklift to remove the old system. Smooth upgrades with powerful and performant step increases will be available through the combination of 64-bit technology, SMP architectures, and clustering techniques. Enterprises who make the move sooner rather than later will be better positioned for success.

Consider push technology to be a way to expand the impact of your web-enabled data warehouse, and if you do not have a web-enabled warehouse, get busy. The economics are too good to ignore. However, there are a few caveats. Only multi-casting is viable, sustainable, or scalable. Multi-casting is a type of broadcast which allows information to be pushed over the network from many sources and to many recipients. This is equivalent to employing a technology in a many to many connection pattern.

Most important of all, adopt a mission-oriented approach, not a project-oriented one, and make your mission nothing less than to enable the decision-support architecture to be the driver of improvement in your organization.

13

INTRANET DATA WAREHOUSE

Introduction

Corporations recognize that information placed in the hands of decision makers is a powerful tool. The data warehouse contains historical data organized by key business dimensions. For example, the data warehouse for a retailer contains daily product sales for each store. The data warehouse for a bank contains customer information for each bank service. Each warehouse summarizes individual transactions into time-series data for monitoring and analyzing performance.

Delivery of data warehouse information to decision makers throughout the enterprise and around the world has been an expensive challenge. The World Wide Web offers a solution. Private corporate Intranet sites are the fastest growing segment of the Web. The opportunity is to introduce a new level of collaborative information sharing among decision makers.

Intranets currently manage unstructured content, including text, image and audio data types, as *static* HTML documents. With the right tools and the right architecture, the data warehouse can be made accessible over the enterprise intranet, forming the basis for a comprehensive enterprise information infrastructure. There are three important advantages of such an infrastructure:

- Information integration
- User collaboration
- Intranet economics

Information Integration

One of the most valuable assets of the enterprise is the operational data used in managing day-to-day business activities. This numeric data provides frequent measures of performance. By developing a data warehouse, corporations are organizing the data in a way that makes the data useful to decision makers.

When the data warehouse is put on the intranet, users can toggle between structured data analysis (producing reports in columns and rows) and unstructured browsing. For example, the marketing manager at a retailer can pull up an advertising image and a report on sales of products featured in the ad on the screen.

Similarly, multiple hospitals and/or application systems are integrated, where a particular hospital information technology staff builds the data warehouse allowing information from various application systems to be stored in real-time. The hospital staff may view patient demographics, lab results, radiology transcriptions, pharmacy and dietary information, using a standard web browser. In addition, users can also create various management and complex utilization reports using the current and/or historical information from the data warehouse.

User Collaboration

The intranet is as much about communicating at an interactive level as it is about making structured and unstructured content easily accessible. There are few that would disagree with the view that decision making improves with timely, accurate, and complete information. The intranet influences how the ideas and experience of a workgroup are exchanged as part of knowledge sharing.

The personal computer era transformed a generation of users into electronic *knowledge seekers*. As knowledge seekers, users seek to load their personal computers with as much data and software as possible. Users want to be self-sufficient analysts—in fact, they have to be self-sufficient.

The network computer era allows users to evolve into *knowledge brokers* and emphasizes the powerful advantage of collaborative problem resolution. Knowledge sharing requires the free flow of all types of information among users—not just text file transfer, but an interactive data analysis capability that encourages the exchange of experience and ideas. The intranet should be the basis for rethinking the enterprise information infrastructure.

Information Technology professionals have struggled with the challenge of delivering fast, accurate, cost-effective and appropriate information to users for many years. With the move to downsizing and open systems, for all the right reasons, most organizations now have *islands of data* within application packages and frequently on different platforms. Often these application packages have different definitions and business structures held within their databases because they have been focused on solving a specific transactional issue.

Intranet Economics

The cost of client/server computing is high when communications, support, and other hidden costs are considered. In fact, some studies suggest that client/server computing is more costly than mainframe computing. Certainly the personal computer has become bloated with processing power, memory, software, and user-managed files of considerable proportions. The result is a "fat" client architecture.

The intranet will change the economics of supporting a large population of knowledge workers. The intranet is a "thin" client architecture. Not only does the intranet reduce communications costs, but the personal computer may very well be replaced with a low-cost intranet device.

The thin client model requires server distribution of applications software. This is where Sun's Java plays a role. Java allows software to be served to the intranet browser in code fragments or applets. Application software no longer needs to be resident on every client. Rather, application software is acquired only when needed, for as long as it is needed, for a specific application.

Application software licensing is shifting from per seat pricing (licensed for each personal computer) to a server-centric licensing model. The result is lower application software licensing costs. Thus, the economics of the intranet are lower communications costs, less expensive thin client hardware, and reduced application software licensing costs.

Internet and the World Wide Web

The Internet is a collection of networks and routers that use the TCP/IP protocol suite and function as a single, large network. The Internet reaches government, commercial, and educational organizations around the world.

Any machine connected to the Internet has a unique Internet (IP) address. The IP address is a four-byte or 32-bit code which is assigned so that all machines belonging to a similar network have the same prefix. This is similar to telephone numbers being grouped into locations; however, location is irrelevant when assigning IP addresses.

An improved IP addressing system will use eight bytes (128-bit), sufficient to make it possible to control any light-switch in any house on the earth without any worries of running out of addresses.

The World Wide Web (WWW)

The web's success has been achieved by creating hypermedia document standards:

- The HyperText Transport Protocol (HTTP) which is used by all web browsers to communicate with web servers.
- HyperText Markup Language (HTML) which is the language used by web page authors to format the hypermedia documents.

Intranets

An intranet can offer a single point of entry into a corporate world of information and applications. The same facets of the Internet that are so compelling to the public can drive an organization to communicate and collaborate at a new level. Intranets are essentially secure mini-internets implemented within organizations. Implementing Internet technology within an organization provides the following benefits:

- Control over storage and retrieval of information within the organization,
- Storage of any document, application, or database in a set location. Authorized users have the potential to get access to this information anywhere. The same hierarchy of information can also be controlled throughout the organization very easily. All affected can be notified of any changes at the same time.
- Elimination of any problems of ambiguity, because only one version of a piece of information is made available. The most up-to-date information can be distributed and shared among users instantly.
- Easily maintained security using firewalls or proxy servers. For example, all users in a particular network group could easily be given or denied access to information depending on their IP address. This network group can range from a single user to all users at a particular site.
- Standardization of all user input, so that common processes, such as filling in company purchase orders, can be easily controlled and modified at will.

Users require only a web browser to be running on their machine to access the whole system. Internet and intranets allow user hardware and software platform independence—there's no specific need for costly hardware or software upgrades to user machines. Users who have access to the Internet at home have the potential to use the company systems at home as they do in the office.

The network and software is easily made more efficient, and can be maintained centrally. Due to the nature of the intranet, there is no problem with splitting work between several servers within the organization around the world.

Server "mirroring" is the preferred technique in larger intranets as a second server can be used if one server goes down. Users can still continue to work by being re-connected to another server.

Software can be easily upgraded without having to organize a mass client upgrade session, because there is essentially only one program, which is located on the server(s).

By implementing various forms on an intranet, the need for paper printing is reduced. This has the benefits of freeing up network resources and saving printing and distribution costs.

Intranets and Web-Based Applications

The most important development in computing since the advent of the personal computer is the explosion of Internet and web-based applications. Somewhat after the fact, the business community has quickly jumped on the Internet bandwagon.

One of the most exciting fields in computing industry today is the development of intranet applications. Intranets are private business networks that are based on the Internet standards, although they are designed to be used internally. The Internet/intranet trend has very important implications for data warehousing applications.

Data warehouses can be made available world-wide on public or private networks at much lower cost. This availability minimizes the need to replicate data across diverse geographical locations. This standard has allowed the web server to provide a middle tier where all the heavy-duty analysis takes place before it is presented to the web-browsing client to use.

The skyrocketing power of hardware and software, along with the availability of affordable and easy-to-use reporting and analysis tools have played the most important role in evolution of data warehouses.

Getting Web-Enabled

While it is true that today's web-enabled decision-support products are evolving, the technology to view previously created reports is readily available now. Even if an organization needs more capability for some users and if a company has an intranet in place, providing users with easy access to web-based reports makes sense.

At this point, some of the available products have been in user environments for some time, and some of these have already been enhanced and upgraded to take advantage of technologies such as Java and ActiveX. In general, products that started with a multi-tier architecture, whether in a client/server or web-enabled environment, are further along the evolutionary path than those that began as client-centric products.

The bottom line is that companies can, and should, get started with web-enabled decision support now. Providing users with access to database reports, interactive viewers and even ad hoc query capabilities in the cost-effective intranet environment is simply good business.

Information Sharing Via the Intranet

Today, most users can communicate via a corporate e-mail system. While an e-mail system allows text files to be exchanged, it does not facilitate true collaboration. True collaboration requires interactive sharing of information in such a way that the recipient can continue an analysis or branch off in an entirely new direction without assistance.

For example, if I receive a data warehouse report from another intranet user, I should immediately be able to drill down or drill up on any report dimension, pivot and rotate the results, add additional calculations as part of my analysis, and then pass my work to others in the organization. This requires dynamic report creation based on data stored in the warehouse.

True collaboration for business decision making requires a higher level of interactive analysis and knowledge sharing than exists today in most text-oriented groupware products.

Putting the Data Warehouse on the Intranet

Data warehouses employ relational database management systems that use SQL to retrieve rows and columns of numeric data, while unstructured content is managed as HTML documents. The challenge in putting the data warehouse on the intranet is in properly enabling SQL data warehouse access from HTML browsers. The following application software services must be provided:

- Analytic layer
- File management
- Agents
- Security

Analytic Layer

Putting structured data content on the intranet requires a server-resident analytic layer to generate SQL *on the fly*, perform computations, and format reports based on user requests. In essence, a specialized structured content web server is required to support data warehouse access from an HTML browser client initiated request.

The analytic layer shares some capabilities with spreadsheet software. The power of a spreadsheet is derived from a user's ability to author custom calculations based on facts stored in cells in the spreadsheet. For example, in Excel, facts (numeric data) are stored in two dimensions. Combining the two dimensions, A1, provides a unique address. This unique address can be used to create a formula for a required calculation, A1-B1. Often the number of calculated rows and columns in a spreadsheet application far outnumber the number of stored facts.

The spreadsheet provides two additional powerful capabilities. First, users can easily replicate formulas for calculations down a column or across a row. Second, the calculation logic is automatically updated if new rows or columns of data are inserted into the spreadsheet.

The data warehouse has multiple dimensions, such as product, vendor, market, outlet, customer, and period, as opposed to the spreadsheet. The combination of multiple data warehouse dimensions still provides a unique address. The analytic layer on the structured content web server allows users to apply calculations, based on database dimensions, to create more useful reports. Furthermore, calculations once authored can be shared with other users much like calculation formulas are replicated within a spreadsheet. And, the calculation logic is maintained as the data warehouse is updated each day, week, or month.

Like the spreadsheet, reports that users request from a data warehouse often contain more calculated rows and columns than raw data. Without a robust analytic layer in front of the data warehouse, the user is limited to a simple listing of stored data elements. The analysis layer is key to addressing business questions that users must answer.

File Management

Data warehousing promotes interactive analysis and knowledge sharing. A report requested by one user is valuable when it is shared with other users to gain their insight and ideas. The recipients should be able to continue the analysis initiated by the original author. In this way, the analysis process becomes an interactive exchange.

Many users can pursue different analysis paths from a common starting point. To meet the challenge of providing interactive analysis of a data warehouse, users must have access and be able to change their copy of the logic used to create the report. A sophisticated server-based file management system is required to support user collaboration at this level. Agents

One of the common complaints about e-mail and even phone mail is that the mail box fills up faster than a user has time to isolate and address the really important issues. Agents are intended to work on behalf of users to isolate important information sought by a user. An agent can be triggered by some predefined event or at a specified time interval. The agent sends an alert to notify specific users on a *need to know basis*.

Agents must have the ability to run continually as background processes on an intranet logic server because each user is almost always disconnected from the web server. This provides a means of automating the routine analysis process. And, when the user signs on to the network, the agents must be smart enough to notify users of conditions that occurred during the disconnect.

Because data warehouses tend to grow exponentially, it is critical that agents proactively monitor and manage activities, alerting decision makers only when specific conditions exist.

An example of the use of triggers, agents, and alerts is a forecast accuracy monitoring application. When each week's actual sales are updated to the data warehouse, the system automatically calculates the mean absolute percent error between forecasted and actual results over the previous six weeks for every product.

The mean absolute percent error is a simple way of representing forecast error over time. An alert is sent to each marketing manager responsible for the product forecast if a threshold for the mean absolute percent error calculation is exceeded. The user can then take appropriate actions to avert out-of-stock conditions or excessive inventory build-up.

Security

The liberal sharing of information and collaboration among users on the intranet immediately raises data security issues. The data warehouse should be viewed as one of the enterprise's most valuable assets. Data must be secured, but if too tightly controlled, the value of the warehouse will never be fully realized.

The security issue is indeed complex. To illustrate, a user has authorization to view financial data at a U.S., region, and territory level. At the territory level, the financial data would include all salary data for sales representatives. If the same user creates a report and decides to share it, the regional managers should have access to only territory information for their region, and be blocked from accessing territory information for other regions. In other words, if a particular user is not authorized to receive and access a report, then that user must not be able to view the report or drill into areas where the user does not have authorization.

In other words, reports that are created from data stored in the warehouse should not simply be shared as text files. All reports should include the underlying logic, giving the recipient the ability to immediately analyze and modify the report as well as the logic and assumptions supporting the analyses. For effective collaboration, reports must be shared throughout the workgroup and enterprise. If the recipients are not authorized, the access to report logic should be denied.

Encryption of data can provide a higher level of security than is generally available for business applications. For example, using the Netscape Secure Socket Layer (SSL), data passing between the client and server can be encrypted. This enables business users to run important applications over unsecured communications lines without worrying about an intruder tapping into the network and viewing the transmitted information.

Structured/Unstructured Content Server

The Common Gateway Interface (CGI) facility of web server software provides a method of executing server-resident software. Building secure applications for the intranet requires a well-thought-out security strategy as well as the appropriate application architecture. Most web applications provide all users with the same access permissions. The information available is either of low or no level of confidentiality.

Business users require a system that maps them to their server account by verifying user names and passwords. When server applications are run, they will have access to their files secured by user, group, and world permission levels. The same issue exists with database security. Users must be mapped to the appropriate entity in the database in order to control the data that a user can access. Since the number of users may be large, the administration of the security system should be centralized at the server and minimized to the extent possible.

A second issue with the CGI interface is that it does not offer a continuous connection to the database. As a result, it is impossible to support an application requiring multiple interactive queries—a data warehousing requirement. One approach to solving this problem is to employ a message-based protocol between the client browser and the server-resident analytic layer using the CGI or through IIOP.

By mapping a user to a server account, a continuous connection is maintained between the logic layer and the database during iterative queries. This facilitates the execution of efficient SQL query strategies and computational routines to meet the user requirements for structured content analysis.

Decision Support and Intranets

Today's businesses are operating in a very different environment from businesses of only a few years ago. Information is proliferating at alarming rates. Data marts and data warehouses are springing up to accommodate the ever-growing stores of data that are the lifeblood of business. Flatter organizations are spawning more users of critical business data. More importantly, these users must quickly turn data into meaningful information on which key business decisions can be based.

Part of the reason for this change is the pervasiveness of the Internet and the World Wide Web which have made fast, easy global communications a reality. The Internet has opened the door to a global business community where being able to make informed decisions and move quickly is key to success. In this environment, finding effective ways to get meaningful information to the people who need it, wherever they are and at any hour of the day or night, is a major business challenge.

Following fast on the heels of the Internet are intranets. In a recent survey, most of the companies surveyed stated that they either already have an intranet in place or plan to implement one. A recent survey showed that companies are installing intranet servers at several times the rate of Internet servers.

The reasons are clear. Intranets are easy to use, fast to implement, cost-effective, and an efficient way to make information available to the people who need it. The fact is that any authorized user can get to information on an intranet with nothing more than a standard web browser, and web browsers are now in widespread use in most organizations.

Intranets are quickly becoming stores of large volumes of information, much of which is static corporate communications materials such as telephone listings, internal memos, corporate communiqués, and similar documents. However, as intranets become more pervasive, the kinds of information on them is changing and expanding. Corporations are now looking for ways to give users *dynamic* access to the information in their databases and data warehouses. These provide them the tools to access real-time information that people can use to improve the speed and quality of their decisions. Web-enabled decision support meets this need.

Web-Enabled Decision-Support Tools

Web-enabled decision-support tools have come a long way in a relatively short time. However, the level of sophistication of the solutions can vary widely. Web-enabled decision-support tools can be classified into three categories:

- *Web-like* tools have the ability to publish static information in HTML format that can be read by browsers. Tools that deliver this level of functionality are usually client-based.
- *Web-lite* tools have the ability to publish static reports on a scheduled basis, deliver on-demand reporting, and/or initiate a report for dynamic execution via the browser. Tools that deliver this level of functionality are client- and server-based. These can be easily integrated as part of "push technology" process.
- *Web-live* tools have the ability to deploy everything available in web-lite implementations in an interactive and content-rich browser environment. Tools that deliver this level of functionality are client- and server-based and have some component written in Java or ActiveX.

Web sites and architectures can be classified according to the following services, in a progression:

1. Provides basic file distribution services using a *two-tier* architecture. These sites save or convert reports and documents as HTML files and store them on the web server.
2. Provides dynamic HTML publishing, which means that HTML documents are created on the fly in response to user requests. The output is a static HTML page or document. Such architectures implement a four-tier architecture (web browsers, web servers, application servers, and databases) and most use Common Gateway Interface (CGI) to link web servers to external programs.
3. Provides Java-assisted publishing, adding Java applets or other client-side programs to the previous architectures to provide an enhanced interface, provide support for localized processing, or convey interface events to back-end CGI servers.
4. Provides dynamic Java publishing. This web architecture is designed, maintained and executed entirely on the web using Java code. It employs a classic *three-tier* architecture (Java applets, a Java application server and a back-end database or resource manager) and is not constrained by HTML and HTTP.

The Web-enabled Solution

These above definitions provide a useful starting point for understanding the functionality of the various web-enabled decision support tools and web architectures available today. However, there are several factors that any organization considering deploying a web-enabled decision support solution should investigate before making a final selection. Some key factors to consider include:

- Consider a solution that can handle all aspects of implementation from designing and building reports to deployment, administration, and management of web applications. Depending upon resources available and the skill level of people who will be using the tools, organizations may also want to look for a solution that requires no programming or scripting. If you are looking for a truly programming-free solution, be sure to verify that the tool also handles any required CGI script generation automatically.

- To be most useful and effective, web-enabled decision-support tools should support Internet standards such as HTML output, hot-linking, and CGI scripts. The tools should also take advantage of JPEG and GIF formats to extend HTML's output capabilities for richer content and should have Java applets and ActiveX controls either in place or planned for the near future. Deployment of Java applets, in particular, will allow the product to provide interactive and content-rich web decision-support environments. Beyond this, be sure that the particular web-enabled solutions allow easy migration as new and emerging technologies and standards mature.

According to many industry experts and analysts, server-based processing is key to successful web-enabled decision support. Web-enabled products that lack server-based processing, including many of the popular client-centric query and reporting tools, are going to be at a distinct disadvantage when it comes to delivering complete web-enabled decision support. Without server-based processing capabilities, users will not be able to take advantage of the benefits of automated scheduling and on-demand reporting.

It is important that the server-based processing is supported on both UNIX and Windows NT platforms. Being able to use the tool with both UNIX and NT increases scalability options and ensures that the large number of medium-to-large organizations that use both platforms can deploy a single seamless solution to all their users.

Some products have the ability to perform all of their processing on the server. Others offer only partial implementations, with only a portion of the processing actually being performed on the server. Since the Internet is a server-based environment, if a web-enabled decision-support solution requires any processing to be executed on the client (SQL generation, calculations, sorting, correlation or result sets, formatting) it may prove unsatisfactory either in terms of performance or functionality.

Whether organizations choose to deploy their web-enabled decision support solution within UNIX or Windows NT environments or both, it is essential that they have complete flexibility in mapping to back-end data sources. This includes access to data warehouses, data marts, and corporate, departmental, and personal databases.

The vast majority of corporate data users are occasional users who do simple information look-ups. For these users, the web is an extremely cost-effective way to meet their needs. Such users' needs are usually addressed most effectively in a client/server environment.

For this reason, it is likely that most organizations will want to deploy both client/server and web-enabled decision-support solutions. Compatibility between the client/server and web solutions is an important consideration. With a single decision-support tool that is architected to provide robust support for both environments, an organization can leverage its client/server and web investments by reusing and redeploying assets for both environments. This eliminates the need to maintain separate systems that require separate administration and training, and saving time and money in the process.

Meeting the Needs

Having a thorough understanding of what a decision support product can really do will help the companies avoid disappointing and sometimes costly mistakes. Whatever else, it is certain that the products available today are precursors of products that will offer greater functionality in the future. For this reason, a clear understanding of how a product's design will accommodate future developments is particularly important.

To evaluate the potential for future capabilities in the product, one of the most important things to look at is the product's underlying architecture. Many of today's Web-enabled tools are based on *fat client* model in which processing is handled on the client. These architectures do not support *server-based* processing, which is integral to every level of dynamic, real-time web-enabled decision support. Products based on a *fat-client model* are poorly matched to the Internet's *thin-client, multi-tier model* and will not grow to accommodate interactive decision support without significant changes.

Some products may already incorporate Java and Active-X capabilities which users need to view sophisticated images with their browsers or to perform web-based ad hoc queries. If Java and Active-X are not already a part of the product, it is important to know whether they will be implemented in an upgrade which will replace the existing tool.

Conclusions

Writing an autobiography and composing a song are not the same, just because you use writing tools to complete both tasks. In much the same way, building an intranet in a decision-support environment is very different from building a public Internet site. Everything from the business case to the user base is different. Some of these differences may seem obvious, but it is certainly easy to get caught up in the rapid pace of intranet development and forget all of the internal systems lessons learned in the past.

Remember, as with client/server, the true cost of your intranet will be back-end loaded with maintenance, content management, and other issues. If you develop your intranet with these differences in mind from the outset, your costs over time will be significantly less and your users will view the system as a success.

It has been recognized that there are not enough analytical personnel to support the decision making of managers. IT departments are now helping by creating a single source of data which is consistent, accurate, and enriched with the types of ratios and measures that enable business professionals to make fact-based decisions. This strategy is called data warehousing.

The Internet provides a number of additional advantages, such as the use of low-cost PCs and standard browsers, and the elimination of expensive remote networks and routers. There is a wealth of data locked up in legacy and relational database systems and now in data warehouses also. The integration of these technologies, intranets and data warehousing, is what we are referring to as data webs.

14

BUILDING AND ACCESSING THE WEB-ENABLED DATA WAREHOUSE

Introduction

It is nearly impossible to read a trade or business publication today without seeing at least one article prodding businesses to get on the web and make money. Certainly, there are many opportunities to exploit the web-enabled data warehouse, but it is not as easy as it sounds. The reality is that while web sites abound, few companies are actually having great success in using their data warehouse resources successfully.

The recent explosion of interest in data warehousing can be attributed to a fortunate synchronicity of new business imperatives with readily available hardware and software tools. While these imperatives have always been goals of successful organizations, the profoundly escalating global competition has brought these imperatives to exponentially higher levels. And through web-enabled data warehousing, organizations are competing at those higher levels.

The primary objective of a data warehouse is to give end users faster, easier, and direct access to corporate data so that they can make quicker, more informed, and better decisions. By so doing, users can find competitive advantages for their organizations resulting in those increased revenues, lowered costs, or both.

Tangential gains in productivity by data warehousing can be realized by removing decision-support burdens from finely tuned operational systems. Thus, data warehousing offers major opportunities for profits and savings on many dimensions. Giving users direct access via the web makes the process even more productive.

The size and scope of warehouse projects vary significantly. For example, a departmental data warehouse project might consist of a centralized warehouse containing extracts from an inventory On-Line Transaction Processing (OLTP) system. An enterprise-wide data warehouse project might draw data from sales, marketing, manufacturing, and financial systems worldwide.

To meet these diverse needs, corporations have acquired many powerful tools, techniques, and expertise for the data warehouse market. In this section, we will discuss some of the requirements for the end user access, data loading, conversion, and information delivery tools for the data warehouse, from ad hoc to production querying and report writing. We will also discuss how these tools can help to optimize the performance of the data warehouse architecture.

Access to Data

Access to a data warehouse needs to be provided for a wide range of users and uses. Data warehouse users range from non-technical end users to business analysts, and their needs vary from ad hoc querying to production report writing. For example, an executive might want to log on and see only canned queries and reports, a production manager might have routine queries, and a financial analyst might want a very sophisticated set of ad hoc querying capabilities to uncover strategic competitive information. From the novice to the power user, the tools need to be able to accommodate the user's needs and skill set.

Data warehousing empowers all of these end users by giving them access to corporate data for decision support. Therefore, all end user tools for decision support need to be evaluated on their facilities for data access, manipulation, and presentation as to how well users are empowered to get the data, to perform analyses and other manipulations on the data, and to present the results in the most informative format.

Ease of Use

The access tool must be easy to use for all levels of users. Advances in user interface technology, such as Microsoft Windows, X/Motif, and Macintosh, have made data access easy. They provide a common set of features that facilitate ease of use, like point- and-click menus and hypertext help. Implementations of these friendly user interfaces along with executive icons, templates, aliases, runtime variable support, and other techniques can shield even the most novice user from having to understand anything about database access or design.

Because data warehousing is based on a dynamic decision-making model, most warehouse users will need tools with robust querying and report writing capabilities. Additionally, the heaviest users of the data warehouse, those with intensive analysis requirements, will need the fastest and most sophisticated set of tools.

A data warehouse user needs to be able to do trend analyses on the data in the warehouse in order to identify patterns and exceptions. Another user needs to be able to perform logical comparisons and see ratios and rankings. A third user needs to be able to perform post-retrieval calculations and other manipulations on the data. Still another needs to be able to compare the results of different queries side by side. And they need to be able to do all of these things iteratively in order to turn the data into valuable information.

Tools

The above scenarios illustrate the need for a powerful and robust set of slicing and dicing capabilities in the end user tool set. At a minimum, the end user tools should support the full SQL SELECT statement. Support for any

SQL-specific extensions is also desirable. The tool should also support a very wide range of mathematical and logical functions and data types. From simple SELECT statements to complex analyses, the end user tools need to provide a powerful, yet easy to use, arsenal of querying capabilities.

Using desktop-publishing-like features, the users should be able to format reports with multiple fonts, images (such as a corporate logo), borders, color highlighting of conditional results, annotated text, odd and even page layouts, master pages, watermarks, and more. Users should be able to create columnar as well as n-dimensional crosstab/matrix reports with multiple pivoting, and design reports that let them view data from separate queries side-by-side.

The primary challenge is to provide an easy-to-use interface while sacrificing as little as possible of the functional richness of SQL or of the tool's capabilities for post-retrieval manipulations and calculations on the data.

Tools are now available that can meet practically all of the data warehouse end users' needs. With web-based access, the time required to create queries and reports can be reduced from weeks to minutes, and the information the users discover can be used to create powerful competitive advantages much more rapidly.

Support for the Data Warehouse

Administration and performance are critical factors in data warehousing where there may be thousands of tables with thousands of rows and hundreds of gigabytes of data. Warehouse access tools must have facilities to manage warehouse metadata and large queries and results sets. From the initial design of the warehouse, end user access tools must be considered for their ability to integrate with the data warehouse's design and optimize its performance.

Over time, the data and the data dictionary in the warehouse will change in response to changing business needs. During the warehouse's creation and ongoing operation, end user access tools that require a separate, redundant data warehouse dictionary, are very costly to implement and maintain.

Tools that read the database metadata do not incur overhead from having to maintain a separate data dictionary. For example, if the multiple dictionaries are not updated at the same time, end users may get no answers or wrong answers to queries and quickly become unproductive and dissatisfied. For the administrator, managing multiple dictionaries is not only an ongoing overhead burden to keep the multiple data dictionaries concurrent, but also an unnecessary additional level of complexity and opportunity for error.

Administrators need to be able to prevent runaway queries and other actions that may overwhelm system resources. Administrative facilities that can help govern resource usage include the ability to cancel queries or to halt queries when a time limit is reached or a certain number of rows are returned.

Client-centric versus Client/Server

By definition, client-centric tools require entire query results sets to be brought back to the client. This can be quite problematic. For example, a query bringing back one million rows of data will adversely affect the performance of a network. If the user wishes to do post-retrieval manipulations on this data set, their desktop system could get tied up for a significant amount of time and it may not be able to even perform the desired operations.

A well-designed client and server tool can enhance data warehouse performance in many ways. It can allow users and warehouse administrators to choose whether to do parts of the processing on the client or on the server. Users can design a report on any client and execute it immediately or schedule it to run on any server and retain the identical fonts and images. For example, customized billing reports can be created on a PC and sent to any server attached to a heavy duty printer that can print out the thousands and thousands of pieces of correspondence required overnight.

This optimizes usage of system processing power, reduces network traffic, and frees up users' desktops for other uses. Other client/server performance-enhancing capabilities include being able to create joins on the server, buffer results, and reformat reports without re-executing queries.

Departmental data warehouses and warehouses in their initial stages of construction are likely to be in a single database source on a single platform. Large organizations with growing data warehousing needs, however, often have several different operational data stores in different databases and on different platforms constituting enterprise-wide data warehouses. Also, with some warehouse designs, highly summarized data is kept in the warehouse. For more detailed data, users need to be able to go to the source of the detailed data for querying. To be truly useful in these environments, the end user tools must be able to access the users'' data in heterogeneous RDBMS from desktop to mainframe.

The querying tool should be able to access the RDBMSs through their native APIs, plus offer access to practically any other source through ODBC and middleware. Native API support not only lets the queries run as fast as the database engine allows, but also gives the user access to the database's

SQL-specific extensions. Access through additional means gives the organization ever more leverage for legacy and new systems.

Application Development

Enterprise-scale applications may be defined as applications which are deployed across an enterprise over heterogeneous platforms, accessed simultaneously by hundreds of users at multiple geographic locations.

Web Support

The enterprise application development environments must permit developers to deploy a web server on any flavor of UNIX, NT, or other platform servers, supporting hundreds or even thousands of users. Application development for the web brings a variety of performance and security-related issues to the forefront. Thus, a development environment which supports cross-platform deployment and offers a wide variety of options (hardware and operating system support) can provide more flexibility and scalability in terms of application size and number of users accessing those applications on the Internet.

In contrast, client-based tool sets are primarily limited to Windows/Intel/Macintosh .architectures. This narrows the choice of servers and server operating systems . which can be used for a web server. A web server based on NT can be a good solution, but the server scalability is tied to the scalability of the selected operating system. Web-based application development and deployment is still in its infancy. Therefore, it is prudent not to make the same mistakes developers did when they developed client/server applications for a limited number of users and later tried to scale up to support more users at more sites.

Deployment of Web-Based Applications

It is essential today for a development environment to support web-based applications development. Software companies are integrating this functionality into their development environments in a variety of ways. The best approach in the short term is to enable current applications to be deployable on the web with minor modifications.

This functionality will become extremely important as the client/sever architecture merges with the intranets. It is unacceptable to have to develop separate applications for two environments. It is prudent to find out if any tool under consideration is planning to support generating HTML, Java, and ActiveX, as appropriate.

Development Environments

The application development environments are targeted toward the development of enterprise-wide applications. Applications developed in these environments are scalable and may be targeted to a large number of users on different operating platforms. They can support a three-tier architecture with varying levels of effort. Following are some critical issues which differentiate application development environments from client-based tool sets:

Repository-Based Development

In the case of GUI-based application development environments, all components are integrated. The integrated repository is the foundation for a complete application architecture. The business logic resides in the repository and, if there is a need for modifying the business logic, it can be done within the repository. The repository may reside either on the application server or within the targeted database. Designing and understanding the correct business logic is most crucial. Once the repository is populated with the business rules and logic, then all applications can be developed very rapidly.

Under normal configurations, the client-based applications do not support an integrated development environment. The complete business logic resides on the client. The database server may be used for stored procedures and triggers. To implement a large-scale application with a client tool set, various components will be needed. However, it becomes a nightmare to keep up with various versions of these components.

Distributed Logic

Application development environments support both two-tier or three-tier application architecture. These normally support some form of partitioning (static or dynamic), where presentation control, business logic, and data logic can be placed separately. Such applications provide a homogeneous development environment that makes coding and debugging easier. Such architecture permits the development of complex and scalable applications which can be used by a large number of users across the enterprise.

Client-based tool sets require that all the application code runs on the workstation and accesses data remotely from the database server. That creates the *fat client* syndrome, where all the executables are placed on the client. Client tool sets usually support only two-tier application architecture. Using this approach for developing enterprise-wide applications may bring the system down because of enormous network traffic. This kind of application architecture may result in the need for continued enhancements in the network architecture and hardware to handle large amounts of message flow. Such an architecture can make it extremely difficult to implement and manage an enterprise-wide application at multiple locations.

File Processing

Most of the GUI-based environments are geared toward interactive online data processing. Thus the tools may not be able to develop and deploy applications which process sequential files in a batch environment. However, the application development environments do support flat-file processing.

The client-based tool sets are not designed for handling any file processing at all. These tools are geared toward small forms-based applications. Additionally, most of the processing is done at the client level, thus server-intensive file I/O cannot be done effectively. Therefore, there will be a need to support two development platforms (one for interactive and another for the batch).

Application Portability

The application development environments provide a homogeneous development environment for both client and server. The developer writes the complete application (presentation logic, control logic, and data logic) using the same language. These high-end tools support multiple platforms, and the application can be ported to a supported platform without any code modifications.

Most application development environments are targeted at developing industrial-strength applications which can be deployed across heterogeneous platforms and access data from different databases. Any solution which is not developed using an enterprise-scale environment will not meet today's business needs. Client-based tool sets are not capable of developing enterprise-scale applications.

Object Orientation (OO)

Even though most of the visual tools market themselves as fully object-oriented (OO), it is important to know the level of OO functionality that is supported. It should be determined if the product strictly follows the object-oriented approach or is a hybrid of object and procedural design.

Currently, most of the tools are object-based. The true object-oriented tool can support the class-based architecture with methods, polymorphism, and inheritance. Inheritance can be a useful feature for most business environments. Therefore, an object-based tool which is not completely OO but supports some nice OO features (such as inheritance capabilities) can be an effective tool. In order to truly reap the benefits of client/server and the web, it is essential to have a tool which can support distributed architecture with ease.

Extraction/Cleansing

One of the most important steps in building a data warehouse is loading data into the warehouse database. Unfortunately, one of the most overlooked and under-scoped steps in building the data warehouse is also loading data into the warehouse database. Most companies grossly underestimate the complexity of the data load process and the effort required.

Businesses look to the decision-support capabilities of the data warehouse to guide them strategically through the marketplace maze. Unreliable, *dirty,* and otherwise bad data can result in misinformed decisions that have direct adverse effects on profit. No business would purposely strive to decrease its bottom line. However, many are doing just that by neglecting to address the extraction, transformation, and data load process thoroughly.

Perhaps even worse are the companies that give only a cursory glance at data quality and then proceed to bulk-load dirty data and base important business decisions on it. These oversights often stem from good intentions, because companies eagerly anticipate the many benefits of the data warehouse. The promise of finding more value in existing data is exciting.

Most businesses think that this discovery process begins after the warehouse is populated, when analysts begin their work with data mining tools and sophisticated query tools. The initial loading of data, however, can yield a dramatic, beneficial discovery process that has a tremendous impact on the business. Loading source data should be the lengthiest and most carefully planned step of warehouse development, but instead it often becomes a simple replication process that duplicates and even exaggerates inconsistencies in the source data.

Many tools on the market facilitate extracting, cleansing, and transforming data as well as analyzing and ensuring data quality. These tools account for a large percentage of the money spent annually on data warehousing. The problem is that no one tool provides all of these services, so in order to maximize the budget dollar, it is extremely important to understand the categories of tools and what each tool has to offer. This knowledge can help you choose the right tools for the job and use existing resources effectively.

The Current State

The first step in loading the data warehouse is to assess the current state of existing source data. Several factors affect this source data, and loading the warehouse repository is a process that varies greatly according to the condition and status of this data. Rarely does the data come from a single source. Multiple sources necessitate matching, blending, and massaging data to shape the final product into something that is usable and meaningful. Data must be accurate to ensure that the decisions being made based on it are good business decisions. Data must be relevant to the business need and consistent across redundant sources. Finally, data must be complete and not lacking required information.

The data quality audit is an assessment of the data itself and the business rules associated with that data. Once the business rules are defined, the data can be measured for consistency and completeness against these rules. A data quality tool must not only assess the current status of the data but provide control for improving and monitoring that data. Analysis of the warehouse data begins by assessing the quality of source data and comparing it to the destination system requirements and answers the following questions:

- What is the structural integrity of both the legacy as well as the new database/data warehouse
- Is the data complete and valid
- How well does your data reflect and work with your business rules and data standards

Data Replication

The simplest way to move data into the warehouse repository is to replicate the data that resides in the source databases. This is fast, simple, and very dangerous. Many companies try this approach, only to find later that the ease of data population is more than offset by the arduous process of cleansing up bad data in the destination database. One way to circumvent this scenario is to use proven data extraction and migration tools along with dependable processes and techniques.

During the transformation process, you can reformat data into new data types that support your end needs. It is also easy to manipulate data values and data types based on existing conditions.

Management Tools

Management tools are software packages that are extremely useful in populating the databases and data marts. These tools are designed and perform at their best when used for managing data marts and small- to medium-scale data warehouses. Such tools provide a solid mechanism for populating and managing the smaller warehouse and the data mart.

The Cleansing

It is crucial to the process of loading the data warehouse that you not just re-arrange the grouping of source data and deliver it to a destination database, but that you also ensure the quality of that data. Data cleansing is vitally important to the overall health of your warehouse project and ultimately affects the health of your company.

The last step prior to mapping and transforming data to the target database is merging, cleansing, and enhancing the data. You can select from several methods to ensure that you are using the best possible source of data. You can even set up merging and cleansing rules that create a source hierarchy that considers each aspect of consolidated data. Finally, the selected, validated, matched, merged, cleansed, and enhanced data is mapped and transformed to the target database using several available methods to populate the target database.

Tool Selection

Tool selection can be time-consuming and frustrating. There is no single tool that does everything. When selecting a tool, your first priority should be to know what you are attempting to accomplish. This should be a natural by-product of designing and planning the data warehouse. Next, set an evaluation period and stick to it. Tool evaluations can go on forever unless you realize that there is no perfect tool and you commit to finding the one that most closely gives you what you need. It can help if you have some established and written guidelines for the product evaluation.

Carefully consider the metadata management. As more and more products are added to the company's list, there is a good chance that more and more metadata repositories are being added as well. Managing multiple metadata repositories can be tedious and frustrating. You should not discount or skip the initial quality and audit step. Finally, select a tool and move forward. No tool does everything, but it will do what it is designed to do. After you know where you are going, know where you are, and know the criteria for the tools selection, make a decision and enjoy the journey.

Data Conversion

The data conversion process for a data warehouse is complex, time-consuming, and unglamorous. It is also the very root of a good, functional data warehouse. After all, *data* is the operative word in *data warehouse*. Quality data conversions are important to the data warehouse because the warehouse holds the information that is key to a corporation's decision-making process. For a corporation to obtain the ultimate goals and promises of a data warehouse, it must understand just how critical the data conversion process is.

The data conversion team examines old and dirty source systems that usually reside on mainframes. Typically, they use good old COBOL for the majority of their work on the mainframe, and they are likely to have the tightest service target of any part of the warehouse. The business users might wait a little longer to obtain the results of their queries, but they will not wait an extra hour for their data loads. In addition, this team faces pressures because the data warehouse is likely to uncover more problems with source data than any other single activity.

Typically, the conversion system is questioned because, as it is the newest system, users assume that the conversion system is what introduced the problems. To truly understand the complexities and resource requirements involved in a quality conversion, you must examine the overall process.

The Conversion Process

Data conversion for a warehouse is usually very large, and you have options that allow different activities to occur simultaneously so that the conversion timeline is as short as possible. However, if you are unaware of or misinterpret the conversion requirements and flow, the activities will not link together smoothly, if at all, at the end of the process.

The conversion plan determines the best route to migrate source data to the data warehouse. It considers available resources, source data volume, number of different source schemas, number and types of different access methods and platforms, data warehouse structure, and the amount of aggregation required.

The strategy for moving data to the common staging area must take into account available machine resources, collective skill set of the data conversion team, and volumes of source data. For example, the source systems are MVS-based, the technical skill set of the data conversion team is MVS and COBOL, and the volume of data is high. In this case, your data conversion plan would recommend a staging area that resides on one of the MVS machines. If, however, the MVS machine resources are limited and your team's technical skill set is strongest with UNIX and C, your plan would recommend a staging area that resides on a UNIX machine and possibly the actual data warehouse server.

The data conversion plan must also consider the structure of the data warehouse and the target database schemas. Typically, data moves from its source system schema to an intermediate schema in the staging area. The intermediate schema is the common interface to which all source systems are extracted. The intermediate schemas do not exactly match the source schemas or the target schemas. They are usually somewhere in between and contain additional fields, such as percentage numbers for use in calculations or key fields to read reference or lookup tables, that enhance the data conditioning, data cleansing, and data transformation routines.

Process Analysis

After establishing a plan, your next step is to analyze the source data carefully. You should determine, on an attribute-by-attribute basis, what source data maps to what target data and what logic is required to migrate from source to target. You should also identify external information such as tables that cross-reference locally used codes to industry-standard codes—for example, health-care procedure codes to use and/or create to transform the source data—and then design any intermediate schemas required to support the conversion plan.

Typically, you can document the conversion for customer review and sign-off. However, if you are using a data migration tool, you can document the conversion specifications directly in the tool and generate conversion specification reports for customer review and sign-off.

Either way, the conversion specifications are extremely important metadata for the data warehouse. Data migration tools automate the process of storing conversion metadata in a central place, tracking the conversion metadata over time, and exporting the conversion metadata to the data warehouse's metadata repository. If you generate the conversion routines manually, you must also generate the conversion metadata manually. The data conversion plan specifies the format of the conversion metadata as well as how you can store, update, and export the metadata.

Whether conversion specifications are generated manually or automatically into program code, you should use conversion specifications to understand the data mapping and required processing logic.

Source Data Extraction

Data extraction routines read the source data, convert it to an intermediate schema, and move it to a common staging area (a temporary work area in which data is held in intermediate schemas). The process of staging data in a common area greatly enhances the reusability of the program code. Some code is necessarily unique because of the source system's access method, platform, and language. However, the code that conditions, cleanses, transforms, and integrates the data is common for all source data if that data is first brought to intermediate schemas in a common place.

You design the data extraction routines to isolate only the data that is migrating to the data warehouse. The design is effective for both the initial load and incremental updates of the data warehouse, and it is important because it reduces the amount of data that migrates to the data warehouse, which in turn reduces computer and network resource requirements for the conversion. The data extraction design should consider how the source system indicates changed and new data, such as time stamps or periodic archives.

Time stamps and periodic archives (such as month-end files of paid claims for an insurance company) are ideal because the data extraction routines easily identify and isolate the changed and new data. If the source system does not indicate changed or new data, you compare the source data with master files of warehouse data to find the changed or new data.

The data extraction routines usually execute within the source system's environment, performing functions that transform, convert from binary, convert from packed decimal, and compare, combine, and parse the source data. These types of data conditioning are more easily performed in the environment that created these types of data than in the target environment that might not support these functions or types of data.

The conditioning process relies heavily on knowledge of the data source; the structure of the data as it resides in the operational systems or in the data warehouse; the structure of the data as perceived by the end user or the warehouse applications; knowledge of the rules required to identify, map, cleanse, transform, and aggregate the data; and security features associated with various metadata objects, such as source system logons and data warehouse database security rules.

Data Loading

Once the source data is gathered to a staging area, it is time to execute the conversion routines that might clean the data. Data cleansing ensures the data's integrity through special programs that correct data, improving the data's accuracy and overall usefulness. You might use software that corrects and enhances errant data fields such as names and addresses. Such data cleansing software is a separate step in a batch job stream, callable subroutines executed in a batch or online environment, or an external service that is not under the control of the traditional batch cycle.

For the data conversion team to implement data cleansing services, the data warehouse architecture design must accommodate constraints imposed by the data cleansing software, such as any platforms on which the data cleansing software does or does not run. You only use this software if you cannot correct the data at the source. In addition, you identify all cleansing requirements in the data conversion plan.

Other data conversion routines transform data. The source systems usually have data attributes that require a transformation process. The transformation process ensures a consistent mapping of codes and keys between the source systems and the data warehouse.

If you are extracting data from more than one subject area or from more than one version within a subject area, you must integrate that data into a single view. In addition, you must address data anomalies and corrections to previously migrated and loaded data.

The techniques of data conditioning, cleansing, transformation, and integration must be applied in an iterative fashion. Once you and the customer are satisfied with the condition of the data, you create load-record images for the atomic-level, dimension, and fact data.

Atomic-level data is the lowest level of data detail in the warehouse and is needed to provide the level of granularity required to effectively condition, cleanse, transform, and integrate the data. If the data warehouse feeds data marts that are typically designed with a star-join schema, you use the atomic-level load data to create the data mart dimension tables. If the processing for this activity is sequential, you sort the resulting files of dimension-load data to eliminate any duplicate records.

To track and generate keys for each of the dimensions of the star-join schema, you must create a key administration application. A variety of key generation and administration strategies exist. Examples are source system key integration and system-generated keys. Source system key integration transforms logical keys from multiple source systems into a unique physical key. A hospital patient might be identified with a social security number in one system and by name and birth date in another system. In the data warehouse, the keys are integrated. System-generated keys are those that the conversion system or RDBMS assigns. The conversion plan documents the strategy that is best suited for the data warehouse and its users.

To create data to load into fact tables, you generate an application that first matches the dimension-load data to the atomic-level load data. Then it populates the fact data records with the keys of the dimensions and the associated quantitative facts contained in the atomic-level data. This application reports any records from the dimension load data that do not match back to the atomic-level load data. If the application performs properly, absolutely no mismatch conditions occur.

Data Aggregation

Load data is aggregated by executing a series of sorts The result is all aggregate dimension load data and all associated aggregated fact load data defined in the data warehouse design.

You must move the data from the staging area to the data warehouse server, if the staging area is not on the server. Once the data is assembled on the data warehouse server, you load it into the database using the RDBMS bulk-load utility. You use referential integrity during the load process to ensure that the fact table key contains true foreign keys from the dimension tables. Fact tables normally contain several million—if not a billion or more—rows. Should the load data contain rows that violate referential integrity, you can easily find the offending records and correct them. Otherwise, you have little chance of even knowing about the problem.

Data Indexing

Whether you decide to update indexes during the bulk load process or later depends on time constraints and the capabilities of the RDBMS Several RDBMSs allow segmenting the table indexes. Then you can drop a portion of the index, bulk load the data, and rebuild the indexes as needed. Segmented table indexes reduce the amount of time needed to bulk load and index the data. Reducing the amount of time spent in the load window has a positive impact on the availability of the warehouse and is especially important if the data warehouse users are located around the world in many time zones.

Quality Assurance

You must ensure the quality of the data not as a separate activity but throughout the data conversion process. The conversion plan specifies customer or end-user reviews and sign-off procedures, data validation and correction procedures, and the process for reconciling data with the source system.

You must work closely with the customer or end user to create the conversion plan and the conversion specifications. As mentioned earlier, you examine the current processing environment to plan the best route by which to move the data from the source systems to the data warehouse. The plan is documented and reviewed with the customer. In this manner, the customer knows up-front what to expect during the data conversion process. To show understanding, the customer formally signs the conversion plan.

To create effective conversion specifications, you should learn as much as possible about the source data, including its structures and the meanings of each of its fields. You should also document how the source data populates the target data, document your understanding, and review it with the internal data warehouse user. Not only will the users be able to validate the meanings of the source data, but they can also better understand how to relate the source data to the data in the data warehouse.

The first place to reconcile the conversion process is after you extract the source data to the intermediate schemas. Total the number of extract records and other additive data, such as counts and monetary amounts, from the intermediate schemas. These figures tie to the totals from the source system. As a rule, reconcile the data early and often in the data conversion process, and strive to find problems as early as possible to avoid having to re-execute multiple steps of the process.

During the conditioning, cleansing, transformation, and integration of the data, you and the user make decisions as the actual values of the data are examined. When you uncover errant data, report the findings to the user. Together you and the user decide to correct the data in the source system or with the data conversion routines. If you correct the data with the data conversion routines, you should also denote the corrections in the conversion metadata.

To reconcile the data, total the number of extract records and other additive data. As you tie the figures from the atomic-level load data to the source systems, consider the actions you took as you conditioned, cleansed, transformed, and integrated the data. Probably, totals no longer match. However, you must reconcile the differences between the source systems and the atomic-level data.

Finally, reconcile the data after you create the fact-load data and the aggregate fact-load data. The totals from all fact tables tie exactly to each other and the atomic-level load data.

Quality Control

With new information continually pouring into warehouses, companies are enlisting business users to help their data pass inspection. For many companies, the quality or lack of it is costly. They spend thousands of dollars and soak up hundreds of hours scrubbing and cleansing data before its gets loaded into a warehouse, but companies often neglect to factor a quality-control function into their budgets for when the warehouse goes live. And with IT rations already strapped, many shops do not have the bandwidth to designate a staffer to watch over data.

As a result, companies are struggling to find ways to incorporate data quality responsibilities into current roles. At a minimum, companies must enlist the user community—typically, analysts—to do its part when it comes to quality control. The users of the data, not IT, are more likely to understand, and therefore uncover, the business reasons why certain information does not make sense or is flat-out wrong.

Given the dire consequences of what can happen with shoddy data, some companies are not comfortable until a formal process is put into place to manage quality control. Short of implementing a formal process, companies are getting by the quality issues with a more ad hoc approach. IT handles it on the production end, while the business analysts, on the other.

No matter how a company decides to approach the issue, it must avoid learning the hard way that it needs better quality control. The controls must be in place to make sure the data is cared for.

Data Sizes

We all know that databases are getting larger, terabyte by terabyte. Server-based reporting engines apply multi-tier architectures to large databases. A user can format a report, structure the query, execute the query, and then wait several seconds (or minutes) for the response from the database. Modern reporting tools have been designed to:

- Address complex SQL statements including multi-table joins and sub-queries
- Access large numbers of database rows
- Employ complex report logic such as summarization routines that involve large numbers of rows
- Transfer large result sets from the database to the end user's workstation

Advanced reporting tools consist of several components. End users run reports from client workstations. Reports are stored and run on a second tier, and database servers are the third tier. Such architecture arrangement is intended to allow reports to run efficiently against large databases and also return large amounts of data.

Reporting System

The heart of an advanced reporting system is a report server that offloads processing from end-user workstations. A report server can run on its own Windows NT or UNIX or another platform, or it can coexist on the database server platform. Coexistence maximizes the speed of data transfer between the report and database servers, but it could degrade DBMS performance because both servers compete for resources. Use of separate platforms gives each server its own dedicated resources, but it requires additional hardware and operating system software. Using separate servers also lengthens the data transfer time between the two servers, therefore, it is a good idea to keep the two servers on adjacent network nodes.

Most users are working to develop tools that let users access reports within web browsers.

Client Components

Client components of reporting tools let users develop, execute, and view reports. In general, the report design and development tool is a separate product from the end user's report viewer.

While end users generally have little control over the performance of the queries they create, developers using a reporting tool's programming language have several options:

- Create custom queries to take advantage of the database
- Allocate input buffer sizes synchronized with the database output buffer size
- Support both static and dynamic SQL
- Select the type of inter-program communication used
- Compile the report code rather than run it through an interpreter at runtime

Microsoft Windows and Macintosh are the most prevalent client operating environments, while Windows NT, UNIX, and web browsers are beginning to be used.

Report Servers

The most interesting advance in reporting against large databases has been the development of report servers that offload data access and report generation from end-user workstations. Windows NT and UNIX or other server platforms are the platforms of choice to run32- bit advanced reporting tool software.

Performance and storage of extracted data and finished reports on the report server is generally limited by memory and disk space, which can be upgraded as needed.

Older report writers restrict the data in a report to the amount that can be selected in one SQL statement. Advanced reporting tools and data warehouse servers reduce query processing time by creating alternatives to single SQL statements. Most reporting tools can now perform this type of query optimization behind the scenes and without users' knowledge or intervention. Similarly, queries for summary information can be directed to aggregation tables on the database or report server instead of resorting to large table scans.

These features require a metadata or semantic layer that resides on the report server. This metadata lets users build queries using data defined in business terminology rather than in cryptic or programmer-oriented database table and column names. The metadata layer translates the business terminology into database access statements that may involve multiple SQL statements or the use of an aggregate table rather than selecting against detail data.

One disadvantage of this approach is the time and effort required to build the metadata layer. Although end users do not need to know physical database details, you need DBA skills to build and maintain the metadata. Database structure changes must be monitored to understand the effect on the metadata layer, which may also require changes.

One critical yet often overlooked aspect of reporting against large databases is the performance impact of report calculations. Calculations that consist of complicated logic, totaling, or OLAP-style slice-and-dice operations require a significant amount of time if large volumes of data are involved. All reporting tools allow calculations to be performed on the report server, eliminating the performance impact on end users.

Some reporting products use native or custom drivers to access the source databases while others use ODBC drivers. Although the first ODBC drivers were slow, it is now unclear whether there is a significant difference between the newer ODBC drivers and native drivers. ODBC's SQL Passthrough capability allows virtually any SQL command to be passed to a data source. The bottom line: both native and newer ODBC drivers provide acceptable performance, but native drivers may still be slightly better.

Most tools can access numerous relational databases by executing the SQL for each report from the server, not the client. The information from each database can then be consolidated on the report server. Be wary of restrictions on the maximum number of database access statements or databases that can be accessed in one query. Concurrent heterogeneous database access, data selection or joining of rows from disparate databases at the same time, is generally not supported.

Other administrative capabilities of report servers include batch processing of multiple reports, query management such as the ability to prioritize queries, error handling, and implementation of security.

Database Server

A common theme in reporting tools is to let the database server undertake as much processing as possible, the theory being that databases have sophisticated query optimization routines, indexing, and partitioning to take advantage of high-performance parallel- processing SMP and MPP hardware. Although this is true to an extent, advanced reporting really requires a coordinated report and database server architecture. In fact, report server capabilities such as stacking multiple SQL queries and caching reports are designed to overcome database performance problems.

Reporting Tools

Reporting tools are becoming more sophisticated as the need to access very large databases becomes more prevalent. The choice of a reporting tool is not as easy as it used be, when performance was not much of an issue and the decision could be based primarily on the user interface. Now, you must have an understanding of the user access requirements, database structure, and LAN/WAN communications capabilities so that you can select the most effective reporting solution, as opposed to a single software tool. You should prototype your reporting tool against a production-size database so that all of the data access and performance tuning capabilities can be exercised.

While server-based reporting engines offload processing from both end-user client machines and database servers, database tuning and an appropriate application design are necessary to take optimal advantage of the architecture. Combined with client viewers, these multi-tier systems make reporting against large data sets more practical than traditional client-based report writers.

Data Mining

The potential payoffs from data mining are enormous if you pick the right tools and use them effectively. These applications can become the foundation of your organization's business strategies—determining credit risk, detecting fraud, managing product warranties, purchasing stock for business stores, and defining new telecommunications products and services.

Traditional database queries are designed to supply answers to simple questions such as "What were my sales in March 1998 in Europe?" Multidimensional analysis, often called online analytical processing (OLAP), lets users do much more complex queries, such as compare sales relative to plan by quarter and region for the prior two years. But in both cases, the results are merely extracted values or an aggregation of values.

Data mining reaches much deeper into databases. Data mining tools find patterns in the data and infer rules from them. Those patterns and rules are used to guide decision-making and forecast the effect of those decisions. And data mining can speed analysis by focusing attention on the most important variables. You might find these patterns with a series of queries against the data, but data mining lets users explore a much wider range of possibilities than even the most sophisticated set of queries.

For example, some grocery chains are encouraging their customers to sign up for cards that give them discounts when the card is presented and scanned at check-out. The store can tell through its scanning system not only what is in each market basket, but who purchased it. This data allows the grocery stores to maintain their customer history with their preferences and frequency (for inventory sake) of purchases of certain products. The grocery store can even determine, if for example, their customer buys a certain brand (e.g. Minutemaid) of orange juice only when on sale or has a real preference for it.

The rise of data warehousing, especially using the web-based applications, also has greatly reduced the barriers to data mining.

Mining Types

There is a large variety of types of information that can be yielded by data mining: associations, sequences, classifications, clusters, and forecasting.

Associations happen when occurrences are linked in a single event. For example, a study of supermarket baskets might reveal that when corn chips are purchased, a majority of the time cola is also purchased, unless there is a cola promotion, in which case cola is purchased more often than corn chips. Knowing this, managers can evaluate the profitability of a promotion.

In sequences, events are linked over time. If a house is bought, then 45% of the time a new oven can be bought within one month and 60% of the time a new refrigerator will be bought within two weeks.

Classification is probably the most common data mining activity today. It recognizes patterns that describe the group to which an item belongs. It does this by examining existing items that already have been classified and inferring a set of rules.

A problem common to many businesses is the loss of their steady customers. Classification can help you discover the characteristics of customers who are likely to leave and provide a model that can be used to predict who they are. It can also help you determine which kinds of promotions have been effective in keeping which types of customers, so that you spend only as much money as necessary to retain a customer.

Clustering is related to classification, but differs in that no groups have yet been defined. Using clustering, the data mining tool discovers different groupings within the data. This can be applied to problems as diverse as detecting defects in manufacturing or finding affinity groups for bank cards.

All of these applications may involve predictions, such as whether a customer will renew a subscription. Forecasting is a different form of prediction. It estimates the future value of continuous variables—like sales figures—based on patterns within the data.

Mining Tools

A number of tools are used in data mining, such as neural networks, decision trees, rule induction, and data visualization. Some tools are based on combinations of these methods.

Neural networks are, essentially, collections of connected nodes with inputs, outputs, and processing at each node. Between the visible input layer and output layer may be a number of hidden processing layers. Some algorithms can translate a neural net model into a set of rules that can help you understand what the neural net is doing. Many neural net products are used beyond the business information arena. Neural networks frequently are applied to more general pattern recognition problems such as handwriting recognition and interpretation of electrocardiograms.

Decision trees divide the data into groups based on the values of the variables. The result is a hierarchy of if-then statements that classify the data. For example, if a customer has made 25% fewer cellular calls each month than the preceding month, for six months, then there is a 60% probability that the customer is going to drop the service. There has been a surge of interest in decision tree-based products, primarily because they are faster than neural networks for many business problems and easier for users to understand.

Decision trees are not foolproof, however, and may not work with some types of data. Some decision trees have problems handling continuous sets of data, like age or sales, and require that they be grouped into ranges. Some combine the features of neural networks and decision trees in an attempt to build a more accurate model and do it faster.

Another type of data mining tool is data visualization software. In some ways, data visualization is not really a data mining tool, because it only presents a picture for users to see rather than automating the process. But the visual representations of as many as four variables in a single picture presents an enormous amount of information in a very concise fashion. Essentially, there is a very wide bandwidth of information presentation to the user that will often make groups stand out as peaks or valleys.

Problem Areas

One potentially serious problem in data mining is the necessity to subset data for performance reasons. You may need to trade off the number of rows in your sample against the number of variables you evaluate to build your model.

First, the data warehouse is distilled into a file of query results by asking all possible combinations of questions for all variables of interest. For example, suppose you had a database with columns of sex, state of residence, age, and income, with one row for each individual. The system asks questions like, such as, how many males in Alaska are age 26. and also looks for the counts with age 27, 28, and so on. It changes the value of every variable until all values have been exhausted. Values like income in this example are used as the basis for metrics, which are kept along with the counts as summaries (e.g., sum or average) in answer to the questions.

The resultant database is typically much smaller than the original data set, because the answers to the questions usually take up much less space than the data itself. Data mining is not magic. Buying a $99 neural net program and throwing it against a terabyte data warehouse is not likely to produce any useful results. It can take forever to get an answer, and that answer will probably be worthless. But when applied properly, data mining can produce the return-on-investment from your data warehouse that you have been waiting for.

Help Desk Data Warehouse—An Example

The web-enabled help desk, used by medium- to large-scale data processing operations, has become the first line of support for a growing number of computer users. The help desk concept delegates responsibility for direct user assistance to a team of specialists whose only mission is answering questions and coordinating the solution of larger problems through other tiers of the data processing organization.

A record of all calls and activities is kept in a database. Such data is required for tracking the activities as well as reporting. Such data is subject-oriented and is historical. This is, in fact, a data warehouse. There is no reason why the data warehousing rules cannot be applied.

The web not only allows the data warehouse user's view and produce reports, but also to maintain their own database activities. This has made the help desk operations more efficient, less people-intensive, and more responsive to users.

One way they have managed that growth is by allowing employees to help themselves through an interactive intranet link to the help desk. This is designed to encourage employees to solve their own problems, reducing the number of calls received by the help desk and lowering overall staff costs. Providing traditional support to computer users is only the beginning of an expanded role for the intranet help desk.

The intranet-based help desk has great potential to serve as a central hub that manages an organization's complete information warehouse needs—from sales and marketing to details on retirement programs. By deploying a customizable, workflow-based system, the intranet-based help desk is well-positioned to support a range of enterprise information needs in the future, such as web publishing, enterprise reporting, and OLAP capabilities.

The Web as an Accelerator (An Example)

In electronic commerce, most business web sites are little more than electronic versions of brochures. A web site that generates genuine value for businesses is one that not only enables them to get standard information, but also delivers feedback tailored to each shopper's history and preferences.

For businesses to be able to do innovative things like suggesting complementary purchases, they must be able to effectively capture and analyze information about shoppers and detect patterns and trends in buying habits. This is best done with a data warehouse tuned to and focused on the Internet experience.

A web-directed data warehouse is not much different from the one used by store managers and buyers. The principal distinction is that, while the internal data warehouse guides store employees in merchandising and promoting their store, the Internet/intranet data warehouse interfaces directly with consumers, to enable them to enjoy a cyber-shopping experience highly tailored to their specific needs.

While we talk about retailers, as a generality, it can be applied to every facet of business, such as banking, help desk, or any such application. Setting up data warehouses to be accessed through the web is a relatively new concept and must be done carefully. Far too many companies establish a web presence without thinking about the implications or understanding the business rationale for doing so. Here are a few guidelines to consider:

- Treat the establishment of a home page with the same deliberate and careful approach you would any new store opening or market expansion.
- Make sure that the information you provide is accurate, and that the information you collect is good and clean. The old computer adage, garbage in, garbage out, still applies.
- Understand the technical and data requirements, and determine who will use the system and the information, what costs will be involved, and what resources will be needed to maintain the system. If you are adding a data warehouse to the web site, you should be able to demonstrate how it can help the site.

    Remember, the data warehouse will not be serving a few dozen or a hundred internal users. It will be subjected to thousands (or potentially millions) of users each day. This, in turn, has significant implications for the amount of resources required to stage data feeds from the web to the data warehouse and vice versa.
- Web data warehousing is a brave new world of cooperation and information into which few have ventured. You should anticipate the need for frequent and numerous adjustments to the site for your business and your users. But if you have done your homework, you should expect some success, too.
- One of the most valuable resources a business has is its user base. Identify the most valuable of these users and include them in your pilot group as you work to establish web data warehousing. These users can give you valuable insight and feedback on what works and what does not. They also will appreciate your attention and feel that you are genuinely interested in retaining them as customers.

Conclusions

Today's new generation of data access and information delivery tools should meet practically all of the data warehouse end user needs for querying and report writing. They can smoothly integrate with various warehouse designs, enhance and optimize the performance of the data warehouses, and are flexible to meet the changing warehouse requirements.

With the proper data warehouse access and delivery solutions, there can be immediate and ongoing paybacks on investment. An IT team can quickly and easily implement the end user tools. And end users can quickly and easily turn the warehouse data into powerful information.

The processes that are enabled by data warehousing represent a compelling goal for organizations that need to compete in today's global business environment. When users can turn data into valuable information, they can help their organizations compete at ever higher levels.

Businesses who want to succeed in making the Internet a viable venue must approach their web sites in the same way they view their stores. They must provide their customers with a compelling and attractive experience that keeps them coming back for more. To help them, the businesses should consider using a data warehouse to give their web sites the kind of features that will make customers view return visits as not only desired, but necessary.

15

MANAGING A WEB WAREHOUSE ENVIRONMENT

Introduction

Delivery of data warehouse information to decision makers throughout the enterprise and around the world has been an expensive challenge. Once data has been extracted and organized for user access, analytic software must be loaded on each user's PC, users must be trained, and ongoing user support staffs must be recruited. User requirements and even the users themselves change constantly, resulting in a significant support burden.

The World Wide Web has come to the rescue. In addition to simplifying the deployment of data warehouse access, intranets have introduced a new level of collaborative interactive analysis and information sharing among decision makers.

Management Issues

Once your data warehouse is finally in place, how do you make sure that the warehouse is correct each day? To make it work and keep it working over the life cycle of the data warehouse is a challenge. Some of the management and operational issues that must be considered are:

- Management of metadata
- Management of information accuracy and consistency across the enterprise
- Management of data availability and system stability
- Backup and recovery plans
- Management of application and database changes from warehouse and operational systems
- Management of the life cycle of the warehouse applications, especially if they are distributed
- Security management for hundreds or thousands of end-users
- Performance tuning and management of hardware, software, network, and interfaces
- Adaptation to changing business environment
- Management of future capacity needs

Operational Requirements

There have been numerous debates whether implementations should be central, distributed, or server-centric, accessed by *thin or fat* clients. With the advent of the Internet and the need for sharing gigabytes of data, in order to manage it effectively, it is imperative that we model our implementations along the following lines:

- Server-centric processing
- Scalable hardware
- Accessibility to business logic
- Analysis and report sharing
- Resource sharing across the enterprise
- Thin-client application partitioning

In most thin-client logical applications, the multidimensional computational layer is partitioned from the graphical user interface and the relational database tiers. This logical multi-tier partitioning can be implemented as a physical three-tier architecture. The multidimensional computational layer resides on a server. This approach allows the middle-tier to execute true background service running agents, reports, and analyses.

A web-based thin-client architecture provides the communications hub to support true collaborative information sharing. What is shared is not just a text file snap-shot of a report, but also the business logic and assumptions supporting the report. Each user has the business logic available to reproduce the report and immediately begin using multidimensional analysis capabilities to set off in a new analytic direction. The original logic is not lost and the results of the new analysis can be shared.

To meet decision makers' need for information, data is being extracted from operational systems and placed in data warehouses. Corporations recognize that information placed in the hands of decision makers is a powerful tool. This section provides information that can be helpful in addressing these issues. It also provides ideas on how to begin implementing management solutions within the organization.

Systems Environment

As decision-support systems mature, numerous systems management issues arise within the enterprise information architecture. Along with maturity comes the increased complexity of managing a more sophisticated decision-support infrastructure. Complexity results from sheer database size as well as the number and diversity of users, making it increasingly difficult to manage availability and performance. As a result, organizations require a new set of tools and techniques to successfully manage a full-scale data warehouse implementation.

As the organization becomes more dependent on a data warehouse's decision-support power, high availability and optimum service levels become increasingly important. Analytical tool sets become more diversified, to keep pace with requirements to support processing outside the traditional database environment. Timely data refresh also increases in significance as the organization uses information to make operational and tactical decisions in addition to purely strategic decisions.

In this section, we examine the impact on systems as data warehousing becomes a critical enterprise resource for decision making.

Multiple Data Marts

Often consolidated into an enterprise data warehouse, data marts deliver information cost-effectively to multiple departments aligned along functional boundaries. Escalating demand for detailed data causes tremendous growth and sometimes causes databases to triple or quadruple in size. Typically the demand for detailed data accelerates within a few months from initial decision-support deployment.

Customized Data Marts

Customized data marts often surface to address specific decision-support requirements within a particular department or functional area. Over time, data mart proliferation can result in duplicated effort and inconsistent content. Moreover, the isolated, departmental nature of some data marts often limits cross-functional decision making. For these reasons, organizations are turning to enterprise data warehouses as a vehicle for consolidating the islands of information embodied in multiple, independent data marts.

The independent data mart infrastructure typically evolves in the early stages of decision support adoption. For example, a financial services organization might deploy individual data marts for:

- Consumer loans
- Mortgages
- Small business banking
- Financial reporting and forecasting
- Consumer banking
- Brokerage products
- Institutional banking
- Credit card product marketing
- Credit risk analysis

Each data mart requires data extracts, transformation programs, and cleansing routines to prepare information for loading into the multiple decision-support environments. Suddenly, the organization becomes overwhelmed with support costs, code maintenance, and production cycles. In addition, multiple data transformation programs result in multiple data definitions across the organizational data marts. The problem is that no single data mart can provide a complete enterprise-wide view of the data.

Although the appropriate data mart can be queried about how many brokerage or credit card customers exist in the bank, there is usually no single way of asking how many total customers the bank has or how many customers have both a credit card and a brokerage account. With stronger customer focus becoming imperative, enterprises must provide an integrated view of the customer across product boundaries. Data marts typically do not support this level of data source integration, nor do they usually provide access to the detailed data necessary to truly understand customer behavior.

An Enterprise Data Warehouse

The enterprise data warehouse can quickly become the source for detailed data that is not practical for independent data marts. Its architecture uses a single data extract and transformation process, with common data definitions targeted to a corporate information model (versus multiple departmental information models). Integration of multiple data sources ensures consistent key structures across product boundaries and common data definitions.

The enterprise data warehouse is usually larger than a data mart, but it eliminates redundancies (for example, common customers across product lines represented multiple times). It should not, however, be viewed as a replacement for data marts. Rather, the enterprise data warehouse can become the source of cleansed, consistent data to populate departmental data marts.

While data marts are designed to optimize performance and usability for well-defined queries, the enterprise data warehouse is designed to provide flexibility in data accessibility. The enterprise data warehouse supports much broader data access requirements and greater diversity of detailed and summarized data elements. An infrastructure, such as a metadata dictionary and data repository, are usually part of an enterprise warehouse, but not often found in departmental data marts.

Design of the data extraction mechanism from the enterprise warehouse to data marts is critical to systems management. Replication tools may help keep smaller lookup tables synchronized between the warehouse and various data marts. However, core entities within the data model will likely require alternative approaches. Most replication tools cannot propagate large amounts of data into a data warehouse or data mart from external sources due to performance restrictions. Usually, high-volume updates and data refreshes rely on tools specifically designed for this purpose.

In addition to data extraction and transformation, it is critical (especially for data mart construction) that these tools aggregate (summarize) and filter data for loading into the target database structures. Most data replication tools not specifically designed for a warehouse environment are incapable of performing the data aggregation required to feed a core set of the tables within a typical warehouse or data mart design.

Setting the Right Environment

Before the human resources can be effective, there are two critical technical elements that must be in place within the warehouse's technical architecture: a metadata strategy and the right warehousing tools. Inappropriate architectures, lack of metadata, or inefficient, non-integrated tools are guaranteed to frustrate support staff, and can more than double staffing requirements, significantly slowing development cycles.

Metadata Management

The warehouse helps organizations proactively monitor trends and patterns in their own business as well as the overall market. Metadata and an efficient infrastructure contributes to the warehouse's success. It is impossible to find an integrated solution on the market, even now. If you can find a way to integrate things around one metadata repository, that is a huge dividend. That is the biggest dividend from the metadata.

The heart of a data warehouse is the metadata. It is fed from several different sources and provides a window to the warehouse. This depicts where the data resides, who owns the data, what the business rules associated with that data are, and what security issues are addressed. The metadata makes the whole warehouse environment usable because without it, when the warehouse starts to grow, it becomes ineffective.

Tool Integration

All data warehousing projects integrate data across the enterprise. The second level of integration comes at the tool level. Warehousing tools today—the database tools, the extract tools, and the scheduling tools—are rarely integrated. The lack of an integrated solution can turn warehouse maintenance into a nightmare.

Depending on the architecture, warehouse maintenance can be manageable or totally impossible. Maintenance has to be part of the architecture from the beginning or the warehouse initiative is guaranteed to fail in 12 months.

Project Management

Once a technological foundation exists that is built around metadata and integrated warehousing tools, there are numerous cultural and environment issues to address. Such issues can just as strongly impact whether the data warehouse becomes the organizations biggest asset or worst nightmare.

These issues center around the shift from structured application development, most often done in a controlled mainframe environment, to a nonstructured environment that is client/server, iterative, fast-paced, and parallel. In this environment, individuals are empowered and more creative. Supporting the data warehousing staff with the right training, consulting help, motivation, and definition of roles and responsibilities can help ensure a smooth transition.

Skills

The skills sets and job responsibilities necessary to maintain the warehouse are varied and complex. Furthermore, they must be coupled with tools and methodologies that are sometimes experimental and are often introduced to an uninitiated team. Supporting the warehouse requires a fundamental change in mindset and values. This usually involves moving from a mainframe-centric environment to the world of client/server, from controlled access to free-form access, from limited distribution to broad access, and from structured applications to ad hoc access in an unstructured environment.

Usually data base administrators are concerned with designing a database in third normal form, and that's the end of it. But now because individual users are going against data that comes from a common source, the data has to be normalized, and then de-normalized, so that users can perform the desired analysis. That usually goes against the grain of traditional DBAs. Within the warehouse environment, there is a lot of data redundancy. But it is okay because warehouse data is read-only, usually for decision support.

To help foster this new mindset quickly, organizations should make a point to select the warehouse team from a variety of different disciplines, such as business analysis, data modeling, data administration, applications development, end user support, or from the IT group. No matter where the resources come from, keeping the group focused and motivated is also important.

Team Motivation

In most organizations, the warehouse project is considered one of the most interesting projects. This is the project with the latest technology, and that is what most technologists want to work with.

Roles and Responsibilities

Proper training, mentoring, planning, motivation, organization, and patience can help ensure that the data warehousing team is positioned to provide the highest level of support, thereby providing the highest return on investment to the organization. Even with this support, if roles, responsibilities, and organizational structure are not clearly defined, disaster can lurk just over the horizon.

The organization and makeup of the data warehousing team can be configured in numerous ways depending upon the organizational processes, management structure, and distribution of resources. Whether the groups number two, three, five, or more also depends upon the size of the organization and the warehouse. Regardless of the size and structure, there are a number of key groups that must be included to ensure adequate and broad-based support. These groups may include:

- The Analysts
- Data Architects
- End users
- Management
- IT department

Each one of these groups plays a pivotal role in each phase of the warehouse development, implementation, and maintenance. Because a data warehouse is never really complete, these roles do not stop and start. They continue throughout the life of the warehouse.

The Analysis Group

A critical role, and the team that initiates the warehouse project, is usually the Analysis Group. This group should be responsible for identifying and defining the purpose and target user group for the warehouse and ensure that the warehouse meets the strategic objectives of the business. The analysts help gather up-front requirements for the warehouse to save time later in redefining and documenting the effort. This group has to be well versed in the technologies employed for the Internet, intranets, and extranets.

It is up to the analysts to ensure that the data warehouse project starts off on the right foot and that the organization is undertaking the effort for the right reasons, that the warehouse can actually fulfill the needs of the business and still be manageable. Analyzing how the warehouse can meet the business objectives early on is critical to preventing the warehouse from growing out of control.

Data Architects

Following requirements gathering, the technical and data architectural support requirements must be defined. The skills required to construct these architectures generally come from different skill sets, backgrounds, and disciplines. In addition to the business requirements, detailed data requirements should be fleshed out before, or as, the technical details are defined. Data collection rates, volumes, and timing from every point-to-point in the warehouse will dictate the needed network capacity, transfer rates, storage volumes, and growth rate of the warehouse. The data architecture will dictate each of these factors.

- Data collection, transformation, distribution and loading must be logically defined by the data architecture team. This group must also possess the skills and experience to define the data models that form the basis of the data warehouse. The initial data model, which supports the business requirements, continues to evolve as operational data is mapped to the physical model during the pilot phase of the warehouse, and continuously changes with modifications and mapping that occur during the warehouse life-cycle.
- Data standards are a critical component of the new data model and data standardization is a responsibility of the data architect.
- Data stewardship is important to enforce those standards.
- Just like the data standards, the data model continues to evolve. Rather than spending months on defining the perfect enterprise data model, the prudent and rapid approach is to develop a frame work that can be built upon.

Symptoms for Lack of Management

Astute managers need to be constantly on the lookout for signs of problems in their warehouse implementations. As is so often the case, the longer one waits to act upon a problem, the more it will cost to remedy that problem. Clearly, the best course is not to allow the problem to occur, but that is not always possible. The following are some the early warning indicators that all is not well with the health of an enterprise's data warehouse or data mart implementations.

Lack of Design Consistency

When different applications or, even worse, different data marts in different departments begin to achieve different results for similar queries or analyses, the organization is in trouble, because it has lost organizational cohesiveness. For example, management wants to find out which cereal types have sold the best in which region over a particular timeframe. East sales and West sales each have implemented their own applications, and each has a different definition. No one can make sense of the two reports answering the same question in which there was such a disparity in basic terms.

Applications can also diverge in the business rules employed to derive certain data. Much time may have to be spent trying to ferret out these differences. Even worse, if users lose confidence in the validity of the data produced from these analyses, they will stop using the system altogether.

System Availability

A data warehouse system must be available and current. Users simply will not tolerate an inability to access historical or current data. There are several dimensions to the management problem which manifest themselves in poorly optimized availability.

There may be times when the system is not available because it is being refreshed with a new update of transactional data. This sometimes happens when refresh scheduling conflicts with operational procedures such as backups. It can also happen if the size of the warehouse has grown to the point where the time required for a refresh has outstripped the available downtime of the system, such as weekends and overnights. Likewise, poor scheduling of backups, or poor planning in terms of backup philosophy can cause a system to be unavailable when users are expecting access to it.

Data Availability

Another kind of availability has to do with maintaining enough disk space on the system to allow table-space requirements to be met for the required analyses. Systems must be monitored continually to free space for tables and other interim results of the analysis which need disk space. History, which must be kept for trend analysis, will continue to take up more and more of the free space, so administrators must maintain a wary vigil to ensure that users have enough system resources available to do their job. Periodic database reorganization will be critical for detecting and correcting disk fragmentation and ensuring maximum data availability.

System Performance

Almost as frustrating as the system which is not available is the system whose response is unacceptably slow. System performance must be maintained, especially in the face of increasing user acceptance of the system. A system whose performance begins to deteriorate will be rejected by those same users who were singing its praises when it was performing well. Performance can be degraded for many reasons:

1. Free-space problems
2. Poorly designed database
3. Poorly written SQL
4. System contention
5. Other resource constraints, such as CPU or memory

Any of the above either singly or in combination is capable of causing sluggish or unacceptable response time for end users. These are typically not issues which arise during the implementation of the warehouse, but rather after the warehouse has been operational for some time and problems of memory allocation and de-allocation (resource contention) begin to surface.

Initially, users are learning the system and SQL statements tend to be relatively simple and not very demanding. As users begin to gain confidence in the system, they will try to build more sophisticated analytical models, which will drive them to more sophisticated SQL scripts. Managers must be on the lookout for all of these possible sources of performance problems, from the sublime to the ridiculous, and from the subtle, unnoticed design flaw in database objects to the operational erosion of free disk space to the users themselves, who can disable a system with a single SQL statement.

Managers must then implement an integrated database performance solution which is capable of monitoring and managing the performance of:

- Servers in distributed environments
- The enterprise network
- Relational databases
- Distributed client/server resources

Only by monitoring all of these potential trouble spots in the system can a manager get the advance warning needed to catch potential problems at a stage where they are still manageable and where their solution is still affordable.

Adaptation to Change

In business today, the only certainty is *change*. Business conditions will change, enterprise organizations will change, business rules will change, business data will change, technology will change. Each of these areas of change impacts the structure and operations of the data warehouse. It means that the warehouse must be able to react to these changes in order to maintain its value to the organization and to leverage the substantial financial and resource investment. Regardless, the issues of managing change are challenging.

Business Rules Changes

Traditionally, business rules have been relatively stable, and have often been coded directly into an application. However, today's global competitive environment means business rules change frequently. Because such a large part of turning data into information involves correctly defining business rules, warehouse projects will require a way to capture and manage business rules as they change so that data warehouse systems can be continually updated.

Applications and Technology Changes

Data warehouse applications require an application development environment for logically complex business applications, speeding time to market, and increasing flexibility for competitive advantage. This can create a new demand for development environments that support the business rule focus of the data warehouse.

Enterprise technology (applications, platforms, and data) must keep pace with demanding business requirements. Unfortunately, enterprise technology improvements often disrupt and impede business, which fosters frustration and resistance to change in IT department practices. The negative side-effects of change must be restricted, but change itself should be encouraged.

Repository

Repository technology can help managers not only manage reference data, but also all data within the data warehouse (or even within the enterprise). If data definitions are stored in the repository, there are two ways to manage database change throughout the enterprise.

The preferred method is to make the changes to the logical model (repository) first. Once the change to a database object is recorded in the repository, a change description and reference list is passed to a database management tool implemented for managing heterogeneous distributed databases and database objects. This tool then creates a strategy that can implement the changes to the physical databases, across the enterprise, for mainframe and client/server databases.

Security Changes

Because many different groups of end users will be accessing different sets of information in the analytical data store, sophisticated security for both the application and the database must be in place. Applications can access multiple servers and multiple objects, thus requiring users to have privileges on multiple servers. A security product that can define privileges through user groups should be considered. By defining privileges for whole groups of users, security administrators define privileges once, then add and delete users as they change jobs.

Changes in security can be made once, to the user group definition, rather than separately to multiple users. Database security needs are similar. A good security tool can help manage the DBMS security, enabling you to define user groups, analyze the effects of changes to security, and analyze the relationship between user security and applications.

In addition to implementing a proactive mechanism that controls and prevents unauthorized access to sensitive system resources (such as files and programs) and to networks, warehouse managers should consider a tool that notifies administrators of attempted violations.

Keeping up with Capacity

A capacity planning software tool can make this effort easier and more accurate. A capacity planning tool should process enterprise-wide data and maintain a historical resource utilization and performance database. Planners should be able to review a wide variety of executive, management, and technical reports and graphs that address system response performance, such as:

- Task availability
- Resource utilization
- Operations analysis

- Trends reporting
- Service level reporting
- Batch window analysis

Managing Change

Change is the only sure thing in a successful data warehouse. However, *unmanaged* change can wreak havoc in a data warehouse environment. Change occurs in the source systems that feed the data warehouse and the data mart. Change occurs as the data warehouse and data marts evolve to support changing business requirements. In both cases, the key to successful change management is the construction of metadata repositories.

In the case of changes to either the source or target systems for populating data warehouse or data marts, it is critical to avoid hard-coded programs that must be modified for data extraction, transformation, or loading. A metadata repository allows source and target structure descriptions, along with data transformations, to be stored in an easy-to-maintain form. That means modifications to extract, transform, and load programs come directly from metadata structures.

The separation of the extract, transform, and load programs from changes in the source or target systems is critical for long-term cost management in the enterprise warehouse environment. The tools for maintaining metadata and automatically generating extract, transform, and load programs are readily available in the marketplace.

Most schema changes relate to expanding attributes or adding subject areas to enhance decision-making capabilities. This, of course, assumes an existing enterprise data model that captures core entities and relationships to support decision making.

To manage evolution of the data model, it is necessary to have a repository for storing the logical data model, business rules and definitions, usage notes, and referential integrity constraints. The repository should be capable of generating physical database structures, based on the metadata. Ideally, the repository should be able to use open systems database products to promote portability.

The repository houses the warehouse database schema (and perhaps data mart schemas as well) on a central server, so that systems management tools can pull down the latest schema and assist in the change management procedures for an evolving warehouse structure. Systems management tools allow a degree of transparency across database packages when managing schema changes.

Along the same lines, front-end web-based data access tools with metadata capability can insulate users from changing database schemas. If a database schema changes, the metadata within the front-end tool would be modified to accommodate evolution. It is critical to avoid impacting users by incidental schema changes in the database. Using metadata front-end tools allow applications to maintain consistency for users in the face of evolving database schemas. A number of database management tools are available to assist in these tasks.

Tool Integration

As techniques and technologies continue to evolve and standards develop, the issues of matching and integrating methodologies and process during the various stages of the project can diminish. In the meantime it is important to select a well-integrated set of tools from companies with a solid track record.

Systems Management

As the enterprise warehouse evolves to encompass multiple databases and data marts, a heterogeneous database environment will likely emerge. The data warehouse database itself can be different from operational databases and everything can run on heterogeneous servers. Productive management of a heterogeneous database environment becomes difficult without proper training and investment in operational personnel for each product and platform. However, specific tools can insulate organizations from product-specific management intricacies and can leverage functionality of various databases with a unified look and feel. The following approaches could enhance system management functions.

Best-of-Breed Tools

A best-of-breed approach to systems management defines each functional requirement for backup and recovery, disk and volume management, and performance monitoring. Then it selects the best tool in each category. With best-of-breed quality for each tool, overall systems management should be best-of-breed as well.

Unfortunately, the lack of integration across independent tools with multiple interfaces presents a systems management challenge. Since there is no automatic mechanism available, it requires functional coordination to be orchestrated manually by operations staff. This could result in errors and prove costly. On the other hand, scripts could be developed to facilitate cooperation between tools. Multiple tool suites also require in-depth knowledge.

Integrated Multiple Toolsets

While the advantage of best-of-breed tools is clear in terms of features and functions, many organizations choose to compromise on bells and whistles to obtain a completely integrated solution that handles the full breadth of systems management.

Using an integrated tool set reduces the education burden and ensures cooperation among tool suites. Reducing the number of sources for these tools may also be an advantage. Although tightly integrated systems management products may not have best-of-breed in every category, their ease-of-use and deployment may outweigh lack of capability in certain areas.

Integrating multiple toolsets under one umbrella provides a single point of reference for systems management, but allows deployment of best-of-breed products beneath the umbrella. This approach to systems management provides transparent cooperation among disparate tools by coordinating event triggers to invoke the appropriate tool. The best-of-breed tools under the umbrella ensure rich functionality, while the umbrella insulates operators from managing multiple tools. Of course, the organization must still deal with heterogeneity woes.

Integrated Meta Models

Implementing small data mart systems designed for a specific user community, built within a short period of time, is a positive thing. However, one must also provide a way for customers to build these systems as part of an enterprise solution.

There has been a lot of promotion of the idea of independent, departmental data marts. However, some organizations that have built these stovepipe (targeted towards a particular product or group of consumers) data warehouse systems are beginning to see that they are incapable of making accurate decisions across the enterprise because they have no way to consistently define data. These organizations are stymied as they must reevaluate data architecture as part of a data warehousing strategy.

When defining data models for your system, select those data definitions that expand outside your business unit and the enterprise reference data. These are definitions that would make sense to roll up into a corporate data warehouse or to integrate with another department's system. Work with a corporate group to ensure that the definitions of these terms are appropriate for the business. Once assured that the data definitions are consistent, there are two different ways to manage those —a partial repository or a full repository. When implementing a departmental data mart, many organizations may not want to consider a full repository implementation as part of the core project.

However, organizations can gain many of the benefits of a repository implementation, particularly those related to data consistency, by implementing a portion of the repository solution. This entails:

- Storing target definitions in the repository for repeatability and reusability. This can be used as sources for the data mart and storing in the metadata.
- Using an end user access tool to understand metadata in business terms.
- Storing key data definitions for multi-department data consistency in the repository.

This methodology provides the benefits of shareable information about data, data consistency throughout the enterprise, and an excellent head start toward a full repository implementation.

As part of the initial data mart implementation, or later as an add-on, organizations may choose to implement a repository. A full repository implementation can provide the data consistency benefits above in addition to the systems and applications management benefits described earlier for the data mart and for other critical applications. Using repositories that support existing languages and CASE tools can help leverage your existing investment in the infrastructure. Relational databases provide an excellent mechanism for tracking changes to metadata.

Managing Database Changes

One of the more complex areas to manage is the area of database change. Because an enterprise data warehouse system may incorporate multiple operational systems, multiple operational data stores, and multiple analytical data stores across multiple platforms, a single database change can affect dozens of other database objects on multiple servers. This is one area, in particular, where strong tools can significantly reduce risk.

Repository technology can help manage not only reference data, but also all data within the enterprise data warehouse. If data definitions are stored in the repository, there are two ways to manage database change throughout the enterprise:

Managing Database Objects

The preferred method is to make the changes to the logical model (repository) first. Once a change to a database object is recorded in the repository, a tool issues a change description and reference list. A number of database administrator (DBA) assist tools can assist in implementing the changes to the physical databases, across the enterprise, for mainframe and client/server databases.

However, many organizations can independently make changes to physical databases throughout the enterprise without notifying the repository or data warehousing group. On the other hand, the independent database administrators can use a tool to make changes to their database objects. This product would store information about the database objects, including server information, and how different data elements relate to one another. Once a change is made to a physical object, the information in the repository can be used to migrate the changes to the appropriate databases.

Managing Database Stability

Enterprise IT must keep pace with the ever-changing business environment (applications, platforms, and data). Unfortunately, enterprise technology improvements often disrupt and impede business processes, which fosters frustration and resistance to change in IT practices. In contrast, some organizations take the view that change is a key ingredient in stability. The negative side-effects of change must be restricted, but change itself must be encouraged. The difference is subtle, but critical.

Many IT professionals restrict change itself to control the side-effects it has on stability. Successful organizations, however, restrict only the side-effects of change and so avoid stagnation. Organizations that embrace data warehousing use their newly acquired information to make changes in their business practices that can bring them competitive advantage. Some technology products offer complete tool-sets in the areas of development, deployment, and support.

The warehouse implementation of application change is particularly challenging because it involves not only the transaction-based operational systems, but also the data warehouse systems and the applications that tie the operational systems with the data warehouse systems. The complexity of the warehouse environment makes the challenge of application vitality even more critical to a business that relies on changing business practices for competitive advantage.

Managing Data Warehouse Delivery

Data warehousing presents tremendous challenges to the existing culture of IT departments. Unfortunately for the unprepared, a data warehouse never returns to the lower regions of the resource curve. By its nature it is extremely iterative, ever changing, and constantly responding to the changing needs of the business.

In building a data warehouse you must have support from the highest levels, adequate funding, adequate resources, and the attention of the organization focused on this latest magic bullet that can save the enterprise from its competition and other unseen dark forces.

The warehouse's ongoing and fluctuating demand requires a vastly different set of IT abilities, outlooks, and metrics than standard OLTP application development.

Optimizing Performance

End users, who include executive management, demand fast response time from a data warehouse system. To succeed with data warehousing, organizations must plan to address these commonly identified potential performance problems discussed earlier. During the planning and implementing phase of your project, look for systems and tools that can optimize SQL and suggest ways to improve it.

Managing Data Availability

Fragmentation and free-space problems can also impact performance and availability. If the available free space falls below a value that does not allow a new segment or extent to be created, processing stops for that task. Therefore, not only does the current available free space need to be monitored, but also history needs to be kept for purposes of trend analysis for determining the effectiveness of the current allocation and storage needs for the future.

Organizations need to implement procedures for detecting and correcting fragmentation through database reorganization to ensure maximum data availability.

Role of IT

Resources from network services, operations, database administration, and application systems must go beyond defining the initial technical architecture and play an active role in expansion, maintenance, and support of the warehouse. The issues in this realm are large and complex. Multiple products are brought together in every facet of information technology to build and support the data warehouse, which is testing the limits of tools on every front.

Administration

If the size of databases has quickly moved from hundreds of gigabytes to the multiple-terabyte range, the stress on the technology is often transferred to the database administration (DBA) staff. The DBA's skills and techniques are being tested along with the tools. Techniques in distribution, security, segmentation, array processing, and other areas that improve performance at all levels are required to meet demands.

Configuration and Network Management

The level of complexity is not isolated to the databases and the server hardware alone, but also spans the desktop Internet environment. Support for the web-based front-end tools and multitude of browsers is especially difficult. Configuration management becomes an issue when dealing with thousands of work stations across the multitude of platforms.

End User Support

The investment in people, technology, and data can all be wasted if data is not delivered to the people who need it to drive, manage and measure the organization. This key role can insure that the highest return on the data warehousing investment is delivered to the business. To truly empower users, they must have the tools and the training to realize their potential.

Once empowered, users often band together to form user groups and learn from one another. User groups are a vehicle for the people using the data warehouse to communicate to warehouse management where their problem areas are as well as what enhancements that they would like to see. It is a chance for IT staff to directly interface with the users.

Leadership and Management

The last important role in managing the warehouse is truly and simply project leadership. Sponsorship at the executive level is one type of leadership that is necessary to make the warehouse a priority within the organization. Project management of the warehouse team is also needed to ensure the warehouse is aligned with the business needs and to develop project plans to support the warehouse as it matures.

Conclusions

As we stated in the beginning, operating a data warehouse smoothly is as challenging as running any sophisticated OLTP system in a day-to-day operational environment. The data warehouse can rapidly turn into a data dump if the business processes to maintain the warehouse are not put in place. The warehouse is of value only if you know how the warehouse fits into the schema of the business. In the end it is the people, the tools, the methods, and their interaction that can get it built and make it last.

Roles and responsibilities of the warehouse management team must be clearly defined and the ground rules for warehouse use must be explained to and understood by the business users and then supported by warehouse management personnel.

The commitment to *staffing* the warehouse team must match or exceed the original commitment it took to build it. Although most organizations with a data warehouse in place today built it themselves, supplementing their efforts with consulting help, the maintenance and support of the data warehouse inevitably becomes the responsibility of the organization's internal resources.

A warehouse that is easy to maintain and able to mature with the business does not just happen by itself. It must be designed that way. During the requirements, architectural design, and construction phase of the warehouse, skills can be developed that can enable the support team to move to a level of independence and self-assurance sufficient to support the day-to-day operation and the never-ending evolution of the data warehouse.

If the data warehouse is properly constructed, with attention paid to metadata and integrated tools, and then is supported by a capable warehouse team with clearly delineated and documented roles and responsibilities, it can become the single most important tool within the organization.

Although an entire foundation must be set in order to construct and manage the warehouse, organizations who have done it successfully say the warehouse can return enormous value to the organization in a relatively short time.

Keeping a data warehouse in order takes more than a conscientious system administrator. Beyond managing the integrity, flow, validity, and usefulness of the data collected, loaded, and extracted, companies need to make sure that the organization is appropriately structured to support the building, management, and maintenance of the warehouse. This takes more than once-a-year spring cleaning or an occasional upgrade.

16

SUMMARY AND CONCLUSIONS

Introduction

Advances in computing technology almost always present a paradox. On one hand, new technology can make a business more competitive, efficient, and profitable. On the other, there is always the threat of an implementation problem brought on by nonstandard components, proprietary platforms, and limited development environments. This paradox is more apparent today than at any other time in computing history.

A number of technologies have advanced over the last several years to present Management Information Systems (MIS) managers with unprecedented opportunities for building state-of-the-art application systems. With the rise of the Internet, distributed objects, object-oriented programming, and client/server and distributed processing architectures, the time is ripe to take advantage of new methods of application development.

We also realize that terabytes of information are locked up in proprietary enterprise systems. Databases and file systems such as DB2, Oracle, VSAM, and IMS/DB contain huge stores of data that can only be accessed by a programmer trained in the intricacies of the transaction processing monitors and the messaging systems that manage programs and information. Add to the mix the complexity of distributed object computing, and it is no wonder that building modern, scalable, reusable applications that access enterprise data can be so challenging.

How can you capitalize on new development environments without redesigning your transaction processing and messaging systems? You must find a way to leverage the immense value of the information in your existing enterprise transaction and messaging systems, while taking advantage of what all the new paradigms of computing have to offer.

Both data warehouses (comprehensive, enterprise-wide) and data marts (subject- or application-specific) must be accessible to a wide variety of users, via the web, with an equally wide variety of application and information needs if they are to provide a high return on investment.

Factors for the Evolution

In reviewing the development of data warehousing, we need to begin with a review of what had been done with the data before of evolution of data warehouses. Let us first look at how the kind of data that ends up in today's data warehouses had been managed historically.

Throughout the history of systems development, the primary emphasis had been given to the operational systems and the data they process. It is not practical to keep data in the operational systems indefinitely; and only as an afterthought was a structure designed for archiving the data that the operational system has processed.

The fundamental requirements of the operational and analysis systems are different; the operational systems need performance, whereas the analysis systems need flexibility and broad scope. It has rarely been acceptable to have business analysis interfere with and degrade performance of the operational systems.

The skyrocketing power of hardware and software, along with the availability of affordable and easy-to-use reporting and analysis tools have played the most important role in evolution of data warehouses. Some of these factors are discussed below.

Data from Legacy Systems

In the 1970s virtually all business system development was done on IBM mainframe computers using tools such as COBOL, CICS, IMS, and DB2. The 1980s brought in the new mini-computer platforms such as AS/400 and VAX/VMS. The late eighties and early nineties made UNIX a popular server platform with the introduction of client/server architecture.

Despite all the changes in the platforms, architectures, tools, and technologies, a remarkably large number of business applications continue to run in the mainframe environment of the 1970's. By some estimates, more than 70 percent of business data for large corporations still resides in the mainframe environment. The most important reason for this is that over the years these systems have grown to capture the business knowledge and rules that are incredibly difficult to carry to a new platform or application.

These systems, generically called *legacy systems*, continue to be the largest source of data for analysis systems. The data that is stored in DB2, IMS, VSAM, etc. for the transaction systems ends up in large tape libraries in remote data centers. A corporation will generate countless reports and extracts over the years, each designed to extract requisite information from the legacy systems. In most instances, MIS groups assume responsibility for designing and developing programs for these reports and extracts. The time required to generate and deploy these programs frequently turns out to be longer than the end users think they can afford.

Information on the Desktop

During the past decade, the sharply increasing popularity of the personal computer on business desktops has introduced many new options and compelling opportunities for business analysis. The gap between the programmer and end user has started to close as business analysts now have at their fingertips many of the tools required to gain proficiency in the use of spreadsheets for analysis and graphic representation.

Advanced users will frequently use desktop database programs that allow them to store and work with the information extracted from the legacy sources. Many desktop reporting and analysis tools are increasingly targeted towards end users and have gained considerable popularity on the desktop.

The downside of this model for business analysis is that it leaves the data fragmented and oriented towards very specific needs. Individual users have obtained only the information that they require. Not being standardized, the extracts are unable to address the requirements of multiple users and uses. The time and cost involved in addressing the requirements of multiple users prove prohibitive.

This approach to data management assumes the end user has the time to expend on managing the data in the spreadsheets, files, and databases. While many of these users may be proficient at data management, most undertake these tasks as a necessity. And given the choice, most users would find it more efficient to focus on the actual analysis and the tools available to them.

Decision-Support Systems

Decision-support systems tend to focus more on detail and are targeted towards lower to mid-level managers. Executive information systems have generally provided a higher level of consolidation and a multi-dimensional view of the data, as high-level executives tend to need the ability to slice and dice the same data rather than drill down to review the data detail.

These two similar and overlapping categories are perhaps the closest precursors to the data warehousing systems. Yet the high price of their development and the coordination required for their production made them an elite product that never entered the mainstream. The following are some characteristics generally associated with decision-support or executive information systems:

- These systems have data in descriptive standard business terms, rather than in cryptic computer field names. Data names and data structures in these systems are designed for use by non-technical users.
- The data is generally preprocessed with the application of standard business rules such as how to allocate revenue to products, business units, and markets.

Consolidated views of the data such as product, customer, and market are available. Although these systems will at times have the ability to drill down to the detail data, rarely are they able to access all the detail data at the same time.

Today's data warehousing systems provide the analytical tools afforded by their precursors. But their design is no longer derived from the specific requirements of analysts or executives; and, as we will see later, data warehousing systems are most successful when their design aligns with the overall business structure rather than specific requirements.

Emerging Technologies

Many factors have influenced the quick evolution of the data warehousing discipline. The most significant set of factors has been the enormous forward movement in the hardware and software technologies. Sharply decreasing prices and the increasing power of computer hardware, coupled with ease of use of today's software, has made possible quick analysis of hundreds of gigabytes of information and business knowledge.

Increasing Desktop Power

Entering the market as a novelty computer in early eighties, the personal computer has become the hotbed of innovation during the past decade. The personal computer was initially used for word processing and other minor tasks, with no links to primary analytical functions. With the help of innovations such as powerful personal productivity software, easy–to-use graphical interfaces, and responsive business applications, the personal computer has become the focal point of all computing today. The powerful desktop hardware and software has allowed for development of the client/server or multi-tier computing architecture.

Almost all data warehouses are accessed by personal-computer-based tools. These tools vary from very simple query capabilities available with most productivity packages to incredibly powerful graphical multi-dimensional analysis tools. Without the wide array of choices available for data warehouse access, data warehousing would not have evolved so quickly.

Power of the Server Software

Server operating systems such as Windows NT and UNIX have brought mission-critical stability and powerful features to the distributed computing environment. The operating system software has become very feature-rich as the cost has been going down steadily. With this combination, sophisticated operating system concepts such virtual memory, multitasking, and symmetric multiprocessing are now available on inexpensive operating platforms. Operating systems such as Windows NT have made these powerful systems very easy to set up and operate, reducing the total cost of ownership of these powerful servers.

Explosion of Intranets and Web-based Applications

The most important development in computing since the advent of the personal computer is the explosion of Internet and web-based applications. Somewhat after the fact, the business community has jumped onto the Internet bandwagon.

One of the most exciting fields in computing industry today is the development of intranet applications. Intranets are private business networks that are based on the Internet standards, although they are designed to be used internally. The Internet/intranet trend has very important implications for data warehousing applications.

First, data warehouses can be available worldwide on public/private networks at a reasonable cost. This availability minimizes the need to replicate data across diverse geographical locations. Second, this standard has allowed the web server to provide a middle tier where all the heavy-duty analysis takes place before it is presented to the web-browsing client to use.

Challenges

As we have seen, a number of new technologies are enabling MIS personnel to quickly and easily build new applications. Distributed objects are emerging as the technology infrastructure for building three-tier client/server applications. It is no longer a matter of whether applications will be built using distributed object models, but when these state-of-the-art systems will be deployed.

On the other hand, object-oriented programming environments do not allow developers to easily leverage existing infrastructure and enterprise data. There are still quite a number of hurdles to overcome in order to build mission-critical applications within this computing environment.

World Wide Web as an Information Accelerator

Throughout history, crucial developments in information technology have accelerated the pace of human endeavor. The spoken word made it possible for us to exchange information in small groups at a single point in time. The tribal culture was born. The written word allowed us to provide information to those who were far away in either time or space.

In the fifteenth century, the invention of the printing press decreased the cost of distributing written information by orders of magnitude, providing an information *broadcast* capability for the first time in human history. What followed was an unprecedented acceleration in rational thought, which we now refer to as The Renaissance. The Scientific Revolution, the Protestant Reformation, European Nationalism, and the Industrial Revolution all trace their roots to Gutenberg's invention, which made possible the dissemination of information critical to their movement.

The World Wide Web represents a paradigm shift of comparable significance to that of the printing press. Rather than broadcast the written word (static information), the WWW broadcasts entire software applications (dynamic information). Similar to the economic impact of the printing press on text, the web decreases the cost of distributing a given piece of software functionality by orders of magnitude. In order to understand this phenomena better, let's consider an example:

In anticipation of the approaching demand for cheap travel in the United States, a group of travel agents joined together to create a program that allowed consumers to search for and book appropriate airline schedules, lodging, and rental cars. They deployed this functionality over the web.

Now, consider the costs to implement the same system via conventional client/server technology. To allow for a pool of even 1,000,000 potential users would require the software developer to ship 2,000,000 floppy disks (assuming two disks to install program), utilize 15,000 gigabytes of hard disk space (assuming the software requires 15 megabytes of disk space on each user's machine), print and ship 500 tons of software manuals (assuming each set of documentation weighs one pound), and staff a help desk to spend 333,333 hours on the telephone answering user questions (assuming one question per user that requires 20 minutes of a staffer's time).

By the time we total the materials, installation, maintenance, and support costs of this configuration, we can quite easily imagine total expenses to distribute our application in excess of $150,000,000. After adjusting for the marketing necessary to convince 1,000,000 people to install our software on their machine, it becomes clear that without a business case likely to generate hundreds of millions, client/server distribution at this scale doesn't make much sense.

Comparing the web vs. traditional client server technology, we see that the web offers massive economic advantages for those needing to distribute software broadly. The break-even point for web development is much lower, which naturally results in much greater application diversity. Additionally, the variable costs of web deployment are also lower, meaning that any applications deployed in this environment will be much more profitable.

As the above example illustrates, the World Wide Web is a superconductor for all those software applications that run effectively through its application programming interface. It plays the same role for software programmers that the printing press played for authors five centuries ago, making it possible for them to project their intellect throughout the society to an unprecedented degree. Before the printing press, the rich man possessed a few books. Today, it is common for a member of the middle class to own a thousand books or more, with quick access to hundreds of thousands.

Before the web, a professional with a home computer was likely to have access to a half-dozen computer programs. After the web, that same professional can now access thousands of programs.

Just as thousands of mass-produced books on subjects such as engineering, manufacturing, and navigation became the building blocks for the industrial age, so shall thousands of massively distributed software programs for communication, engineering, and decision making become the building blocks for the coming information age.

In an instant, the web has emerged as the low-cost distribution channel for software. In many cases, the cost is so low that it allows knowledge workers to self-publish their work. The result is a drastic increase in the velocity of information flow. Software expertise is distributed, tuned, modulated, and amplified with frightening speed over the global Internet. The collective intellect of humanity, which is our fundamental engine of growth, thinks faster and grows wiser.

Two 20th Century Innovations Collide

As we have discussed above, the success of the data warehousing movement has resulted in a massive increase in the amount of data being captured for decision support, as well as an increase in the number of decision-support applications available. The more recent proliferation of the World Wide Web has provided the world with a revolutionary distribution channel for software programs. The lack of effective distribution channels and production capabilities for any industry an cripple the industry development for many years. That was true in case of heavy products as well as crude oil.

By 1875, with the arrival of the first modern rail transportation systems, the critical distribution bottle-neck was broken, and John D. Rockefeller was rapidly building the Standard Oil Company. The distribution leverage provided by those railroads provided the revenues necessary to perfect Standard's refinery technology, and those refineries turned out increasing quantities and varieties of petroleum byproducts. By exploiting previously untappable oil deposits, he soon accumulated more wealth than any person of his generation.

The massive accumulations of commercial data are analogous to the above crude oil example. Hardware, databases, and decision-support software constitute the essential technologies for *mining* and *refining* this raw data. Building a data warehouse is similar to building an oil refinery. The World Wide Web is the transportation system for refined product. The critical shift that occurs at this point is the creation of a merchant decision-support business. In other words, with the Internet as a distribution channel, it has become possible for corporations to use their data warehouse as a revenue-generating, rather than cost-reducing, asset.

Consider the opportunities available to a telecommunications company to obtain value from its database of telephone calls. By providing decision-support applications over the web against a comprehensive data warehouse containing call level details for all customers, the telecommunications firm can offer its customers answers to a horde of questions on a continuous basis. They can, in an instant, determine the call distribution by region, city, street, or even zip code.

Other merchants could ascertain the percentage of the time their telesales reps spent on the phone or the average length of their phone calls or which prospects they speak with or how many calls they spend on average with each prospect.

Once this sort of analytical functionality has been implemented, it is not difficult to imagine how the system might evolve into a more active management control system that allows the client to react and to take immediate remedial action or change policy on the fly.

Telecommunications firms can benefit from commercial decision-support offerings in the following ways:

- Bundle these services with their basic phone service in order to differentiate their offering and obtain some combination of enhanced rates or market share.

- Sell these services for a fee, since some will be extremely valuable to the customer.

- Obtain enhanced customer loyalty and "lock-in" by building enough customizable reporting, analysis, and control features into the system so that the customer does not wish to switch to a new service because the current telecommunication firm's software has become "mission critical" to the customer's own day-to-day operations.

Of course, providing a commercial data warehouse online in not without its costs. It may cost tens of millions of dollars or more to provide high concurrency access to massive amounts of data. However, the wisdom of this investment for the telecommunications provider becomes clear when we consider the economics of scale involved.

No one can provide a call detail analyzer as cheaply as the provider of the phone service. They have a natural low-cost position in this business, since they can build a particular decision-support application once and then distribute it to tens of thousands of corporations with only slight charges for marginal sales, marketing, and billing expenses. The decision-support service becomes just one more line item on a bill that they already send to each of these customers every single month and they amortize their development costs over a huge user base.

This sort of success encourages commercial data warehouse providers to invest more effort in decision-support application development and to collect more diverse and greater volumes of data for analysis.

Explosive growth is imminent because the value of a data warehouse is proportional to the number of people who query it, the frequency of their queries, and the sophistication of the analysis. As the number of users on the World Wide Web increases, the number of customers for the commercial data warehouse also increases. This results in more revenue to the data warehouse owners, encouraging them to invest in their decision-support offerings. As their decision-support applications improve, they draw more customers, encourage more frequent usage, and in turn perpetuate this cycle.

Data Warehouses Adjusting to the Web

What was initially a trend toward consolidating corporate information in data warehouses and making it available through user-friendly query tools has now become a necessity. This premise is based on providing users the ability to get access to corporate information, particularly information that has been consolidated from multiple production databases into data warehouses optimized for query processing. The field includes online analytical processing (OLAP) solutions, in which information is moved into a multidimensional database that allows it to be examined from many angles, and ROLAP, an adaptation of OLAP technology that works with relational databases.

The Internet and data warehousing are both hot issues. Companies are increasingly aware that the Internet can help them reach out to new markets and increase their value to customers, particularly by offering individualized, one-to-one marketing. Data warehousing technology allows companies to develop marketing models that focus on customers instead of products. It seems natural, therefore, that data warehousing is converging with the Internet. This convergence is resulting in a new category of decision-support tool, the web-enabled warehouse.

Putting a data warehouse on the web offers tremendous benefits, but it also presents some serious technical and organizational challenges.

Security

The first issue is security. You must have a clearly defined security policy and understand how to make Internet access to an internal data warehouse consistent with that policy. If your organization does not have a security policy, stop reading and get to work on one! The Internet is used by many unscrupulous people. The impact of a security breach in a mission-critical system can be devastating. Make sure your solution has strong encryption, authorization, and authentication services.

Business Value

Success also depends on having a sponsor for the warehouse, someone who will help develop a clear business case for putting the warehouse on the web.

Companies often start by putting warehouses on their intranet. Some companies are also cautiously venturing into the extranet environment, which allows them to provide access to business partners, such as suppliers or distributors. Other companies have gone straight to web-enabled warehouses that allow consumers to access the warehouse from the Internet. These include retail companies, such as mail order, packaged goods, and direct marketing; and service companies, such as banks, overnight delivery services, and travel agents.

But in each of these cases, you are not likely to succeed unless you clearly articulate the business value of the project and find an executive sponsor in the appropriate department (sales, marketing, product management, or customer service and support).

Impact Assessment

You also need to assess what impact a web-enabled warehouse will have on your MIS organization and infrastructure. This includes considering changes in utilization patterns and the number of active clients. Changes also include the need to learn new skills, such as how to integrate a warehouse database with a web server and which tools are necessary. Other items to consider include networks, servers, failure/recovery procedures, development and test-ing tools, and training for programmers and operators.

Usage and Management

Consider how people will use the warehouse and what impact their behavior will have on elements such as performance, availability, throughput, and net-work bandwidth. For example, you need to select among three basic query ap-proaches, such as static pages, dynamic pages, or dynamic queries.

Many companies begin by putting up a static, canned set of reports. Most of the production reporting packages available on the market can generate HTML pages that can be hosted by a web server. If your users require routine reports and do not need the ability to modify or query these reports, the static approach can be sufficient.

On the other hand, dynamic parameter entry, using a simple dialog box, allows the user to request a report and modify its behavior. For example, a company may put up a web site on which sales personnel can measure their performance relative to a quota. The site administrator can allow a sales repre-sentative to enter a date range, such as this month or quarter, and generate a report specific to that information. A more privileged user, such as a regional sales manager, can request the same data for more than one sales represen-tative.

More powerful and flexible query tools allow the user to browse the warehouse, view data definitions, and generate multidimensional queries that may result in a significant server load. The warehouse server needs to support either a multidimensional database or a relational DBMS using a star or snowflake schema, to handle these kinds of queries. The multi-variant nature of the queries and the significant impact they can have on overall system de-sign and management typically require more planning, administration, and system capacity.

In all cases, keep in mind that users are very demanding. You will need a flexible, high-performance web server and tight integration with your ware-house DBMS in order to provide quality service.

You also need to consider how to deliver data to end users. In many in-stances, it will be sufficient for the user to run a query or report from a browser. To do this, however, the user must start the browser, locate the proper web site, and then select and run the query or report. This is a classic example of pull technology, because the user needs to actively request, or pull, the data from the warehouse.

There are times when users want information to be delivered without having to actively request it. To achieve this, companies can set up push models that use triggers to initiate reports. Triggers can be caused by a regular or irregular event. A regular trigger might automatically send an inventory report at the end of every quarter. An event trigger might notify a manager when regional sales drop below a predefined threshold. Then there is the question of how to get this information to the user who needs it. Publish-and-subscribe packages, for example, let users indicate interest in the data, so that when the data becomes available, it is automatically transmitted-via fax, e-mail, or a broadcast server, as the result of a trigger.

Tools and Support

Since putting your warehouse on the web will stress its capacity, you will need good tools for managing the system, especially the network and various servers. And you must ensure that your vendors' support services will meet your global support requirements.

Supporting Technologies

There are a number of technologies that play an important role in building and implementing a data warehouse. Some of these are summarized in the following sections.

Metadata

One of the most important components of the data warehouse is that of metadata. Metadata allows the decision support user to find out where data is in the process of discovery and exploration. Metadata contains the following components:

- Identification of the source of data
- Description of the customization that has occurred as the data passes from the data warehouse to the data mart
- Simple descriptive information about the data mart, including tables, attributes, relationships
- Definitions

Metadata is created by and updated from the load programs that move data into the data marts or data warehouses. There needs to be linkage between the metadata found in the data mart and the metadata found in the data warehouse. Among other things, the metadata linkage between the two environments needs to describe how the data in the two environments is related.

OLAP

Data warehousing is not a product, but a strategy that accommodates the need to consolidate and store data in information systems dedicated to improving the performance of the corporation by providing end users with timely access to critical information.

Within a data warehousing strategy, online analytical processing (OLAP) supports strategic applications. The role of the OLAP is best understood in the context of the five key components of a data warehousing or data marting strategy, which are:

Policy

Rules governing business issues like goals and scope of the data warehouse; operational issues like loading and maintenance frequency; and organizational issues like information security are as critical to successful data warehouse and data mart implementations as are product and technology choices.

Transformation

Before raw data can be stored in a data warehouse, it must be transformed and cleansed so that it has consistent meaning to users who access it. This transformation may involve restructuring, redefining, filtering, combining, recalculating and summarizing data fields from a range of disparate transaction systems.

Storage

As data is moved from various transaction systems into the warehouse, it must be stored in order to maximize system flexibility, manageability and overall accessibility. The information stored in the warehouse is historical in nature and includes detailed transactional data and detail. The technology best suited to serve the role of historical data repository in the data warehouse is the relational database.

Analysis

This is the component of a data warehousing solution which addresses the corporate need to understand what is driving business performance. The analytical component must support sophisticated, autonomous end user queries, rapid calculation of key business metrics, planning and forecasting functions, and what-if analyses on large data volumes. Unlike the data warehouse storage component, the analytical solution must encompass historical, derived, and projected information. The technology best suited to serve this role as the analytical engine in the data warehouse is the OLAP server.

Presentation and Access

The ability to select, view and manipulate data refers to data presentation and access. Desktop tools such as spreadsheets, query tools, web browsers and report writers meet this need by presenting a graphical interface for navigating warehouse data.

Data Warehouse Access

In general, the user tools for accessing data warehouses and data marts can be placed in one of two main categories:

1. *Personal productivity tools* (such as spreadsheets, word processors, statistical packages and graphics tools) are characterized by the requirement to manipulate and present data on individual PCs. Developed for stand-alone environments, personal productivity tools address applications requiring desktop manipulation of small volumes of warehouse data.

2. Data query and reporting tools deliver warehouse-wide data access through simple interfaces that hide the SQL language from end-users. These tools are designed for list-oriented queries, basic drill down analysis and generation of reports. These tools provide a view of simple historical data but do not address the need for multidimensional reporting, analysis and planning, nor are they capable of computing sophisticated metrics.

By combining standard access tools with a powerful analytical engine, users are able to gain real insight from the data in the warehouse. OLAP addresses warehouse applications such as performance reporting, sales forecasting, product line and customer profitability, sales analysis, marketing analysis, what-if analysis and manufacturing mix analysis—applications that require historical, projected, and derived data. A key characteristic of OLAP is that historical data is made vastly more useful to the business user by transforming it through OLAP calculation into derived and projected data.

Query Tools

The success of a data warehouse depends on your query tool. If end users cannot easily answer key business questions using the tools they have been given, even the most elegant design and heroic load efforts will be judged failures. Choosing a tool that empowers users to ask a wide array of questions, rather than limiting them to the basics, can be a challenge.

Today, most organizations no longer set out to build an enterprise data warehouse on a grand scale. Instead, the warehouse is built a piece at a time, through single subject-area data marts. The team responsible for building the first pilot data mart is often charged with identifying the technology that will be used by business people for query, reporting, and analysis.

But not all needs will be obvious during a pilot. Some requirements will not make themselves known until users begin working with the data warehouse. Others will not be an issue at all until your second or third data mart is built, long after a decision has been made.

Your choice of query tools will have significant short- and long-term impact, such as:

Ease of Use and Flexibility of Setup

The query tool must be easy to use, easy to set up, and flexible in its presentation of the database. If it falls short, your data warehouse will not be used.

Aggregate Awareness

To minimize response time, the query tool must make use of pre-calculated summary tables when appropriate, without bothering business users to make decisions on how data is fetched.

Multiple Heterogeneous Data Sources

Your users will want to combine data from multiple sources within a report. Some of those sources may be in data marts on different platforms, and some may not be in the data warehouse at all.

Integrated Analysis

Your tool should provide analytic capabilities without requiring ongoing support of developers. It should allow users to slice, dice, and drill through data, without enforcing a single predefined hierarchical view.

Whether you implement data marts or a data warehouse, design stars or snowflakes, or centralize enterprise data by any other method, you will need to select a query tool that facilitates the analysis via the web.

The passage of time and the progress of industry consists of long periods of execution, punctuated by intermittent bursts of metamorphosis. We are currently entering one such transitional phase in the information technology industry. The concept of the data warehouse is being redefined by the Internet. That system of open networking protocols has forever changed the economics of information dissemination, catalyzing a entirely new class of software programs. The result is the commercial decision-support application—a concept so simple that a child can understand its significance, so powerful that it will remake entire sectors of our economy forever, and so compelling that every knowledge worker will grow dependent upon at least one of these within the decade.

Securing Inter/Intra/Extranet Applications

Securing a distributed web-enabled environment will always require a combination of physical security and logical security (authentication, authorization, and encryption). All the physical and logical security in the world will not help you if some authorized person gives the information away. Technical security must always be part of a complete security system that incorporates proven protocols and manual procedures.

There are a vast number of security protocols to protect against various scenarios, including eavesdropping, man-in-the-middle attacks, repudiation, and message alteration. Kerberos is a private key encryption approach developed at the Massachusetts Institute of Technology. It is based upon a central (possibly replicated) security server that is trusted by everyone.

Most attention in the commercial world has been directed to securing messages. This is understandable in a distributed environment, especially given the open nature of the Internet. One area that has had very limited attention is securing databases. Most commercial implementations use simple password protection for access with no encryption and no single sign-on. Also, most database security routines available with commercial DBMSs are stand-alone and cannot integrate easily with other security mechanisms.

Messages are short-lived, but data in databases can be around for many years. Today, assuming that steps have been taken to secure the transaction messages, the easiest way to do damage or act fraudulently would be to access the relatively unprotected databases and alter the data. DBMSs do have secure-database capabilities, usually directed to military use, but it is rare for commercial databases to be encrypted or protected using public key techniques.

Probably the biggest problem in securing distributed systems is the integration of disparate security systems. Your web site may use SSL, your mainframe may use ACF2 password protection, and your internal servers may use Kerberos. There is no general solution to this problem today, although there are some proprietary solutions that cover a wide range of environments.

The Internet

The Internet is perceived as a hostile place, and as such it is a great proving ground for Intranet and extranet security. If security technology works on the Internet, it will work anywhere. Right now, the emphasis on the Internet is providing secure financial transactions.

The state of the art requires very careful coding of applications, firewalls, and servers and browsers with Secure Sockets Layer (SSL) capabilities. SSL is a flexible protocol that supports various encryption algorithms, including RSA and DES. Unfortunately, it only addresses the securing of HTTP traffic today, namely regular web pages. This is not currently a problem because most Internet transactions are forms-based and as such, use HTML/HTTP. With the introduction of CORBA/IIOP as an Internet transaction protocol, there is another channel to secure. At this time IIOP is in the clear (unencrypted), but secure IIOP is planned. This will be critical to the use of IIOP for transactions over the Internet.

SSL, as used in the standard versions of the popular browsers, provides only server authentication based on public key technology and not public-key-based user authentication. Although the software to have password protection for certain web pages is available on many web servers, the software uses passwords stored on the server, making them vulnerable to interception if someone uses the same password on many sites.

Middleware

Beyond physical security and the provision of dedicated connections between machines, the simplest—but probably least flexible and most expensive—way to secure middleware communications is to use hardware. Assuming the servers are in a secure environment, encryption boxes can be used to communicate securely over public connections. This could be an intranet or even the Internet.

This approach provides solid point-to-point security. The more flexible approach is to secure the middleware communications at a software level. This is potentially more vulnerable than the hardware approach, but it is cheaper and more flexible when new connections are needed. The potential extra vulnerability is a result of the software running in relatively insecure operating system environments.

Managing Security

As mentioned earlier, technical security alone cannot provide appropriate security at an acceptable cost. Before implementing technical solutions, you must resolve two areas of security management. One involves managing the risk during the design and implementation stage, and the other involves managing the risk during operations.

Technical security does not work unless it is supported by appropriate processes, the right control structure, and educated attitudes toward security. Operational security addresses these issues.

Today, securing distributed systems requires a combination of several different types of products. SSL provides link encryption for the Internet and some authentication. Products based on Kerberos or RSA technology can be used to secure the middleware environment, albeit with some integration effort. Standards are emerging for at least securing the messaging part of distributed systems, with secure IIOP being one of the more important areas.

Distributed systems security is an exciting and important area. Providing rock-solid security for the Inter/Intra/Extranet is essential for it to reach its enormous potential.

Data Warehouse as Corporate History

The data warehouse, like most successful technological innovations, is the beneficiary of a fortunate change in economic circumstance. Corporations exist to perform transactions, the most significant of these generally being the sale to a customer of either products or services. Having succeeded in performing these transactions, the next great challenge is to optimize the process and innovate new varieties of the offering.

The status quo at the dawn of the data warehouse era (early 90s) was proprietary hardware and database software from vendors such as IBM, Teradata, and Tandem. The cost to accumulate and analyze 100 gigabytes of data (approximately one years' worth of store-item-week information for a typical retail chain) might exceed $25 million.

After discounting for the risk of in-house development, delays between project initiation and completion, and the attendant management drain of such a large undertaking, it is easy to see why an experienced executive would be reluctant to go forward with any project that did not promise to deliver a return in excess of $100 million. With an economic hurdle this high, experimentation by IT visionaries was effectively stifled, and large database development remained the province of a few mega-organizations.

All of this changed with the advent of parallel processing hardware running the UNIX operating system, coupled with merchant RDBMSs capable of exploiting multiple threads simultaneously for processes such as data loads, indexing, aggregation, cleansing, and queries. UNIX introduced competition for the hardware platform. Merchant RDBMSs introduced competition for the software platform. As might be expected, prices plummeted.

By mid 1990s, it was possible to put together an open systems configuration capable of hosting over 100 gigabytes of data for a few million dollars, and companies could get started with pilot projects for a fraction of that cost. As conventional economics dictates, when the cost of a commodity decreases by an order of magnitude, demand normally increases even faster (assuming any pent-up demand).

We need not have worried about any lack of demand. Retail, consumer packaged goods, insurance, healthcare, telecommunications, transportation, entertainment, manufacturing, government, and financial services organizations embraced this technology with a vengeance. The justification was generally improvement of operational efficiency in areas such as merchandising, category management, logistics, promotions, marketing & sales programs, asset management, cost containment, pricing, and product development.

As of today, data warehouses either exist or are in the process of being created in many of the midsize and large corporations in the US. They represent the corporate memory, and grow in both size as well as asset value with every day that passes.

Impact on MIS

Decision Support Systems (DSS) and Executive Information Systems (EIS), although not new, are becoming more and more prevalent as the technology of data warehousing becomes widely accepted. Thanks to recent innovations in storage technology, improved PC capabilities, web-enabled interfaces, and more powerful database servers, the concept of a data warehouse has become a reality. Data warehousing is now considered an enabling technology that makes powerful DSS and EIS implementations practical.

Building a data warehouse is no small undertaking. Consider the basic premise of the warehouse. This may entail collecting and storing from 50 to

500 gigabytes to terabytes of disparate data taken from a variety of operational source systems, and then making that data quickly available to users across the entire enterprise. Data extraction tools have made collecting data from disparate operational systems less daunting.

Warehouse administration tools provide a lot of help with managing the data warehouse and associated metadata. Web-based data access tools are providing business users with easy access to the information stored in the warehouse. With software packages like these, building a data warehouse has become a more manageable and less intimidating undertaking.

The tools are great, but before you rush out to buy them, and before you invest in the latest parallel data servers or mega-CPUs to run everything on, consider the impact a data warehouse effort will have on it. In a decision-support environment, development begins at the data analysis stage, where all work flows from the data modeling and analysis activities. When the model is complete, the data warehouse is built. In most case, only after testing are user requirements determined. Given the powerful access tools utilized with the data warehouse, securing the data is much more difficult.

Data quality is a major concern. Two issues, consistency and currency, are keys to high quality in the warehouse. Consistency of the data, regardless of the source, is absolutely required. Currency must be continually verified since the data is never updated, only refreshed.

Techniques must be devised to gather and transform the data that populates the warehouse. Metadata must be created and maintained. Integration with operational data stores has to be defined and database management policies implemented.

Determining the Value

Data warehouse development, unlike transactional system development, is a highly iterative process. It would be foolish to attempt to build the entire warehouse all at once, as is done with application systems. As a result, priorities have to be evaluated to determine which pieces of the warehouse to implement first. Ideally, the warehouse is built in small increments. Above all else, consistency of design and consistency across the data is essential.

Architectural Considerations

Data warehouse implementations are often associated with some sort of a reengineering effort or a shift to client/server development environments. The warehouse operates in the world of PCs, networks and database servers.

Warehouses are not ordinarily associated with mainframe environments except to the extent that they capture data from mainframe source systems.

Building this infrastructure is a major component of warehouse development. Unlike a typical transaction application system where knowledge of the application is paramount, data warehouse support requires a staff of integration specialists who can track and resolve problems across a wide spectrum of software and hardware segments.

A New Paradigm

The theme prevalent throughout the present economy is commoditization. In every sector, leading providers are finding that their transactions are losing their differentiation. Consumers can obtain the same services from a variety of banks, insurance firms, ticketing agencies, airlines, hotels, mortgage firms, shipping companies, telecommunications firms, etc. Vendors have their choice of distribution channels, advertising channels, and marketing venues. Retailers are flooded with products, all vying for the same shelf space. Capitalism has been a success, and we are nearly crippled by the number of options presented to us. Emerging from this cacophony of choice is a common strategy across all these lines of business: differentiation through bundled decision-support services.

A bank can rise above its competition by providing decision-support software that analyzes receipts from customers, payments to suppliers, and asset flows. Health insurance companies can insure the loyalty of a corporate client by providing better expense reporting and therapeutic treatment statistics for area caregivers.

A travel agency can provide a system to control costs, analyze business travel patterns, and centrally manage a worldwide travel policy. A consumer packaged goods firm can provide their retail buyer with a category-management decision-support system which allows the retailer to obtain a higher rate of inventory turns for that product line. The intended result of these commercial decision-support initiatives is a happy customer, leading to more transactions with that customer (i.e. more "shelf-space" and market share).

One useful technique for visualizing the way the world will appear following this transformation is to extrapolate from the example set by automated teller machines (ATMs). ATMs are fairly simple devices, providing rudimentary transaction and decision-support services for banks. Yet, they have become a business necessity for any bank that expects to prosper and grow.

A web-enabled commercial decision-support system is like an ATM on steroids. It can process much more sophisticated transactions, provide rich analytical decision-support capabilities, is available in tens of millions of locations, can be upgraded every week if desired, is applicable to nearly every industry, and the core technology is supported by thousands of computer industry vendors and an army of system integrators. For many of us, our only interface with our bank is the ATM. In the future, our primary and perhaps only interface with our vendors may be a software application running over the web, providing data warehouse access and transaction services.

Conclusions

Historically, data warehousing has been a technical initiative in order to control cost or optimize operations. While there are many thousands of internally focused data warehouse initiatives which represent valid IS investments, firms should benefit significantly more over the long term by finding ways to deploy data warehouse access outside of their own employee base to their customers, partners, suppliers, and investors. With the advent of the World Wide Web, the data warehouse is destined to become a profitable, integral part of the revenue generating function for many firms.

Web-enabled data warehousing is a best-in-class corporate strategy that addresses a broad range of decision-support requirements served by a variety of personal productivity, query and reporting, and OLAP tools. OLAP fulfills a set of user-driven functional requirements for reporting, analysis and planning applications. The inherent organizational requirement for planning and analysis is to help drive improved business performance. Successfully meeting this need requires that the company understand its past performance and prepare for its future. There is no better way than through the use of web-enabled interactive data warehousing applications.

Two of the hottest items on almost every organization's to-do list these days are building an Internet presence and building a data warehouse. The Internet has officially arrived, with over one million web sites. Statistics show that users of the Internet continue to double annually, and the number of World Wide Web sites is doubling every three months.

The adoption of data warehousing technology by all types of organizations is reaching epic proportions. With no surprises, these two popular technologies are joining forces, enabling one another with the byproduct being easy access to integrated information by a very large and geographically-distributed set of users. Some organizations currently developing data warehouses are looking to the web to supply the user interface.

Web browsers, coupled with powerful web-enabled decision-support analysis, provide access to server-based warehouses. This has eliminated the need for multiple, dispersed applications on user desk tops that are impossible to configure and support. This has simplified the data warehouse architecture and offers other advantages to traditional warehouse interface tools, including:

- Unlike many custom-built interfaces, web browsers are cheap and easy to install
- Problems posed by multiple operating systems are eliminated
- Web browsers are intuitive and simple to use, reducing user training and ramp-up time significantly
- Server-based browsers mean easier maintenance and fewer support issues
- Decision-support analysis and reporting tools are web enabled
- The cost associated with expanding an organization's network to reach all of its warehouse users is greatly reduced when the Internet serves as the vehicle for access.

Many organizations are taking steps now that will help down the road when they decide to adopt warehousing technology. Organizations that are readying their intranets today to disseminate organization-specific information are setting up protocols that will give them an advantage when they are ready to link their workforce to a data warehouse.

But the issue of security still looms large. What company wants to be among the first to put their mission-critical information out in cyberspace and make security less of an issue? Putting sensitive data on the web is still a scary thought, but the benefits of doing so are beginning to outweigh the risks.

A number of products are being developed to leverage web warehouse technology. Some allow for SQL to be embedded in HTML documents, which generates the results of queries directly to the web in the form of text, video, images, or other data types. Links to relevant information can be dynamically generated from the database. From the user's point of view, what could be better than generating a report of raw numbers that shows an increase in customer support response time, then clicking a hotlink to a graph depicting the improvement over the last quarter, and then sending the company pundits an e-mail sharing the good news.

A few industry experts are predicting that the marriage of the web and the data warehouse may indeed be the trend of the future. Although it's in its infancy, the combined technology of data warehousing and the Internet offers great potential to organizations looking to leverage information across the enterprise. With increasing investment in company-wide intranets, the next possible step is using that investment to harness the power of information through the data warehouse. Whether organizations use their web warehouses to transfer knowledge or as a revenue-generating data storefront, the benefits in terms of competitive advantage cannot be underestimated.

After the rapid acceptance of data warehousing systems during past few years, there will continue to be many more enhancements and adjustments to the data warehousing system model. Further evolution of the hardware and software technology will also continue to greatly influence the capabilities that are built into data warehouses.

Data warehousing systems have become a key component of information technology architecture. A flexible enterprise data warehouse strategy can yield significant benefits for a long period to come.

Glossary

64-Bits. A measure of the processing capacity of computer systems which refers to the number of bits which it can process simultaneously. 64-bit machines have the ability to move data between the CPU and memory and peripherals eight bytes at a time. Likewise, they have the ability to process data, such as in integer and floating point mathematics, in eight byte increments simultaneously.

Abstract Class. A specialized class used solely for subtyping. It defines a common set of behaviors to be inherited by its subtypes. It has no instances. (Synonymous with Virtual Class in C++.)

Access Control List (ACL). Most network security systems operate by allowing selective use of services. An Access Control List is the usual means by which access to, and denial of, services is controlled. It is simply a list of the services available, each with a list of the hosts permitted to use the service.

Activation: Copying the persistent form of methods and stored data into an executable address space to allow execution of the methods on the stored data.

Active Data Warehouse: A data warehouse that searches for trends and patterns in evaluational data. It is an active process that searches an evaluational database for trends, patterns, and exceptions.

Ad Hoc Query. Request or query about which the system has no prior knowledge or built-in functions for servicing. Ad hoc queries are distinguished from standard reports, where specific information is sought in a specific format about specific subjects on a regular basis.

Ad Hoc Query Tool. An end user tool that accepts an English-like or point-and-click request for data and constructs an ad-hoc query to retrieve the desired result.

Ad Hoc View. A view of a data set constructed "on the fly." Commonly used in OLAP technology to follow a query line and slice and dice the data to support an analyst's line of reasoning

Adapter. A board installed in a computer system to provide network communication capabilities to and from that computer system. Also called a Network Interface Card (NIC).

Administrative Data. In a data warehouse, the data that helps a warehouse administrator manage the warehouse. Examples of administrative data are user profiles and order history data.

Agent. An entity that performs operations on behalf of other objects, systems, and agents.

Aggregate Data. Data that is the result of applying a process to combine data elements. Data that is taken collectively or in summary form.

Aggregation. Used in the broad sense to mean aggregating data horizontally, vertically, and chronologically.

Alerts. A notification from an event that has exceeded a pre-defined threshold.

Alternate Routing. A mechanism that supports the use of a new path after an attempt to set up a connection along a previously selected path fails.

American Standard Code for Information Interchange (ASCII). This is the code that most computers use to represent displayable characters. An ASCII file is a straightforward text file without special control characters.

Attribute. Structural information about data that serves to establish its context and give meaning to it. The term is also used to refer to descriptive structural information about a data field in a record.

Analytical Data Store. Useful in making strategic decisions, this data storage area maintains summarized or historical data. This stored data is time variant, unlike operational systems which contain real-time data. Information contained in this data store is determined and collected based on the corporate business rules. and for representation of business rules. Its source for distribution and use is a data warehouse.

Applet. A small application program written in Java and commonly distributed in an attachment in a Web document to be executed by a Java-enabled web browser.

AppleTalk. A networking protocol developed by Apple Computer for communication between Apple Computer products and other computers.

This protocol is independent of what network it is layered on. Current implementations exist for LocalTalk (235 Kbps) and EtherTalk (10 Mbps).

Application Layer. Layer seven of the OSI Reference Model; implemented by various network applications including file transfer, electronic mail, and terminal emulation.

Application Lifecycle. Includes the following three stages—process and change management, analysis and design, construction and testing.

Application Objects. Applications and their components that are managed within an object-oriented system. Example operations on such objects are "Open," "Install," "Move," "Re-move, and remove".

Application Program Interface (API). The programming interface used to access and control a library or program.

Application. A program or a set of programs that provides functionality to the end user.

Application-Level Firewall. A firewall system in which service is provided by processes that maintain complete TCP connection state and sequencing. Application level firewalls often re-address traffic so that outgoing traffic appears to have originated from the firewall rather than the internal host.

Architecture. A definition and preliminary design which describes the components of a solution and their interactions. An architecture is the blueprint by which implementers construct a solution which meets the users' needs.

Assignment. The activity of copying the values of one object into another object. The details of such an assignment vary according to the implementation language used.

Associations. A statistical measure that shows the degree to which two variables are related.

Asynchronous. Referring to two or more signals which, though they have the same nominal rates, actually operate at different rates.

Asynchronous Message Communication. Asynchronous message communication provides the capability for objects to send messages, even without the existence of the receiving object at the instant the message is sent. The receiving object can retrieve messages at its convenience. There is no blocking or synchronization required between objects. Asynchronous message communication is a foundation for constructing concur-rent computing environments.

Asynchronous Protocol. A type of transmission where information is sent at any speed and at random with no routing information.

Asynchronous Request. A request in which the client object does not pause or wait for delivery of the request to the recipient, nor does it wait for the results.

Asynchronous Transfer Mode (ATM). (1) The CCITT standard for cell relay wherein information for multiple types of services (voice, video, data) is conveyed in small, fixed-size cells. ATM is a connection-oriented technology used in both LAN and WAN environments. (2) A fast-packet switching technology allowing free allocation of capacity to each channel. The SONET synchronous payload envelope is a variation of ATM. (3) An international ISDN high speed, high-volume, packet switching transmission protocol standard. ATM currently accommodates transmission speeds from 64 Kbps to 622 Mbps.

Atomic Data. Data elements that represent the lowest level of detail. For example, in a daily sales report, the individual items sold would be atomic data, while rollups such as invoice and summary totals from invoices are aggregate data.

Attribute. An identifiable association between an object and a value. An attribute A is made visible to clients as a pair of operations—get_A and set_A. Read-only attributes only generate a get operation. A characteristic or property of an object. Usually implemented as a simple data member or as an association with another object or group of objects.

Audience. The consumer (caller) of an interface. An interface might be intended for use by the ultimate user of the service (functional interface), by a system management function within the system (system management interface), or by other participating services in order to construct the service from disparate objects (construction interface).

Authentication. The process of assuring that data has come from its claimed source, or of corroborating the claimed identity of a communicating party.

Authentication Token. A portable device used for authenticating a user. Authentication tokens operate by challenge/response, time-based code sequences, or other techniques. This may include paper-based lists of one-time passwords.

Authorization. The process of determining what types of activities are permitted. Usually, authorization is in the context of authentication—once you have authenticated a user, they may be authorized different types of access or activity.

Authorization Rules. Criteria used to determine whether or not an individual group or application may access reference data or a process.

Automatic Data Partitioning. The process of automatically partitioning data and metadata based on a client's request for data at a specific data site.

Availability. A measure of the percentage of time that a computer system is capable of supporting a user request. A system may be considered unavailable as a result of events such as system failures or unplanned application outages.

Bandwidth. (1) Measure of the information capacity of a transmission channel. (2) The difference between the highest and lowest frequencies of a band that can be passed by a transmission medium without undue distortion, such as the AM band, 535 to 1705 kilohertz. (3) Information carrying capacity of a communication channel. Analog bandwidth is the range of signal frequencies that can be transmitted by a communication channel or network. (4) A term used to indicate the amount of transmission or processing capacity possessed by a system or a specific location in a system (usually a network system).

Bi-directionall Extracts. The ability to extract, cleanse, and transfer data in two directions among different types of databases, including hierarchical, networked, and relational databases.

Binding. The selection of the method to perform a requested service and of the data to be accessed by that method. (See also dynamic binding and static binding)

Bit-mapped Indexes. Indexing techniques which use binary encoding to represent data. Originally used only for low cardinality data, recent advances such as Sybase IQ have allowed this technique to be used for high cardinality data as well.

Bridge/Router. A device that can provide the functions of a bridge, router or both concurrently. Bridge/router can route one or more protocols, such as TCP/IP and/or XNS, and bridge all other traffic.

Browser. A software facility used to view and modify classes, attributes and methods.

Bulk Data Transfer. A software-based mechanism designed to move large data files. It supports compression, blocking, and buffering to optimize transfer times.

Business Architecture. One of the four layers of an IT architecture—information, business, applications and technology. Describes and defines the business processes used within an organization.

Business Data. Information about people, places, things, business rules, and events, which is used to operate the business. It is not metadata. (Metadata defines and describes business data.)

Business Rules. The statements and stipulations that a corporation has set as "standard" in order to run the enterprise more consistently and smoothly.

Business Schema. A schema that represents the structure of business transactions used by clients in the real world. It is considered to be unnormalized data.

Cache. A high-speed dynamic memory used as a buffer between the CPU and physical disk storage to mitigate or eliminate potential speed differences between access times to physical disks and faster system memory. In storage arrays cache implementation is usually non-volatile to ensure data integrity.

Capacity Planning. The process of considering the effects of a warehouse on other system resources such as response time, DASD requirements, etc.

Cardinality. The number of data occurrences allowed on either side of a data relation. In the common data architecture, cardinality is documented with data integrity, not with the data structure.

CASE. Computer Aided Software Engineering.

CASE Management. The management of information between multiple CASE "encyclopedias," whether the same or different CASE tools.

Catalog. A component of a data dictionary that contains a directory of its DBMS objects as well as attributes of each object.

CDR. Common Data Representation.

Central Warehouse. A database created from operational extracts that adheres to a single, consistent, enterprise data model to ensure consistency of decision-support data across the corporation. A style of computing where all the information systems are located and managed from a single physical location.

Centralized Data Warehouse. A data warehouse implementation in which a single warehouse serves the need of several business units simultaneously with a single data model which spans the needs of the multiple business divisions.

Change Data Capture. The process of capturing changes made to a production data source. Change data capture is typically performed by reading the source DBMS log. It consolidates units of work, ensures data is synchronized with the original source, and reduces data volume in a data warehousing environment.

Character Set. A grouping of alphanumeric and special characters used by computer systems to store data. Different sets of characters are used to support different user languages and different applications. The various groupings have been codified by ANSI (American National Standards Institute).

Chargeback. The process that data warehouse managers use to ensure appropriate costs are correctly distributed to the corresponding business units and users so that they can meet financial reporting requirements.

Churn. A term applied to a class of customers who constantly join and then subsequently leave an organization as a customer.

CIOP. Common Inter-ORB Protocol.

Circuit. A two-way communications path. A communication path or network; usually a pair of channels providing bi-directional communication.

Class. In object programming, a type or group of objects, all having the same properties, operations, behavior. Types classify objects according to a common interface; classes classify objects according to a common implementation.

Class Attribute. A characteristic or property that is the same for all instances of a class. This information is usually stored in the class type definition.

Class Hierarchy. Embodies the inheritance relationships between classes.

Class Inheritance. The construction of a class by incremental modification of other classes.

Class Member. A method or an attribute of a class.

Class Method. A class method defines the behavior of the class. Such a method performs tasks that cannot or should not be done at the instance level, such as providing access to class attributes or tracking class usage metrics.

Class Object. An object that serves as a class. A class object serves as a factory. (See factory.)

Classification. The process of dividing a dataset into mutually exclusive groups such that the members of each group are as "close" as possible to one another and different groups are as "far" as possible from one another, where distance is measured with respect to specific variable(s) you are trying to predict. For example, a typical classification problem is to divide a database of customers into groups that are as homogeneous as possible with respect to a creditworthiness variable with values "Good" and "Bad."

Client/Server. A distributed technology approach where the processing is divided by function. The server performs shared functions, managing communications, providing database services, etc. The client performs individual user functions, providing customized interfaces, performing screen to screen navigation, offering help functions, etc.

Client/Server Processing. A form of cooperative processing in which the end user interaction is through a programmable workstation that must execute some part of the application logic over and above display formatting and terminal emulation.

Client. An object that requests a service from a server object in a client/server relationship. The code or process that invokes an operation on an object.

Collaboration. Two or more objects that participate in a client/server relationship in order to provide a service.

Collection. A set of data that resulted from a DBMS query.

COM. DEC's and Microsoft's Common Object Model.

Common Meta-metadata. The architecture component of the common data architecture consisting of formal data names, comprehensive data definitions, common data structure, and consistent data quality. The common meta-metadata provides the framework for the development of common metadata.

Common Object Request Broker Architecture (CORBA, CORBA 2). A specification for objects to locate and activate one another through an object request broker. CORBA 2 extends the specification to facilitate object request brokers from different vendors to inter-operate.

Component. A conceptual notion. A component is an object that is considered to be part of some containing object. Classes, systems or subsystems can be designed as reusable pieces. These pieces can then be assembled to create various new applications.

Composition. The creation of an object that is an aggregation of one or more objects.

Compound Object. A conceptual notion. A compound object is an object that is viewed as standing for a set of related objects.

Computer Aided Software Engineering (CASE). A collection of software tools that support and automate the process of analyzing, designing and coding software systems.

Conceptual Schema. A schema that represents a common structure of data that is the common denominator between the internal schema and external schema.

Configuration. The phase in which the LE client discovers the LE Service.

Conformance. A relation defined over types such that type x conforms to type y if any value that satisfies type x also satisfies type y.

Connectivity. The ability of a device to connect to another. This includes the physical issues associated with the busses, connector topologies, and other components as well as the support of the protocols required to pass data successfully over the physical connection.

Consistent Data Quality. The state of a data resource where the quality of existing data is thoroughly understood and the desired quality of the data resource is known. It is a state where disparate data quality is known, and the existing data quality is being adjusted to the level desired to meet the current and future business information demand.

Constraint. A relational or behavioral restriction or limit. Usually regarded as a property that must always hold true.

Consumer. An individual, group, or application that accesses data/information in a data warehouse.

CORBA. Common Object Request Broker Architecture.

Coupling. A dependency between two or more classes, usually resulting from collaboration between the classes to provide a service. Loose coupling is based on generic behavior and allows many different classes to be coupled in the same way. Tight coupling is based on more specific implementation details of the participating classes and is not as flexible as loose coupling.

Critical Success Factors. Key areas of activity in which favorable results are necessary for a company to reach its goal.

Cross Selling. The business techniques of associating like products to customer purchases. For example, if a customer buys letterhead, there is an opportunity to sell envelopes in the same transaction.

Crosstab. A process or function that combines and/or summarizes data from one or more sources into a concise format for analysis or reporting.

Data. Items representing facts, text, graphics, bit-mapped images, sound, or analog or digital live-video segments. Data is the raw material of a system supplied by data producers and is used by information consumers to create information.

Data Access Tool. An end-user-oriented tool that allows users to build SQL queries by pointing and clicking on a list of tables and fields in the data warehouse.

Data Access. Equipment and/or software applications that permit connection and attachment to data stores. Commonly used to mean access to relational databases.

Data Accuracy. The component of data integrity that deals with how well data stored in the data resource represents the real world. It includes a definition of the current data accuracy and the adjustment in data accuracy to meet the business needs.

Data Administration. The processes and procedures by which the integrity and currency of the data in the warehouse are maintained.

Data Aggregation. A type of data derivation where a data value is derived from the aggregation of two or more contributing data characteristics in different data occurrences within the same data subject.

Data Analysis and Presentation Tool. Software that provides a logical view of data in a warehouse. Some create simple aliases for table and column names; others create data that identify the contents and location of data in the warehouse.

Data Architecture. (1) The science and method of designing and constructing an integrated data resource that is business-driven, based on real world objects and events as perceived by the organization, and implemented in appropriate operating environments. The overall structure of a data resource that provides a consistent foundation across organizational boundaries to provide easily identifiable, readily available, high-quality data to support the business information demand. (2) The component of the data resource framework that contains all activities, and the products of those activities, related to the identification, naming, definition, structuring, quality, and documentation of the data resource for an organization.

Data Attribute. Represents a data characteristic variation that is used in a logical data model.

Data Capture. The collection of information, usually at the time a transaction occurs, in a form that can be used by a computer system (for example, the recording of a sale or of a withdrawal from an automated cash machine). The term also applies to saving on a storage medium (a disk) a record of the interchanges between the user and a remote information utility.

Data Cardinality. Cardinality is a property of data elements which indicates the number of allowable entries in that element. For example, a data element such as "gender" only allows two entries—"male" or "female." Data elements which have few allowable entries are said to possess "low cardinality." Those, such as "age" or "income," for which many allowable entries are possible, are said to have "high cardinality."

Data Characteristic. An individual characteristic that describes a data subject. It is developed, directly through measurement or indirectly through derivation, from a feature of an object or event. Each data subject is described by a set of data characteristics.

Data Cleansing. The process of manipulating the data extracted from operational systems so as to make it usable by the data warehouse. When loading data from existing operational systems, it is likely that few if any of the operational systems will have data to present in a format which is compatible with the data model developed for the warehouse. For example, a product number may be held as a numeric field in one system while a second system appends an alpha suffix to the number for reporting purposes.

Data Cluster. A temporary group of data subjects for a specific purpose. It can be any useful combination of data subjects for any specific purpose that cannot be met by any of the other categorical levels.

Data Collection. The process of acquiring source documents or data. The grouping of data elements into a coherent whole through classification, sorting, ordering, and other organizational techniques.

Data Collection Frequency. The frequency at which data is collected.

Data Compression. Mathematical techniques used to reduce the amount of storage required for certain data.

Data Concurrency. The situation where the replicated data values are synchronized with the corresponding data values at the official data source. When the data values at the official data source are updated, the replicated data values must also be updated so they are consistent with the official data source.

Data Consistency. The result of using a repository to capture and manage data as it changes so that decision-support systems can be continually updated.

Data Conversion. The process of changing data from one physical environment to another. This process makes any changes necessary to move data from one electronic medium or database product to another.

Data Definition. Enabling the structure and instances of a database to be defined in a human- and machine-readable form.

Data Delivery. The electronic movement of data stored in remote locations to a user's desktop.

Data Denormalization. The process of developing the internal schema from the conceptual schema.

Data Derivation. The process of creating a data value from one or more contribution data values through a data derivation algorithm.

Data Dictionary. A database about data and database structures. A catalog of all data elements, containing their names, structures, and information about their usage. A central location for metadata. Normally, data dictionaries are designed to store a limited set of available metadata, concentrating on the information relating to the data elements, databases, files, and programs of implemented systems.

Data Dimension. A representation of a single set of objects or events in the real world.

Data Dissemination. The process of getting data from the data resource to a client, within or without the organization, through appropriate application and telecommunication networks. Data are disseminated through client/server applications, electronic mail, and traditional business applications.

Data Distribution. The placement and maintenance of replicated data at one or more data sites on a mainframe computer or across a telecommunications network. The part of developing and maintaining an integrated data resource that ensures data is properly managed when distributed across many different data sites. Data distribution is one type of data deployment, which is the transfer of data to data sites.

Data Element. The most elementary unit of data that can be identified or described in a dictionary or repository and which cannot be subdivided.

Data Encryption. Encoding of file contents so that they are unreadable or difficult to read without the original encoder key.

Data Encryption Standard (DES). A popular standard encryption scheme.

Data Entity. Represents a data subject from the common data model that is used in the logical data model.

Data Explosion. A term given to express the increase in stored data when using multiDimensional database systems. The amount of data stored in these systems is often a multiple of the size of the raw data entered into the systems from the existing operational databases. Hence, the data undergoes an "explosion" to several times (or many times) its original size.

Data Extract. Data which normally resides on an operational system and which is removed from that system for loading into a data warehouse.

Data Extraction. The process of moving data from one database source to one database target (either from an operational database to a data mart, or from one data mart to another).

Data Extraction Software. Software that reads one or more sources of data and creates a new image of the data.

Data File. A representation of a data entity from the logical data model that is implemented with a physical data model. It is a physical file of data that exists in a database management system, as a computer file outside a database management system, or as a manual file outside a computer that represents a data entity.

Data Flow Diagram. A diagram that shows the normal flow of data between services as well as the flow of data between data stores and services.

Data Fragmentation. A nonorderly process of placing data at various data sites. It is not done within the common data architecture, is not well-managed or documented, and results in unknown, undocumented, redundant data.

Data Generalization. The process of creating successive layers of summary data in an evaluational database. It is a process of zooming out to get a broader view of a problem, trend, or situation. It is also known as rolling up data.

Data Integrity. The formal definition of comprehensive rules and the consistent application of those rules to assure high integrity data. It consists of techniques to determine how well data is maintained in the data resource and to ensure that the data resource contains data that has high integrity. Data integrity includes techniques for data value integrity, data structure integrity, data retention integrity, and data derivation integrity.

Data Key. A set of one or more data characteristics that have a special meaning and use in addition to describing a feature or trait of a data subject. Data keys are important for uniquely identifying data occurrences in each data subject and for navigating through the data resource.

Data Layer. A separate and distinct set of related spatial data that is stored and maintained in a spatial database. It represents a particular theme or topic of interest in the real world and is equivalent to a data subject.

Data Loading. The process of populating the data warehouse. Data loading is provided by DBMS-specific load processes, DBMS insert processes, and independent fastload processes.

Data Management. Controlling, protecting, and facilitating access to data in order to provide information consumers with timely access to the data they need. The functions provided by a database management system.

Data Management Software. Software that converts data into a unified format by taking derived data to create new fields, merging files, summarizing and filtering data; the process of reading data from operational systems. Data management software is also known as data extraction software.

Data Mapping. The process of assigning a source data element to a target data element.

Data Mart. A subset of the data resource, usually oriented to a specific purpose or major data subject, that may be distributed to support business needs. The concept of a data mart can apply to any data whether it is operational data, evaluational data, spatial data, or metadata.

Data Mining. (1) The process of utilizing the results of data exploration to adjust or enhance business strategies. It builds on the patterns, trends, and exceptions found through data exploration to support the business. It is also known as data harvesting. (2) A technique using software tools geared for the user who typically does not know exactly what he's searching for, but is looking for particular patterns or trends. Data mining is the process of sifting through large amounts of data to produce data content relationships. This is also known as data surfing.

Data Mining Methodology. A set of processes and tools that, in combination, provide a means of implementing a data mining application. Methodologies are primarily used to standardize the approach to implementing products, and, as a byproduct, increase consistency and reduce error.

Data Model. A logical map that represents the inherent properties of the data independent of software, hardware, or machine performance considerations. The model shows data elements grouped into records, as well as the association around those records.

Data Modeling. A method used to define and analyze data requirements needed to support the business functions of an enterprise. These data requirements are recorded as a conceptual data model with associated data definitions. Data modeling defines the relationships between data elements and structures.

Data Movement. The transportation of data from disparate sources ranging from various mainframes, client/server machines, and network files servers to a central location, the data warehouse, in order to create a reliable source of information, usable for strategic decision making.

Data Normalization. A process to develop the conceptual schema from the external schema.

Data Optimization. A process that prepares the logical schema from the data view schema. It is the counterpart of data deoptimization.

Data Partitioning. (1) The formal process of determining which data subjects, data occurrence groups, and data characteristics are needed at each data site. It is an orderly process for allocating data to data sites that is done within the same common data architecture. (2) The process of logically and/or physically partitioning data into segments that are more easily maintained or accessed. Current RDBMS systems provide this kind of distribution functionality. Partitioning of data aids in performance and utility processing.

Data Pivot. A process of rotating the view of data.

Data Propagation. The distribution of data from one or more source data warehouses to one or more local access databases, according to propagation rules.

Data Quality. Indicates how well data in the data resource meet the business information demand. Data quality includes data integrity, data accuracy, and data completeness.

Data Refining. A process that refines disparate data within a common context to remove data variability and redundancy, and develop an integrated data resource. Disparate data is the raw material and an integrated data resource is the final product.

Data Refreshing. The process of updating active data replicates based on a regular, known schedule. The frequency and timing of data refreshing must be established to match business.

Data Replication. (1) A formal process of creating exact copies of a set of data from the data site containing the official data source and placing those data in at other data sites. (2) The process of copying a portion of a database from one environment to another and keeping the subsequent copies of the data in sync with the original source. Changes made to the original source are propagated to the copies of the data in other environments.

Data Repository. A logical (and sometimes physical) partitioning of data where multiple databases which apply to specific applications or sets of applications reside. For example, several databases (revenues, expenses) which support financial applications (A/R, A/P) could reside in a single financial data repository.

Data Resource. A component of information technology infrastructure that represents all the data available to an organization, whether automated or nonautomated.

Data Restructuring. The process to restructure the source data to the target data during data transformation.

Data Scrubbing. The process of filtering, merging, decoding, and translating source data to create validated data for the data warehouse.

Data Sharing. The process of understanding the content and meaning of data, identifying and selecting the appropriate data to meet business needs, and sharing that data.

Data Source. A specific data site where data is stored and from which it can be obtained. Any source of data from a specific organization, such as a data base or data file. A data source may include nonautomated data, but it does not include unpublished documents containing data.

Data Store. A place where data is stored. A generic term that includes databases and flat files.

Data Structure. A representation of the arrangement, relationship, and contents of data subjects, data entities, and data files in the common data architecture. It includes all logical and physical data within the common data architecture.

Data Summarization. The process of summarizing primitive evaluational data or derived evaluational data to create more generalized derived evaluational data.

Data Surfing. See data mining.

Data Synchronization. The process of identifying active data replicates and ensuring that data concurrency is maintained. Also known as data version synchronization or data version concurrency because all replicated data values are consistent with the same version as the official data.

Data Terminal Equipment (DTE). The part of a data station that serves as a data source, destination, or both, and that provides for the data communications control function according to protocol. DTE includes computers, protocol translators, and multiplexers.

Data Transfer. The process of moving data from one environment to another environment. An environment may be an application system or operating environment. See data transport.

Data Transformation. The formal process of transforming data in the data resource within a common data architecture. It includes transforming disparate data to an integrated data resource, transforming data within the integrated data resource, and transforming disparate data. It includes transforming operational, historical, and evaluational data within a common data architecture.

Data Translation. The process of converting data from one form into another when moving between different DBMSs.

Data Type. The form of a data value, such as date, number, string, floating point, packed, and double-precision.

Data Value. The individual facts and figures contained in data characteristics, data characteristic variations, data attributes, and data items.

Data Visualization. The process of creating and presenting a chart from a set of data based on a set of attributes. It deals with understanding patterns, trends, and relationships in historical data and providing visual information to the decision maker.

Data Warehouse. (1) A subject-oriented, integrated, time-variant, non-volatile collection of data in support of management's decision making process. A repository of consistent historical data that can be easily accessed and manipulated for decision support. (2) An implementation of an informational database used to store sharable data sourced from an operational database-of-record. It is typically a subject database that allows users to tap into a company's vast store of operational data to track and respond to business trends and facilitate forecasting and planning efforts.

Data Warehouse Architecture. An integrated set of products that enables the extraction and transformation of operational data to be loaded into a database for end user analysis and reporting.

Data Warehouse Engines. Relational database management systems (RDBMS) and multidimensional database management systems (MDBMS). Data warehouse engines require strong query capabilities, fast load mechanisms, and large storage requirements. Database technology is referred to as database engine.

Data Warehouse Infrastructure. A combination of technologies and the interaction of technologies that support a data warehouse environment.

Data Warehouse Management Tool. Software that extracts and transforms data from operational systems and loads it into the data warehouse.

Data Warehouse Network. An integrated network of data warehouses that contain sharable data propagated from a source data warehouse on the basis of information consumer demand. The warehouses are managed to control data redundancy and to promote effective use of the sharable data.

Data Warehouse Orientation. A SOFTWARE AG program that provides an orientation to business and technical management on opportunities and approaches to data warehousing. The orientation program encompasses a high-level examination of solutions to business problems, return on investment, tools, and techniques as they relate to data warehouse implementation. In addition, the program's objective is to assist customers in determining their readiness to proceed with data warehousing and to determine the appropriate data warehouse for their environment.

Database. A collection of data which is logically related.

Database Administrator (DBA). The individual or group of individuals responsible for a database. Typically, the DBA is responsible for determining the information content of the database; determining the internal storage structure and access strategy for the database; defining data security and integrity checks; and monitoring database performance and responding to changing requirements.

Database Machine. A computer peripheral device that, from the viewpoint of the computer, directly executes database-related tasks, relieving the main computer of the execution of these tasks. Database machines can be attached to the computer responsible for application tasks via a channel or local area network (LAN). The database machine is itself a computer. However, because it has only database management tasks to perform, its hardware and software can be highly optimized for the job at hand. A database server that performs only database functions is sometimes referred to as a database machine.

Database Management System (DBMS). A layer of software between the physical database and the user. The DBMS manages all requests for database action (for example, queries or updates) from the user. Thus, the user is spared the necessity of keeping track of the physical details of file locations and formats, indexing schemes, and so on. In addition, a DBMS permits centralized control of security and data integrity functions.

Database Schema. The logical and physical definition of a database structure.

DBA. Database Administrator.

DBMS. Database Management System.

Decentralized Database. A centralized database that has been partitioned according to a business- or end-user-defined subject area. Typically ownership is also moved to the owners of the subject area.

Decision Support. A set of software applications intended to allow users to search vast stores of information for specific reports which are critical for making management decisions.

Decision-Support Database. A database that contains historical and summary data to support on-line analytical processing.

Decision-Support Processing. See on-line analytical processing.

Decision-Support Systems. Systems which allow decision makers in organizations to access data relevant to the decisions they are required to make.

Decision-Support Systems (DSS). Software that supports exception reporting, stop light reporting, standard repository, data analysis, and rule-based analysis. A database created for end user ad hoc query processing.

Decision trees. A tree-shaped structure that represents a set of decisions. These decisions generate rules for the classification of a dataset.

Deferred Synchronous Request. A request where the client does not wait for completion of the request, but does intend to accept results later. Contrast with synchronous request and one-way request.

Delegation. (1) The ability of a method to issue a request in such a way that self-reference in the method performing the request returns the same object(s) as self-reference in the method issuing the request. (See self-reference.) (2) The ability of an object to issue a request to another object in response to a request. The first object therefore delegates the responsibility to the second object.

Demographic. A term derived from "demos" meaning population and "graphein" meaning to write or describe. Literally it means describing populations.

Demographic Data. Any data that locates, identifies, or describes populations.

Denormalized Data Store. A data store that does not comply to one or more of several normal forms. See normalization.

Derived Data. Data that is the result of a computational step applied to reference or event data. Derived data is the result either of relating two or more elements of a single transaction (such as an aggregation), or of relating one or more elements of a transaction to an external algorithm or rule.

Design. A process that uses the products of analysis to produce a specification for implementing a system. **Design Pattern**. See pattern.

Desktop Applications. Query and analysis tools that access the source database or data warehouse across a network using an appropriate database interface. An application that manages the human interface for data producers and information consumers.

Dial Up. A type of communication that is established by a switched-circuit connection using the telephone network.

DII. Dynamic Invocation Interface.

DIR. Dynamic Implementation Routine.

Disparate Data. Data items that are essentially not alike, or are distinctly different in kind, quality, or character. They are unequal and cannot be readily integrated to adequately meet the business information demand. Disparate data is heterogeneous data.

Disparate Databases. Databases or database management systems that are not electronically or operationally compatible. Disparate databases are known as heterogeneous databases.

Disparate Operational Data. The current-value operational data that supports daily business transactions. It is the disparate data, including both tabular and nontabular data, that most organizations currently use to support their daily business operations.

Distributed Data Set. A data set from one data subject or data occurrence group that is distributed.

Distributed Database Management System. A software product that manages and maintains the distributed database and makes it transparent to clients. Data flows freely over any network or combination of networks using one or more network protocols.

Distributed Database System. (1) A combination of distributed databases and distributed database management systems. Any database management system can interact with any other database management system across multiple system configurations to provide data to clients. (2) Systems in which the database storage is dispersed across multiple machines and multiple physical locations.

Distributed Database Systems. Systems in which the database storage is dispersed across multiple machines and multiple physical locations.

Distributed Object Computing (DOC). A computing paradigm that distributes cooperating objects across a heterogeneous network and allows the objects to inter-operate as a unified whole.

Domain. A formal boundary that defines a particular subject or area of interest.

Drill Down. A method of exploring detailed data that was used in creating a summary level of data. Drill down levels depend on the granularity of the data in the data warehouse.

Drilling Down. The process of viewing data in more detail.

DSS. See Decision-Support System.

DSU/CSU. Equipment used to terminate a Switched 56 line and convert a PC's digital data signal into a digital transmission signal.

Dynamic Invocation. Constructing and issuing a request whose signature is not known until runtime.

Dynamic Link Library (DLL). A dynamically loaded run-time library.

Dynamic Object-Based Application. The end user functionality provided by one or more programs consisting of inter-operating objects.

Dynamic Password Authentication Servers. Products consisting of server software that generates constantly changing passwords and two-factor, software or hardware-based password.

Dynamic Queries. Dynamically constructed SQL that is usually constructed by desktop-resident query tools. Queries that are not pre-processed and are prepared and executed at run time.

DCE. OSF's Distributed Computing Environment.

Dynamic Routing. Routing that adjusts automatically to changes in network topology or traffic.

EIS. Executive Information System.

Embedding. Creating an object out of a non-object entity by wrapping it in an appropriate shell.

Encapsulation. The technique used to hide the implementation details of an object. The services provided by an object are defined and accessible as stated in the object contract.

Encryption. Applying a specific algorithm to data so as to alter the data's appearance and prevent other devices from reading the information. Decryption applies the algorithm in reverse to restore the data to its original form.

End User Data. Data formatted for end user query processing; data created by end users; data provided by a data warehouse.

Enhanced Data. Data which is based on the raw atomic data of captured transactions, but which has been manipulated to add value. This implies the addition of mathematical manipulations such as the derivation of averages, standard deviations, or the appending of special fields or code to enhance comprehension such as adding a region code to a product number to allow for regionalization of queries.

Enhanced Data Extraction. The ongoing process that extracts snapshots of operational data on a regular basis for enhancing the evaluational database.

Enterprise. A complete business consisting of functions, divisions, or other components used to accomplish specific objectives and defined goals.

Enterprise Data. Data that is defined for use across a corporate environment.

Enterprise Data Model. A blueprint for all of the data used by all departments in the enterprise. An enterprise data model has resolved all of the potential inconsistencies and parochial interpretations of the data used and presents a consistent and commonly understood and accepted view and definition of the enterprise data.

Enterprise Data Warehouse. An enterprise data warehouse is a centralized warehouse which services the entire enterprise.

Enterprise Data. Data that is defined for use across a corporate environment.

Enterprise Modeling. A technique for modeling an entire business enterprise from the business manager's point of view. An enterprise model is composed of the objects, events, and business rules that describe the enterprise. Separate but related business systems can be built from this model to enhance the efficiency and consistency of the operation of the enterprise.

Enterprise Storage. A shared central repository for information, connected to disparate computer systems, that provides common management, protection and information sharing capabilities.

Enterprise System Connection Architecture (ESCON). An IBM mainframe channel architecture commonly used to attach storage devices.

ESIOP. Environment-Specific Inter-ORB Protocol.

Ethernet. (1) A baseband LAN specification invented by Xerox Corporation and developed jointly by Xerox, Intel, and Digital Equipment Corporation. Ethernet networks operate at 10 Mbps using CSMA/CD to run over coaxial cable. Ethernet is similar to a series of standards produced by IEEE referred to as IEEE 802.3. (2) A very common method of networking computers in a local area network (LAN). Ethernet will handle about 10,000,000 bits per second and can be used with almost any kind of computer.

Event. (1) A happening in the real world. (2) A significant change in the environment or the state of an object that is of interest to another object or system.

Exchange Format. The form of a description used to import and export objects.

Executive Information Systems (EIS). Tools programmed to provide canned reports or briefing books to top-level executives. They offer strong reporting and drill-down capabilities. Today these tools allow ad hoc querying against a multidimensional database and most offer analytical applications along functional lines such as sales or financial analysis.

Expert System. A rule-based program that implements the domain knowledge of a human domain expert. It is usually able to "reason" through new problems by applying its rules.

Exploratory Data Analysis. The use of graphical and descriptive statistical techniques to learn about the structure of a data set.

Export. To transmit the description of an object to an external entity.

Externalized Object Reference. An object reference expressed as an ORB-specific string. Suitable for storage in files or other external media.

Extract. A set of data which resides normally on the operational systems which is uploaded into the data warehouse.

Extract Frequency. The latency of data extracts, such as daily versus weekly, monthly, quarterly, etc. The frequency that data extracts are needed in the data warehouse is determined by the shortest frequency requested through an order, or by the frequency required to maintain consistency of the other associated data types in the source data warehouse.

Extract Specification. The standard expectations of a particular source data warehouse for data extracts from the operational database system-of-record. A system-of-record uses an extract specification to retrieve a snapshot of shared data, and formats the data in the way specified for updating the data in the source data warehouse. An extract specification also contains extract frequency rules for use by the data access environment.

Extranet. Extranet is an instantiation of an Internet where an organization allows its external partners to participate in the internal data warehouse.

Fault-tolerance. The characteristic of a system that allows it to handle the loss of a particular component without interrupting normal operations.

File Transfer Protocol (FTP). (1) An IP application protocol for transferring files between network nodes. (2) An Internet protocol that allows a user on one host to transfer files to and from another host over a network.

Filters. Saved sets of chosen criteria that specify a subset of information in a data warehouse.

Firewall. (1) Isolation of LAN segments from each other to protect data resources and help manage traffic. (2) Hardware or software that restricts traffic to a private network from an unsecured network.

Fractional T-1. A WAN communications service that provides the user with some portion of a T1 circuit which has been divided into 24 separate 64 Kbps channels. Fractional E-1 is in Europe.

Fragmentation. The process in which a packet is broken into smaller pieces, fragments, to fit the requirements of a physical network through which the packet must pass.

Frame Relay. High-performance interface for packet-switching networks. Considered more efficient than X.25 which it is expected to replace. Frame relay technology can handle "bursty" communications that have rapidly changing bandwidth requirements.

Framework. A set of collaborating abstract and concrete classes that may be used as a template to solve a specific domain problem.

Fraud Detection. The use of technologies such as data mining to look through large amounts of data and discern patterns that may indicate fraudulent use of a company's product. For example, credit card companies review transaction data to see if a customer's usage profile has suddenly changed.

Frequently Asked Questions (FAQ). Usually appears in the form of a "readme" file in a variety of Internet formats. New users are expected to read the FAQ before participating in newsgroups, bulletin boards, video conferences and so on.

FTP. File Transfer Protocol.

Functional Data Warehouse. A warehouse that draws data from nearby operational systems. Each functional warehouse serves a distinct and separate group (such as a division), functional area (such as manufacturing), geographic unit, or product marketing group.

Functional Decomposition. The process of refining a problem solution by repeatedly decomposing a problem into smaller and smaller steps. The resulting steps are then programmed as separate modules.

Functional Interface. Interfaces that define the operations invoked by users of an object service. The audience for these interfaces is the service consumer, the user of the service. These interfaces present the functionality (the useful operations) of the service. An object service definition.

Garbage Collection. The recovery of memory occupied by unreferenced objects, usually implemented by the language or environment.

Gateway. A software product that allows SQL-based applications to access relational and non-relational data sources.

Geographic Information System. An organized collection of computer hardware, software, geographic data, and personnel designed to efficiently capture, store, update, manipulate, analyze, and display all forms of geographically referenced information.

Graphical User Interface (GUI). Any interface that communicates with the user, primarily through graphical icons.

Handle. A value that identifies an object.

Hash. Data allocated in an algorithmically randomized fashion in an attempt to evenly distribute data and smooth access patterns.

Heterogeneous Data. See disparate data.

Heterogeneous Databases. See disparate databases.

Heuristic. A rule of thumb or guideline used in situations where no hard and fast rules apply. An empirical rule, or educated guess based upon past experiences.

Highly Summarized Data. Evaluational data that are summarized by removing many data characteristics from the primary key of the data focus. Highly summarized data have coarse granularity.

Historical Database. A database that provides an historical perspective on the data.

HyperText Transfer Protocol (HTTP). (1) The protocol most commonly used in the World Wide Web to transfer information from web servers to web browsers. (2) The protocol that negotiates document delivery to a web browser from a web server.

HyperText Mark Up Language (HTML). Coding language used to create hypertext documents for the World Wide Web.

IDL. Interface Definition Language.

IIOP. Internet Inter-ORB Protocol.

Implementation. A definition that provides the information needed to create an object and allow the object to participate in providing an appropriate set of services. An implementation typically includes a description of the data structure used to represent the core state associated with an object, as well as definitions of the methods that access that data structure. It will also typically include information about the intended interface of the object.

Implementation Definition Language. A notation for describing implementations. The implementation definition language is currently beyond the scope of the ORB standard. It may contain vendor-specific and adapter-specific notations.

Implementation Inheritance. The construction of an implementation by incremental modification of other implementations. The ORB does not provide implementation inheritance. Implementation inheritance may be provided by higher level tools.

Implementation Object. An object that serves as an implementation definition. Implementation objects reside in an implementation repository.

Implementation Repository. A storage place for object implementation information.

Import. Creating an object based on a description of an object transmitted from an external entity.

Information. (1) A collection of data that is relevant to one or more recipients at a point in time. It must be meaningful and useful to the recipient at a specific time for a specific purpose. Information is data in context, data that has meaning, relevance, and purpose. (2) Data that has been processed in such a way that it can increase the knowledge of the person who receives it. Information is the output, or "finished goods," of information systems. Information is also what individuals start with before it is fed into a data capture transaction processing system.

Information Systems. A component of information technology infrastructure that represents the implementation of business activities, using the data resource, and residing on the platform resource.

Information Warehouse. IBM's approach to data warehousing that supports the implementation of either functional, central, or decentralized warehouses.

Informational Data. Data which has been extracted, summarized, and stored in a Data Warehouse for purposes of supporting Informational Applications.

Inheritance. The construction of a definition by incremental modification of other definitions. (See also Implementation Inheritance)

Initialization. Setting the initial attribute values of a new object.

Input/Output (I/O). Transmittal of information between a computer processor and its peripherals, such as terminals and storage devices.

Instance. An object created by instantiating a class. An object is an instance of a class.

Instantiation. Object creation.

Integrated Digital Network (IDN). The integration of transmission and switching functions using digital technology in a circuit-switched telecommunications network.

Integrated Services Digital Network (ISDN). (1)The recommendation published by CCITT for private or public digital telephone networks where binary data, such as graphics, digitized voice, and data transmission, pass over the same digital network that carries most telephone transmissions today. (2) An overall application of the technology to provide for both newer digital and more traditional telephone services in an integrated network, incorporating the new network and interfacing standards which are being adopted worldwide. (3) Method for carrying many different services over the same digital transmission and switching facilities. (4) A digital telephone system made up of two 64 Kbps "B" channels for data and one "D" channel for message trafficking.

Integration. Used here in the broad sense to mean the transformation of disparate data into an integrated data resource.

Intelligent Agent. A software routine that waits in the background and performs an action when a specified event occurs. For example, agents could transmit a summary file on the first day of the month or monitor incoming data and alert the user when certain transactions have arrived.

Intelligent Caching. Prefetching and storing disk-resident data in memory based on algorithms which identify access patterns, rather than on simple frequency of access.

Interface Definition Language (IDL). When used in conjunction with an ORB, IDL statements describe the properties and operations of an object.

Interface Inheritance. The construction of an interface by incremental modification of other interfaces. The IDL provides interface inheritance.

Interface Type. A type that is satisfied by any object (literally, by any value that identifies an object) that satisfies a particular interface. (See also object type.)

Interface. A description of a set of possible uses of an object. Specifically, an interface describes a set of potential requests in which an object can meaningfully participate. (See also object interface, principal interface, and type interface.)

Interior Gateway Routing Protocol (IGRP). Learns best routes through LAN Internet (TCP/IP).

International Organization for Standardization (ISO). Best known for the 7-layer OSI Reference Model.

Internet. A collection of networks interconnected by a set of routers which allow them to function as a single, large virtual network.

Internet Access. The method by which users connect to the Internet.

Internet Address. Also called an IP address. It is a 32-bit address assigned to hosts using TCP/IP. The address is written as four octets separated with periods (dotted decimal format) that are made up of a network section, an optional subnet section, and a host section.

Internet Protocol (IP). A Layer 3 (network layer) routing protocol that contains addressing information and control information that allows packets to be routed. Documented in RFC 791.

Internet Service Provider (ISP). (1) Any of a number of companies that sell Internet access to individuals or organizations at speeds ranging from 300 bps to OC-3. (2) A business that enables individuals and companies to connect to the Internet by providing the interface to the Internet backbone.

Internetwork. A collection of networks interconnected by routers that function (generally) as a single network. Sometimes called an Internet, which is not to be confused with the Internet.

Internetworking. General term used to refer to the industry that has arisen around the problem of connecting networks together. The term can refer to products, procedures, and technologies.

Inter-operability. The ability for two or more ORBs to cooperate to deliver requests to the proper object. Inter-operating ORBs appear to a client to be a single ORB.

Intranet. A private network that uses Internet software and standards.

IOP. Inter-ORB Protocol.

IOR. Inter-operable Object Reference.

IP Spoofing. An attack whereby a system attempts to illicitly impersonate another system by using its IP network address.

IPX. Novell's Internet Packet Exchange.

ISDN. Integrated Services Digital Network.

ISDN Centrex. A service provided by local telephone companies to customer premises, in which a central office digital switch performs in lieu of a customer PBX in an ISDN system. ISDN Centrex uses one "B" channel and one "D" channel to provide an array of digital voice and data capabilities.

ISO. International Organization for Standardization.

Iterative Analysis. A technique whereby a researcher uses the results of a previous query to refine the parameters of subsequent queries.

Java Database Connectivity (JDBC). A standard implemented by Sun Microsystems that allows developers to write applications in the Java language, without having to use environment-specific code.

Joins. An operation performed on tables of data in a relational DBMS in which the data from two tables are combined in a larger, more detailed joined table.

Legacy Data. Another term for disparate data because they support legacy systems.

Legacy System. A previously existing system or application.

Link. Relation between two objects (a concept).

Literal. A value that identifies an entity that is not an object. (See also object name.)

Local Area Network (LAN). (1) A network covering a relatively small geographic area (usually not larger than a floor or small building). Compared to WANs, LANs are usually characterized by relatively high data rates. (2) Network permitting transmission and communication between hardware devices, usually within one building or complex.

Logical Data Model. (1) A data model that represents the normalized design of data needed to support an information system. Data are drawn from the common data model and normalized to support the design of a specific information system. (2) Actual implementation of a conceptual module in a database. It may take multiple logical data models to implement one conceptual data model.

Logical Data Structure. The structure of data in the logical data model. It is a subset of the common data structure that supports a single information system and usually represents a single real world perspective. It contains data entities and data attributes needed in the information system.

Manageability. The collective processes of storage configuration, optimization, and administration, including backup and recovery and business continuance.

Managed Object. Clients of system management services, including the installation and activation service and the operational control service (dynamic behavior). These clients may be application objects, common facilities objects, or other object services. The term is used for compatibility with system management standards (the X/Open GDMO specification and ISO/IEC 10164 System Management Function, Parts 1 to 4). An object service definition.

Mapping. A rule or process, the OO equivalent of a mathematical function. Given an object of one set, a mapping applies its associative rules to return another set of objects. Member function (see method).

Market Basket Analysis. A technique employed in the retail industry where the contents of "typical" sets of purchases are analyzed to determine statistically which products are selling best, what kinds of affinities might exist between and among products, and similar associations.

Massively Parallel Processing (MPP). The "shared nothing" approach of parallel computing. Massively parallel processing is a technology which tightly couples many processors, each with their own copy of the operating system and memory. Coupling the processors and coordinating their activity allows the processors to work in parallel on complex or large problems which would otherwise take too long on a single processor machine. MPP is a competing technology to Symmetric MultiProcessing (SMP), in which multiple processors share a single copy of the operating system and also share memory and peripherals.

Message. The mechanism by which objects communicate. A message is sent by a client object to request the service provided by the server object.

Metadata — (1) Traditionally, metadata was data about the data. In the common data architecture metadata is all data describing the foredata, including meta-predata and the meta-paradata. It comes after or behind the foredata and supports the foredata. (2) Metadata is data about data. Examples of metadata include data element descriptions, data type descriptions, attribute/property descriptions, range/domain descriptions, and process/method descriptions. The repository environment encompasses all corporate metadata resources, database catalogs, data dictionaries, and navigation services. Metadata includes things like the name, length, valid values, and description of a data element. Metadata is stored in a data dictionary and repository. It insulates the data warehouse from changes in the schema of operational systems.

Metadata Synchronization. The process of consolidating, relating, and synchronizing data elements with the same or similar meaning from different systems. Metadata synchronization joins these differing elements together in the data warehouse to allow for easier access.

Metadata Warehouse. A database that contains the common metadata and client-friendly search routines to help people fully understand and utilize the data resource. It contains common metadata about the data resource in a single organization or an integrated data resource that crosses multiple disciplines and multiple jurisdictions. It contains a history of the data resource, what the data initially represented, and what they represent now.

Meta-model. A model that defines other models.

Meta-object. An object that represents a type, operation, class, method or object model entity that describes objects.

Meta-type. A type whose instances are also types.

Method. Code that can be executed to perform a requested service. Methods associated with an object are structured into one or more programs.

Methodology. A system of principles, practices, and procedures applied to a specific branch of knowledge.

Middleware. A communications layer that allows applications to interact across hardware and network environments.

Mid-tier Data Warehouses. To be scalable, any particular implementation of the data access environment may incorporate several intermediate distribution tiers in the data warehouse network. These intermediate tiers act as source data warehouses for geographically isolated sharable data that is needed across several business functions.

Mini Marts. A small subset of a data warehouse used by a small number of users. A mini mart is a very focused slice of a larger data warehouse.

MIPS. An acronym for millions of instructions per second. MIPS is mistakenly considered a relative measure of computing capability among models and vendors. It is a meaningful measure only among versions of the same processors configured with identical peripherals and software.

Model. A formula or algorithm that computes outputs from inputs. A statistical model also includes information about the conditional distribution of the targets given the inputs.

Modeling. A model is a representation of an object. Modeling answers questions about objects. Modeling is the use of a structure and process for analyzing a data set. For example, a decision tree is a model for the classification of a data set.

Modem. Contraction of modulator-demodulator. A device which modulates and demodulates signals transmitted over communication facilities.

MPP. Massively Parallel Processing.

Multidimensional Analysis. Informational analysis of data which takes into account many different relationships, each of which represents a dimension. For example, a retail analyst may want to understand the relationships among sales by region, by quarter, by demographic distribution (income, education level, gender), by product. Multidimensional analysis will yield results for these complex relationships.

Multidimensional Database. (1) A database which has been constructed with the multiple dimensions pre-filled in hyper-dimensional "cubes" of data rather than the traditional two-dimensional tables of relational databases. (2) A database concept designed for decision support systems in which related data is stored in multidimensional "hypercubes." This data organization allows for sophisticated and complex queries and can provide superior performance in certain cases over traditional relational structures.

Multidimensional Database Management System(MDBS and MDBMS). A powerful database that lets users analyze large amounts of data. An MDBS captures and presents data as arrays that can be arranged in multiple dimensions.

Multiple Dimension Analysis. See multiple dimension processing.

Multiple Dimension Processing. On-line analytical processing for decision support that uses a combination of single dimension and multiple dimension data subjects. It is also referred to as static data analysis because the data values do not change. It is also known as multiple dimensional analysis.

Multiple Inheritance. The construction of a definition by incremental modification of more than one other definition.

Multithreading. A program execution environment that takes instruction from multiple independent execution "threads."

Multi-tiered Data Marts. Data is passed through more than one staging area database and subjected to different levels of transformations. In this way, a data mart may act as both a target and a source.

Multi-way Joins. A join operation which involves more than two tables.

Network. A collection of computers and other devices that are able to communicate with each other over some network medium.

Network-driven Data Distribution. The situation where the existence of a data site on a telecommunications network drives the distribution of data to the data site to support a business need.

Neural Networks. Non-linear predictive models that learn through training and resemble biological neural networks in structure.

Normalization. The process of removing all model structures that provide multiple ways to know the same fact; a method of controlling and eliminating redundancy in data storage.

Normalized Data. Data that has been through data normalization. The data in the data view schema and the external schema.

Object. A person, place, thing, or concept that has characteristics of interest to an environment. In terms of an object-oriented system, an object is an entity that combines descriptions of data and behavior. A combination of a state and a set of methods that explicitly embodies an abstraction characterized by the behavior or relevant requests. An object is an instance of a class. An object models a real world entity and is implemented as a computational entity that encapsulates state and operations (internally implemented as data and methods) and responds to requests for services. An object is a self-contained software package consisting of its own private information (data), its own private procedures (private methods), which manipulate the object's private data, and a public interface (public methods) for communicating with other objects.

Object Adapter. The ORB component that provides object reference, activation, and state-related services to an object implementation. There may be different adapters provided for different implementations.

Object-based. A characteristic of a programming language or tool that supports the object concept of encapsulation, but not inheritance or polymorphism.

Object Component. A group of collaborating objects or a discrete repackaged application that provides a large-grained piece of business application functionality.

Object Creation. An event that causes an object to exist that is distinct from any other object.

Object Data Base Management System (ODBMS). A system that provides for long-term, reliable storage, retrieval, and management of objects.

Object Implementation. The code executed for an object or a component.

Object Interface. A description of a set of possible uses of an object. Specifically, an interface describes a set of potential requests in which an object can meaningfully participate as a parameter. It is the union of the object's type interfaces.

Object Library/Repository. A central repository established expressly to support the identification and reuse of software components, especially classes and other software components.

Object Management Group. A non-profit group, consisting of users, vendors, and university researchers, dedicated to promoting object-oriented technology and the standardization of that technology.

Object Name. A value that identifies an object. (See handle.)

Object-oriented Analysis. The process of specifying what a system does by identifying domain objects and defining the behavior and relationships of those objects.

Object-oriented Design. The process of developing an implementation specification that incorporates the use of classes and objects. It encourages modeling the real world environment in terms of its entities and their interactions.

Object-oriented. Any language, tool or method that focuses on modeling, real world systems using the three pillars of objects, encapsulation, inheritance, and polymorphism.

Object Reference. A value that precisely identifies an object. Object references are never reused to identify another object.

Object Request Broker (ORB). Provides the means by which objects make and receive requests and responses. The middleware of distributed object computing that provides a means for objects to locate and activate other objects on a network, regardless of the processor or programming language used to develop and implement those objects.

Object Services. The basic functions provided for object lifecycle management and storage such as creation, deletion, activation, de-activation, identification, and location.

Object Type. A type the extension of which is a set of objects (literally, a set of values that identify objects). In other words, an object type is satisfied only by (values that identify) objects. (See also interface type.)

ODBC (Open Database Connectivity). A standard for database access co-developed by Microsoft from the SQL Access Group consortium.

OLAP. On-Line Analytical Processing.

OLTP. On-Line Transaction Processing.

OMG. Object Management Group

On-Line Analytical Processing (OLAP). Processing that supports the analysis of business trends and projections. It is also known as decision-support processing. Originally introduced in 1994 in a paper by E. F. Codd, OLAP is a decision-support counterpart to On Line Transaction Processing. OLAP allows users to derive information and business intelligence from data warehouse systems by providing tools for querying and analyzing the information in the warehouse. In particular, OLAP allows multidimensional views and analysis of that data for decision-support processes.

On-Line Transaction Processing (OLTP). Processing that supports the daily business operations. Also know as operational processing.

Open Systems Interconnection (OSI). A 7-layer architecture model for communications systems developed by ISO and used as a reference model for most network architectures.

Operation. A service that can be requested. An operation has an associated signature, which may restrict which actual parameters are possible in a meaningful request.

Operational Data. Data used in the operational processing of business transactions that support day-to-day business operations. It is detailed, largely primitive data necessary to keep the organization operating.

Operational Data Store (ODS). An integrated database of operational data, containing timely, current, and integrated information. The data is typically very granular. These systems are subject-oriented, not application-oriented, and are optimized for looking up one or two records at a time for decision making. Their sources include legacy systems and it contains current or near term data. An ODS may contain 30 to 60 days of information, while a data warehouse typically contains years of data.

Operational Database. The database-of-record, consisting of system-specific reference data and event data belonging to a transaction-update system. It may also contain system control data such as indicators, flags, and counters. The operational database is the source of data for the data warehouse. It contains detailed data used to run the day-to-day operations of the business. The data continually changes as updates are made, and reflect the current value of the last transaction.

Operational Metadata. Metadata about operational data.

Operational System or Database. An information or transaction processing system used to store data such as bank balances, inventories, payroll, manufacturing OLE - Microsoft's Object Linking and Embedding.

Optimized Data. Data that has been through data optimization. The data in the logical schema and conceptual schema.

ORB. Object Request Broker.

ORB Core. The ORB component that moves a request from a client to the appropriate adapter for the target object.

Ordinary Least Squares. A technique for fitting a regression equation to the observed data.

OSF. Open Software Foundation.

OSI. ISO's Open Systems Interconnection.

Overloaded Operation. Multiple methods of the same name, each having a unique signature. This allows the methods of the same name to be invoked with various argument types.

Packet. (1) A logical grouping of information that includes a header and (usually) user data. (2) A continuous sequence of binary digits of information, switched through the network as an integral unit. Consists of up to 1024 bits (128 octets) of customer data plus additional transmission and error control information.

Packet Switching. (1) Type of data transfer that occupies a communication link only during the time of actual data transmission. Messages are split into packets and reassembled at the receiving end of the communication link. (2) A transmission technique that segments and routes information as discrete units. Packet switching allows for efficient sharing of network resources as packets from different sources can all be sent over the same channel in the same bitstream.

Paradigm. A broad framework for thinking about and perceiving reality. A theoretical, philosophical model composed of identifiable theories, laws, and generalizations used in defining and solving problems.

Parallel Processing. A technique of tightly coupling multiple processors and associated software to coordinate the efforts of the multiple processors so that they may act in parallel to solve problems which are too large and/or complex for single processors.

Parallelism. The ability to perform functions in parallel.

Partition. Decomposing a type into its disjoint subtypes, parts, etc.

Password. A group of characters assigned to a user by the System Administrator and used for accessing or entry to a system or database.

Password Authentication Protocol (PAP). A simple password protocol that transmits a user name and password across the network, unencrypted.

Path. One or more Sonet lines, including network elements at each end capable of accessing, generating, and processing Path Overhead. Paths provide end-to-end transport of services.

Pattern. A pattern describes a problem, a solution to a problem, and when to apply the solution. Patterns may be categorized as design patterns, business process patterns, and analysis patterns.

PCI-Bus. The Peripheral Component Interconnect Bus is a set of industry standards which define the mechanical, electrical, and protocols, required to interface peripheral controllers to a CPU. PCI allows data transfers at a clock rate of 33 Mhz. PCI puts a complex managing layer between the CPU and peripherals which buffers the signals allowing ten peripherals (max of five add-in cards) to maintain high performance.

Performance Management Tools. Tools that help warehouse managers monitor, maintain, and manage warehouse performance in distributed, heterogeneous environments.

Perimeter Firewall. There are two types of perimeter firewalls, static packet filtering and dynamic. Both work at the IP address level, selectively passing or blocking data packets. Static packet filters are less flexible than dynamic firewalls.

Persistent Object. An object that can survive the process or thread that created it. A persistent object exists until it is explicitly deleted.

Physical Data Model. A data model that represents the denormalized physical implementation of data that support an information system. The logical data model is denormalized to a physical data model according to specific criteria that do not compromise the logical data model but allow the database to operate efficiently in a specific operating environment.

Pointer. A variable that can hold a memory address of an object.

Polymorphism. The concept that two or more types of objects can respond to the same request in different ways.

Population. See data loading and data replication.

Port. The identifier (16-bit unsigned integer) used by Internet transport protocols to distinguish among multiple simultaneous connections to a single destination host.

Primary Data Source. The first data site where the original data is stored after its origination.

Primary Key. A set of one or more data characteristics whose value uniquely identifies each data occurrence in a data subject. A primary key is also known as a unique identifier.

Profile. A set of information about a user, such as name, password or department, set up by the system administrator.

Protection. The ability to restrict the clients for which a requested service will be performed.

Protocol. (1) A formal description of a set of rules and conventions that govern how devices on a network exchange information. (2) The set of rules governing interactions between two or more parties. These rules consist of syntax (header structure), semantics (actions and reactions that are supposed to occur), and timing (relative ordering and direction of states and events).

Protocol Address. Also called a network address. A network layer address referring to a logical, rather than a physical, network device.

Protocol Stack. Related layers of protocol software that function together to implement a particular communications architecture. Examples include AppleTalk and DECnet.

Proxy. The mechanism whereby one system "fronts for" another system in responding to protocol requests. Proxy systems are used in network management to avoid having to implement full protocol stacks in simple devices, such as modems.

Public. A security permission criteria used to make member access available to other objects.

Query. A (usually) complex SELECT statement for decision support. See ad hoc query.

Query Response Time. The time it takes for the warehouse engine to process a complex query across a large volume of data and return the results to the requester.

Query Tools. Software that allows a user to create and direct specific questions to a database. These tools provide the means for pulling the desired information from a database. They are typically SQL-based tools and allow a user to define data in end user language.

RDBMS. Relational Database Management System.

RDBMS Concurrence. Overlapping, concurrent execution of code segments.

Redundancy. The storage of multiple copies of identical data.

Redundancy Control. Management of a distributed data environment to limit excessive copying, update, and transmission costs associated with multiple copies of the same data. Data replication is a strategy for redundancy control with the intention to improve performance.

Redundancy. The storage of multiple copies of identical data.

Redundant Data. The situation where the same data characteristic exists at two or more data sites. Redundant data is created, stored, and maintained independently and the existence of the redundancy is often unknown to the organization.

Reference Data. Business data that has a consistent meaning and definition and is used for reference and validation (process, person, vendor, and customer, for example). Reference data is fundamental to the operation of the business. The data is used for transaction validation by the data capture environment, decision support systems, and for representation of business rules. Its source for distribution and use is a data warehouse.

Refining. A process that removes impurities from crude or impure material to form useful products, such as refining crude oil.

Refresh. Once a data warehouse is implemented, the contents of the warehouse must be periodically updated to reflect changes in the legacy systems from which the data is gathered. These update cycles are known as refreshes..

Relation. An object type that associates two or more object types. A relation is how associations are formed between two or more objects.

Relational Database Management System (RDBMS). A database management system which uses the concept of two-dimensional "tables" to define "relationships" among the different elements of the database.

Relational Database. A type of database that stores information in tables (rows and columns of data) and conducts searches by using data in specified columns of one table to find additional data in another table. In a relational database, the rows of a table represent records and the columns represent fields. In conducting searches, a relational database matches information from a field in one table with information in a corresponding field of another table to produce a third table that combines requested data from both tables.

Relational Model. A data model in which the data is organized in relations (tables). This is the model implemented in most modern database management systems.

Remote Access. The process of allowing remote workers to access a corporate LAN over analog or digital telephone lines.

Remote Access Server. Access equipment at a central site that connects remote users with corporate LAN resources.

Replicated Data. Data that is copied from a data source to one or more target environments based on replication rules. Replicated data can consist of full tables or rectangular extracts.

Replication. The process of keeping a copy of data, either through shadowing or caching.

Repository. A location, physical or logical, where databases supporting similar classes of applications are stored.

Repository Environment. Contains the complete set of a business's metadata. It is globally accessible. As compared to a data dictionary, the repository environment not only contains an expanded set of metadata, but can be implemented across multiple hardware platforms and database management systems (DBMS).

Request. An event consisting of an operation and zero or more actual parameters. A client issues a request to cause a service to be performed. Also associated with a request are the results that can be returned to the client. A message can be used to implement (carry) a request and/or a result.

Requirements. A statement of the capabilities a system is supposed to offer, from a user's point of view. This statement is input into the object-oriented analysis process, where it will be transformed into a much more precise description.

Return on Investment. A financial measure used to quantify the desirability of promoting a particular effort. Return on investment compares the benefits returned to the enterprise against the cost required to implement it. It is usually expressed as a ratio.

Reuse. Reuse is the process of locating, understanding, and incorporating existing knowledge, design, and components into a new system. Reuse should occur at all levels of system development analysis, design, implementation, testing, documentation, and user training.

Reverse Data Denormalization. A process that transforms the physical schema to the distribution schema. It undoes the database to its distributed schema or to the logical schema if there is no data distribution.

Reverse Data Modeling. Movement from the physical schema to the distribution schema to the logical schema to the data view schema to the business schema.

RFP. Request For Proposal.

ROLAP (Relational OLAP). Performing OLAP functions against a relational DBMS. Many relational products will offer star and snowflake schema for allowing OLAP queries in a relational environment.

Role. A sequence of activities performed by an agent.

Route. A path through an internetwork.

Routed Protocol. A protocol that can be routed by a router. To route a routed protocol, a router must understand the logical internetwork as perceived by that routed protocol. Examples of routed protocols include DECnet, AppleTalk, and IP.

Router. (1) An OSI Layer 3 device that can decide which of several paths network traffic will follow based on some optimality metric. Also called a gateway (although this definition of gateway is becoming increasingly outdated), routers forward packets from one network to another based on network-layer information. (2) A dedicated computer hardware and/or software package which manages the connection between two or more networks.

Routing. The process of finding a path to the destination host. Routing is very complex in large networks because of the many potential intermediate destinations a packet might traverse before reaching its destination host.

Routing Information Protocol (RIP). An IGP supplied with Berkeley UNIX systems. It is the most common IGP in the Internet. RIP uses hop count as a routing metric. The largest allowable hop count for RIP is 16.

Routing Metric. The method by which a routing algorithm determines that one route is better than another. This information is stored in routing tables. Metrics include reliability, delay, bandwidth, load, MTUs, communication costs, and hop count.

Routing Protocol. A protocol that accomplishes routing through the implementation of a specific routing algorithm. Examples of routing protocols include IGRP, RIP, and OSPF.

Routing Table. A table stored in a router or some other internetworking device that keeps track of routes (and, in some cases, metrics associated with those routes) to particular network destinations.

Scalability. (1) The ability to scale to support larger or smaller volumes of data and more or fewer users. The ability to increase or decrease size or capability in cost-effective increments with minimal impact on the unit cost of business and the procurement of additional services. (2) The ability of a system to accommodate increases in demand by upgrading and/or expanding existing components, as opposed to meeting those increased demands by implementing a new system.

Schema. (1) A diagrammatic representation of the structure or framework of something. (2) The logical and physical definition of data elements, physical characteristics and inter-relationships.

Secure HTTP (SHTTP). An extension of HTTP for authentication and data encryption between a web server and a web browser.

Security. Protection against unwanted behavior. The most widely used definition of (computer) security is *security = confidentiality + integrity + availability*.

Security Policy. A security policy is the set of rules, principles, and practices that determine how security is implemented in an organization. It must maintain the principles of the organization's general security policy.

Segmentation. Techniques for deriving clusters and classes by creating two-way and multi-way splits from a dataset according to specified variables.

Server. A service that provides standard functions for clients in response to standard messages from clients. *Note*: A commonly used definition of server also refers to the physical computer from which services are provided.

Server Object. An object providing response to a request for a service. A given object might be a client for some requests and a server for other requests. (See also client object.)

Simple Mail Transfer Protocol (SMTP). Protocol governing mail transmissions. It is defined in RFC 821, with associated message format descriptions in RFC 822.

Single Inheritance. The construction of a definition by incremental modification of one definition. (See also multiple inheritance.)

Skeleton. The object-interface-specific ORB component that assists an object adapter in passing requests to particular methods.

Small Computer System Interface (SCSI). A standard for connecting peripheral devices to computers. The standard defines a physical connection scheme as well as a set of protocols for controlling the flow of data across the interface.

SMP. Symmetrical Multiprocessing.

SNA. IBM's System Network Architecture.

Software Engineering Institute (SEI). The SEI is located at Carnegie Mellon University. Originally a U.S. Air Force project, the SEI objective was to provide guidance to the military services when selecting capable software contractors. The resulting method for evaluating the strengths and weaknesses of contractors proved valuable for assessing other software organizations. Since the late 1980s, SEI has been addressing the maturity of software within commercially developed applications.

Source Database. An operational, production database or a centralized warehouse that feeds into a target database.

Spatial Data. A type of nontabular data with a spatial component that allows them to be precisely located on some base, such as the Earth. Sometimes referred to as aspatial data. Includes both geospatial data and structospatial data.

Spatial Data Hierarchy. A data subject hierarchy for defining spatial data themes and subthemes that includes both current and future spatial data needs.

Specific Object. An object (relative to a given object service) whose role is to provide a part of the object service whose interface it carries. The concept is that a limited number of implementations (and potentially a limited number of instances) of these objects exist in the system, commonly as "servers." An object service definition.

SQL (Structured Query Language). A structured query language for accessing relational, ODBC, DRDA, or non-relational compliant database systems.

SQL Query Tool. An end user tool that accepts SQL to be processed against one or more relational databases.

SQL-Compliant. Conforms to ANSI standards for Structured Query Language specifications.

Standard Query. A stored procedure of a recently executed query. Technically, a standard query may be stored on the desktop as "canned" SQL and passed as dynamic SQL to the server database to execute. This is undesirable unless the stored query is seldom executed.

Star Schema. A database design characterized by its simplicity, allowing users to navigate through the data easily, and its rapid response time. Unlike traditional relational schemas, normalization is not a goal of star schema design. Star schemas are usually divided into fact tables and dimensional tables, where the dimensional tables supply supporting information, such as the demographics of the buyers who made up the entries in the primary fact table.

State. The information about the history of previous requests needed to determine the behavior of future requests.

Static Query. A stored, parameterized procedure, optimized for access to a particular data warehouse.

Stovepipe Decision-Support Systems. Independent, departmental data marts incapable of making accurate decisions across the enterprise because they have no way to consistently define data.

Striping. A RAID technique which breaks up blocks of data into parallel "stripes" which are stored on different disks in order to enhance performance.

Stub. A local procedure corresponding to a single operation that invokes that operation when called. Subclass (See subtype.)

Subnetwork. Collection of OSI end systems and intermediate systems under the control of one administrative domain and using a single network access protocol. For example, private X.25 networks, a series of bridged LANs.

Subtype. A specialized or specific object type.

Summaries. Data that is aggregated according to specific criteria. For example, individual daily sales may be aggregated to weekly totals, or averaged to a single per/day number rather than maintaining all of the individual data elements.

Summarization Tables. These tables are created along commonly used access dimensions to speed query performance, although the redundancies increase the amount of data in the warehouse. See aggregate data.

Summary Data. Data that are aggregated according to specific criteria. For example, individual daily sales may be aggregated to weekly totals, or averaged to a single per/day number rather than maintaining all of the individual data elements.

Summary Statistics. Statistics that are aggregated according to specific criteria.

Symmetrical Multiprocessing (SMP). The "shared everything" approach of parallel computing.

Synchronous Request. A request in which the client object pauses to wait for completion of the request.

System Object Model/ Distributed System Object Model (SOM/DSOM). SDM is a class library, and DSOM is an ORB. Both provided by IBM.

Systems Architecture. One of the four layers of the information systems architecture. The systems architecture represents the definitions and inter-relationships between applications and the product architecture.

T1. (1) Digital transmission facility operating with a nominal bandwidth of 1.544 Mbps. Also known as Digital Signal Level 1 (D1). Composed of 24 DS-0 channels in many cases. The T1 digital transmission system is the primary digital communication system in North America. (2) A high-speed 1.5 Mbps leased line often used by companies for access to the Internet.

Table Partitioning. The process of identifying the tables needed at each data site.

Target Database. The database in which data will be loaded or inserted.

Target Object. An object that receives a request. (Synonymous with server object.)

Targeted Marketing. The business technique for isolating the most likely set of potential customers for a given product and/or product profile.

TCP/IP. Transmission Control Protocol/Internet Protocol.

Temporal Data. Any data that represents a point in time or a time interval. They are data with a time component.

Temporal Database. A database that has the capability to store temporal data and manage data based on those temporal data. It can recreate data values for past or future dates based on the temporal data values. These databases are also known as time-relational databases.

Test Data. Data that contains input and target values and is not used for training a model. Test data is used to estimate generalization and to compare models. See also training data and validation data.

TPC-D Benchmark. A benchmark developed by the Transaction Processing Performance Council to measure the performance of decision-support applications. The TPC approved its fourth benchmark in April 1995. It differs from the existing benchmarks which focus on light and mid-weight customer-oriented transactions. TPC-D represents a broad range of decision-support applications that require complex, long-running queries against large complex data structures. Real-world business questions were written against this model, resulting in 17 complex queries.

Traditional Data Sharing. The situation where individual physical files and independent translation schemes are only useful as long as the source and target databases retain the same content and structure.

Transaction. The occurrence of two or more related actions which result in a transfer from one party to another, or from each party to the other. Transactions include order entry, point-of-sale exchanges, teller machines, etc.

Transaction Data. Data captured during an exchange between two or more systems that accomplishes a particular action or result. For example, a point-of-sale terminal will provide data about the latest sale processed.

Transmission Control Protocol/Internet Protocol (TCP/IP). (1) The common name for the suite of protocols developed by the U.S. Department of Defense in the 1970s to support the construction of world-wide internetworks. TCP and IP are the two best-known protocols in the suite. TCP corresponds to Layer 4 (the transport layer) of the OSI reference model. It provides reliable transmission of data. IP corresponds to layer 3 (the network layer) of the OSI reference model and provides connectionless datagram service. (2) The collection of transport and application protocols used to communicate on the Internet and other networks. (3) A protocol (set of rules) that provides reliable transmission of packet data over networks.

Trigger Rule. A cause-and-effect relationship. When a certain event type occurs, a specific operation will be performed.

Type Interface. Defines the requests in which instances of this type can meaningfully participate as a parameter. For example, if given a document type and a product type in which the interface to document type comprises "edit" and "print," and the interface to product type comprises "set price" and "check inventory," then the object interface of a particular document that is also a product comprises all four requests.

Type. A predicate (Boolean function) defined over values that can be used in a signature to restrict a possible parameter or characterize a possible result. Types classify objects according to a common interface; classes classify objects according to a common implementation.

Uniform Resource Locator (URL). Standard way to state address of any resource located on the World Wide Web.

UNO. Universal Networked Objects.

Update. One of the four actions associated with data (CRUDÑCreate, Read, Update, and Delete). Not allowed in a data warehouse because a data warehouse depends on a time series of data.

Use Case/Scenario. A description of the sequence of actions that occurs when a user participates in a dialogue with a system. It describes the behavior that is invoked by a system function.

Validation Data. Data that are is indirectly during training for model selection, for early stopping, or for other methods intended to improve generalization. See also test data and training data.

Value-dependent Operation. An operation in which the behavior of the corresponding request depends upon which names are used to identify object parameters (if an object can have multiple names). Virtual class (See abstract class)

Versioning. The ability for a single definition to maintain information about multiple physical instantiations.

Vertical Data Aggregation. The summarization of data to higher levels of generalization.

Vertical Data Layer Aggregation. The combination of two or more data layers to form a more enhanced data layer. Aggregation may occur with either geospatial data layers or structospatial data layers.

Virtual Private Network (VPN). A network service offered by public carriers in which the customer is provided a network that in many ways appears as if it is a private network (customer-unique addressing, network management capabilities, dynamic reconfiguration, etc.) but which, in fact, is provided over the carrier's public network facilities.

Warehouse Business Directory. Provides business professionals access to the data warehouse by browsing a catalog of contents.

Warehouse Technical Directory. Defines and manages an information life cycle, a definition of warehouse construction, change management, impact analysis, distribution, and operation of a warehouse.

Web Gateway. An interface between some external source of information and a web server.

Web Page. An HTML document on the Web.

Web. Web, used as a noun, is shorthand for the World Wide Web.

Workflow. The structured flow of information through the well-defined steps of a business process where tasks are performed on elements of the information. Typical workflows have both sequential and concurrent tasks.

WWW. World Wide Web.

BIBLIOGRAPHY

Adriaans, Pieter and Zantiage, Dolf, *Data Mining*, Addison-Wesley, Reading, MA, 1996.

Agarwal, S., Agrawal, R., Deshpande, P.M., Gupta, A., Naughton, J.F., Ramakrishnan, R., Sarawagi, S., *On the Computation of Multidimensional Aggregates*, Proc. VLDB '96, 506–521.

Agrawal, R., Gupta, A., Sarawagi, S., *Modeling Multidimensional Databases*, Research Report, IBM Almaden Research Center, San Jose, California, 1995. Appeared in Proc. ICDE '97. Abstract

Aiken, Peter, *Data Reverse Engineering: Slaying the Legacy Dragon*, McGraw-Hill, New York, 1995.

Anahory, Sam, and Murray, Dennis, *Data Warehousing in the Real World*, Addison-Wesley Longman, Reading, MA, 1997.

Baker, Sean, *CORBA Distributed Objects, using Orbix*, Addison-Wesley, Reading, MA, 1997.

Baralis, E., Paraboschi, S., Teniente, E., *Materialized view selection in a multidimensional database*, Proc. VLDB '97, 156–165.

Barquin, Ramon, and Edelstein, Herb (editors), *Building, Using, and Managing the Warehouse*, Prentice-Hall, Saddle River, NJ, 1997.

Barquin, Ramon, and Edelstein, Herb (editors), *Planning and Designing the Data Warehouse*, Prentice-Hall, Saddle River, NJ, 1996.

Berners-Lee, Tim, Fielding, Roy, and Nielsen, Henryk Frystyk, *Hypertext Transfer Protocol-HTTP/1.0*, work in progress within the HTTP Working Group of the IETF, 1996.

Berry, Michael, and Linoff, Gordon, *Data Mining Techniques, For Marketing, Sales and Customer Support*, John Wiley & Sons, New York, 1997.

Berson, Alex, *Data Warehousing: Architecture and Technology*, McGraw-Hill, New York, 1997.

Bischoff, Joyce, and Alexander, Ted (editors), *Data Warehouse: Practical Advice from the Experts*, Prentice-Hall, Saddle River, NJ, 1997.

Bitterer, Andreas, et al, *Transaction Processing in a Client/Server Environment*, Prentice Hall PTR, Saddle River, NJ, 1996.

461

Blattberg, Robert C., Glazer, Rashi, and Little, John D.C., Editors, *The Marketing Information Revolution*, Harvard Business School Press, 1994.

Bontempo, Charles J., and Saracco, Cynthia, *Database Management: Principles and Products*, Prentice-Hall, Saddle River, NJ, 1996.

Brackctt, Michael H., *Data Sharing*, John Wiley & Sons, New York, 1994.

Brackett, Michael H., *The Data Warehouse Challenge*, John Wiley & Sons, New York, 1996.

Brodie, Michael L., and Stonebreaker, Michael, *Migrating Legacy Systems: Gateways, Interfaces, and the Incremental Approach*, Morgan Kaufmann, 1995.

Burleson, Donald, *High Performance Oracle Data Warehousing*, Coriolis Group, 1997.

Cabena, Perter, *Discovering Data Mining: From Concept to Implementation*, Prentice-Hall, Saddle River, NJ, 1997.

Chatziantoniou, D., and Ross, K.A., *Querying Multiple Features of Groups in Relational Databases*, Proc. VLDB '96, 295–306.

Codd, E.F., *A Relational Model of Data for Large Shared Data Banks*, Communications of the ACM, 13:6, June 1970, pp. 377–387.

Corey, Michael, and Abbey, Michael, *Oracle Data Warehousing*, McGraw-Hill, New York, 1996.

Cox, Brad J., *Object-Oriented Programming, An Evolutionary Approach*, Addison-Wesley Longman, Reading, MA, 1986.

Data Warehousing for Dummies, IDG Books, 1997.

Dec, K., *A Guide for Estimating Client/Server Costs*, Gartner Group, Stamford, Conn., 1995.

DeGeus, Arie, *Planning as Learning*, Harvard Business Review, p. 74 (March–April 1988).

Deshpande, M., Naughton, J.F., Ramasamy, K., Shukla, A., Tufte, K., Zhao,Y., *Cubing Algorithms, Storage Estimation, and Storage and Processing Alternatives for OLAP*, IEEE Data Engineering Bulletin, 20(1):3–11, March 1997.

Devlin, Barry, *Data Warehouse: From Architecture to Implementation*, Addison-Wesley Longman, Reading, MA, 1997.

Dhar, Vasant, and Stein, Roger, *Intelligent Decision Support Methods: The Science of Knowledge Work*, Prentice-Hall, Saddle River, NJ, 1997.

Dhar, Vasant, and Stein, Roger, *Seven Methods for Transforming Corporate Data Into Business Intelligence*, Prentice-Hall, Saddle River, NJ, 1997.

Dyer, Robert, and Forman, Ernest, *An Analytic Approach to Marketing Decisions*, Prentice Hall, Saddle River, NJ, 1995.

Dyreson, A., *Information Retrieval from an Incomplete Data Cube*, Proc. VLDB '96, 532–543.

Dyreson, A., *Using an Incomplete Data Cube as a Summary Data Sieve*, IEEE Data Engineering Bulletin, 20(1):19–26, March 1997.

Faloutsos, H.V., Jagadish, N.D., Sidiropoulos, R.L., *Recovering information from summary data,* Proc. VLDB '97, 36–45.

Fang, Walter, et. al, *VisualAge for Smalltalk Distributed-Developing Distributed Object Applications,* Prentice Hall PTR, Saddle River, 1996.

Fayyad , Usama M., Piatetsky-Shapiro, Gregory, Smyth, Padhraic, and Uthurusamy, Ramasamy, *Advances in Knowledge Discovery and Data Mining,* MIT Press, 1995.

Fingar, Peter, *The Blueprint for Business Objects,* SIGS Books, 1996.

Gill, Harjinder and Rao, Prakash, *The Official Client/Server Computing Guide to Data Warehousing,* Que, Indianapolis, IN, 1996.

Golfarelli, M., Maio, D., Rizzi, S., *Conceptual design of data warehouses from E/R schemes,* Proc. 31st Hawaii Intl. Conf. on System Sciences, 1998.

Gray, Jim, and Reuter, Andreas, *Transaction Processing Concepts and Techniques,* Morgan Kaufmann, San Francisco, CA, 1993.

Gray, J., Bosworth, A., Layman, A., and Pirahesh, H., *Data cube: a relational aggregation operator generalizing group-by, cross-tabs and subtotals,* Int'l Conf. on Data Engineering '96. Technical report.

Groth, Robert, *Data Mining: A Hands On Approach for Business Professionals,* Prentice-Hall, Saddle River, NJ, 1997.

Gupta, Vivek R., *Data Warehousing with MS SQL Server Unleashed,* SAMS, Indiana, 1997.

Gupta, H., *Selection of Views to Materialize in a Data Warehouse,* Proc. Intl. Conf. on Database Theory, January 1997.

Gupta, H, Harinarayan, V., and Quass, D., *Aggregate query processing in data warehousing environments,* Proc. VLDB '95, 358–369.

Gyssens, M., and Lakshmanan, L.V.S., *A foundation for multi-dimensional databases,* Proc. VLDB '97, 106–115.

Hacid, M. S., Marcel, P., and Rigotti, C., *A Rule Based CSQL for 2-Dimensional Tables,* Proc. 2nd Intl. workshop on Constraint Database Systems (CDB'97), January 1997, 92–104.

Hacid, M. S., Marcel, P., and Rigotti, C., *A Rule-Based Language for Ordered Multidimensional Databases,* Proc. 5th Intl. Workshop on Deductive Databases and Logic Programming (DDLP'97), July 1997, 69–81.

Hacid, M. S., Marcel, P., and Rigotti, C., *A rule based data manipulation language for OLAP systems,* Proc. 5th Intl. Conf. on Deductive and Object-Oriented Databases (DOOD'97), December 1997.

Hackathorn, Richard D., *Web Farming for the Data Warehouse,* Morgan Kaufmann, San Francisco, CA, 1998.

Hackney, Doug, *The Seven Deadly Sins of Data Warehousing,* Addison-Wesley Longman, Reading, MA, 1997.

Hackney, Doug, *Understanding and Implementing Successful Data Marts,* Addison-Wesley Longman, Reading, MA, 1997.

Hammer, J., Garcia-Molina, H., Labio, W., Widom, J., and Zhuge, Y., *The Stanford Data Warehousing Project*, IEEE Data Engineering Bulletin, 18(2):41–48, June 1995.

Hammergren, Thomas C., *Data Warehousing on the Internet*, International Thomson Computer Press, Phoenix, AZ, 1997.

Hammergren, Thomas C., *Data Warehousing: Building the Corporate Knowledge Base*, International Thomson Computer Press, Phoenix, AZ, 1997.

Harinarayan, V., Rajaraman, A., and Ullman, J.D., *Implementing Data Cubes Efficiently*, Proc. ACM SIGMOD '96, 205–216.

Harinarayan, V., *Issues in Interactive Aggregation*, IEEE Data Engineering Bulletin, 20(1):12–18, March, 1997.

Harold, Elliotte R., *JAVA Network Programming, Emeryville*, O'Reilly, 1997.

Ho, C.T., Agrawal, R., Megiddo, N., Srikant, R., *Range queries in OLAP data cubes*, Proc. ACM SIGMOD '97, 73–88.

Ho, T., Bruck, J., and Agrawal, R., *Partial-Sum Queries in OLAP Data Cubes Using Covering Codes*, Proc. ACM PODS '97, 228–237.

Hull, R., and Zhou, G., *A Framework for Supporting Data Integration Using the Materialized and Virtual Approaches*, Proc. ACM SIGMOD '96, 481–492.

Humphreys, Patrick, Bannon, Liam, Migliarese, Piero, Pomerol, Jean-Charles, and McCosh, Andrew, *Implementing Systems for Supporting Management Decisions*, Chapman & Hall, New York, NY, 1996.

Huyn, N., *Multiple-view self-maintenance in data warehousing environments*, Proc. VLDB '97, 26–35.

Inmon, W.H., and Hackathorn, Richard D., *Using the Data Warehouse*, New York, John Wiley & Sons, Inc, New York, NY, 1994.

Inmon, W.H., Imhoff, Claudia, and Battas, Greg, *Building the Operational Data Store*, John Wiley & Sons, New York, NY, 1996.

Inmon, W.H. Imhoff, Claudia, and Sousa, Ryan, *Corporate Information Factory*, John Wiley & Sons, New York, NY, 1997.

Inmon, W.H., Zachman, John, and Geiger, Jonathon, *Data Stores, Data Warehousing, and the Zachman Framework*, McGraw-Hill, New York, NY, 1997.

Inmon, W.H., Welch, J.D., and Glassey, Katherine, *Managing the Data Warehouse*, John Wiley & Sons, New York, NY, 1997.

Inmon, W.H., *Building the Data Warehouse*, QED Publishing Group, 1996.

Jacobson, Ivar, et al, *The Object Advantage, Business Process Reengineering with Object Technology*, Addison-Wesley Longman, Reading, MA, 1995.

Jagadish, H.V., Narayan, P.P.S., Seshadri, S., Sudarshan, S., Kanneganti, R., *Incremental organization for data recording and warehousing*, Proc. VLDB '97, 16–25.

Johnson, T., and Shasha, D., *Some Approaches to Index Design for Cube Forests*, IEEE Data Engineering Bulletin, 20(1):27–35, March 1997.

Kelly, Brian W., *AS/400 Data Warehousing: The Complete Implementation Guide*, CBM Books, Oslo, Norway, 1996.

Kelly, Sean, *Data Warehousing in Action*, John Wiley & Sons, New York, NY, 1997.

Kelly, Sean, *Data Warehousing: The Route to Mass Customization*, John Wiley & Sons, New York, NY, 1994.

Kimball, Ralph, *The Data Warehouse Toolkit*, John Wiley & Sons, New York, NY, 1996.

Kimball, Ralph, and Strehlo, Kevin, *Why decision support fails and how to fix it*, ACM SIGMOD Record 24(3), September 1995.

Koulopolous, Thomas M., and Frappolo, Carl, *Electronic Document Management Systems*, McGraw-Hill, New York, NY, 1995.

Labio, W., Quass, D., Adelberg, B., *Physical Database Design for Data Warehousing*, Proc. ICDE '97.

Labio, W.J., and Garcia-Molina, H., *Efficient Snapshot Differential Algorithms for Data Warehousing*, Proc. VLDB '96, 63–74. Technical report.

Lau, Christina, *Object-Oriented Programming Using SOM and DSOM*, Van Nostrand Reinhold, New York, NY, 1994.

Li, C., and Wang, X.S., *A data model for supporting on-line analytical processing*, in Proc. Conf. on Information and Knowledge Management, November 1996, pp. 81–88.

Li, C., and Wang, X.S., *Optimizing Statistical Queries by Exploiting Orthogonality and Interval Properties of Grouping Relations*, Proc. Eighth Intl. Conf. on Scientific and Statistical Databases, June 1996.

Martin, James, *Enterprise Engineering, Vol. 1–4*, Savant Institute, London, 1995.

Mattison, Rob, *The Object-Oriented Enterprise*, McGraw-Hill, New York, NY, 1994.

Mattison, Rob, *Data Warehousing and Data Mining for Telecommunications*, Artech House, Cambridge, MA, 1997.

Mattison, Rob, *Data Warehousing: Strategies, Tools and Techniques*, McGraw-Hill, New York, NY, 1996.

Mowbray, T.J., and Zahavi, R., *The Essential CORBA: Systems Integration Using Distributed Objects*, Wiley/OMG, New York, NY, 1995.

Mowbray, Thomas J., and Brando, Thomas J., *Interoperability and CORBA-Based Open Systems*, Object Magazine, 3(3), September–October 1993, pp. 50–54.

Mowbray, Thomas J., and Malveau, Raphael C., *CORBA Design Patterns*, John Wiley & Sons, New York, NY, 1997.

Mowbray, Thomas J., and Zahavi Ron, *The Essential CORBA*, John Wiley & Sons, New York, NY, 1995.

Mumick, I.S., Quass, D., and Mumick, B.S., *Maintenance of data cubes and summary tables in a warehouse*, Proc. ACM SIGMOD '97, 100–111.

Object Management Group, Inc., *OMG Business Application Architecture*, 1995.

OMG, *Universal Networked Objects*, OMG Document Number 95.3.10., The Object Management Group, Farmingham, MA., March 10, 1995.

OMG, *Common Facilities Architecture*, Revision 3.0, OMG TC Document 94-11-9, The Object Management Group, Framingham, MA, November 14, 1994.

OMG, *Common Facilities Roadmap*, Revision 2.0, OMG TC Document 94-11-10, The Object Management Group, Framingham, MA, November 15, 1994.

OMG, *Common Object Request Broker: Architecture and Specification*, Revision 1.2, OMG TC Document 93-12-43, The Object Management Group, Framingham, MA, 1994.

OMG, *CORBA 2 Compliance, OMG TC Document 94-12-2*, The Object Management Group, Framingham, MA., December 2, 1994.

OMG, *CORBA Services: Common Object Services Specification*, Object Management Group, Inc. 1995.

OMG, *Object Management Architecture Guide, Revision 2.0, Second Edition*, OMG TC Document 92-11-1, The Object Management Group, Framingham, MA, September 1, 1992.

OMG, *Object Services Architecture, Revision 8.0, OMG TC Document 94-11-12*, The Object Management Group, Framingham, MA, December 9, 1994.

OMG, *The Common Object Request Broker Architecture and Specification*, Revision 2.0: Object Management Group, Inc. 1995.

O'Neil, Patrick, *Database: Principles, Programming, Performance,* Morgan Kaufmann, San Francisco, 1994.

O'Neil, Bonnie, *Oracle Data Warehousing Unleashed.* Sams, Indiana, 1997.

O'Neil, P., Quass, D., *Improved query performance with variant indexes*, Proc. ACM SIGMOD '97, 38–49.

Orfali, Robert, and Harkey Dan, *Client/Server Programming with JAVA and CORBA*, John Wiley & Sons, New York, NY, 1997.

Orfali, Robert, Harkey, Dan, and Edwards, Steve, *Instant CORBA*, John Wiley & Sons, New York, NY, 1997.

Orfali, Robert, Harkey, Dan, and Edwards, Steve, *The Essential Client/Server Survival Guide, Second Edition*, John Wiley & Sons, New York, NY, 1996.

Orfali R., Harkey D., Edwards J., *The Essential Distributed Objects Survival Guide*, John Wiley & Sons, New York, NY, 1996.

Otte, Randy, et. al, *Understanding CORBA*, Prentice-Hall, Saddle River, NJ, 1996.

Parsaye, Kamran, and Chignell, Mark, *Intelligent Database Tools and Applications,* John Wiley & Sons, New York, NY, 1993.

PC Week, *The Data Warehouse Advantage*, Ziff-Davis Press, Indianapolis, IN, 1997.

Poe, Vidette, *Building a Data Warehouse for Decision Support*, Prentice Hall, Saddle River, NJ, 1996.

Poolet, Michelle A. and Reilly, Michael D., *Data Warehousing with Microsoft SQL Server*, Que, Indianapolis, IN, 1997.

Pope, Allan, *The CORBA Reference Guide, Understanding the Common Object Request Broker Architecture,* Addison-Wesley Longman, Reading, MA, 1997.

Quass, D., Gupta, A., Mumick, I.S., and Widom, J., *Making Views Self-Maintainable for Data Warehousing*, Proc. Fourth Intl. Conf. On Parallel and Distributed Information Systems (PDIS '96), December 1996.

Quass, D., and Widom, J., *On-Line Warehouse View Maintenance for Batch Updates,* Proc. ACM SIGMOD '97, 39–404.

Raden, Neil, *Performance is Everything*, John Wiley & Sons, New York, 1997.

Rao, S.G., Badia, A., Van Gucht, D., *Providing Better Support for a Class of Decision Support Queries*, Proc. SIGMOD '96, 217–227. Technical Report.

Redman, Thomas C., *Data Quality For The Information Age*, Artech House, 1996.

Ross, K.A., and Srivastava, D., *Fast Computation of Sparse Datacubes*, Proc. VLDB '97, 116–125.

Ryan, Timothy, *Distributed Object Technology: Concepts and Applications,* Prentice Hall, Saddle River, NJ, 1996.

Sarawagi, S., Agrawal, R., Gupta, A., *On Computing the Data Cube,* Research Report 10026, IBM Almaden Research Center, San Jose, California, 1996. Abstract

Sarawagi, S., *Indexing OLAP Data*, IEEE Data Engineering Bulletin, 20(1):36–43, March 1997.

Sauter, Vicki L., *Decision Support Systems*, John Wiley & Sons, New York, 1996.

Sessions, Roger, *Object Persistence-Beyond Object-Oriented Databases*, Prentice Hall PTR, Saddle River, NJ, 1996.

Shelton, Robert E., *Business Objects & BPR*, Data Management Review, 4:11, pp. 6–20 (November 1994).

Shoshani, A., *OLAP and Statistical Databases: Similarities and Differences*, in Proc. ACM PODS '97, 185–196.

Shukla, A., Deshpande, P.M., Naughton, J.F., and Ramasamy, K., *Storage Estimation for Multidimensional Aggregates in the Presence of Hierarchies*, Proc. VLDB '96, 522–531.

Siegel, Jon, et al, *CORBA Fundamentals and Programming,* John Wiley & Sons, New York, NY, 1996.

Silverston, Len, Inmon, William H., and Graziano, Kent, *The Data Model Resource Book: A Library of Logical Data Models and Data Warehouse Designs*, John Wiley & Sons, New York, NY, 1997.

Simon, Alan R., *Strategic Database Technology: Management for the Year 2000*, Morgan Kaufmann, San Francisco, CA, 1995.

Singh, Harry S., *Data Warehousing: Concepts, Technology, and Applications,* Prentice Hall, Saddle River, NJ, 1997.

Singh, Harry, *Heterogeneous Internetworking*, Prentice-Hall, Saddle River, NJ, 1996.

Singh, Harry, *UNIX for MVS Programmers*, Prentice-Hall, Saddle River, NJ, 1996.

Sprague, Ralph H. and Watson, Hugh, *Decision Support For Management*, Prentice-Hall, Saddle River, NJ, 1996.

Stikeleather, Jim, *Why Distributed Object Computing is Inevitable*, Object Magazine, p. 35 (March-April 1994).

Sutherland, Dr. Jeffrey, *Distributed Object Architecture for IS Applications*, Distributed Object Computing, SIGS Publications (1994).

Sutherland, J., *Business Objects and the Evolution of the Internet. CRC Handbook of Object Technology*, CRC Publications.

Tanler, Richard, *The Intranet Data Warehouse: Tools and Techniques for Connecting Data Warehouses to Intranets*, John Wiley & Sons, New York, 1997. John Wiley & Sons, New York, NY, 1995.

Taylor, Dr. David A., *Business Engineering with Object Technology*, John Wiley & Sons, New York, NY, 1995.

Theodoratos, H., and Sellis,T., *Data warehouse configuration*, Proc. VLDB '97, 126–135.

Thomsen, Erik, *OLAP Solutions: Building Multidimensional Information Systems*, John Wiley & Sons, New York, NY, 1997.

Turban, Efraim, *Decision Support Systems and Expert Systems*; Prentice-Hall, Englewood Cliffs, NJ, 1995.

Watson, Hugh J., Houdeshel, George, and Rainer, Rex Kelly, *Building Executive Information Systems and Other Decision Support Applications*, John Wiley & Sons, New York, 1997.

Weiss, Sholom M., and Indurkhya, Nitin, *Predictive Data Mining: A Practical Guide*, Morgan Kaufmann, San Francisco, 1997.

Wiener, J.L., Gupta, H., Labio, W.J., Zhuge, Y., Garcia-Molina, H., and Widom, J., *A System Prototype for Warehouse View Maintenance*, Proc. ACM Workshop on Materialized Views: Techniques and Applications, 26–33, June 1996.

Wright, Robert. *The Man Who Invented the Web*, TIME 149:20, May 19,1997.

Yazdani, Sima and Wong, Shirley, *Data Warehousing with Oracle: An Administrator's Handbook*, Prentice-Hall, Saddle River, NJ, 1997

Zhao, Y., Deshpande, P.M., and Naughton, J.F., *An Array-Based Algorithm for Simultaneous Multidimensional Aggregates*, Proc. ACM SIGMOD '97, 159–170.

Zhou, G., Hull, R., King, R., and Franchitti, J.C., *Supporting Data Integration and Warehousing Using H2O*, IEEE Data Engineering Bulletin, 18(2):29–40, June 1995.

Zhou, G., Hull, R., and King, R., *Generating Data Integration Mediators that Use Materialization*, Journal of Intelligent Information Systems 3:2/3, May 1996, 99–221.

Zhuge, Y., Garcia-Molina, H., Hammer, J., and Widom J., *View Maintenance in a Warehousing Environment*, Proc. ACM SIGMOD '95, 316–327.

Zhuge, Y., Wiener, J.L., and Garcia-Molina, H., *Multiple View Consistency for Data Warehousing*, Proc. ICDE '97.

INDEX

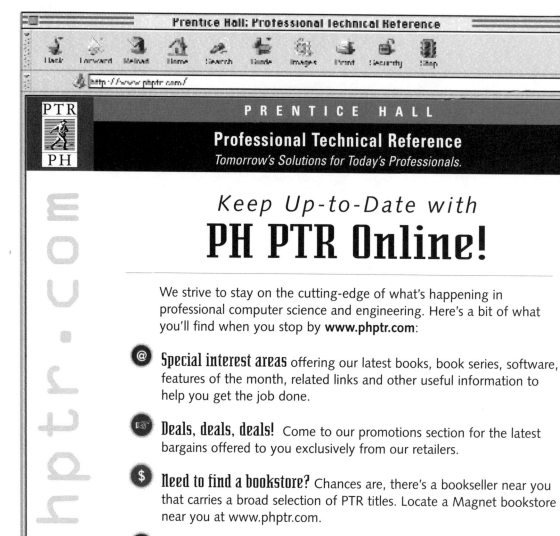